OUTSIDE AutoCAD

A Nonprogrammer's Guide to Managing AutoCAD's Database

Dale Evans

VENTANA PRESS

AutoCAD Reference Library™

Outside AutoCAD: A Nonprogrammer's Guide to Managing AutoCAD's Database
AutoCAD Reference Library™

Library of Congress Cataloging-in-Publication Data

Evans, Dale, 1951-
Outside AutoCAD: a nonprogrammer's guide to managing AutoCAD's database / Dale Evans.
p. cm.
Includes index.
ISBN 1-56604-041-8
1. Computer graphics. 2. AutoCAD (Computer file) I. Title.
T385.E982 1993
620'.0042'02855369--dc20 92-46279
CIP

Book design: Karen Wysocki
Cover design: Spring Davis-Charles, One-of-a-Kind Design
Cover illustration: Line drawing of sextant, courtesy of Autodesk, Inc.
Index Services: Dianne Bertsch, Answers Plus
Editorial staff: Charles Hutchinson, Linda Pickett, Pam Richardson
Proofreaders: Jean Kaplan, Virginia Phelps
Production staff: Rhonda Angel, John Cotterman, Karen Wysocki
Technical editor: Brian Matthews, Architectural Technology Dept. Head, Wake Technical Community College

First Edition 9 8 7 6 5 4 3 2 1
Printed in the United States of America

Ventana Press, Inc.
P.O. Box 2468
Chapel Hill, NC 27515
919/942-0220
FAX 919/942-1140

Limits of Liability and Disclaimer of Warranty

About the Author

Dale E. Evans is an author and columnist living in Shelley, Idaho. His articles are regularly featured in *Cadence* and *DesignNet* magazines, focusing on maximizing CAD productivity. The author of *The PC-DOS Mini Series*, a three-volume DOS course and reference guide, he is employed by EG&G Idaho, Inc. and is Principal of Evans and Associates, a CAD consulting firm and Registered AutoCAD Developer. He guided the establishment of an Authorized AutoCAD Training Center at the University of Idaho, Idaho Falls Center for Higher Education and sits on advisory boards for two colleges in southeastern Idaho. He holds a B.S. degree in Engineering Technology from Brigham Young University.

Trademarks

Acknowledgments

I could never have written this book alone. Very special thanks to Cindy and our children who gave me their wholehearted encouragement, love and patience during this entire project.

Thanks to the many people at Ventana Press who helped from start to finish: to Pam Richardson for advice, coordination and direction; to Brian Matthews for his assistance in editing, mentoring and preparing the illustrations; to the entire production and editing staff; and a special thanks to Josef and Elizabeth Woodman who invited me to write this book.

Thanks also to Neele Johnston at Autodesk, Kathleen Maher and friends at *Cadence*, Loren Casper and Bob Lurker at Lucero and to my many friends and associates for their constant support in this fast-moving industry.

CONTENTS

Introduction xix

SECTION I: The AutoCAD Database

CHAPTER 1

The AutoCAD Database 1

Benefits of Understanding the Database 1
The AutoCAD Entity—The Main Element in the Database 2
- Line Entity Data 2
- Circle Entity Data 3
- The Line in Detail 5
- The Circle in Detail 6
- Other Entity Types 7
- The Block Entity 7

Applying the Knowledge 10

CHAPTER 2

AutoLISP as a Database Tool 13

Why AutoLISP? 13
Some AutoLISP Basics 14
- Storing Real Values in AutoLISP Variables 15
- Strings & AutoLISP Variables 16
- Storing AutoCAD Point Values in AutoLISP Variables 17

User Input to an AutoLISP Routine 18
- (getint & (getreal 18
- The (getstring Function 19
- Creating a Sentence With (getstring 20
- The (getpoint Function 21

Association Lists 21
- The (assoc Function 22

Applying AutoLISP Into the Database 23
- Substituting Data 24
- Substituting New Data for Old Data 25
- Applied AutoLISP Programs 27
- Modifying a Block 27
- Renaming a Block 28

Searching a Blocks Database 28
Creating BLK_LIST.LSP 28
Comments 29
Program Listing 29
Program Explanation 30

CHAPTER 3 **The Power of Selection Sets 35**
Selection Sets—The Tools You've Always Wanted 35
The Selection Set Filters Dialogue Box 35
AutoLISP Tools Behind the Dialogue Box 39
The (ssget Function 39
More Power With SSGET! 40
The Flexibility of (ssget "X") 41
Rational Arguments for (ssget "X") 42
Sample Applications 42
FIND_BLK.LSP 43
FIND_TXT.LSP 44

SECTION II: Attributes

CHAPTER 4 **The Value of Attributes 49**
What are AutoCAD Attributes? 49
Defining Attributes 51
Using the Attribute Definition Dialogue Box 52
The Mode Dialogue Area 53
The Attribute Dialogue Area 55
The Text Options Dialogue Area 57
The Insertion Point Dialogue Area 59
Completing the Attribute Definition 60
Adding the Next Attribute 61
Defining the Block 62
Inserting the Block With Attributes 62
Editing Attributes 65
The Edit Attributes Dialogue Box 65
Editing Attribute Values at the Command Prompt 65
Editing Attribute Definitions 66
Editing Attribute Definitions Using the DDEDIT Command 66
Editing Attribute Definitions Using the CHANGE Command 67

Displaying Attributes ... 68
Creating ATT_DEF.LSP ... 68
Using ATT_DEF.LSP ... 68

CHAPTER 5 **Attribute Extraction ... 71**
Attribute Extraction Explained ... 71
Start From the Desired Result ... 72
Extraction Format ... 72
CDF Format ... 72
SDF Format ... 72
DXF Format ... 73
Defining the Format—An Example of a Template File ... 74
General Template File Format & Rules ... 74
Extraction File Planning & Block Creation ... 76
Time Out! Create the Blocks With Attributes ... 76
Creating the Extract File ... 78
The Final Step—Uploading to a DBMS ... 80

CHAPTER 6 **Attributes in the AutoCAD Database ... 81**
Changing Attribute Text Styles ... 81
The CA_STYLE.LSP Program ... 81
Loading & Running the Program ... 83
How the Program Works ... 84
Changing an Attribute Layer Assignment ... 88
The C:CH_LAYER.LSP Program ... 88
Loading & Running the Program ... 89
How the Program Works ... 89
Locating Attribute Text Strings ... 91
The C:FIND_ATT.LSP Program ... 91
Loading & Running the Program ... 93
How the Program Works ... 93
Rapid Entry of Text Into Attributes ... 97
The C:FILL_ATT.LSP Program ... 97
Loading & Running the Program ... 100
How the Program Works ... 102

SECTION III: AutoCAD for Windows

CHAPTER 7 **AutoCAD for Windows** **111**
The Benefits of Windows 111
Why Use Windows? 111
Loading & Using Special Applications 112
Context-Sensitive Help 114
DOS Versus Windows 115
Your Own Custom Menu 116
Shortening the Learning Curve 117
Why AutoCAD for Windows? 117
The Write Text Editor 117
Capturing the AutoCAD Screen 119
Other Desktop Tools 122
Windows-based AutoCAD Help 122
Dynamic Data Exchange 122

CHAPTER 8 **Opportunities for Customization** **123**
The Look & Feel of Windows 123
Multiple AutoCAD Sessions 124
Resizing Graphics Windows 124
Introducing OLE 124
An OLE Example 125
Updating an Embedded Object 126
The Client/Server Concept 126
Comparing Linking & Embedding 126
Updating Linked & Embedded Drawings 127
Customization 127
Creating a Custom Toolbar 128
Other Buttons in the Toolbar Customization Dialogue Box 130
Special Command Characters 130
Creating a Custom Toolbox 130
Customizing the Pull-Down Menus 132
Pull-Down Menu Control Codes 134
Accelerator Keys 134
Check Marks 135
Graying-out a Menu Item 138
Creating a Cascading Menu 139

CHAPTER 9 **Using Dynamic Data Exchange** **141**
DDE Applications 141
Other Applications 141
Exporting a Drawing 142
Shutting Down DDE 144
The DDE Menu Explained 144
DDE via AutoLISP 146
Export Modes in Detail 147
Shut-down via DDE.LSP 148
Additional DDE.LSP Information 149
More Customization 149

SECTION IV: ASE

CHAPTER 10 **Overview** **153**
ASE: The AutoCAD Sequel Extension 153
A Review of Database Basics 153
Designing a Database 154
SQL—What Is It? 155
Why Combine SQL & AutoCAD? 155
What's ASE? 156
Applications for ASE 157

CHAPTER 11 **Learning & Applying ASE Commands** **161**
ASE Commands 161
Administrative Commands 162
Utility Commands 175
Link Commands 183
Manipulative Commands 190

CHAPTER 12 **ASE: A Hands-On Example** **195**
Creating a Sample Drawing 195
Database Requirements 197
Preparing the DOS Environment 197
The FACILITY Database Structure 198
A Sample Data Set 200

The ACADASE Layer 201
Dialogue Box Usage 201
Initializing ASE 202
Setting the DBMS Driver 203
Setting the Current Database 204
Setting the Current Table 207
ASE's Viewing & Editing Tools 210
Adding a Row to the EMPLOYEE Table 213
Setting a Row by Key Value 215
Deleting a Row in a Table 217
Linking Your Drawing to the Database 219
Linking with Quick Link (ASEQLINK) 222
Linking to Two or More Rows 222
Linking Occupants to the Offices 226
Displayable Attributes 227
Selection Using ASE 230
Using SQL and the SQL Editor 230
Exporting Your Data 232

SECTION V: The AutoCAD Development System

CHAPTER 13
ADS—Is It for You? 237
ADS—What Is It? 237
How Do I Use It? 237
Is ADS a Programming Language? 241
Do You Have to Use C? 241
Why Use ADS? Why Not AutoLISP? 241
Inexpensive ADS Development 244

CHAPTER 14
ADS—Getting Involved 247
The ADS Concept 247
How Much ADS Do You Need to Know? 248
Creating an ADS Application in BASIC 248
Creating a Sample ADS Application 251

Compiling the Source (.BAS) Code 252
Linking Files 253
Running a Real Mode ADS Application 254
Writing a Real Mode ADS Application 255
Running DRW_CIR.EXE 258

SECTION VI: Proteus

CHAPTER 15
Proteus—The Fundamentals 263
Introducing Proteus 263
Languages Behind the Buttons 263
DCL 264
AutoLISP/ADS 266
Building the Sample 267
Changing Dialogue Attributes 267
Some Helpful Dialogue Box Guidelines 268

CHAPTER 16
Putting Proteus to Work 271
Planning for Proteus 271
Defining the Application 271
Controlling the DCL File 273
Writing & Examining the DCL File 273
Displaying & Using the Dialogue Box 277
MOD_BLK.LSP Explained 280
Running the Program 281
Testing as You Program 282
On-line Resources: BASE.DCL & ACAD.DCL 282
Summary 283

APPENDIX A
Fundamentals of AutoLISP 285
Database Toolkit Listing 286
AutoLISP Tips & Tricks 287
Loading a Single AutoLISP File 288
Loading Multiple AutoLISP Files 289
Finding Your AutoLISP Files 290
The DBTOOLS.LSP File 291
DBTOOLS.LSP 292

LINE_MOD.LSP 293
BLK_SCAL.LSP 294
BLK_NAME.LSP 295
BLK_LIST.LSP 295
FIND_BLK.LSP 297
FIND_TXT.LSP 298
ATT_DEFF.LSP 300
CA_STYLE.LSP 301
CH_LAYER.LSP 303
FIND_ATT.LSP 305
FILL_ATT.LSP 306
Functionality 309

APPENDIX B **AutoLISP Function Listing** **311**
The AutoCAD Database Codes 313

APPENDIX C **Drawing Interchange & File Formats (Release 12)** **325**
Group Codes 327
Comments 330
File Sections 330
HEADER Section 331
Writing DXF Interface Programs 338
Error Occurrences With DXFIN 340

APPENDIX D **Programming References** **341**
ADS LIBRARY 341
Synopsis of Basic ADS Library Subroutines 341
Establishing the Interface to AutoLISP 341
External Function Handling 342
Error Handling 342
Linked List Handling 342
AutoCAD Queries & Commands 344
Geometric Utilities 344
User Input 344
External Function Value Returns 345
Conversion 346
Coordinate System Transformation 346

Display Control 346
Low-Level Graphics 347
Wild-Card Matching 347
Selection Sets 347
Entity Handling 348
Extended Entity Data 349
Symbol Tables 349
PROTEUS CODE LIST 349
Programmable Dialogue Box Functions 349
ACAD.INI LISTING 351
Example File Listing 351
SQL COMMAND LIST 354
SQL Syntax 354
SQL Commands 354

Companion Disk Sneak Preview 357

Index 359

The Database...Inside-Out

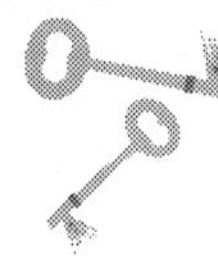

How far the personal CAD world has come in ten short years! I remember the days when just seeing lines, arcs and circles generated on a black & white monitor sent everyone through the roof. Only a handful of AutoCAD users even bothered with the non-graphic information behind the drawing. These were brave souls indeed, grappling with the .DXF database, .DXB files and complex AutoLISP programming, not to mention trying to tie it all into early dBASE or Lotus 1-2-3.

AutoCAD's Release 12, augmented by important new Windows database features, lets even the "all-thumbs" AutoCAD user work behind his or her drawing to get at critical data behind the drawing, whether to create an attribute, generate a report or concoct a full-blown bill of materials.

While much has been written about AutoCAD's database, *Outside AutoCAD* was created specifically for those who wish to access and manage AutoCAD's non-graphic information—often to accomplish relatively simple tasks—without having to acquire the skills of a programming guru.

Computer Aided Design has become a proven means to higher productivity in every field it touches. Its highly functional command sets allow the automation of repetitive tasks, reduced design time and improved accuracy. Superior functionality is especially seen in systems that provide productive programming tools.

AutoCAD offers high-productivity tools for every level of user. These tools include easily programmed menus, intuitive commands, user-programmable script files and AutoCAD's own graphics programming language: AutoLISP. To allow further productivity, programmable dialogue boxes can be created and accessed through the graphical user interface via AutoLISP and the new DCL language.

Advanced tools let the user create complex programming applications via ADS, tie AutoCAD drawings to textual databases using ASE and even create custom applications within the Microsoft Windows environment by using AWE. Further advanced tools can exist because of the accessibility of the AutoCAD database. AutoCAD's open software design is an open door to design productivity.

While extreme levels of complexity may be reached through the use of any of the above tools, high productivity can also be achieved by using these tools in simple ways.

What's Inside

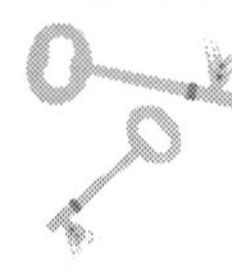

To both programmers and nonprogrammers this book will be useful. Your road to productivity will start by using AutoLISP in a basic way to work through the entity database. If you're a beginner and not experienced with AutoLISP or any of the language applications, you'll find each chapter builds upon the preceding chapter.

If you're an experienced programmer with the various program languages, you'll find the book useful in order to interpret the inside data from AutoCAD into output file data.

Outside AutoCAD begins by removing much of the AutoCAD database mystique that often stands in the way of the customization you would like to do. Database elements are explained through the use of hands-on examples, geared for nonprogrammers who desire higher productivity. AutoLISP's functions are introduced as database tools and are taught in just the right amount of detail so you can understand and use the examples now and in your own programs.

While attributes have been a part of AutoCAD since most users can remember, they remain one of the most valuable elements of the AutoCAD system. Section II explores and explains the value and use of attributes. Starting with the basics and progressing through attribute extraction, the section concludes by teaching you how to build and use tools that will help you increase your effective and productive use of attributes.

Since the introduction of personal computers, users have searched for a friendly interface to their programs. After thousands of hours and millions of development dollars have been spent in an attempt to fill the need for a friendly user interface, the most popular solution that has emerged is Microsoft Windows. Section III assists you in learning the advantages of the AutoCAD for Windows Extension, or AWE. You'll also learn how to use Dynamic Data Exchange (DDE) to tie your AutoCAD graphics data to outside data managed by other tools such as a spreadsheet system.

Section IV introduces you to ASE, the AutoCAD SQL Extension. ASE is the means which by you can unite SQL-based data with AutoCAD to build such applications as Facility Management and Geographic Information Systems. AutoCAD makes access to SQL data available to all users.

Section V opens the door to ADS. This book concentrates on helping you learn how to use this powerful and versatile tool. Through the use of AutoLISP, you can start using ADS to fill your own requirements.

Attractive and functional integration is the mark of professionalism in CAD application development. Section VI teaches you how to achieve a custom look and feel in your own applications through the use of AutoCAD's programmable Proteus GUI.

How to Use This Book

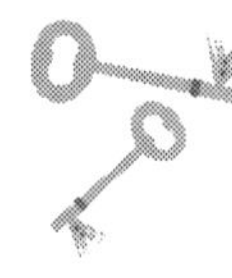

Overall this book will be an invaluable tool as you learn how to start putting productivity to work in your own applications. Intermediate and advanced AutoCAD courses will rely on *Outside AutoCAD* as an excellent basis for course work and reference material. Outside the classroom, you will learn from, and refer to the book for database principles and techniques that will add to your AutoCAD productivity.

This book is not intended to be a complete AutoLISP reference manual but attempts to explain the areas of AutoLISP used herein. *AutoLISP in Plain English*, published by Ventana Press, is a good basic introduction to the subject. (Purchase details are located in the back of the book.)

Best wishes as you learn and apply *Outside AutoCAD* in your own business!

— Dale Evans
Shelley, Idaho

SECTION I

The AutoCAD Database: Opening the Door to Productivity

CHAPTER 1

The AutoCAD Database

Database. Don't let the term baffle you. If you're an AutoCAD user, *database* is just a fancy term that stands for the contents of an AutoCAD drawing file. As designers, you're accustomed to seeing AutoCAD's database as a picture on a graphics display—but the real database is a list that describes each line, arc, circle and so forth in a drawing.

When you move or change the location of an item in a drawing, you change the database list; the AutoCAD program sees the change in the list and thus displays it as a change in the picture on the screen.

This chapter presents AutoCAD's entity concepts—blocks, lines, circles, arcs and text—to give you a basic understanding of the AutoCAD database. The principles presented here will help you visualize what's behind a drawing so you can take advantage of the database as an everyday AutoCAD user. Initially, you'll concentrate on the more familiar entities and how to use AutoCAD's tools with those entities to cut design time and increase productivity. As you learn these basic techniques, you'll create a foundation for working with AutoCAD's database. So let's get started...

Benefits of Understanding the Database

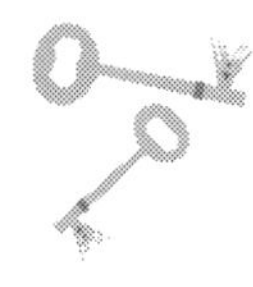

Understanding the AutoCAD database offers several benefits. You'll be able to scale blocks by individual axis, edit entity properties by program control, substitute blocks for other blocks by name, count entities and search for text or entities in a drawing, among other things. Let's take a closer look at a few of these capabilities, starting with a simple block as an example.

Suppose you've used a certain block throughout your drawing and then decide to substitute another block for it everywhere it's found. Your initial problem is that AutoCAD has no command for making such a substitution without redefining the block that's on your drawing. Here's where understanding the database comes in handy: you can make this substitution by going into the database, where you can alter any block you choose by using a command that you define. To do this, you'll substitute one block for another by changing its name in the database.

Next, say you scale a block during block insertion but want to scale the block again, in a single direction, after insertion. There is no AutoCAD command that allows you to do this. Again, by using a few AutoCAD database concepts, you can scale one or more blocks independently in any axis.

The AutoCAD Entity—The Main Element in the Database

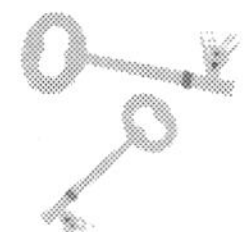

Everything you see in an AutoCAD drawing—lines, circles, arcs, text, blocks—is an AutoCAD *entity*. *Abstract* entities, like viewports, aren't easy to imagine but are also entities nevertheless.

Let's start with using AutoCAD's tools on the more familiar entities. As you use and master these techniques, you'll be building a strong foundation for working with AutoCAD's database.

Line Entity Data

Let's begin by starting a NEW drawing. Name the drawing DBASE1= (use no prototype). Create and set a layer called LINES. When you've completed the exercise, make sure you SAVE the drawing.

Here are the settings for the drawing:

UNITS	Decimal
Precision	2
LIMITS	0,0
Upper-right	12,9
GRID	.25
SNAP	.25

Now, let's try a quick example of an AutoCAD entity: a line. Create a single line from an x,y,z location of 3,4,0 and end it at 2,6,0 (see Figure 1-1). Then use an AutoLISP function to list the data of the line.

The list describing the line is called an *entity data* (or *association*) *list* and will look something like this:

```
((-1 . <Entity name: 6000001a>) (0 . "LINE") (8 . "LINES")
(10 3.0 4.0 0.0) (11 2.0 6.0 0.0) (210 0.0 0.0 1.0)
```

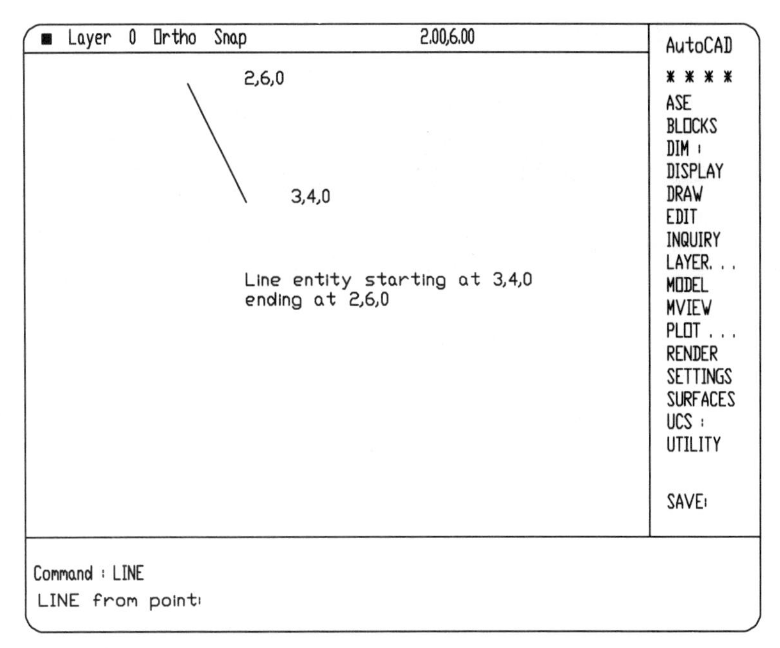

Figure 1-1: Line entity starting at 3,4,0 and ending at 2,6,0

You can display this information yourself. If you want your listing to look as much as possible like the one above, first create a new layer called LINES. Then draw a line that starts at location 3,4,0 and ends at location 2,6,0. After drawing the line, switch to your text screen (either use the TEXTSCR command or press the F1 key), then at the Command prompt enter the following:

Type: `(entget (entlast)) <Return>`

Your response to the entity data list will look almost identical to the example above. Your list may have more information, but don't be concerned about complexity yet.

Circle Entity Data

Let's try a circle now. Repeat the above exercise, but for a circle instead of a line. Set layer 0 as the current layer. Draw a circle with the center at location 5,7 and with a radius of 1.50 (see Figure 1-2). To display the database information that defines the circle entity you just created, switch to your text screen and enter the following:

Type: `(entget (entlast)) <Return>`

You should see an entity data listing that looks something like the response below. Remember, your list may have more information, but don't worry about that yet.

Response:
```
((-1 . <Entity name: 60000034>) (0 . "CIRCLE") (8 . "0")
(10 5.0 7.0 0.0) (40 1.5) (210 0.0 0.0 1.0)
```

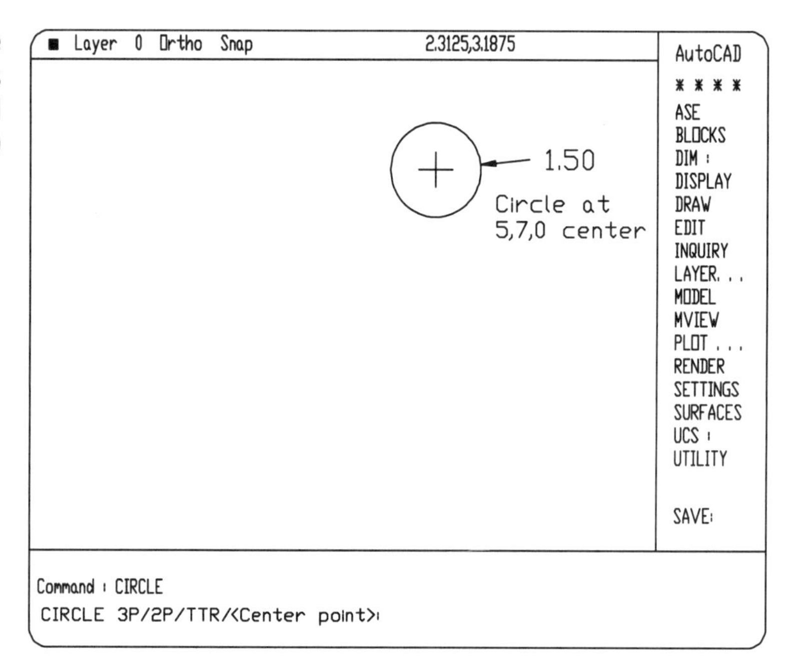

Figure 1-2: Circle entity with its center at 5,7,0 and a radius of 1.50

You now have a drawing that consists of a line on the LINES layer and a circle on layer 0. If you could look at the textual listing of the database, you'd see something like this list:

```
((-1 . <Entity name: 6000001a>) (0 . "LINE") (8 . "LINES")
(10 3.0 4.0 0.0) (11 2.0 6.0 0.0) (210 0.0 0.0 1.0)

((-1 . <Entity name: 60000034>) (0 . "CIRCLE") (8 . "0")
(10 5.0 7.0 0.0) (40 1.5) (210 0.0 0.0 1.0)
```

As you can see, a listing for each entity appears in the order in which you drew it: first the line, then the circle. Now let's see what makes up each entity data list, starting with the line definition.

The Line in Detail

The complete line entity data list is shown below:

```
((-1 . <Entity name: 6000001a>) (0 . "LINE") (8 . "LINES")
(10 3.0 4.0 0.0) (11 2.0 6.0 0.0) (210 0.0 0.0 1.0)
```

The list of data shown, which defines the line, is made up of several *sublists*. Let's look at each of the sublists, breaking them into their various parts. Pay close attention to the first number in each of the lists, as it is the sublist key.

Entity Name

```
(-1 . <Entity name: 6000001a>)
```

This sublist is made up of two parts, divided by a period. This type of sublist is called a *dotted pair*. The **–1** is a code that means the entity name is contained in the other part of the list. The entity name is a unique identifier, assigned by AutoCAD to the entity (in this case, the line). Sometimes the identifier contains numbers and letters, sometimes only numbers. Only the AutoCAD software can assign the entity name; you cannot assign it yourself. But you can use it to modify the entity to which it belongs.

Entity Type

```
(0 . "LINE")
```

This sublist is also a dotted pair (a list made up of two parts, divided by a period). The first part is the number **0**, which is a code that means the entity type is given in the other part of the list. In this case, the other part of the list tells us that the entity type is a **LINE**.

Layer on Which the Entity Resides

```
(8 . "LINES")
```

Once again, the sublist is a dotted pair. The **8** is a code indicating that the name of the layer on which the entity resides is shown in the other part of the list. In this example, the layer on which the entity resides is called **LINES.**

Starting Point of the Line

```
(10 3.0 4.0 0.0)
```

By now, you've probably gathered that the first number in each of the sublists is a code that tells you the meaning of the following items in the sublist. Since the entity is a line, the **10** means that three numbers will follow which will be the x, y and z location of the beginning of the line. In this example, the beginning of the line is at an x,y,z location of **3,4,0**.

Ending Point of the Line

```
(11 2.0 6.0 0.0)
```

The **11** at the beginning of this sublist means that the following three numbers will be the x, y and z location of the ending point of the line. The ending point for this line is at **2,6,0**.

Extrusion Direction

```
(210 0.0 0.0 1.0)
```

The set of three numbers that follows the **210** code represents a vector that specifies the *extrusion direction* of the entity. The extrusion direction is given by an x,y,z coordinate. In this case, the x and y directions are **0** and the z direction is **1**, indicating that this entity lies on AutoCAD's x,y coordinate plane.

The Circle in Detail

The complete circle entity data list is shown below:

```
((-1 . <Entity name: 60000034>) (0 . "CIRCLE") (8 . "0")
(10 5.0 7.0 0.0) (40 1.5) (210 0.0 0.0 1.0)
```

You'll find that the circle's database definition shown above is similar to the line definition in the following ways:

- –1 Contains the AutoCAD-assigned entity name.
- 0 Contains the entity type (CIRCLE).
- 8 Contains the name of the layer on which the entity resides (layer 0).
- 210 Contains the circle's extrusion direction (the circle lies on AutoCAD's x,y coordinate plane).

The next two sublists differ in purpose from those in the line definition. Remember, pay attention to the first number in the list—it's the key.

Circle Center Point

```
(10 5.0 7.0 0.0)
```

Because this sublist applies to the definition of a circle, the **10** code at the beginning of the list means that the three numbers that follow it represent the x, y and z location of the center of the circle. In this example, the center of the circle is located at an x,y,z location of **5,7,0**.

Circle Radius

```
(40 1.5)
```

This small sublist has a code of **40**, which means that the radius of the circle is the second number in the list. The radius in this example is **1.5**.

Other Entity Types

Each AutoCAD entity has a definition similar to those described above. Some are more complex, some less. Each list that defines an entity obeys the following rules:

- Each entity definition list begins with the entity name.
- The entity name is followed by the entity type.
- The entity type is followed by the name of the layer on which the entity resides.
- The layer assignment is followed by a description of the entity.

The Block Entity

Let's look at one more entity type: a block. To best understand the block, create and use a 1-inch-square block of your own, naming it BL. Follow these steps:

1. Set layer 0 as the current layer.
2. Insert your block at x,y location 6,5.
3. When prompted, enter an X scale factor of 2 and a Y scale factor of 3.

4. The rotation angle should be zero (0).
5. Save the drawing under the name DBASE1 so you can use it in a later chapter.

Figure 1-3 shows an example of a block that has been placed into the drawing at the specified location. The block name for this example is BL. The resulting definition that appears in the AutoCAD database looks like the following:

```
((-1 . <Entity name: 60000088>) (0 . "INSERT") (8 . "0")
(2 . "BL") (10 6.0 5.0 0.0) (41 . 2.0) (42 . 3.0) (50 . 0.0)
(43 . 2.0) (70 . 0) (71 . 0) (44 . 0.0) (45 . 0.0)
(210 0.0 0.0 1.0))
```

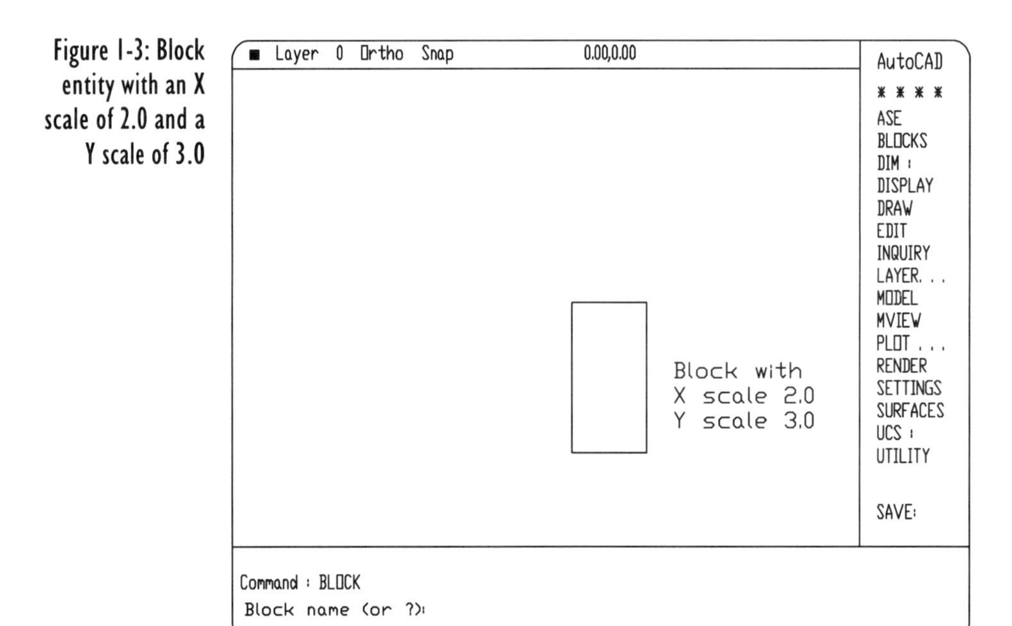

Figure 1-3: Block entity with an X scale of 2.0 and a Y scale of 3.0

The block's database definition shown above is similar to the line and circle definitions shown previously and below. Remember, pay attention to the first code number in each of the sublists.

–1 Contains the AutoCAD-assigned entity name.

0 Contains the entity type. The entity type is INSERT, indicating that the entity is a block.

8 Contains the name of the layer on which the entity resides (layer 0).

Block Name

```
(2 . "BL")
```

The data belonging to a block will have a code **2** in this sublist, followed by the user-defined name of the block. **BL** is the name of the block in this example.

Insertion Point of the Block

```
(10 6.0 5.0 0.0)
```

This sublist begins with the code number **10**, indicating (since the entity is a block) that the x,y,z insertion point is **6,5,0**.

Remember, the meaning of the first code number varies depending on the type of entity being defined.

X Scale Factor of the Block

```
(41 . 2.0)
```

The code **41** indicates that the X scale factor is contained in this sublist. Your scale factor of **2.0** appears here.

Y Scale Factor of the Block

```
(42 . 3.0)
```

As you can see, the Y scale factor is set up just like the X scale factor above, except the code number is **42** and the scale factor is **3.0**.

Block Rotation

```
(50 . 0.0)
```

The code **50** in this sublist means that the other number in the sublist is the rotation of the block in radians.

Z Scale Factor of the Block

```
(43 . 2.0)
```

The code **43** indicates that this is the sublist that contains the Z scale factor.

Other Block Definition Sublists

```
(70 . 0) (71 . 0) (44 . 0.0) (45 . 0.0) (210 0.0 0.0 1.0)
```

The codes **70, 71, 44** and **45** each have zero values, indicating that the block was inserted with the INSERT command. If positive values were present, it would indicate that the block was inserted with the MINSERT command.

The code **210** has the same purpose and meaning as it does in the line and circle definitions explained earlier.

Applying the Knowledge

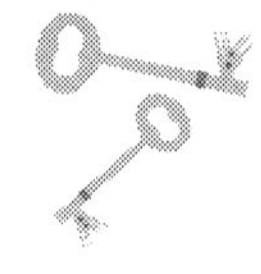

To take the chore out of working within the database and to help you with database information, I've included the following AutoLISP programs in Chapter 2, "AutoLISP as a Database Tool": LINE_MOD.LSP, BLK_SCAL.LSP, BLK_NAME.LSP and BLK_LIST.LSP. Complete documentation on these programs is also found in Chapter 2.

Before moving on, let's take a quick look at BLK_LIST.LSP. The BLK_LIST.LSP program gives you a simple way to use the information you've gleaned from this chapter.

If you have the *Outside AutoCAD Companion Disk*—and if it's properly installed—all you need do is type in the name of the program. The *Companion Disk* will save you hours otherwise spent typing in and debugging your programs.

If you don't have the *Outside AutoCAD Companion Disk*, turn to Chapter 2 of this book to see how to create the programs. In Release 12, use the APPLOAD command to load your program.

You'll find complete instructions on creating and loading these programs in Chapter 2.

Here's how the BLK_LIST.LSP program works to help you take the chore out of searching the database for block information. The program searches the drawing database for each block used in the drawing and prints the name of each block on the text screen. Each block name is listed one time, followed by the number of times it occurs in the drawing.

If you've created the file BLK_LIST.LSP, place it in the directory where your AutoCAD files are located so AutoCAD can find it when you attempt to load it. After you create the file and it's saved in the correct directory, load any drawing file that has blocks in the drawing; then use APPLOAD, or at the Command prompt:

Type: `(load "blk_list") <Return>`

If you made no mistakes typing the program in the text editor, the program will be loaded and ready for you to use. To use the program, type the following at the Command prompt.

Type: `blk_list <Return>`

If you use this program with a large drawing file, be patient. The program searches the entire AutoCAD database!

Moving On

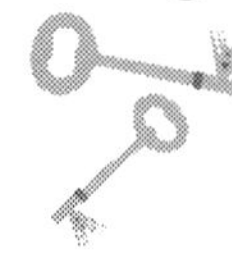

Remember that everything you see in an AutoCAD drawing is an entity, and that every entity is defined in the AutoCAD database in a form similar to the examples shown in this chapter. By understanding the way entities are defined, you can work directly with the AutoCAD database to increase your AutoCAD talent and productivity.

The next step in learning about the AutoCAD database is to become more familiar with AutoLISP, which is one means we'll use to bring more flexibility to the AutoCAD database.

CHAPTER 2

AutoLISP as a Database Tool

AutoLISP is one of several ways to gain entry to AutoCAD's database and, as you'll soon find out, has an excellent set of tools you can use to sharpen your database abilities.

Programs written in AutoLISP are easy to test and debug without leaving the AutoCAD drawing editor. That's why you don't have to be an AutoLISP expert to use AutoLISP. By the time you've finished this chapter, you'll be prepared to start using AutoLISP within the AutoCAD database.

Why AutoLISP?

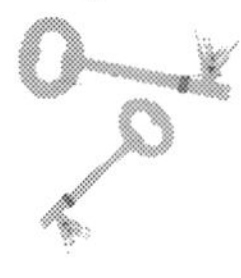

While AutoCAD commands are very powerful tools for the creation and editing of a wide variety of designs and drawings, AutoLISP opens up the world of customization. Let's look at a few good reasons to use AutoLISP. You can:

- Create your own commands.
- Perform calculations.
- Import and export data.
- Automatically create designs based on parameters you enter or read from a file.

In addition, AutoLISP lets you "look" into the database, make a copy of the part you're interested in, change the copy and then use your altered copy to replace the part of the database you looked at. This lets you edit your drawings faster and increase your productivity more than you thought possible.

You can make endless improvements to everyday design tasks with AutoLISP. Any activity you repeat over and over again is a candidate for a productivity increase; and if an activity is laborious or needs shortening, AutoLISP can speed it up.

Some AutoLISP Basics

The best way to introduce yourself to AutoLISP is to try it out. In fact, you already used AutoLISP, without knowing it, when you typed and used the (entget (entlast)) function in Chapter 1, "The AutoCAD Database." Let's try some more.

The following example uses an AutoLISP *function*, an AutoLISP *variable* (sometimes called an AutoLISP *symbol*) and an integer. You can think of a function as a routine or subroutine. Each function performs a specialized job—and if the function you need doesn't exist, AutoLISP lets you define your own.

An AutoLISP variable stores a value. For example, say you use a variable called *counter* to keep track of the number of times your AutoLISP program draws a line. The *counter* variable starts out by storing the value *1*. Each time AutoLISP draws a line, the counter is incremented by 1 and is checked to see if the desired number of lines have been drawn. When the program detects that the desired value is reached, it stops drawing lines. An AutoLISP variable can store several types of values, such as an integer or real number, a string (one or more text characters) or an AutoCAD point value.

Let's get started with the first fundamental AutoLISP example. Enter the drawing editor in a NEW drawing (you don't need a prototype). Flip to the text screen and enter the following at the Command prompt:

Type: `(setq a 10) <Return>`

Response: `10`

To understand what you just did, let's look at each part of the simple line of code above. You used the AutoLISP function **(setq** to place the value of **10** into the variable **a**. Notice the system's response: **10** was printed on the screen. Whenever you type an AutoLISP function, the system will return the final result of the function. You can force AutoLISP not to print the final result if you use the (princ function after the last function. For example:

Type: `(setq a 10)(princ) <Return>`

Response: There will be no response. You forced it not to print.

Now let's print the value that's been saved in the **a** variable. At the Command prompt, enter this next line:

Type: `(print a)(princ) <Return)`

Response: `10`

The value **10** will again be printed. If you don't include the **(princ** function, the **10** will be printed twice; first in response to the print instruction, and next as the final result of the function. You can also cause AutoLISP to print the value stored in a variable by preceding the variable name with an exclamation mark (!). For example, if you enter the following, the result will be the same as in the preceding example:

Type: `!a <Return>`

Response: `10`

It's easy to recognize an AutoLISP function because it's always preceded by a left paren (. You'll always find a matching right paren), either later in the line or at the end of the program. In fact, every AutoLISP program must have an equal number of left and right parentheses.

Storing Real Values in AutoLISP Variables

Often you need to store "real" (instead of integer) values within AutoLISP variables. Here's how it's done.

In the above example, the number **10**, an integer value, was stored in the variable **a**. To store the **10** as a real number, you'd represent the value with a decimal point (10.0), as shown below:

Type: `(setq a 10.0) <Return>`

Response: `10.0`

NOTE: If you want to represent a number that falls between a minus 1 and a positive 1 as a real number in AutoLISP, you'll need to place a leading zero in the number or AutoLISP will give you an error. For instance, to save the value 0.30 in an AutoLISP variable, you'd enter:

Type: `(setq a 0.30) <Return>`

Response: `0.3`

In the above case, the floating point value of **0.3** is stored in the variable **a**. To print out the value that's stored in the variable, enter:

Type: `(print a)(princ) <Return>`

or

Type: `!a <Return>`

Response: `0.3`

Strings & AutoLISP Variables

Storing a string in an AutoLISP variable isn't much different than saving numbers, although it may appear so. Look at this example that saves the text string **ABC** in the AutoLISP variable **some_txt**. Go ahead and enter the following:

Type: `(setq some_txt "ABC") <Return>`

Response: `"ABC"`

The text string **ABC** (in uppercase letters) is stored in the variable **some_text**. Notice that the way the variable is written is no different than in the earlier examples, but the string **ABC** is surrounded by quotation marks. If the string isn't enclosed by quotation marks, the string won't be saved and an error will result.

Also notice that when a string is stored into a variable, AutoLISP remembers whether you typed uppercase or lowercase characters. Case sensitivity can make a big difference. To print the value to the display:

Type: `!some_text <Return>`

The AutoLISP (print function sees the variable **some_text** and prints the value stored in it on the screen. The (princ supresses the result of the function that is returned. The result looks like the following:

Response: `"ABC"`

Storing AutoCAD Point Values in AutoLISP Variables

You store coordinates in a variable by using an apostrophe (') within a list. Let's look at a simple x,y,z set of coordinates.

An x,y,z set of numbers that represents a point in AutoCAD would look like the following:

```
(2.4 5.1 0.0)
```

You'd store this point definition in an AutoLISP variable called **pt1** as follows:

Type: `(setq pt1 '(2.4 5.1 0.0)) <Return>`

Response: `(2.4 5.1 0.0)`

The apostrophe (') that precedes the three point values lets AutoLISP know that the numbers in the parentheses should not be evaluated as a function would be, but should be stored in the variable exactly as they appear. The apostrophe is a shorter way of writing the (quote function. If the (quote function were used to write the above example, it would look like this:

Type: `(setq pt1 (quote (2.4 5.1 0.0))) <Return>`

Response: `(2.4 5.1 0.0)`

Suppose you've stored a point location in an AutoLISP variable, as in the above example. Now you want to display the location of the point in your drawing. You can enter:

Type: `Blipmode <Return>`

Response: `OFF/ON <On>: ON <Return>`

Type: `ID <Return>`

Response: `Point:`

Type: `!pt1 <Return>`

Response: `X = 2.4000      Y = 5.1000      Z = 0.0000`

The system responds by displaying a "blip" at the x,y,z location that was saved in the **pt1** variable. (You don't need to turn on BLIPMODE if it's already on.)

User Input to an AutoLISP Routine

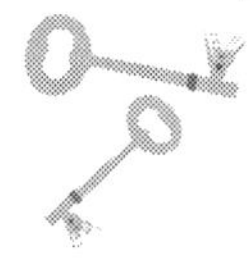

So far, we've talked about storing values in AutoLISP variables by using the (setq function directly. However, you'll often want AutoLISP to prompt you to enter text, a number or a point from the keyboard. To do this, you'll use the (getstring, (getint, (getreal and (getpoint functions.

Let's look at the (getint and (getreal functions first.

(getint & (getreal

Suppose you had a program that created views of a predetermined size and location, according to the number of views you asked for. You'd be prompted to enter the number of views. While you did that, AutoLISP would wait for your input and the program would then continue running.

The part of the program that prompted you and accepted your input might look something like this:

Type:
```
(setq n_views
(getint "\nEnter number of views to create: ")) <Return>
```

Response:
```
Enter number of views to create:
```

Type:
```
2 <Return>
```

Go ahead and type this example. When you do, the above prompt will be printed on your screen, and AutoLISP will wait for you to type an integer followed by a Return.

You can see the value that was stored in the **n_views** variable by entering:

Type:
```
!n_views <Return>
```

Response:
```
2
```

The backslash-n (**\n**) that precedes the prompt in the (getint example above causes AutoLISP to go to a new line before typing the rest of the prompt enclosed by the quotation marks.

NOTE: The n that follows the backslash MUST be a lowercase letter, or it won't make AutoLISP go to a new line.

Now retype the (getint example. When you're prompted to enter a number, try entering an alpha character or a real number (such as 3.5). Notice how AutoLISP won't accept any input but an integer.

The following example is similar to the one above but asks you to enter a real number. Enter the following:

Type:
```
(setq temperature
(getreal "\nEnter temperature in degrees: ")) <Return>
```

Response:
```
Enter temperature in degrees:
```

Type:
```
70 <Return>
```

Just as before, you'll be given a prompt, and AutoLISP will wait for you to enter a real number. This time, you're allowed to enter either an integer or a real number. If you enter an integer, AutoLISP's (getreal function will convert it to a real (floating point) number. As you might expect, string values are not accepted as input. Now, if you enter the following, AutoLISP will print the floating point value that's stored in the **temperature** variable:

Type:
```
!temperature <Return>
```

Response:
```
70.0
```

The (getstring Function

As you'd expect, the (getstring function is the way to interactively enter text from the keyboard into an AutoLISP program as it prompts you to do so. The following example is an illustration of how this function might be used:

Type:
```
(setq newtxt
(getstring "\nEnter text: ")) <Return>
```

Response:
```
Enter text:
```

Type: `Getstring_enters_text <Return>`

You'll be able to enter a string of text that contains no spaces. You can enter alpha or numeric characters, since the (getstring function converts whatever you type into text. AutoLISP will remember if any text you type in was in uppercase or lowercase characters.

Now let's instruct AutoLISP to type the contents of the **newtxt** variable.

Type: `!newtxt <Return>`

Response: `"Getstring_enters_text"`

Notice the quotation marks around the response. Also notice that the uppercase and lowercase letters have been preserved, and that you had no spaces in the text sentence string.

Creating a Sentence With (getstring

If you want to enter a string of text that contains spaces (a sentence, for instance), you'll need to restructure your AutoLISP instruction as the following:

Type:
```
(setq sentence
(getstring 2 "\nEnter a sentence: ")) <Return>
```

Response: `Enter a sentence:`

Type: `Getstring enters text <Return>`

Type a sentence in response to the prompt and press the Return key at the end of the sentence. Your sentence is limited to 132 characters.

In this example, the variable name **sentence** is later followed by the **(getstring** function and a number. The actual number you choose to place behind the function and variable name has no meaning; just the fact that a number is there causes the (getstring function to let you type text and spaces. Without a number, AutoLISP considers a space to be a Return.

The contents of the **sentence** variable can be displayed as in the preceding examples.

Type: `!sentence <Return>`

Response: `"Getstring enters text"`

Notice that the uppercase and lowercase characters and text spacing are preserved.

The (getpoint Function

The (getpoint function is similar to the other functions that request user input, as we've already discussed. But the (getpoint function also lets you enter your input from the keyboard, from the tablet or from the mouse. Enter the following:

Type: `(setq pt1 (getpoint "\nEnter a point: ")) <Return>`

When you're prompted to enter a point, type the following:

Type: `4,4,0 <Return>`

The location of the x,y,z point **4.0,4.0,0.0** will be stored in the **pt1** variable.

Now type the example again, but this time when you're prompted to enter a point, digitize a point by using the mouse or tablet cursor. Once again, the point value that you entered will be stored in the **pt1** variable.

The new **pt1** value will take the place of the value you already entered.

The (getpoint function also lets you use AutoCAD's *rubber band* feature. Enter the following:

Type: `(setq pt2 (getpoint pt1 "\nSecond point: ")) <Return>`

In response to the prompt, use your mouse or cursor to digitize the point. The rubber band feature will be activated because of the **pt1** argument that is placed after the **(getpoint** function. If you leave out the **pt1** argument, rubber banding will not be activated.

Association Lists

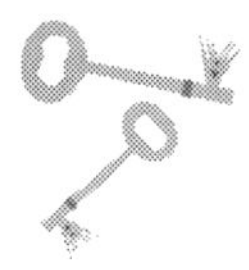

Another part of the database that the above program relies on is the entity sublist, or *association list*. (Remember those numbers you were asked to pay special attention to in Chapter 1? They came at the beginning of each entity—or association—list and were referred to as "keys" or "codes").

As you'll now probably recall, the entity list defines an entity. An entity list for a line has six association lists, shown here (each list is contained within parentheses):

```
((-1 . <Entity name: 6000001a>) (0 . "LINE") (8 . "LINES")
(10 3.0 4.0 0.0) (11 2.0 6.0 0.0) (210 0.0 0.0 1.0)
```

An association list is often used where an *identifier key* is needed. In the AutoCAD database, the *key* is the first item in each entity sublist (association list). Look at the association list below:

```
(8 . "LINES")
```

This is an association list shown in the example just above. The **8** is the key. You may recall that the text string following it is a layer name: the line resides on the **LINES** layer.

The (assoc Function

You can use the (assoc function to find information in an entity list. Let's use the line entity list below:

```
((-1 . <Entity name: 6000001a>) (0 . "LINE") (8 . "LINES")
(10 3.0 4.0 0.0) (11 2.0 6.0 0.0) (210 0.0 0.0 1.0)
```

Start out by loading the file you saved from Chapter 1 (DBASE1). Remember? You drew a line from 3,4 to 2,6 on a layer called LINES. Get a copy of the line entity list by following these steps:

1. Go to the text screen:

Type: `(setq e (car (entsel "\nSelect entity: "))) <Return>`

2. Select the line entity. (You'll see that AutoLISP prints the AutoCAD-assigned entity name, as below.)

Response: `<Entity name: 6000001a>`

NOTE: If you miss the line when you try to select it, the AutoCAD-assigned entity name will not be printed, and you'll have to go back to step 1. Remember, the line listing may alter slightly on your machine.

3. Now get a working copy of the line entity list by entering:

Type: `(setq edata (entget e)) <Return>`

A copy of the line entity data, similar to the one below, is printed to your screen:

Response:
```
((-1 . <Entity name: 6000001a>) (0 . "LINE") (8 . "LINES")
(10 3.0 4.0 0.0) (11 2.0 6.0 0.0) (210 0.0 0.0 1.0)
```

It's stored in the variable called **edata** (any variable name could have been chosen, but **edata** is a good abbreviation for "entity data").

Now use the (assoc function to copy an association list from the entity list. Let's make a copy of the association list that contains the location of the ending point of the line and store the copy in a variable called **end_point_data**. Here's how it's done:

Type:
```
(setq end_point_data (assoc 11 edata)) <Return>
```

The variable **end_point_data** now contains a copy of the association list that tells where the endpoint of the line is. You can tell AutoLISP to print the contents of the **end_point_data** variable to the screen by entering:

Type:
```
!end_point_data <Return>
```

If your line is located in the same position as the line in this example, you'll see the following association list displayed:

Response:
```
(11 2.0 6.0 0.0)
```

The x,y,z coordinate locations of the endpoint of the line are **2,6,0.**

Applying AutoLISP Into the Database

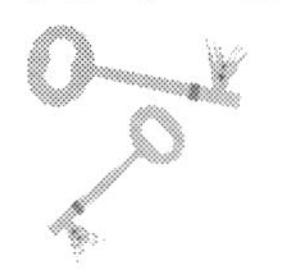

So far, you've looked at some AutoLISP basics. It's time to apply what you've learned. First, you'll see how to substitute new for old entity data; then you'll try your hand at scaling and renaming blocks.

If you've purchased the *Outside AutoCAD Companion Disk*—and if it's properly installed—all you need do is use the Release 12 APPLOAD command, then type in the name of the programs that follow. The four AutoLISP programs on the *Companion Disk* are:

- LINE_MOD.LSP (modifies a line)
- BLK_SCAL.LSP (rescales a block)
- BLK_NAME.LSP (rename a block)
- BLK_LIST.LSP (searches the database for blocks)

If you don't have the *Outside AutoCAD Companion Diskette*, you can create the programs as you work through the book. You'll find complete instructions on creating and loading these programs in Appendix A. Make certain the files are loaded and ready to use. Use the Release 12 command of APPLOAD to load the files.

Substituting Data

What would happen if you could change one of an entity's x, y or z values?

Well, if the entity were a line, the endpoint would move. If it were a block, you could scale a block in a single axis at a time!

Let's start with the line entity you're familiar with. Draw a line from 3,4,0 to 2,6,0. Perform the three steps as you work the example. Follow the explanations closely.

First, flip to your text screen:

Type:
```
(setq e (car (entsel "\nSelect entity: "))) <Return>
```

The **(entsel** function returns a list, consisting of the AutoCAD-assigned entity name, followed by the x,y,z location where you selected the entity. The **(car** function gets the entity name from the list and passes it to the **(setq** function, which stores it in the **e** variable.

Second, select the line entity. You'll see that AutoLISP prints the AutoCAD-assigned entity name.

Response:
```
Select entity:
```

(Pick the line with your mouse.)

Response:
```
<Entity name: 6000001a>
```

(You may get a slightly different number in your machine.)

Third, to get a working copy of the line entity list:

Type:
```
(setq edata (entget e)) <Return>
```

Once again, the entity list should look like this:

Response:
```
((-1 . <Entity name: 6000001a>) (0 . "LINE") (8 . "LINES")
(10 3.0 4.0 0.0) (11 2.0 6.0 0.0) (210 0.0 0.0 1.0)
```

Substituting New Data for Old Data

Now you'll use the (subst function to substitute a new value for one of the existing values in the association list where the line endpoint values are stored. We'll change the x value from 2.0 to 8.0 in this association list:

(11 2.0 6.0 0.0).

You'll also be using the (cons function, which you haven't used before, to construct a new association list that you'll substitute for an existing one.

Since the y and z values won't change, save them so you can use them with the instructions provided later. You can save the y value by entering:

Type:
```
(setq y_value (caddr (assoc 11 edata))) <Return>
```

Response:
```
6.0
```

In this instruction, the **(caddr** function picks out the third item (the y value of 6.0) in the association list and sends it on to the **(setq** function, which stores it in the variable called **y_value**.

Save the z value by entering:

Type:
```
(setq z_value (cadddr (assoc 11 edata))) <Return>
```

Response:
```
0.0
```

Operating in the same manner as the previous instruction, this instruction goes into the association list with the key of **11**. The **(cadddr** function gets the fourth item (the z value of 0.0) and stores it in the variable called **z_value**.

To make the substitution,

Type:
```
(setq edata
(subst
(cons 11 (List 8.0 y_value z_value)) (assoc 11 edata)
edata)
) <Return>
```

The instructions above may look complicated, but they're simple when you look at them one piece at a time. Let's look at the far right inside sets of parentheses in the third line:

```
(assoc 11 edata
```

The **(assoc** function, as explained earlier, finds the association list that has the key of **11** stored in the **edata** variable.

```
(cons 11 (List 8.0 y_value z_value))
```

The list constructor function, **(cons**, creates a list that begins with the association list key, **11**. The key is followed by the function **(List**, and the new x value that will eventually be assigned to the endpoint of the line. Following the new x value are the existing y and z values, which were each stored in variables.

```
(subst
(cons 11 (List 8.0 y_value z_value)) (assoc 11 edata) edata)
```

You already know what the **(cons** and **(assoc** functions do. Now the **(subst** function substitutes the new association list for the old one that was found by the **(assoc** function. The **edata** variable is the last argument that appears in the instruction. It tells the **(subst** function which entity list will receive the substitution. The change has now been made to a copy of the entity list.

Remember, up to this point, you've been making changes to a *copy* of the entity list, not the entity list itself. You won't see any changes to the line entity. In the next step, we'll make the change to the line.

The last step is to use the **(entmod** function to modify the entity whose name appears at the beginning of the entity list. In this case, it's the line. When the following command is typed, the data in the copy of the entity list takes the place of the data belonging to the entity itself.

Type: `(entmod edata) <Return>`

You'll see the endpoint of the line entity "move" from its original location to the new location, specified by the new x values, but the same y and same z values.

Applied AutoLISP Programs

If the example you just completed were placed into a real AutoLISP program, it would look similar to the following one. Now would be a good time to QUIT your editing session and create the program, using your ASCII text processor. Go to the directory where you keep your AutoCAD drawing files. Copy the program, just as it appears, and save it under the name LINE_MOD.LSP.

Type:
```
(defun C:LINE_MOD ()
(setq e (car (entsel "\nSelect entity: ")))
 (setq edata (entget e))
 (setq y_value (caddr (assoc 11 edata)))
 (setq z_value (cadddr (assoc 11 edata)))
 (setq edata (subst
  (cons 11 (List 8.0 y_value z_value)) (assoc 11 edata)
 edata)
 )
 (entmod edata)
 (princ)
)
```

Modifying a Block

This program is an illustration of how you can scale a block entity independently in x and y. It's actually a modification of the LINE_MOD.LSP program above. You can copy this program using your text editor and save it to your AutoCAD drawing directory. Call it BLK_SCAL.LSP.

Type:
```
(defun C:BLK_SCAL ()
 (setq new_x_scal (getreal "\nEnter new x scale: "))
 (setq new_y_scal (getreal "\nEnter new y scale: "))
 (setq e (car (entsel "\nSelect block: ")))
 (setq edata (entget e))
 (setq edata
  (subst (cons 41 new_x_scal) (assoc 41 edata) edata)
 )
 (setq edata
  (subst (cons 42 new_y_scal) (assoc 42 edata) edata)
 )
 (entmod edata)
 (princ)
)
```

Renaming a Block

What do you think would happen if you substituted a new block name for the old one? The new block appears in the old block's place, like magic! Try to find an AutoCAD command that will do this. (There isn't one!)

This next program is an illustration of how you can rename a block entity. It's actually a modification of the BLK_SCAL.LSP program above. You can copy this program using your text editor and save it to your AutoCAD drawing directory. Call it BLK_NAME.LSP.

Type:
```
(defun C:BLK_NAME ()
  (setq new_bname (getstring "\nEnter new block name: "))
  (setq e (car (entsel "\nSelect block: ")))
  (setq edata (entget e))
  (setq edata
    (subst (cons 2 new_bname) (assoc 2 edata) edata)
  )
  (entmod edata)
  (princ)
)
```

Searching a Blocks Database

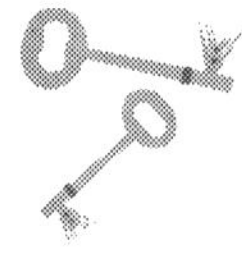

The *Outside AutoCAD Companion Disk* provides you with an AutoLISP program called BLK_LIST.LSP that takes the chore out of searching the database and helps you search the database for block information. This is the most complicated program and so is saved until last.

In Chapter 1, I referred to the BLK_LIST.LSP file as an example of an AutoLISP-based database utility program. The program is shown below, followed by a line-by-line explanation of its functions.

Creating BLK_LIST.LSP

If you've purchased the *Outside AutoCAD Companion Disk,* load the BLK_LIST.LSP file with the Release 12 APPLOAD command. If you don't have the *Companion Disk,* you'll have to create the program. Appendix A gives you complete instructions on how to do this. Use an ASCII text editor such as the DOS 5.0 editor, Norton Editor or the KETIV editor to create the file. Whatever editor you use, make sure you can operate it in ASCII mode or that it can output an ASCII text file.

Notice how the program uses indenting. If a function cannot be completed on one line, it continues on the next line, indented by two spaces. The program's ending parenthesis is on a line by itself and is aligned with the opening parenthesis of the program. Create the BLK_LIST.LSP file as follows (don't type in the line numbers—they're just reference numbers).

Comments

All comments in the program begin with the semicolon character (;). Comments aren't needed for the program to run, but they help you remember your train of thought as you write the program. Always use comments that are easily understood so another person can understand the program with a minimum of effort.

Program Listing

Here's how the program looks line by line.

```
 1 (defun C:BLK_LIST (/ e enttyp ename blkexist blkname blknum
    selset)
 2   (setq e (entnext))        ; Set e to the first entity name
 3   (while e                  ; Loop as long as there are entities
      ;; Look at the entity type code
 4     (setq enttyp (cdr (assoc 0 (entget e))))
 5     (if (equal enttyp "INSERT") ; Is the entity a Block?
 6       (progn                    ; ...if so, do the following...
          ;; Save the block name in "ename"
 7         (setq ename (cdr (assoc 2 (entget e))))
          ;; if we haven't seen the block before...
 8         (if (not (member ename blkexist))
            ;; Append ename to list of existing blocks
 9           (setq blkexist (append blkexist (list ename)))
          ) ;endif
        ) ; endprogn
      ) ; endif
10     (setq e (entnext e))  ; Set e to the next entity
    ) ; endwhile
11   (princ "\n")                    ; blank line
12   (princ "\n    Block    -    No.") ; heading
```

```
13    (princ "\n    ---------") ; heading
14    (foreach blkname blkexist        ; for each block found...
        ;; create selection set
15      (setq selset
          (ssget "X" (list (cons 0 "INSERT") (cons 2 blkname)))
        ) ; endsetq
        ;; count number of blocks in SS
16      (setq blknum (sslength selset))
17      (princ "\n    ")                ; blank line
18      (princ blkname)                 ; print block name
19      (princ "     ")                 ; spaces
20      (princ blknum)                  ; print number of blocks found
      ) ; endforeach
21    (princ)                         ; suppress nil message to screen
22 ) ; end BLK_LIST
```

Program Explanation

To help you understand the program in depth, here's a line-by-line explanation of how it functions and runs.

```
1 (defun C:BLK_LIST (/ e enttyp ename blkexist blkname blknum
    selset)
```

The **(defun** function creates a user-defined function. A set of parentheses following the name of the new function contains the variables that will be used in the new function. Since the variables are declared in the parentheses following a slash (/), they will exist only while this new program is running.

> *NOTE:* The slash *must* be followed by a space.

```
2 (setq e (entnext))
```

When the **(entnext** function is called with no arguments, it finds the AutoCAD-assigned name of the first entity in the database. In this case, the entity name is stored in the variable called **e**.

```
3 (while e
```

A **(while** loop begins here. The **(while** function looks at the expression following it (**e**, in this case) to see if it is true. Here, it looks to see if something is stored in the **e** variable. As long as there is something stored in the **e** variable, we haven't yet looked at the entire database.

```
4 (setq enttyp (cdr (assoc 0 (entget e))))
```

This is a set of nested AutoLISP instructions. When you see a nested function like this, it's easiest to start with the inner-most set of parentheses and work your way out.

The **(entget** function is used to extract the database description from the entity.

The **(assoc** function separates out a specific part of the database description so that (in this case) information can be obtained from it. In this instance, **(assoc** is used to extract the name of the entity type.

The **(cdr** function divides the entity type from the **0**, which identifies it as the entity type. The **(cdr** function looks at a list and returns all but the first element of the list.

The list only had 2 parts, so **(cdr** returned the entity type, which was the second part.

Finally, the **(setq** function stores the entity type in the variable called **enttyp**.

```
5  (if (equal enttyp "INSERT")
```

The **(equal** function compares two values to see if they evaluate to the same thing.

The **(if** function tests an expression to see if it's true. In this instance, if the value stored in the variable called **enttyp** is the same as the string **INSERT**, then the expression is true (**INSERT** indicates that the entity type is a block). If the expression is true, the expression following the **(if** function is carried out. If it isn't true, the second expression is carried out (if it exists).

```
6  (progn
```

The **(progn** function is followed by a set of parentheses. Everything inside these parentheses is counted as a single expression. It's used here so that multiple expressions can be enclosed inside its parentheses, making them count as a single expression.

```
7 (setq ename (cdr (assoc 2 (entget e))))
```

This nested expression works like line 4, except this one uses the **(assoc** function to extract the name of the block by using the block code **2**. The block name is saved in the **ename** variable.

```
8 (if (not (member ename blkexist))
```

The **(member** function checks to see if the value stored in the first variable (**ename**) is found in the "list" named by the second variable (**blkexist**). (See line 9 for explanation.)

```
9 (setq blkexist (append blkexist (list ename)))
```

The purpose of this nested set of instructions is to create a list consisting of the names of all the blocks in the AutoCAD drawing database. The **(list** function turns whatever expressions follow it into a list.

```
10 (setq e (entnext e))
```

When the **(entnext** function is called with the name of an entity, the next entity name is found. This instruction stores the AutoCAD-assigned entity name in the variable **e** so it can be examined as the previous entity was.

```
11 (princ "\n")
```

When the **\n** argument is used with **(princ**, a blank line is printed on the display.

```
12 (princ "\n    Block    -    No.")
```

Lines 12 and 13 are similar. Each uses the **(princ** function to print the text contained in the quotation marks.

```
13 (princ "\n    ————") ; heading
```

(See the line 12 description.)

```
14 (foreach blkname blkexist
```

The **(foreach** function looks at each item in the list named by the second argument (**blkexist**) and performs the expression that follows. The **blkname** variable can be considered a temporary storage variable for each item found in the list.

```
15 (setq selset
     (ssget "X" (list (cons 0 "INSERT") (cons 2 blkname)))
   )
```

This set of instructions creates a "selection set" through the **(ssget** function. A selection set is a group of entities that AutoLISP remembers is a group. In this case, the **(list** and **(cons** functions tell the **(ssget** function which entities to remember as a selection set. The entities to be remembered are blocks and are called by the block name that is stored in the **blkname** variable. In other words, all the blocks in the drawing that have the block name that is stored in the **blkname** variable will be remembered as a selection set. The selection set will be stored in the variable **selset**.

```
16 (setq blknum (sslength selset))
```

In this line of instructions, the **(sslength** function looks to see how long the list called **selset** is. In other words, **(sslength** is looking to see how many block entities were found by the **(ssget** function. The number of blocks having the name specified in line 15 above are counted using this routine. The number is stored in the variable called **blknum**.

```
17 (princ "\n     ")
```

This is similar to a previous function. It causes the cursor to go to a new line and then prints a few blank characters.

```
18 (princ blkname)
```

The **(princ** function is used in this case to print the block name belonging to the blocks that were just counted. The **(princ** function, without the **\n**, will not go to the next line.

```
19 (princ "      ")
```

Here, the **(princ** function prints a few blank characters to put some space between the block name and the next item that will be printed.

```
20 (princ blknum)
```

The **(princ** function now prints the contents of the **blknum** variable. In this case, the **blknum** variable contains the number of blocks that were found by the **(ssget** function.

```
21 (princ)
```

The **(princ** variable, when used by itself just before the end of the program, suppresses the value that would normally be returned by the function. Its purpose in this case is to give a more pleasing output.

```
22 )
```

The right parenthesis is the final closing paren that closes the program.

Moving On

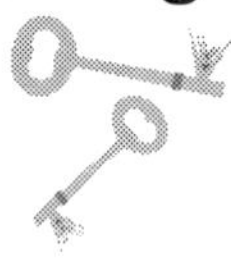

AutoLISP is one of the most popular ways to add flexibility and programmability to AutoCAD's database. It's an excellent tool to use in becoming acquainted with AutoCAD's database from your vantage point outside AutoCAD. In Chapter 3, "The Power of Selection Sets," you'll get acquainted with the concept of selection sets and why you'll want to use them often as you create and edit your designs and drawings.

The Power of Selection Sets

In this chapter, you'll learn how to use AutoCAD's built-in *selection set* tools for selecting and editing a drawing based on layers, colors, entity names and more! You'll also discover the power and flexibility of selection sets and will soon be using these tools in nearly every editing session. And you'll learn how easy it is to build your own selection set tools.

Selection Sets—The Tools You've Always Wanted

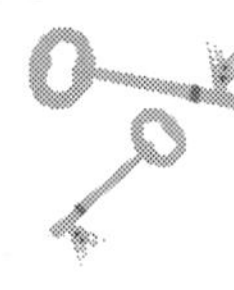

Selection sets are one of AutoCAD's most powerful editing tools. Have you ever wanted to select all the geometry on a certain layer, or according to block name or entity type? What about selecting all the yellow text that falls inside a windowed area? Did you know that all these capabilities and more have been available since AutoCAD Release 9, and continue to get more powerful with each release?

Many AutoCAD users have never heard of these tools because few courses teach about them, and few users discover them in the AutoCAD documentation. You're about to find out that the tools you've always wanted have been there all along! And they're ready for you to use and customize for your own needs.

The Selection Set Filters Dialogue Box

The quickest way to create and use selection sets is by using AutoCAD's built-in selection set filters dialogue box (see Figure 3-1). Here's an example of how it works.

Suppose you wanted to select all the text on two layers (TEXT1 and TEXT2) of your drawing in order to move all of it onto another layer (TEXT3). You could use the filters dialogue box to find all the text to be changed without disturbing any other geometry that may reside on the same layer as the text. Let's bring up the filters dialogue box to see how to use it.

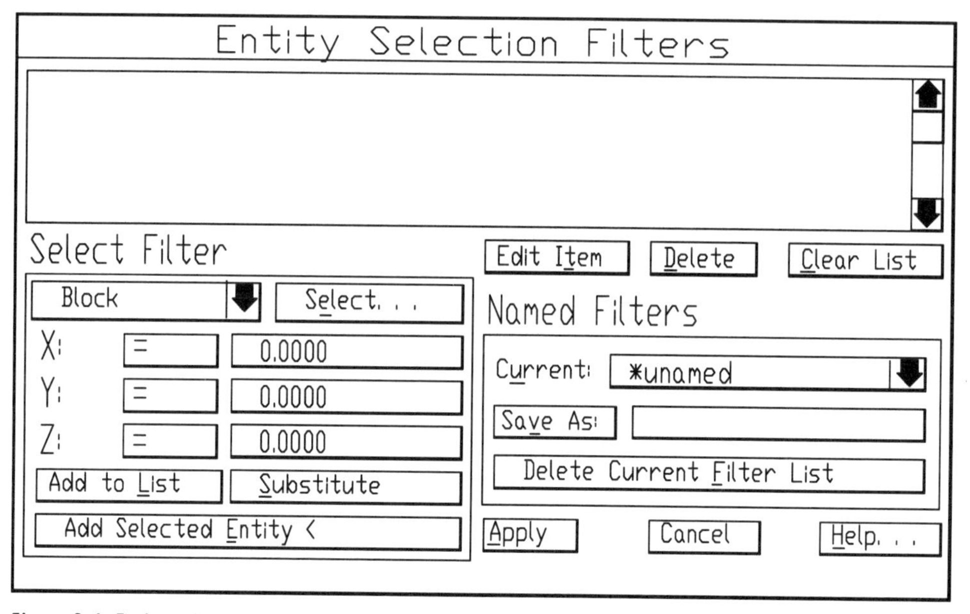

Figure 3-1: Entity selection filters dialogue box

1. Start a NEW drawing and at the Command prompt:

Type: `Filter <Return>`

The filters dialogue box will appear. It looks similar to the dialogue box shown in Figure 3-1. The top portion of the dialogue box, where you'll write your selection *filter list* (explained in step 4, below) will be blank if you haven't used it before.

2. Now you can tell the dialogue box what you want to select. Find the Select Filter box and, just below it, point to the down arrow and click the mouse (or cursor) button.

Clicking on the down arrow makes a list of filters appear, as shown in Figure 3-2.

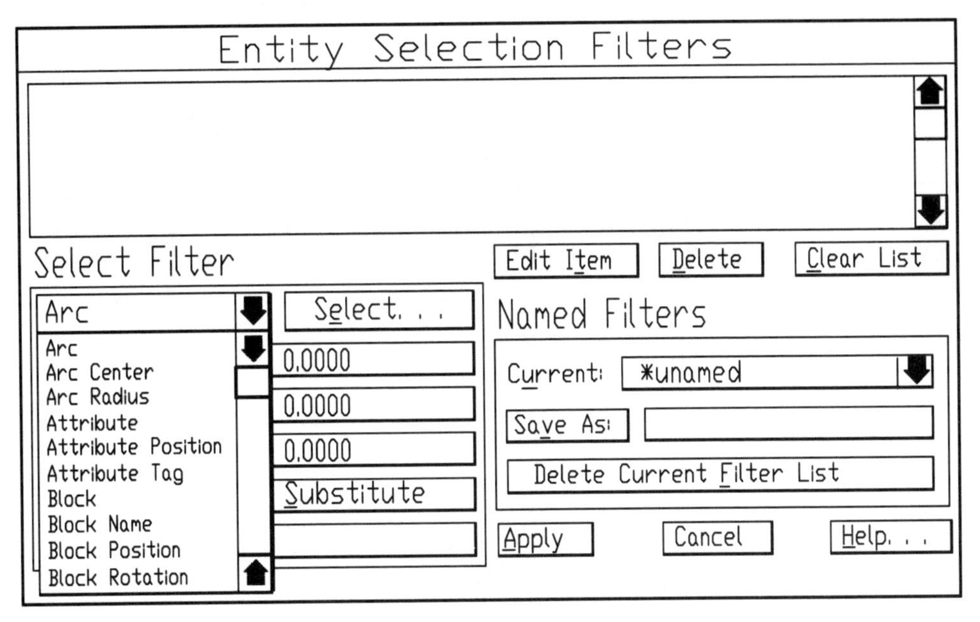

Figure 3-2: Filter list

3. Use the scrolling arrows or scroll bar on the right side of the list to find the *text* filter. When it appears, pick it.

When you pick the text filter, it will be highlighted and will appear in the Select Filter box.

4. Pick the Add to List box. Picking this box causes the filter you've chosen—the text filter, in this case—to be added to the filter list area of the dialogue box. When your selection appears there, it will be one of the items used to create the selection set in the drawing.
5. Go back to the Select Filter down arrow and pick it again. Once again, the list of filters reappears.
6. In the list of filters, find and select *layer*. Notice that the layer filter now appears in the Select Filter box.
7. Pick the Select... box. When you pick the Select... box, a list of the layer names appears, as shown in Figure 3-3.

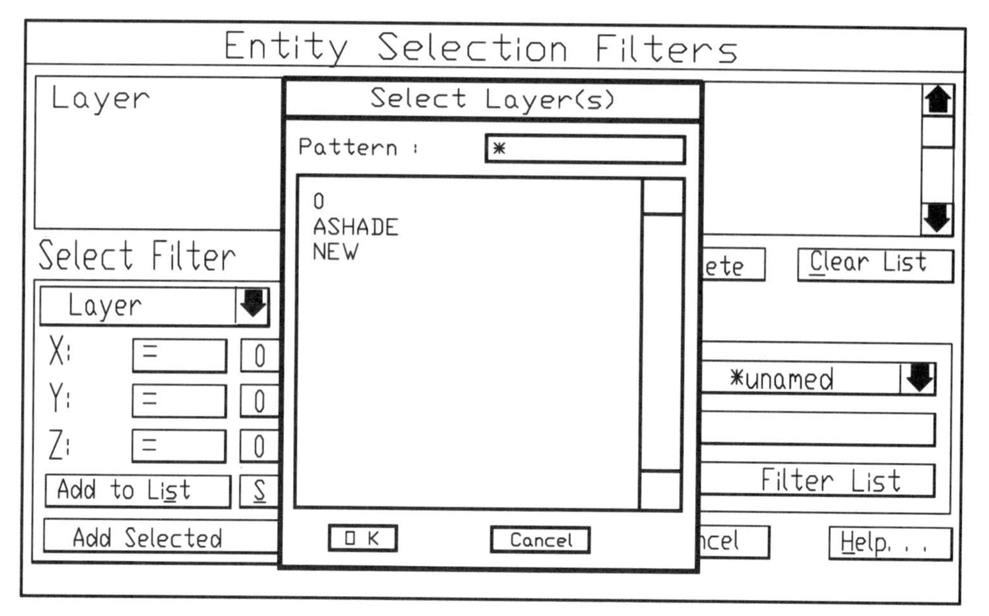

Figure 3-3: Layer name list

8. Pick each of the layers on which the text resides.

9. Pick OK.

10. Pick the Add to List box. Picking this box enters your new selection filter into the filter list area at the top of the dialogue box. Now there are two items in the filter list.

11. Pick the Apply box. This makes the dialogue box disappear.

12. Press the Return key to finish the process.

The selection set has now been created. You may have been surprised to see that no entities were selected. When you create a selection set, it doesn't select the entities in the familiar way. The thing to remember is that editing commands and the SELECT command do the selecting—the selection set just gathers a list of entities that can be selected by one of these commands.

The final step is to use the AutoCAD CHPROP command to move the text entities to the desired layer.

13. At the Command prompt:

Type: `CHPROP <Return>`

14. When the system prompts you to select objects:

Type: `P <Return>`

This causes the set of previously selected objects to be selected. Now you can easily finish the CHPROP command and move the text entities onto the desired layer.

The selection set filters dialogue box has a great deal of flexibility and power. It makes it easy to select a group of entities at the same time.

AutoLISP Tools Behind the Dialogue Box

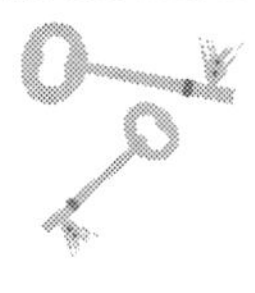

The selection set filters dialogue box is often the right tool to use. But there will be times when you'll want to bypass the dialogue box and use the selection set tools directly. Following are short descriptions of the selection set tools that control the dialogue box, along with some tips for using each of them.

The (ssget Function

You create selection sets with AutoLISP's (ssget function. You can use it with a variety of arguments or with no argument at all. For instance:

Type: `(ssget) <Return>`

Response: `Select objects:`

You'll be prompted to select objects. If you want to save the selection set to use as input to a later command, you can add a variable (**saved_set**) to the above function, as shown below:

Type: `(setq saved_set (ssget)) <Return>`

Response: `Select objects:`

Again, you're prompted to select objects. After you select the desired objects and press the Return key, the group of entities that were selected will be remembered by the **saved_set** variable. You can use the MOVE command to move that group of entities later on in the editing session. When the system asks you to select objects:

Type: `!saved_set <Return>`

This selects the group of entities in the **saved_set** selection set for easy moving.

More Power With SSGET!

In this example, we'll create a selection set that will help us move all circles that reside on a specific layer and that lie inside a certain area on the drawing.

Start a new drawing and create new layers called ONE, TWO and THREE (or simply load the drawing file, DBASE3, from the *Outside AutoCAD Companion Diskette*). Assign colors to the layers as follows:

LAYER	COLOR
ONE	Red
TWO	Yellow
THREE	Green

Figure 3-4: Dbase 3

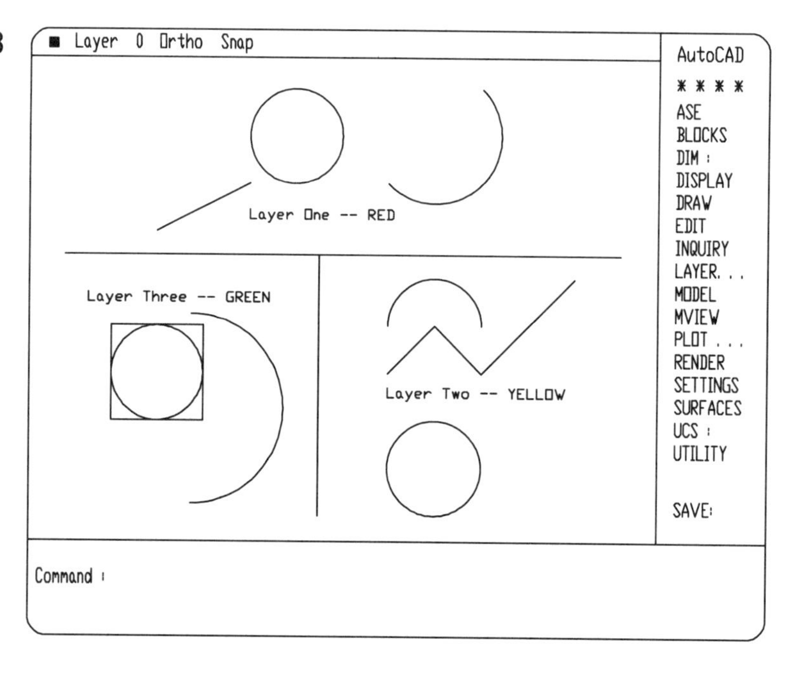

Set the ONE layer as the current layer and place several entities on the ONE layer. Use lines, arcs, circles (be sure to use circles), text and other entities as you wish.

Now set the TWO layer as the current layer and, just as you did in the previous step, add the same variety of entities to that layer.

Finally, repeat the above procedure for the THREE layer. You should now have a drawing with a variety of red, yellow and green entities, each color occupying a layer.

Before proceeding, save the drawing under the name DBASE3 (unless you already have the *Outside AutoCAD Companion Diskette*).

Now you're ready to use the (ssget function in combination with the AutoCAD "window" selection option to select only the circles you want to move. Enter the following:

Type: `MOVE <Return>`

The system will prompt you to select objects:

Type: `(ssget '((0 . "circle") (8 . "one"))) <Return>`

The system will continue to prompt you to select objects.

Now use your cursor or mouse to select a group of entities by window.

NOTE: You won't need to type a **w** for "window." Release 12 allows you to select by window or crossing without typing a **w** or **c**.

Notice that only the circles on layer ONE are selected, even though the selection window included many of the other entities, some of which are on the same layer and some of which are on other layers!

The Flexibility of (ssget "X")

Adding the X argument to the (ssget function creates a selection set according to a filter list that follows the function. Here's an example you can use with your DBASE3 drawing file.

Type: `(setq selset (ssget "X" '((0 . "circle")))) <Return>`

Now if you wanted to delete (or otherwise edit) all the circles in the drawing, you'd enter:

Type: `erase <Return>`

At the prompt to select objects:

Type: `!selset <Return>`

. . . and all of the circles will be selected!

NOTE: The above example will find and select ALL circles in the drawing database. Furthermore, if you type **(ssget "X")** with no filter arguments, ALL entities in the drawing database will be selected—even if they're on frozen layers.

Rational Arguments for (ssget "X")

In the above examples, (ssget always looked for conditions (entities) that matched, or were "equal," to the request. A special *key*, or *group code*, in Release 12 allows you to test for "less than," "greater than," "less than or equal," "greater than or equal," "not equal" and other conditions.

If you wanted to create a selection set of all circles with a radius greater than 0.5, you'd enter:

Type:
```
(setq selset_cir
  (ssget "X" '((0 . "circle") (-4 . ">") (40 . 0.5)))
) <Return>
```

The special group code is the **–4** that appears in the above example. The group code (or key) of **40** specifies the radius of a circle. In this example, all circles with a radius greater than **0.5** will be placed in the selection set. Refer to the *AutoLISP Programmer's Reference Manual* for an explanation of all of the group codes.

Sample Applications

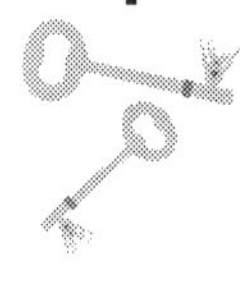

The following examples are two ways that you can use the (ssget function to assist you in editing a drawing or design. Both programs are found on the *Outside AutoCAD Companion Diskette*, or you can create them yourself with an ASCII text editor.

Some of the concepts used in these programs aren't covered in this book, but all AutoLISP functions that appear in the example programs are listed in Appendix B.

FIND_BLK.LSP

The FIND_BLK program searches the drawing database for the block named by the user and reports the number of times it occurs in the drawing. It also highlights the blocks that are found by using the AutoCAD SELECT command.

The FIND_BLK program is run by placing it in your drawing directory (or another directory from which it can be loaded), then loading it as follows:

Type: (load "find_blk") <Return>

To run the program:

Type: find_blk <Return>

The program will prompt you for the name of the block you wish to find. As you review the program, refer to the information in this chapter and in the previous chapter, "AutoLISP as a Database Tool," on AutoLISP. You'll find that it isn't hard to modify to meet your specific needs.

```
(defun C:FIND_BLK (/ blkname numberofblocks selset)
  ;; get name of block(s) to be found
  (setq blkname (getstring "\nEnter Block name: "))
  ;; convert blkname to upper case
  (setq blkname (strcase blkname))
  ;; find blocks with name specified by user
  (setq selset
    (ssget "X" (list (cons 0 "INSERT") (cons 2 blkname)))
  ) ; endsetq
  (if (equal selset nil)  ; if none found...
    (setq selset 0)       ; set "selset" to acceptable value
    (progn                ; otherwise do the following...
      ;; highlight the selected blocks with the SELECT command
      (command "SELECT" selset "")
      ;; count number of blocks selected
      (setq numberofblocks (sslength selset))
    );endprogn
  );endif
  ;; report number of blocks found
  (prompt "\nNumber of blocks named ") (princ blkname)
  (princ " = ") (princ numberofblocks) (princ)
) ; end FINDBLK
```

FIND_TXT.LSP

The FIND_TXT program works in a similar manner to the FIND_BLK program, but finds user-specified text. When the text is found, it flashes a box around the text. The program is really two programs in one. The first, called HILITEBOX, is what you might call a *subroutine* that draws the flashing box around the text. The second program is the main program that finds the text and then tells the subroutine to flash the box around the text.

Although the following example is quite complex, it is offered in anticipation that it will be of help to you as you collect design and editing tools.

```
;;; subroutine...
(defun hilitebox (searchdata Yval1 Yval2)
  (setq counter 0)
  ;; calculate highlight box
  (setq dotX1 (- (cadr (assoc 10 searchdata)) 5.) ; X1
        dotX2 (+ dotX1 10.) ; X2
        dotY1 (- (caddr (assoc 10 searchdata)) Yval1) ; Y1
        dotY2 (+ dotY1 Yval2) ; Y2
        pt1 (list dotX1 dotY1)
        pt2 (list dotX2 dotY1)
        pt3 (list dotX2 dotY2)
        pt4 (list dotX1 dotY2)
  ) ; endsetq

  ;; draw highlight box - color: dark grey
  (while (<= counter 10)
    (grdraw pt1 pt2 8)
    (grdraw pt2 pt3 8)
    (grdraw pt3 pt4 8)
    (grdraw pt4 pt1 8)
    (setq counter1 0)
    ;; draw highlight box - color: white
    (while (< counter1 200)
      (setq counter1 (1+ counter1))
    ) ; delay
    (grdraw pt1 pt2 7)
    (grdraw pt2 pt3 7)
    (grdraw pt3 pt4 7)
    (grdraw pt4 pt1 7)
    (setq counter1 0)
```

```
    (while (< counter1 200)
      (setq counter1 (1+ counter1))
    ) ; delay
    (setq counter (1+ counter))
  ) ; endwhile
) ; endhilitebox
 ;;; main function...

(defun C:FINDTEXT ()
  (setq srchtxt
    (strcase (getstring "\nEnter string to search for: "))
  ) ; endsetq
  ;; create selection set made up of only text
  (setq selset
    (ssget "X" (list (cons 0 "TEXT")))
  ) ; endsetq
  (if (equal selset nil) ; if nothing in selection set,
    (setq selset 0)      ; set selset to 0 for sslength function
    (setq nfound (sslength selset)) ; else, count the number found
  ) ; endif
  (setq indx 0)          ; set counter index
  ;; while items in selset, do the following
  (while (< indx (sslength selset))
    ;; Save entity name in "ename"
    (setq ename (ssname selset indx))
    ;; if right text is found,
    (if (equal srchtxt (cdr (assoc 1 (setq edata (entget ename)))))
      (progn             ;  do the following...
        ;; draw hilite box around matching text
        (hilitebox edata 5 5)
        ;; ask the user to keep looking or not...
        (setq look (strcase (getstring "\nKeep looking? y/n: ")))
          (if (= look "Y")
            ;; if yes, increment index
            (setq indx (1+ indx))
            ;; if no, set value to stop
            (setq indx (1+ (sslength selset)))
          ) ; endif
```

```
            (setq indx (1+ indx)) ; else, increment index
          ) ; endprogn
          (setq indx (1+ indx))   ; else, increment index
        ) ; endif
      ) ; endwhile
      (princ)
    ) ;end FINDTEXT
```

Moving On

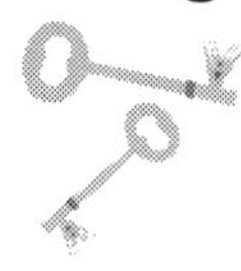

With the conclusion of this section, we're ready to begin learning about AutoCAD *attributes*. Attributes are often used to create bill-of-material listings, but in the following chapter, "The Value of Attributes," we'll explore some additional applications that will let you take advantage of principles you've already learned. You'll find that you'll be able to look even further into AutoCAD's database, where attributes are defined and stored.

SECTION II

Attributes: Adding Functionality and Intelligence

The Value of Attributes

Attributes have been a part of AutoCAD since most users can remember, yet they remain one of the most valuable elements of the software. Starting here, with the basics, you'll learn how to set up attributes and so build a foundation for using them. As you learn basic attribute concepts, you'll recognize areas in your work where their use can lighten your workload and enhance your productivity.

Also, with attribute intelligence, your drawings will finally consist of more than just graphics and text that can only be viewed and plotted. Whether you've only tried to use attributes or have used them extensively, you'll discover in this section how attributes can be of more value to you. You'll also learn numerous attribute applications. The listing below shows just a few of them. They're a fast and easy means to:

- Work with facilities management applications.
- Place text into predefined areas of a drawing.
- Create a bill of materials.
- Work in mapping applications.
- Add "intelligence" to a drawing.

You'll not only learn how to set up your drawing to work with attributes but also see how to extract them to a non-AutoCAD file that can be imported into a spreadsheet or database system. You'll also begin using attributes to save time, to ensure quality and to improve not just productivity but also the reliability of your products.

Let's take a look at some attribute basics.

What are AutoCAD Attributes?

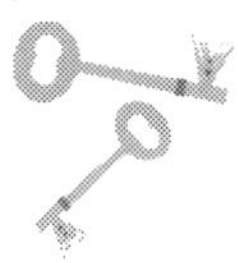

Attributes allow you to place text and/or text-based information into a drawing at predefined locations. You'll define the placed text by rules that control style, orientation, visibility and other features.

Attributes have to be contained in a block. An attribute may appear by itself, as text, but it more commonly appears as part of a block symbol.

To illustrate: attributes are used in electrical schematic applications where discrete components are labeled with a reference designation and a value for the component. Figure 4-1, for example, shows you a resistor with a reference designation of R1 and a resistance value of 50,000 ohms.

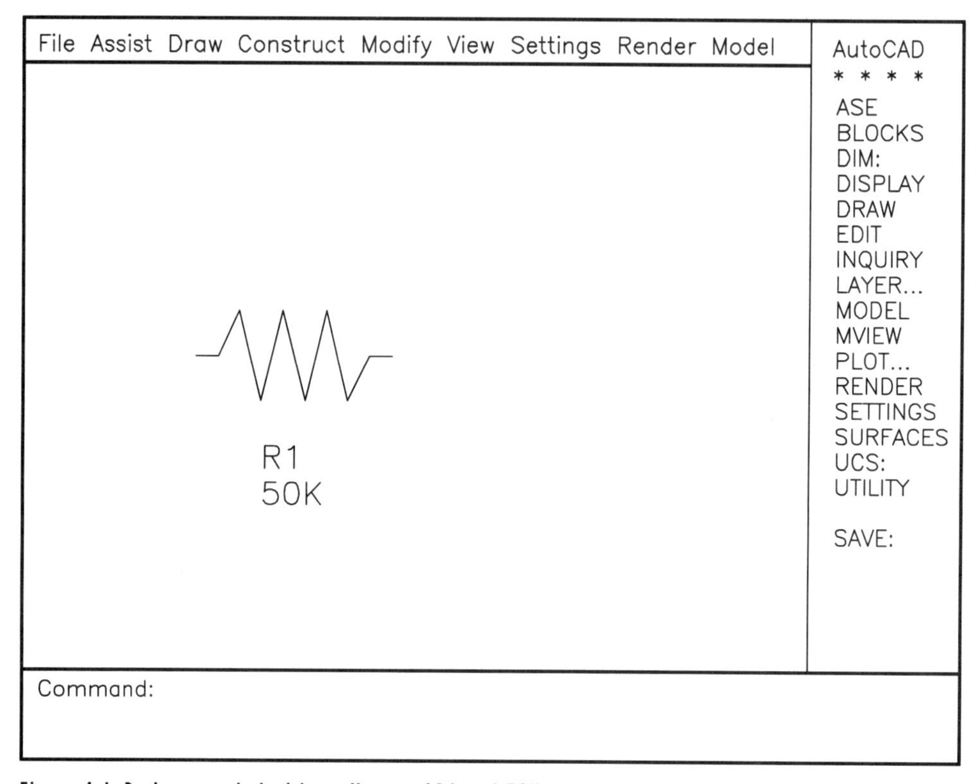

Figure 4-1: Resistor symbol with attributes of R1 and 50K

Figure 4-1 shows you that both the reference designation (R1) and the value (50K) are attributes. They occupy a user-defined location.

As you move through this chapter and the examples that follow, you'll learn how to define the various kinds of attributes. You'll also find out about the text variables you can use when defining attributes. For example, text can be in one of six modes: changeable, constant, visible, invisible, preset or not preset.

Defining Attributes

AutoCAD Release 12 gives you two ways to define attributes: you can use the ATTDEF (attribute define) command at the Command prompt; or you can use the DDATTDEF (dynamic dialogue attribute define) command, which brings up a dialogue box. Let's look at the dialogue box, keeping in mind that you can also use all of the key items in the dialogue box at the Command prompt with the ATTDEF command.

Figure 4-2 shows the Attribute Definition dialogue box after being filled in. This chapter will guide you in selecting options and entering information into the box. You can check the accuracy of your entries against the figure. Note that the X, Y and Z attributes in the Insertion Point dialogue area have not been filled in.

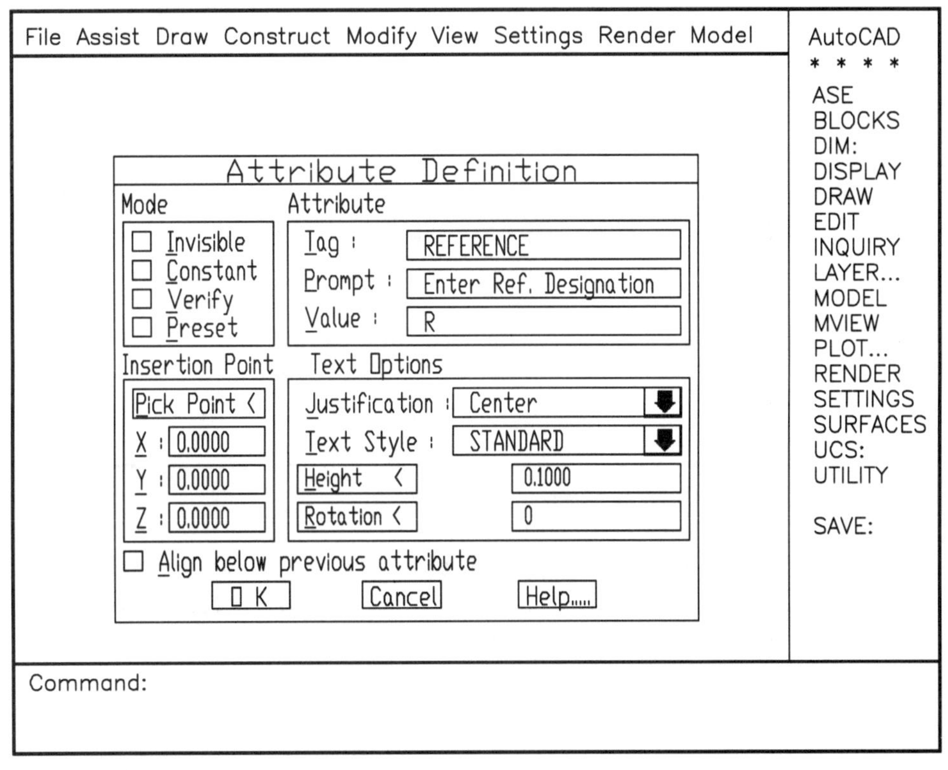

Figure 4-2: The AutoCAD Attribute Definition dialogue box

Using the Attribute Definition Dialogue Box

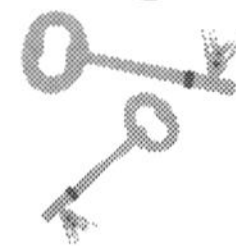

Let's create a resistor symbol with two attributes, like the one shown in Figure 4-1. First, start a NEW drawing and create the resistor (you can use lines or polylines). Its size is shown in Figure 4-3.

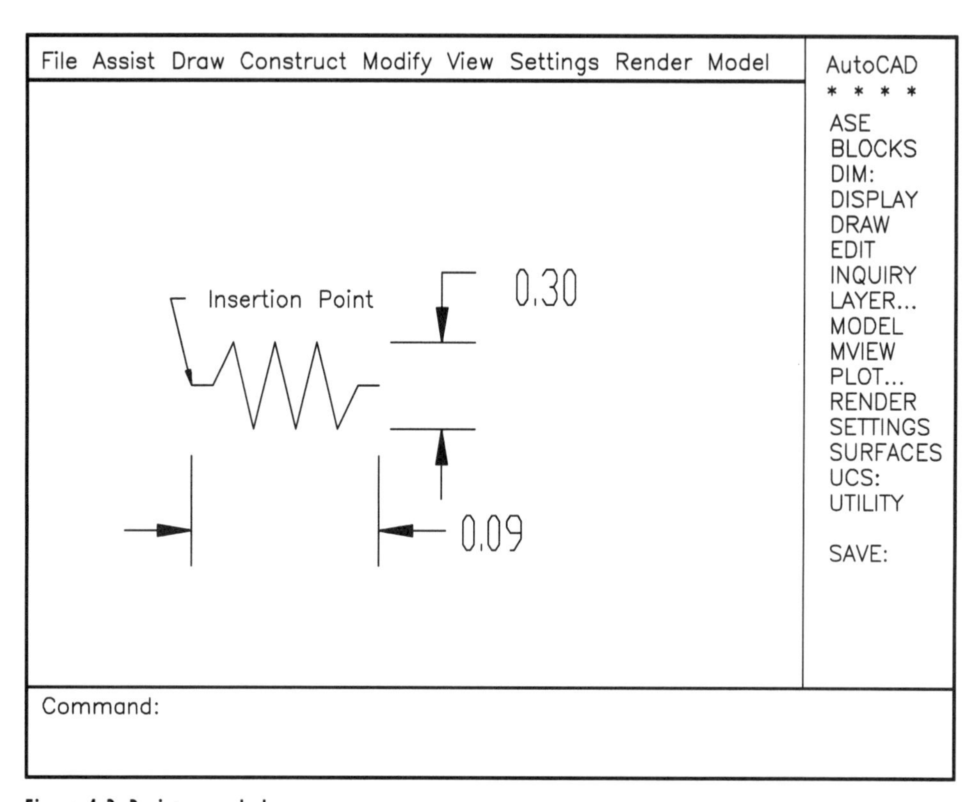

Figure 4-3: Resistor symbol

Don't worry if your drawing isn't perfect. The purpose of this exercise is to define a set of attributes. After you've created the resistor symbol, enter the command:

Type: `DDATTDEF <Return>`

The Attribute Definition dialogue box appears, as shown in Figure 4-4. Now you can fill in the information that's requested in the box. You can select the item to change by picking it with the mouse (or cursor) or by typing the underlined character.

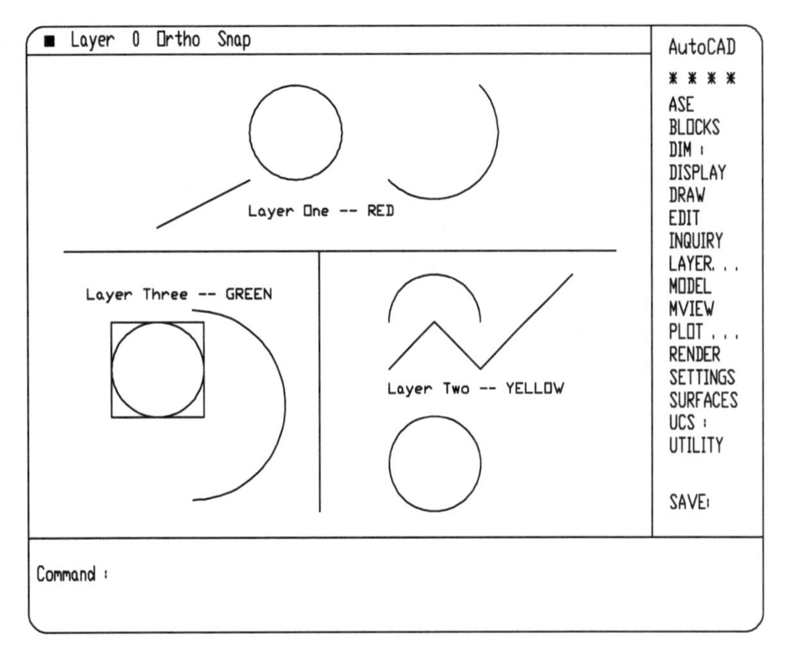

Figure 4-4: The four Attribute Definition dialogue box areas: Mode, Attribute, Insertion Point and Text Options

As you'll see from Figure 4-4, the dialogue box is divided into four areas: Mode, Attribute, Insertion Point and Text Options. Each of the areas is explained below.

NOTE: Use the mouse to pick each location in which you want to enter text. No Return is needed.

The Mode Dialogue Area

The Mode dialogue area, shown in Figure 4-5, contains instructions that specify whether the text (or *value,* in other words) contained in the attribute will be invisible/visible, constant/variable, verified/not verified and preset/not preset.

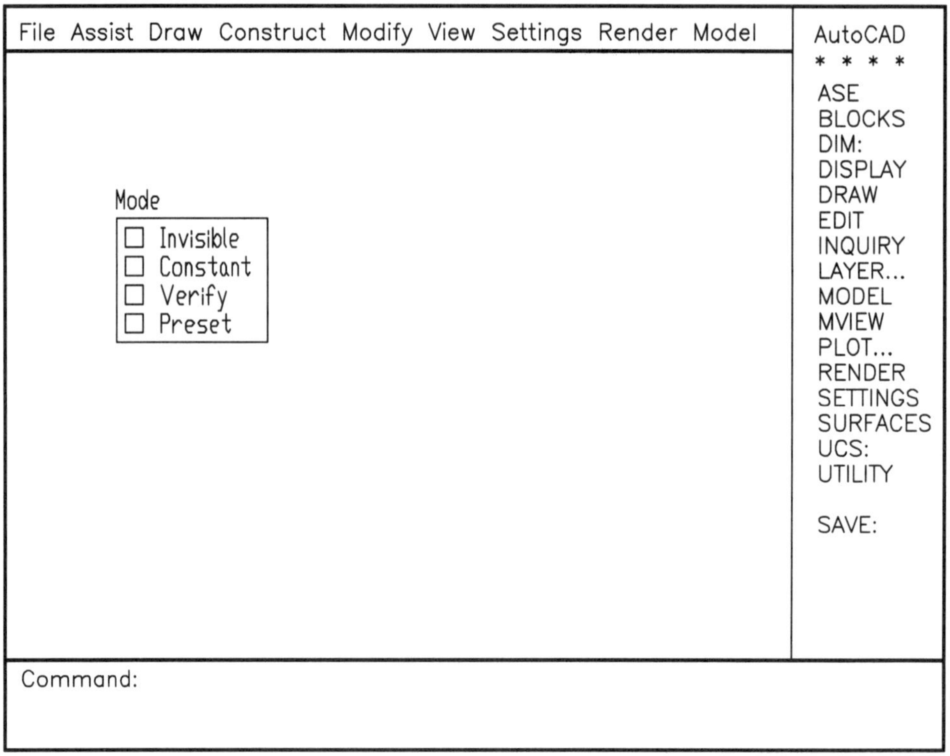

File Assist Draw Construct Modify View Settings Render Model

AutoCAD
* * * *
ASE
BLOCKS
DIM:
DISPLAY
DRAW
EDIT
INQUIRY
LAYER...
MODEL
MVIEW
PLOT...
RENDER
SETTINGS
SURFACES
UCS:
UTILITY

SAVE:

Mode
☐ Invisible
☐ Constant
☐ Verify
☐ Preset

Command:

Figure 4-5: Mode dialogue area

Invisible

The default for this setting is for visible text, but if you pick the Invisible setting (an X appears in the box next to it), the value (text) assigned to the attribute will be invisible. Picking the box again makes the X disappear, meaning the text will be visible again. Try it a few times to see how it works.

Invisible text is useful for "attaching" invisible information such as cost, model number, manufacturer, etc., to a block. To see invisible text, use the ATTDISP command.

Our example is visible, so we'll leave the box empty.

Constant

The default for this setting is Off, meaning you can enter text into the attribute at any time. If you pick this box, turning the Constant setting

On, you'll be required to place a text value (alpha or numeric) into the attribute, and the value you enter will become permanent. That is, each time the block is inserted into the drawing, the same text will be assigned as the attribute value. Constant attribute values are often used with the invisible setting and contain information such as cost or model number.

Our example has a variable value, so we'll leave the box empty.

Verify

If you create the attribute with the Verify setting On, you'll be asked to verify the attribute value when you insert the block that contains it. The default is Off.

Our example won't need to be verified, so leave the box empty.

Preset

When defining a variable attribute, you can enter a default attribute value. If you select Preset, you won't be prompted to enter text into the attribute when inserting the block that contains the attribute. Rather, the default text will be entered for you. Remember, however, that you can also enter attributes at the Command line.

If you enter attributes at the Command line, preset attribute values will be placed on the block for you. If you use a dialogue box, the preset attribute values will be placed into the dialogue box for you as you add the block. Either way, you save time! You should use preset values whenever you can.

Our example won't use a preset attribute, so leave the box empty.

The Attribute Dialogue Area

The Attribute dialogue area, the main part of the Attribute Definition dialogue box, is shown in Figure 4-6. It is here that you enter the default value contained in the attribute—and where you identify the meaning of the value. Here, also, you enter the prompt you want to see when you insert the block containing the attribute into your drawing.

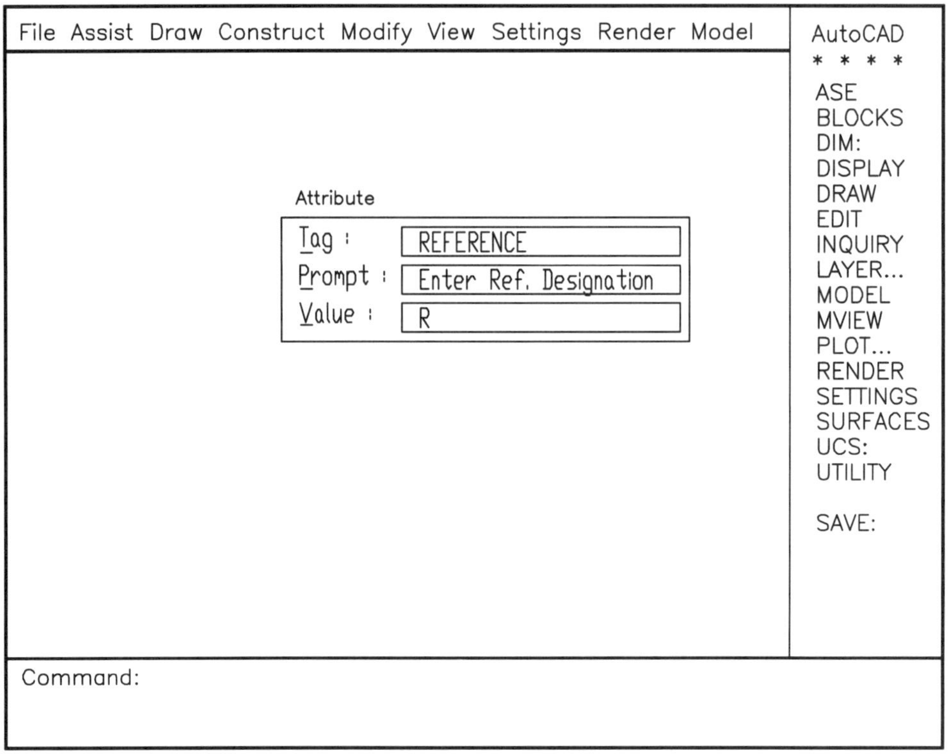

File Assist Draw Construct Modify View Settings Render Model

Attribute

Tag : REFERENCE
Prompt : Enter Ref. Designation
Value : R

AutoCAD
* * * *
ASE
BLOCKS
DIM:
DISPLAY
DRAW
EDIT
INQUIRY
LAYER...
MODEL
MVIEW
PLOT...
RENDER
SETTINGS
SURFACES
UCS:
UTILITY

SAVE:

Command:

Figure 4-6: Attribute dialogue area

Tag

The Tag area contains the description, or meaning, of the text (or value) that will be placed into the attribute. For instance, if you wish the attribute to contain the price of an item, you might type **price** for the attribute tag. (Remember, use the mouse to pick the location where you'll type the tag.)

For our example, the tag should be **REFERENCE**.

Type: `REFERENCE`

The tag will always be converted to uppercase characters and can contain no spaces. You can't leave this area blank because it gives meaning to the value placed in the attribute.

Prompt

This is where you place the prompt you'll see when you insert the block into your drawing. If you've specified a Constant attribute value, you won't be allowed to enter anything here. If you leave this area blank, the attribute tag will be used for the prompt.

For our example, the prompt should be **Enter Ref. Designation**:

Type: `Enter Ref. Designation`

Value

This is where the default value goes. If you leave this area blank, no default value will be placed in the attribute when you insert the block containing this attribute into your drawing. If you don't enter a value when prompted, no value will be placed for you. You can later enter a value by using the DDATTE command.

For our example, the value should be **R**:

Type: `R`

The Text Options Dialogue Area

In the Text Options dialogue area, you select the justification, text style, height and rotation for the text contained in the attribute value (see Figure 4-7). This lets you define attribute values that are the same as the text in your drawing.

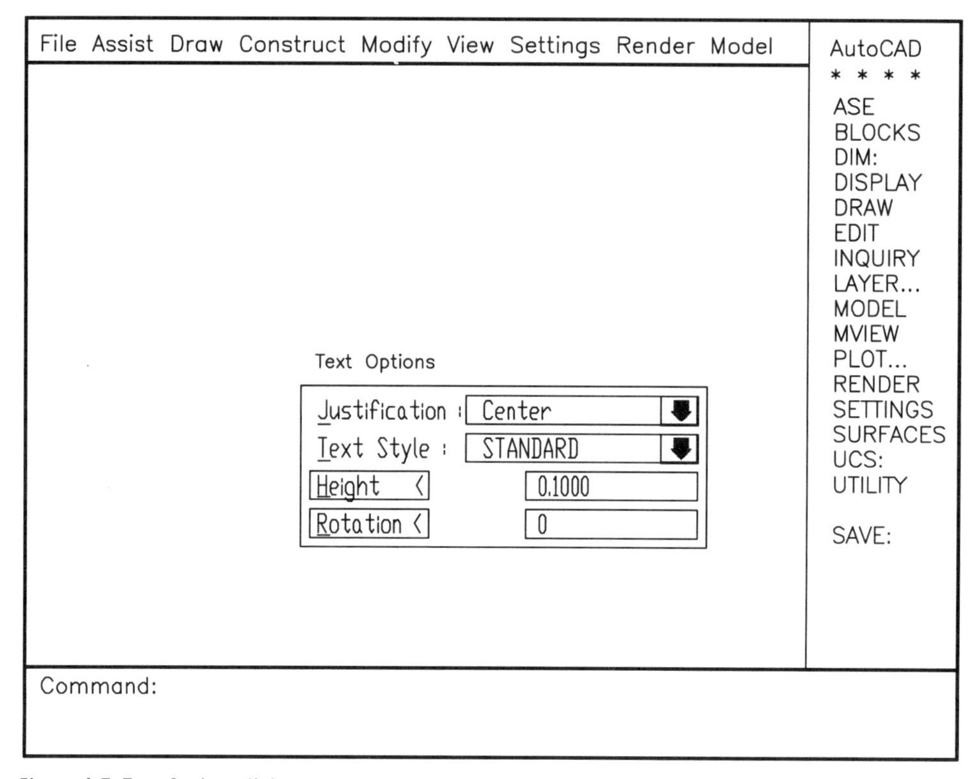

Figure 4-7: Text Options dialogue area

Justification

You can specify any Justification setting that you'd use for ordinary text. To look at the possible settings, pick the down arrow next to the Justification box. Picking Fit or Aligned as the text justification will affect your ability to use the Height and Rotation buttons.

For our example, we'll specify Center as the justification, so pick Center.

Text Style

Click on the down arrow next to the Text Style box to see the available text styles. You can then pick any style from the list.

If a style doesn't appear on the list, it means it hasn't been defined in your current drawing. In order to use it, you'll have to cancel your attribute definition routine and define the style you wish to use.

Our example will use Standard as the text style, so pick Standard.

Height <

Each setting that allows input from the graphics screen has a left arrow (<) by it. You can keep the default text height, type in a new value or pick the Height < button and digitize a new text height.

For our example, pick in the box to the right of the button and to the right of the default value (0.200). Then backspace over the height shown and enter the height.

Let's use 0.1000 as the text height.

Type: `0.1000`

Rotation <

This setting can be changed the same way as the text height.

For our example, the rotation should be zero (0).

The Insertion Point Dialogue Area

The Insertion Point dialogue area (see Figure 4-8) allows you to type the x, y and z coordinates of the attribute. Or you can pick the Pick Point < button, whereupon the Attribute Definition dialogue box disappears, allowing you to pick the location on the screen.

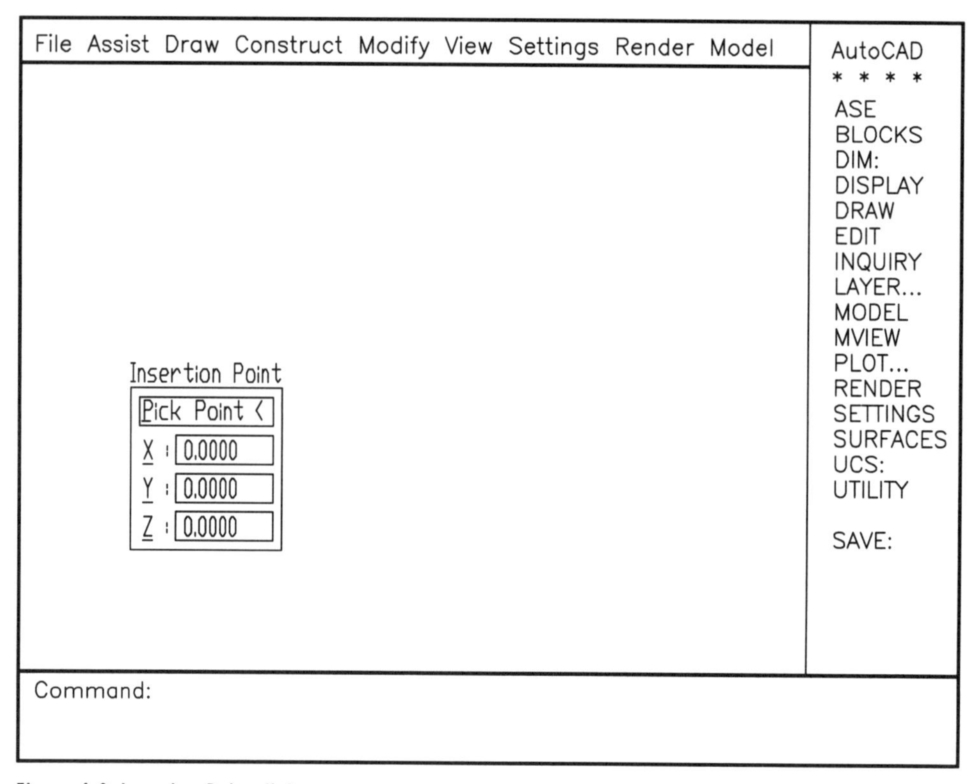

Figure 4-8: Insertion Point dialogue area

After picking the location, the Attribute Definition dialogue box reappears so you can finish the attribute definition process. Just below the Insertion Point dialogue area is a box labeled "Align below previous attribute." If you're defining the second or following attribute in a block, and you want it to be vertically aligned with the attribute immediately above it, pick this box and the attribute you're defining will be aligned. If the attribute you're defining is the first in the block, the "Align below previous attribute" option is disabled.

For our example, specify the attribute insertion point by picking the Pick Point < button. Then pick a point below the resistor symbol, leaving enough room for the text height you've chosen.

Completing the Attribute Definition

The final step in defining the attribute is to pick the OK button. This returns you to the editing area, where you'll see the attribute tag appear in the location you specified.

Adding the Next Attribute

The following attribute is defined in the same way as the first, with a few modifications. Begin the second attribute definition by typing:

Type: `DDATTDEF <Return>`

The dialogue box will appear again, ready to accept new information. The second attribute will contain the resistance value of the resistor. Enter new attributes as follows.

The second attribute's Tag should be: **VALUE_IN_OHMS**

Type: `VALUE_IN_OHMS <Return>`

The Prompt should be: **Enter value in ohms**

Type: `Enter value in Ohms`

The Value should be: **Ohms**

Type: `Ohms`

The Justification should be: **Center**

Pick: `Center`

The Text Style should be: **Standard**

Pick: `Standard`

The Height should be: **0.10**

Type: `0.10`

The Rotation should be zero.

You won't need to pick an Insertion Point. Instead, pick the "Align below previous attribute" box.

Now, pick the OK box. The second attribute is now defined.

Defining the Block

The next step is to create the block definition.

Type: `BLOCK <Return>`

The name of the block is **Res:**

Type: `RES <Return>`

The Insertion Point of the block is located at the left end of the symbol. See Figure 4-3 for its location.

Now use a Window to select the entire symbol. Include the graphics that belong to it as well as the attribute tags that you defined. Press the Return key, and the block with attributes will be created.

Inserting the Block With Attributes

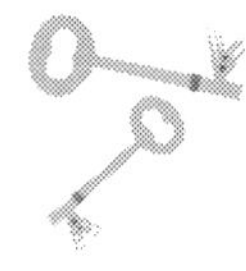

A block that contains attributes can be inserted at the Command prompt or by using a dialogue box. Likewise, values can be placed in the attributes at the Command prompt or by using the Enter Attributes dialogue box. We'll insert our sample block at the Command prompt and use the Enter Attributes dialogue box to fill in the attribute information.

The system variable ATTDIA must be set to 1 if we are to use the dialogue box. The default for this system variable is 0, so turn it on by typing:

Type: `ATTDIA <Return>`

You'll be prompted to enter a zero (0) or a one (1). At the prompt:

Type: `1 <Return>`

Now the ATTDIA variable is on.

The ATTREQ variable must also be on to give you the opportunity to enter values into the attributes. The default value for this system variable is 1, so you shouldn't need to change it. If you have to change it, just type the variable name, hit Return, type 1 and hit Return again.

Now you're ready to insert the block. At the Command prompt:

Type: `INSERT <Return>`

Response: `Block name:`

Type: `RES <Return>`

Digitize the insertion point, then give the X and Y scales and rotation angle as follows:

Type: `1 <Return>` (This is the X scale.)

Type: `1 <Return>` (This is the Y scale.)

Type: `0 <Return>` (This is the rotation angle.)

The Enter Attributes dialogue box will appear (see Figure 4-9).

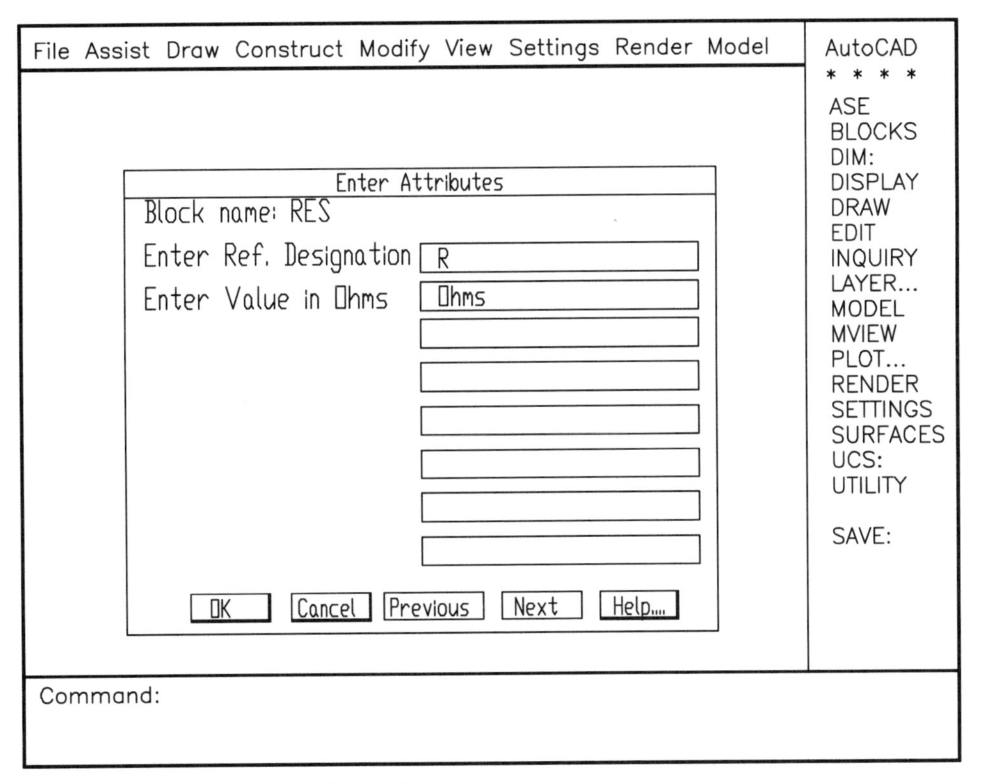

Figure 4-9: The Enter Attributes dialogue box

You can change information in the dialogue box by picking the text you wish to change and deleting it with the Backspace and/or Delete key. Then type the new text into the location you chose. Click on the Previous or Next buttons at the bottom of the dialogue box to see each attribute and its default value. After you've entered all the attribute values, pick the OK box to return to the graphics screen, where you'll see your block with attributes. Your example should look similar to the one shown in Figure 4-10.

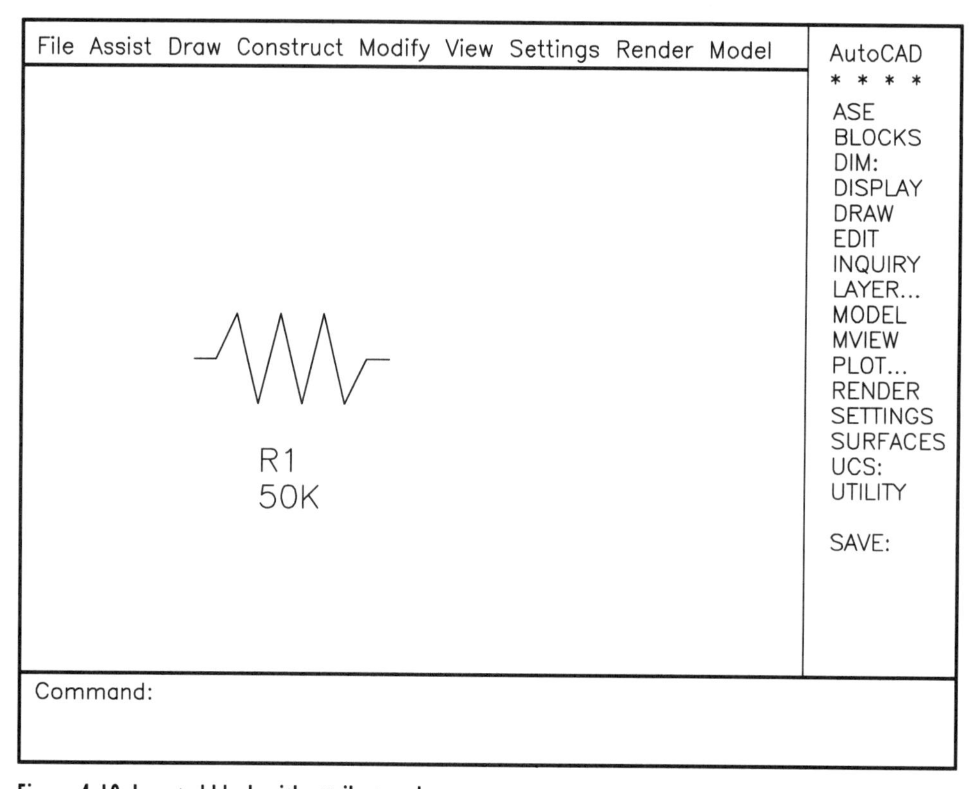

Figure 4-10: Inserted block with attribute values

Editing Attributes

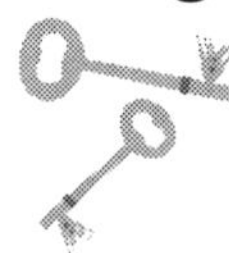

AutoCAD gives you two commands for editing attribute values. Each of the commands are discussed below.

The Edit Attributes Dialogue Box

The easiest and quickest way to edit an attribute value is to use the DDATTE command, which brings up the Edit Attributes dialogue box. To change attribute text, give the DDATTE command and select the attribute text, and the dialogue box will appear. Use the cursor to select which text to change, then pick OK when you've finished making changes. The Edit Attributes dialogue box doesn't give you a way to change the text style, placement or rotation. Those settings must be changed with the ATTEDIT command.

Editing Attribute Values at the Command Prompt

The ATTEDIT command, which you use at the Command prompt, lets you change the following attribute settings:

Attribute text (attribute value)

Position

Height

Angle

Style

Layer

Color

Although the ATTEDIT command is often considered to be less user-friendly than the DDATTE command, it's more flexible. If a certain text string appears in many (or all) attributes, for instance, you can change them all at once. After typing the ATTEDIT command, specify whether you wish to edit attribute values according to block name, attribute tag or attribute value. You can tell the ATTEDIT command to edit only the attributes that appear on the screen; you can specify that you want to edit only the visible attributes; you can edit all attributes; or you can edit individual attributes.

Editing Attribute Definitions

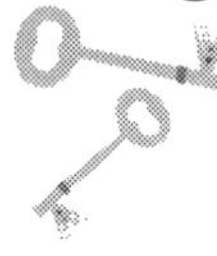

We've just discussed how to edit attribute values. But what if you want to make changes to the attribute definition itself? AutoCAD gives you several ways to make those changes, two of which we'll discuss in this chapter (DDEDIT and CHANGE). The third way to make changes is with AutoLISP, which we'll discuss in a later chapter.

NOTE: Before you can edit an attribute definition using the commands explained below, you must first EXPLODE the block in which the attribute is defined. After you edit the attribute definition, you must use the BLOCK command to redefine the block. If the block resides in a file by itself (as it would if it were created using the WBLOCK command), you can go into that file and edit it directly.

Editing Attribute Definitions Using the DDEDIT Command

The simplest way to edit an attribute definition is with the DDEDIT command. It brings up the Edit Attribute Definition dialogue box. Figure 4-11 shows what the dialogue box looks like when you prepare to edit the first attribute definition from the resistor example you created earlier.

File Assist Draw Construct Modify View Settings Render Model

AutoCAD
* * * *
ASE
BLOCKS
DIM:
DISPLAY
DRAW
EDIT
INQUIRY
LAYER...
MODEL
MVIEW
PLOT...
RENDER
SETTINGS
SURFACES
UCS:
UTILITY

SAVE:

Edit Attribute Definition

Tag : REFERENCE
Prompt : Enter Ref. Designation
Default : R

OK Cancel

Command:

Figure 4-11: Edit Attribute Definition dialogue box

You can use the DDEDIT command to edit normal text. When you edit attribute information, though, the DDEDIT command knows it should bring up the Edit Attribute Definition dialogue box instead of the Edit Text dialogue box.

It's easy to use the Edit Attribute Definition dialogue box, but its capabilities are limited. It only allows you to edit the attribute tag, the prompt and the default value.

To use the DDEDIT command, make sure you're working on an exploded block. You can tell if the attribute information has been exploded, because the attribute tag(s) will be displayed while you're in the drawing editor.

Type: `DDEDIT <Return>`

Then select the attribute tag you wish to edit. When you select the tag, the dialogue box will be displayed as in Figure 4-11. After making the desired changes, pick the OK button. The changes will be made to the attribute definition. Now redefine the block by using the BLOCK command.

Editing Attribute Definitions Using the CHANGE Command

The CHANGE command is the most versatile command for editing attribute definitions. It allows you to change any of the following settings:

Attribute Location

Text Style

Text Height

Rotation Angle

Attribute Tag

Prompt

Default Value

Remember—you can only edit attribute definitions if the block in which they're defined is exploded. To use the CHANGE command to edit attribute definitions:

Type: `CHANGE <Return>`

Select the attribute you wish to change. Press Return when you're asked if you want to change "Properties" or to "Change point." You'll then be led through each of the settings listed above, and you'll be able to change each setting as it's presented. If you don't want to change a setting, bypass it by pressing the Return key. You'll notice that some settings, like Text Justification or attribute Visibility, are not changeable. Those settings can only be changed by using AutoLISP, which is discussed later.

Displaying Attributes

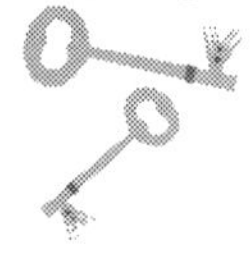

You can use the ATTDISP command to change the visibility of attributes. The command has three settings: On, Off and Normal. When ATTDISP is On, all attribute values are visible, even if they were defined as invisible. The Off setting causes all attribute values to be invisible, even if they were defined as visible. When ATTDISP is set to Normal, each attribute is set to the visibility state it was given when it was defined.

Creating ATT_DEF.LSP

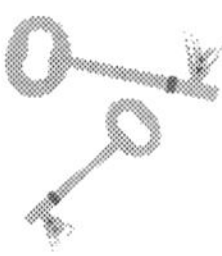

You can find the ATT_DEF.LSP program in Appendix A. As you would with other AutoLISP programs, make sure it's properly loaded. If you have the *Outside AutoCAD Companion Disk*, and it has been properly installed, all you need do is type in the name of the program.

If you don't have the *Outside AutoCAD Companion Disk*, turn now to Appendix A and create the program ATT_DEF.LSP. Make certain the file is loaded and ready to use. As always, you'll find complete instructions on creating and loading these programs in Appendix A.

I've included the following lisp file to show you how to automate something as simple as multiple attributes. It will automate the attribute input you worked through in this chapter.

Using ATT_DEF.LSP

The ATT_DEF.LSP file will pause to allow you to enter a start point for text, then allow you to set a text height, then pause again to allow you to set a text rotation value. Once loaded and run, it will put in both the attributes at one pass. You can even modify it to add more attributes.

All you need do then is BLOCK your resistor with the attributes.

To load the file, use the Release 12 APPLOAD command or do as follows:

Type:
```
(load "att_def") <Return>
att_def <Return>
```

The file will pause for the origin point, height and rotation value of your text.

Response:
```
<Start point>:
```

Pick or digitize a point. Press Return.

Response:
```
Height <2.0000>:
```

Enter a text height. Press Return.

Response:
```
Rotation angle <0>:
```

Enter **0** (zero). Press Return.
The attributes will be placed after the third Return.
You can create the ATT_DEF.LSP file as follows:

Type:
```
(defun C:ATT_DEF () (graphscr)
  (setq att_1 "REFERENCE")
  (setq att_1a "Enter Ref. Designation... ")
  (setq att_1b "R")
  (terpri)
  (setq att_2 "VALUE_IN_OHMS")
  (setq att_2a "Enter value in Ohms... ")
  (setq att_2b "Ohms")
  (terpri)
  (command "attdef" "" att_1 att_1a att_1b pause pause pause)
  (command "attdef" "" att_2 att_2a att_2b "")
  (princ)
)
```

Moving On

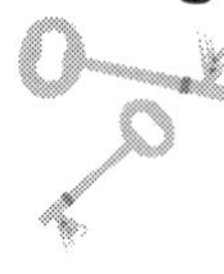

The attribute basics introduced to you in this chapter will let you begin to use attributes to save time and effort in your drawings. You've now established a foundation that will help you use attributes in more advanced ways.

In the next chapter, "Attribute Extraction," you'll be extracting attribute values from AutoCAD and placing them into a file that can be read by database management and spreadsheet systems.

Attribute Extraction

This chapter focuses on how to prepare attributes within the drawing database so they can be transferred outside AutoCAD into the world of database management and other analysis applications.

A powerful feature toward enhancing your attribute productivity within your database is that attributes can contain information that later may be used by AutoLISP applications within AutoCAD. One illustration is a facility management application, others are external applications, such as bill-of-materials or mapping applications.

By properly defining and setting up attributes within a drawing, or set of drawings, you can expand the utility of your AutoCAD system far beyond the realm of drawing creation alone.

Attribute Extraction Explained

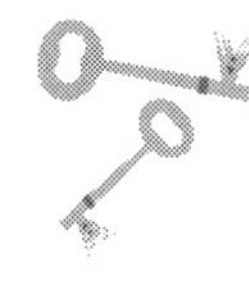

Attributes are pieces of text that are an integral part of an AutoCAD block entity. Some attribute values (text), such as manufacturer names or model numbers, may never change; others, such as unique identifiers like reference designations, may change with each block insertion.

Say you had a set of house plans in AutoCAD that included attributes as part of each commercially purchased item. You could categorize all of the items into an "intelligent" list: a bill of materials for the items required to build the house. The list would show the model number of each item, the manufacturer or supplier and the cost of each item. You can often create such a list by using an AutoCAD command that will read all of the attributes in the drawing, choose the ones you specify and copy the attribute information to a file on the hard disk. In other words, the command "extracts" attribute information and places it into a file that can be read by another program, such as a database management system. You can tell the command which information from which attributes to extract, and you can specify the file format (how the information will look).

Start From the Desired Result

Suppose you're working on an interior design and want a bill of materials containing the item name, model, supplier and cost. By determining the results you want, you've begun defining the requirements of your attribute extraction system. Now you can define the remaining requirements and begin designing the format of the extracted information.

Extraction Format

The extraction format is the way the attribute text appears when it's saved into a file on the hard disk. The format you choose controls what items are written, where they're written in relationship to each other and how many characters are reserved for each item. AutoCAD gives you three choices of formats: Comma Delimited File (CDF), Space Delimited File (SDF) and Drawing Interchange File (DXF).

CDF Format

CDF format requires each piece of information written to a file to be enclosed by quotation marks (single or double—single are the default) and separated from a neighboring piece of information by commas. Actually, other characters are allowed, but quotation marks and commas are the default. The format of the above example might appear as follows:

```
'Item_Name','Model','Supplier','Cost'
```

When actual data is placed in a file on the hard disk in CDF format, it would look something like this:

```
'chair','2320A','XYZ Furniture','879.00'
```

Notice how each item is placed inside single quotation marks and separated by commas. CDF format uses a comma as the default separator. Likewise, single quotes are CDF's default characters for enclosing each piece of information. You'd only use other characters if commas or quotation marks were included in your data.

SDF Format

SDF format requires each piece of information written to a file to be of a defined width, and it's up to you to define the width. In other words, if a piece of information contains the cost of an item, you might reserve (or define) a certain number of characters in which the cost would be written. If the cost would never exceed $999.99, for example, you'd reserve at least six characters in which the cost would be written (the dollar sign isn't included). The six characters would include the dollar amount, the cents amount and a character for the decimal point. But to make the information more readable, you'd probably reserve at least eight characters so the information would have a space on either side of it.

Information in SDF format would look like this:

```
Item_Name   Model     Supplier      Cost
```

Here's how the actual data would look:

```
chair       2320A     XYZ Furniture     879.00

couch       3350T     XYZ Furniture     1237.00

table       1517Y     Tables Are Us     649.00
```

Notice how easy it is to read each of the items. SDF format is the most commonly used format in the personal computer world, probably because it's easy to read and easy to define.

DXF Format

If you're familiar with the appearance of AutoCAD's Drawing Interchange File format, this format will look familiar to you. When you extract information from AutoCAD attributes into a DXF format, however, this form of DXF only includes block references, attributes and *sequence end* entities. (A sequence end isn't visible to the user but marks the end of an attribute definition in the database.) You might say that AutoCAD has two types of DXF formats, one for files and one for attribute extraction. When the attribute extraction file is created, it will have a .DXX extension instead of the familiar .DXF extension that belongs to the more common DXF files created by the DXFOUT command. Reading a DXF attribute extraction file is also more difficult than reading similar information in CDF or SDF format.

Defining the Format—An Example of a Template File

Now let's look at the instructions you'll use to place the extracted information into one of these formats. Before you can create a CDF or SDF file, you must create a *template* file that describes how the CDF or SDF file will look. We'll choose SDF as our format since it's the most popular. You should also be aware that a template file is not required by the DXF format because it has its own predefined structure.

The template file is an ASCII file. You can create it using any ASCII text editor, such as the MS-DOS "EDIT" editor or the "Write" editor in Microsoft Windows. Or you can use a text processor such as WordPerfect—as long as you save the file in ASCII format, making sure no control characters are saved with the file. A template file would look like this:

```
ITEM_NAME   C011000
MODEL       C010000
SUPPLIER    C016000
COST        N009002
```

Let's give the template file the name FURNTMP.TXT. In the above example, the attribute tag is shown on the left, with a description of how the data will be represented on the right. In database terms, each attribute tag represents one "field" in a database. The ITEM_NAME will consist of alpha characters (designated by the "C" in the description) and will allow up to eleven characters in the item name. The MODEL will also consist of alpha characters and will allow up to 10 characters. The SUPPLIER will allow up to 16 alpha characters. The COST must consist of numeric characters and will accommodate up to 9 characters. But two of those 9 characters will be the decimal places, and one will be the decimal point, leaving 6 places for "dollars" and two places for "cents."

General Template File Format & Rules

A template file can be much more inclusive than it is in the above example. As you can see in the following list, it can allow you to extract the block name and layer; the x, y and z location of the block; the number of blocks found; the block's handle identifier, orientation and x, y and z scale. (More categories are listed in the *AutoCAD Reference Manual*.)

BL:NAME	Cwww000
BL:X	Nwwwddd
BL:Y	Nwwwddd
BL:Z	Nwwwddd
BL:NUMBER	Nwww000
BL:LAYER	Cwww000
BL:XSCALE	Nwwwddd
BL:YSCALE	Nwwwddd
BL:ZSCALE	Nwwwddd
tagname	Cwww000
tagname	Nwwwddd

The field names are on the left with the description of the data to be contained in each field on the right. The field names are explained as follows:

BL:NAME BL: indicates that the information to be extracted for this field is part of the block but not part of an attribute. In this case, it's the block name.

Tagname You wouldn't actually type **tagname** in your template file. This is where you'd place the name of the attribute tag whose information you wanted to extract.

The data descriptions are explained as follows:

C A character field. If numbers appear in this field, they'll be converted to ASCII characters.

N A numeric field. If you specify a numeric field and one or more ASCII characters are in the item to be extracted, AutoCAD will display an error.

www The maximum number of characters in the field. The decimal point counts as one character if it's a floating point field. For example, if 023 appears here, it means that 23 characters are allowed in the field, including the decimal point.

ddd The number of decimal places in the field. If 002 appears here, two places past the decimal are specified.

000 If the field is an integer or an ASCII field, no decimals are needed—these zeros are placeholders.

Your file may include as many of the above categories (fields) as you wish, but you must include at least one attribute tag name.

The template file can contain no tab characters. If you want to line up the characters from line to line, use spaces.

The name of the template file *must* have a .TXT file extension. The fields may be in any order you desire.

The output of the information will be in the same order you used to specify the field names.

You cannot use any field more than once.

The same template file can be used for CDF or SDF format output.

Extraction File Planning & Block Creation

It may seem that the information in this chapter is given in reverse order, but it has been given in the order you should follow when designing your own database extraction system. If you began your AutoCAD extraction steps by creating blocks, taking no thought for how your extracted file output would look, the results would seldom be satisfactory. On the other hand, if you plan from the desired outcome to the very design of the blocks used to define the drawing, your final output will most often meet your expectations with few or no modifications. Perhaps the best time to design your blocks and their attributes is when you determine what information to extract and what form it will finally take upon extraction.

Time Out! Create the Blocks With Attributes

In a real application, you probably would have created the blocks by now. But, for this example, you'll need to create the blocks with the attributes that match the content of this discussion.

Figure 5-1 shows three blocks with attributes that match our example. Actually, each of the blocks has been exploded so you can see the attribute tag names. All of the attributes are visible. Only the attribute containing the cost is not constant; all the others will contain text as it is shown in Figure 5-2.

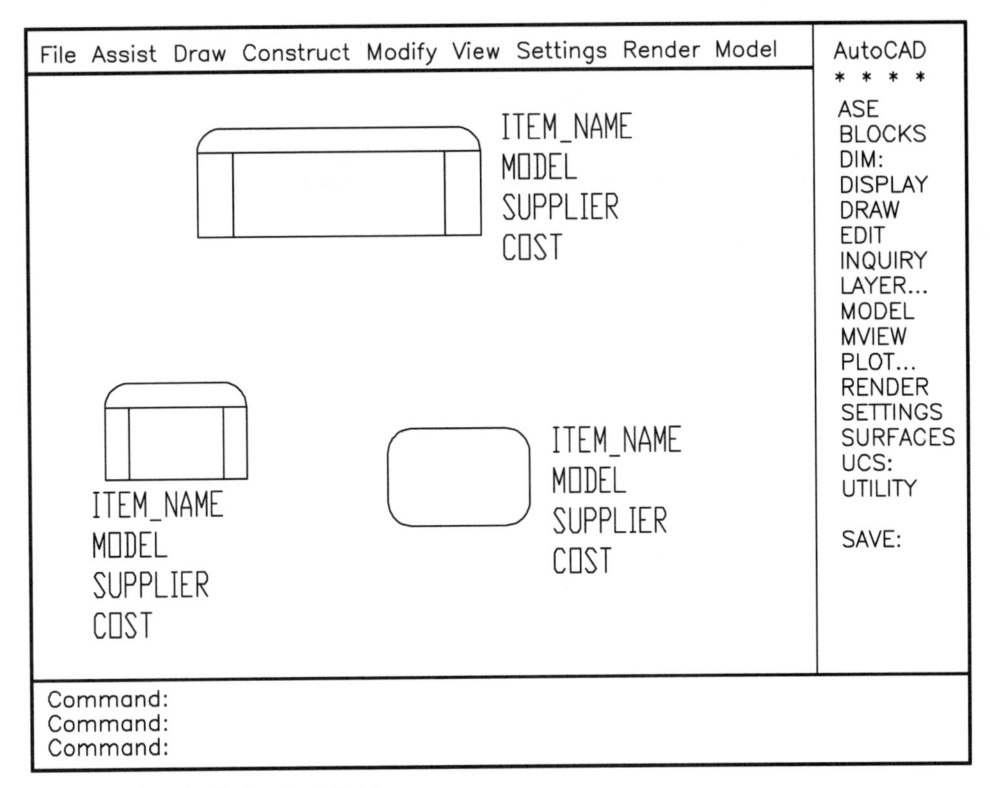

Figure 5-1: Sample blocks with definitions

Now create the geometry for each of the three blocks yourself, defining and placing attributes in each of the locations shown. After the geometry and attributes have been created, make each symbol into a block. Remember to include the appropriate attribute definitions with each block you define. Call one block TABLE, another CHAIR and the last COUCH.

After all the blocks have been defined, insert each of them into the drawing and enter the cost of each item, if you're prompted to do so. You may place as many blocks in your drawing as you wish, but this discussion will assume you inserted each block one time.

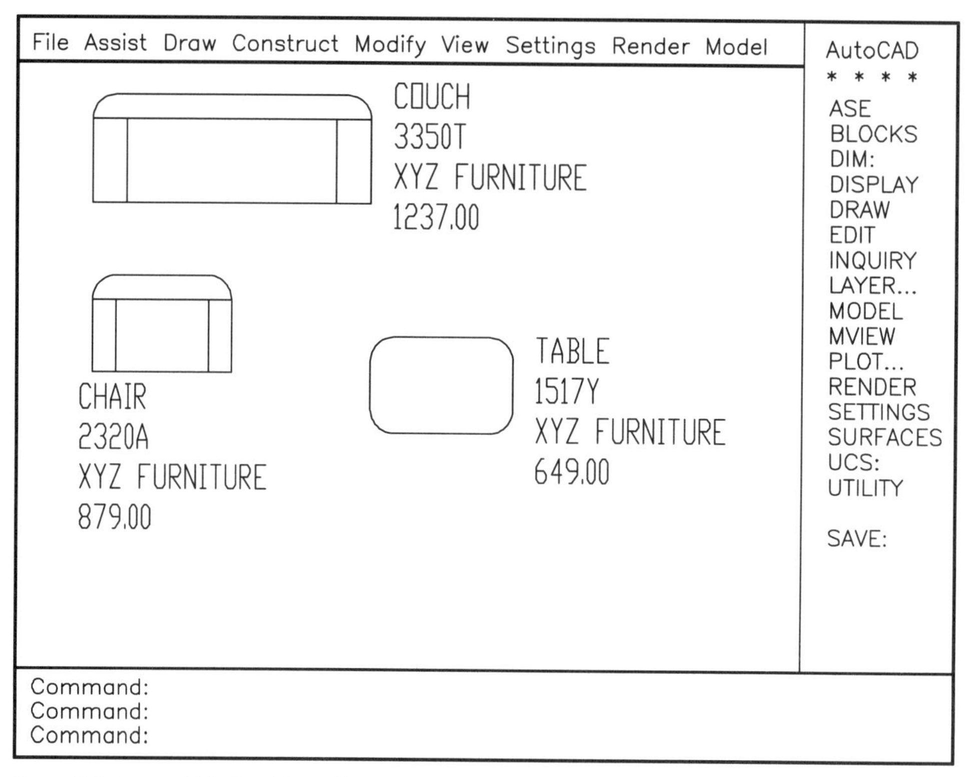

Figure 5-2: Inserted blocks with attribute text

Creating the Extract File

Now, if the blocks in your drawing are well-defined and include the attribute information you'll need for the attribute extraction, you can give the attribute extract command.

AutoCAD gives you two commands for extracting attribute information. You can type the ATTEXT command at the Command prompt, or you can bring up the Attribute Extraction dialogue box (shown in Figure 5-3) by using the DDATTEXT command.

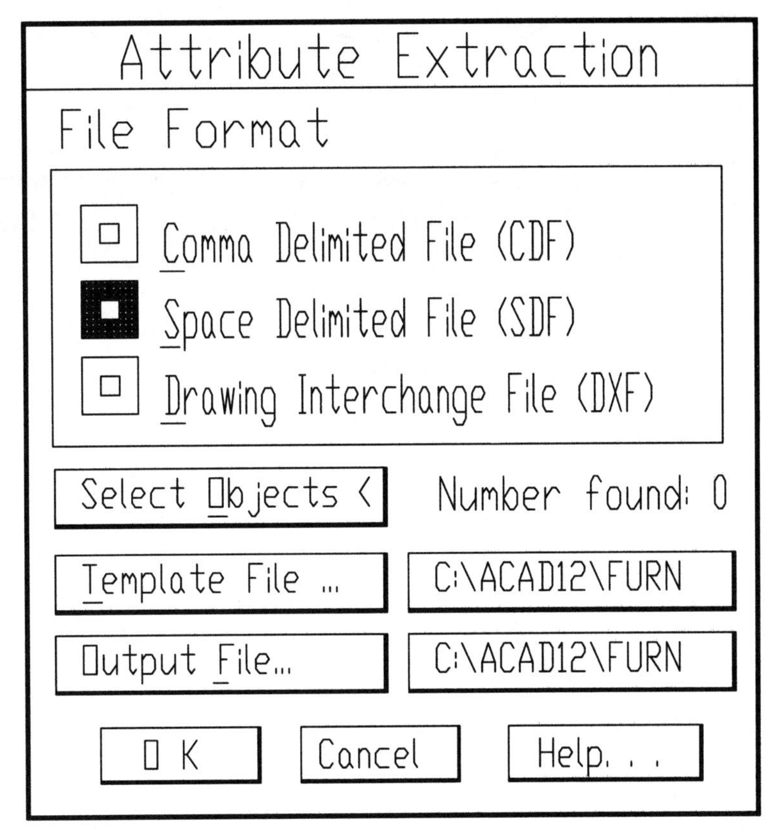

Figure 5-3: Attribute Extraction dialogue box

The dialogue box allows you to specify the file format for your extracted data. You can hit a button and type the name of the template file (the name of the template file is displayed to the right of the button). You can specify the name of the output file in the same way, whereupon it is also displayed.

For the example we've been using, specify the name FURNITUR.TXT.

The Select Objects button allows you to select specific blocks from which attribute text will be extracted if it matches the criteria in your template file.

The ATTEXT command allows you to enter the same information as does the dialogue box, and requires you to type the file format (CDF, SDF or DXF), the name of the template file and the extract file name. You can also pick specific blocks if you desire.

The Final Step—Uploading to a DBMS

If you've performed the preceding steps properly, uploading your file to Database Management System (DBMS) is almost trivial. Your extract file is compatible with most database management systems, most of which have a built-in utility for loading SDF- and/or CDF-formatted files into their data structure. If you were working in the dBASE III database management system in a database called FURN, and the name of your SDF-format extract file was FURNITUR.TXT, you could type the following instructions in the dBASE III program to load the contents of the extract file into the database.

Type:
```
use furn <Return>
append from furniture.txt sdf <Return>
```

The system response will indicate how many records (lines or rows of information) were loaded.

Once the information is loaded into the database system, you can use it for reporting purposes, cost tracking or as a system to generate a bill of materials.

Moving On

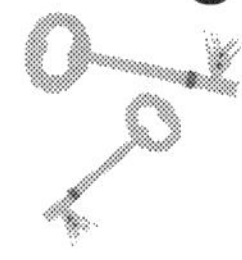

The information and exercises contained in this chapter are a small sample of what you can do with attribute extraction using AutoCAD. By carefully planning your drawing applications, and realizing the power of attributes and attribute extraction, you can apply these principles to almost any AutoCAD design and drafting discipline. As we move on, we'll learn how to add more functionality and flexibility to attributes. You'll find that with the help of a few applied AutoLISP concepts, you'll be able to more fully control AutoCAD's attribute capabilities.

Attributes in the AutoCAD Database

In the previous chapter you learned how to prepare attributes to be transferred outside AutoCAD. In this chapter you'll find out how to access attributes and some of their internally defined features. You'll see how to change parts of attribute definitions more easily by applying and using AutoLISP instead of AutoCAD commands.

You'll use an AutoLISP program to help you change your attribute text styles according to block name. You can even change your attribute text layer assignments with it. You'll also learn of a utility that will help you locate attribute text strings in your drawing. And, by using a simple program, you'll be able to move existing AutoCAD text into pre-defined attributes—and rapidly increase your skill level.

Changing Attribute Text Styles

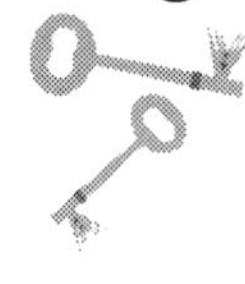

If you've ever tried to change attribute text styles by using the old ATTEDIT command, you'll be glad to know about a faster and easier way. The following program (CA_STYLE.LSP) prompts you to enter the name of the text style you wish to substitute and to enter the name of the block where the text style is found. (The text style to be substituted must already be created for your current drawing/editing session.)

The program finds each attribute occurrence from block names identified by you and replaces it with the new text style. To keep it simple, this program works on a maximum of three attributes per block.

The CA_STYLE.LSP Program

The following program is CA_STYLE.LSP, or Change Attribute Style. Use an ASCII text editor or a text processor in ASCII format to create the file.

The line numbers are for reference only and aren't part of the program. Any words to the right of a single, double or triple semicolon (;) are comments—AutoLISP doesn't evaluate anything appearing on a line following a semicolon. You place comments in the program to make it easier to read and understand.

```
1  (defun C:CA_STYLE (/ new_style blk_name s_set indx
2                     e e_att1 edata1 e_att2 edata2
3                     e_att3 edata3)
4
5    ;;; Variable
6    ;;;   Name          Description
7    ;;; =========       ===========
8    ;;; new_style     name of new text style.
9    ;;; blk_name      name of blk whose attrib style will change
10   ;;; s_set         selection set containing all blks to change
11   ;;; indx          counter - counts number of blocks to change
12   ;;; e             AutoCAD-assigned entity name of block
13   ;;; e_att1        AutoCAD-assigned entity name of 1st attrib
14   ;;; edata1        entity data of 1st attribute
15   ;;; e_att2        AutoCAD-assigned entity name of 2nd attrib
16   ;;; edata2        entity data of 2nd attribute
17   ;;; e_att3        AutoCAD-assigned entity name of 3rd attrib
18   ;;; edata3        entity data of 3rd attribute
19
20   (setq new_style (getstring "\nEnter new text style name:  "))
21   (setq blk_name (getstring "\nEnter block name:  "))
22   ;; create selection set of specific blocks
23   (setq s_set
24     (ssget "X" (list (cons 2 blk_name)))
25   ) ; endsetq
26   (if s_set                          ; if block is found,
27     (progn
28       (setq indx 0)                  ; initialize counter
29       (repeat (sslength s_set)       ; for each block,
30         (setq e (ssname s_set indx))  ; get entity name
31         (setq e_att1 (entnext e))     ; get attrib_entity name
32         (setq edata1 (entget e_att1)) ; get data
33         ;; substitute new style
34         (setq edata1
35           (subst (cons 7 new_style) (assoc 7 edata1) edata1)
36         ) ; endsetq
37         (entmod edata1)               ; modify entity
38         (setq e_att2 (entnext e_att1)); get attrib_entity name
39         (setq edata2 (entget e_att2)) ; get data
```

```
40          ;; substitute new style
41          (setq edata2
42            (subst (cons 7 new_style) (assoc 7 edata2) edata2)
43          ) ; endsetq
44          (entmod edata2)                ; modify entity
45          (setq e_att3 (entnext e_att2)); get attrib_entity name
46          (setq edata3 (entget e_att3)) ; get data
47          ;; substitute new style
48          (setq edata3
49            (subst (cons 7 new_style) (assoc 7 edata3) edata3)
50          ) ; endsetq
51          (entmod edata3)                ; modify entity
52          (entupd e)                     ; update block
53          (setq indx (1+ indx))          ; increment counter
54        ) ; endrepeat
55      ) ; endprogn
56      (princ "\nNo attributes found: ")  ; print msg if none found
57    ) ; endif
58    (princ)
59 ) ; end CA_STYLE
```

Loading & Running the Program

Before the program will work, you must define the new text style. Use the STYLE command to do this, or use the pull-down menu, which leads you to the Select Text Font icon menu.

Place the program in your drawing directory or in a directory from which you can easily load it. Use Release 12's APPLOAD command to load it, or at the Command prompt:

Type: `(load "ca_style") <Return>`

After the program is loaded, invoke it by typing the program name at the Command prompt:

Type: `ca_style <Return>`

When the program prompts you, enter the name of the new (previously defined) text style, then type the name of the block that contains the text style you wish to be changed.

The program will look at every occurrence of the named block and if there is attribute text in the block, it will be assigned the new style you specified.

How the Program Works

Here's a line-by-line explanation of the CA_STYLE.LSP program. Remember, the line numbers are for reference only.

Lines 1–3

```
1  (defun C:CA_STYLE (/ new_style blk_name s_set indx
2                       e e_att1 edata1 e_att2 edata2
3                       e_att3 edata3)
```

The program begins by defining the new function name: **C:CA_STYLE**. The **C:** indicates that the function will become an AutoCAD command. The variables used in the program are all declared to be local variables so that if the program is used twice in a row, the variables won't need to be initialized.

Lines 5–18

```
5    ;;; Variable
6    ;;;   Name            Description
7    ;;; =========         ===========
8    ;;; new_style       name of new text style.
9    ;;; blk_name        name of blk whose attrib style will change
10   ;;; s_set           selection set containing all blks to change
11   ;;; indx            counter - counts number of blocks to change
12   ;;; e               AutoCAD-assigned entity name of block
13   ;;; e_att1          AutoCAD-assigned entity name of 1st attrib
14   ;;; edata1          entity data of 1st attribute
15   ;;; e_att2          AutoCAD-assigned entity name of 2nd attrib
16   ;;; edata2          entity data of 2nd attribute
17   ;;; e_att3          AutoCAD-assigned entity name of 3rd attrib
18   ;;; edata3          entity data of 3rd attribute
```

Each of the variables is listed, not as part of the executable program but as information in comment form to help the user understand the purpose of each variable.

Lines 20–21

```
20   (setq new_style (getstring "\nEnter new text style name:  "))
21   (setq blk_name (getstring "\nEnter block name:  "))
```

You're prompted to enter the new style name, which the program stores in the variable called **new_style**. Then you're prompted to enter a block name so the program will know where to look for attribute text styles to change.

Lines 22–25

```
22   ;; create selection set of specific blocks
23   (setq s_set
24     (ssget "X" (list (cons 2 blk_name)))
25   ) ; endsetq
```

A selection set is created that includes all the blocks in the drawing that have the specified name.

Lines 26–29

```
26   (if s_set                              ; if block is found,
27     (progn
28       (setq indx 0)                      ; initialize counter
29       (repeat (sslength s_set)           ; for each block,
```

If at least one block was found matching the specified name, the program counts the number of blocks found and starts a **(repeat** function so that each block's attributes will be modified.

Lines 30–32

```
30         (setq e (ssname s_set indx))  ; get entity name
31         (setq e_att1 (entnext e))     ; get attrib_entity name
32         (setq edata1 (entget e_att1)) ; get data
```

The **(ssname** function looks into the selection set and finds the AutoCAD-assigned entity name belonging to each block. AutoCAD's database is structured so that the next entities following each block description are the attributes that belong to the block. By using the **(entnext** function, the program gets the first attribute belonging to the block. The **(entget** function is used to read the information belonging to the attribute.

Lines 33–36

```
33          ;; substitute new style
34          (setq edata1
35            (subst (cons 7 new_style) (assoc 7 edata1) edata1)
36          ) ; endsetq
```

A new list is built, containing the name of the new style that you entered earlier. Then the new list is substituted for the list containing the currently assigned style name.

Line 37

```
37          (entmod edata1)                 ; modify entity
```

The changed information is transferred back to the entity, modifying the entity.

Lines 38–39

```
38          (setq e_att2 (entnext e_att1)); get attrib_entity name
39          (setq edata2 (entget e_att2)) ; get data
```

The **(entnext** function is used with the name of the attribute we just looked at, causing the program to go to the next entity. When a block has several attributes, the attributes always follow the block definition, one after the other. The **(entget** function reads the data belonging to the attribute.

Lines 40–44

```
40          ;; substitute new style
41          (setq edata2
42            (subst (cons 7 new_style) (assoc 7 edata2) edata2)
43          ) ; endsetq
44          (entmod edata2)                 ; modify entity
```

Same as lines 33–37, but with the second attribute.

Lines 45–51

```
45          (setq e_att3 (entnext e_att2)); get attrib_entity name
46          (setq edata3 (entget e_att3)) ; get data
47          ;; substitute new style
48          (setq edata3
```

```
49          (subst (cons 7 new_style) (assoc 7 edata3) edata3)
50         ) ; endsetq
51         (entmod edata3)                ; modify entity
```

Same as lines 40–44, but with the third attribute.

Line 52

```
52         (entupd e)                     ; update block
```

When changes are made to attributes as the previous lines did, the **(entupd** function is used to redraw the block with its attributes so the changes can be seen.

Line 53

```
53         (setq indx (1+ indx))          ; increment counter
```

The counter that keeps track of the number of blocks that were found is incremented, so the next block's attribute style can be modified.

Lines 54–55

```
54       ) ; endrepeat
55     ) ; endprogn
```

These are the closing parentheses for the (repeat and (progn functions.

Line 56

```
56     (princ "\nNo attributes found: ")  ; print msg if none found
```

The message is printed if no blocks by the specified name were found.

Line 57

```
57   ) ; endif
```

This is the closing parenthesis for the (if function.

Line 58

```
58   (princ)
```

The **(princ** function prevents the function from printing "nil" when the program ends.

Line 59

```
59 ) ; end CA_STYLE
```

This is the closing parenthesis for the definition of the program.

Changing an Attribute Layer Assignment

Sometimes an attribute was defined with an incorrect layer setting. If the block only has one attribute and you wish to move the attribute text to a different layer, the following program allows you to easily make such a change.

The C:CH_LAYER.LSP Program

The following program allows you to change the layer assignment of a single piece of attribute text.

The line numbers are for reference only and aren't part of the actual program. Any words to the right of a single, double or triple semicolon (;) are comments—AutoLISP doesn't evaluate anything appearing on a line following a semicolon. You place comments in the program to make it easier to read and understand.

```
1  (defun C:CH_LAYER (/ newlayer blkname e edata e1)
2    (setq newlayer
3      (strcase (getstring "\nEnter name of new layer: "))
4    ) ; endsetq
5    (setq blkname
6      (strcase (getstring "\nEnter name of block to look at: "))
7    )
8    (setq e (entnext))
9    (while e
10     (setq edata (entget e))
11     (if (and (= (cdr (assoc 0 edata)) "INSERT")  ; block found
12              (= (cdr (assoc 2 edata)) blkname) ; by name
13         ) ; endand
14       (progn
15         (setq e1 (entnext e)) ; go to attribute info
16         (setq edata (entget e1)) ; get attribute data
17         (setq edata
```

```
18          (subst (cons 8 newlayer) (assoc 8 edata) edata)
19        ) ; endsetq
20        (entmod edata) ; modify entity
21        (entupd el)    ; update attribute
22      ) ; endprogn
23    ) ; endif
24   (setq e (entnext e)) ; go to next entity
25   ) ; endwhile
26   (princ)
27 ) ; endCH_LAYER
```

Loading & Running the Program

Create the program with an ASCII text editor and save it in a directory on your hard disk from which it is easy to load AutoLISP programs. Load the program into your editing session by typing at the Command prompt:

Type: `(load "ch_layer") <Return>`

After the program is loaded, invoke the program by typing the program name at the Command line as follows:

Type: `ch_layer <Return>`

The program will prompt you to enter the name of the layer to which you want the attribute reassigned.

After you enter the name of the new layer, the program will prompt you to enter the name of the block whose attribute layer assignment you wish to change. Enter the name of the block, press Return, and the attribute layer will be assigned.

NOTE: This program will change the layer of all "first" attributes in all blocks by the specified name throughout the drawing.

How the Program Works

Here's a line-by-line explanation of the CH_LAYER.LSP program.

Line 1

```
1  (defun C:CH_LAYER (/ newlayer blkname e edata el)
```

The program will become a new AutoCAD command called **CH_LAYER**. The program's variables are listed behind the program name (function) definition.

Lines 2–7

```
2     (setq newlayer
3       (strcase (getstring "\nEnter name of new layer: "))
4     ) ; endsetq
5     (setq blkname
6       (strcase (getstring "\nEnter name of block to look at: "))
7     )
```

You're prompted to enter the name of the new layer and the name of the block to see if it has an attribute.

Line 8

```
8     (setq e (entnext))
```

Get the next entity.

Line 9

```
9     (while e
```

A loop is entered to detect when the process is complete.

Lines 10–13

```
10     (setq edata (entget e))
11     (if (and (= (cdr (assoc 0 edata)) "INSERT")  ; block found
12              (= (cdr (assoc 2 edata)) blkname) ; by name
13         ) ; endand
```

The entity is checked to see that it's a block.

Lines 14–22

```
14       (progn
15         (setq e1 (entnext e)) ; go to attribute info
16         (setq edata (entget e1)) ; get attribute data
17         (setq edata
18           (subst (cons 8 newlayer) (assoc 8 edata) edata)
```

```
19          ) ; endsetq
20          (entmod edata) ; modify entity
21          (entupd e1)    ; update attribute
22        ) ; endprogn
```

The new layer assignment is substituted for the old. Then the entity is modified and updated.

Lines 23–27

```
23      ) ; endif
24    (setq e (entnext e)) ; go to next entity
25    ) ; endwhile
26    (princ)
27 ) ; endCH_LAYER
```

The program goes to the next entity. Eventually, the program finishes running and the program ends.

Locating Attribute Text Strings

It's not uncommon during the drawing process to want to know exactly where a certain attribute text string is. Perhaps the attribute text is invisible, but you don't want to turn on the attribute display feature. You might be working on a floor plan that has attributes attached to each of the windows and doors, and you'd like to know where all of the windows are that will be supplied by a certain manufacturer. If the manufacturer's name is listed as attribute text, the following program will flash the block(s) it belongs to.

The C:FIND_ATT.LSP Program

The following program assists you in locating attribute text on your drawing, by flashing the block to which the text belongs. After starting the program, you enter the text string you wish to find (the string is not case-sensitive) and then enter the number of times you wish the block to flash.

Remember, the line numbers are for reference only, and words to the right of a semicolon are comments.

```
1  (defun C:FIND_ATT (/ str1 e enttyp edata att_value)
2    (setq old_cmdecho (getvar "cmdecho"))
```

```
3    (setvar "cmdecho" 0)                    ; turn cmdecho off
4    (setq str1
5      (strcase (getstring "\nEnter exact string to search for: "))
6    ) ; endsetq
7    (setq num_flashes
8      (getint "\nEnter number of times to flash block/text: ")
9    ) ; endsetq
10   (setq e (entnext))                ; start at beginning of database
11   (while e                           ; loop... look at every entity
12     (setq enttyp (cdr (assoc 0 (entget e)))) ; Save entity type
13     (if
14       (and
15         (equal enttyp "INSERT") ; If current entity is a Block
16         (equal (cdr (assoc 66 (entget e))) 1) ; & has attribute
17       ) ;endand
18       (progn                             ;Evaluate every list
19         (setq blk_ent_name e)            ; remember entity name
20         (setq e (entnext e))             ; next entity
21         (setq edata (entget e))          ; get data
22       ) ; endprogn
23     ) ; endif
24     (setq edata (entget e))
25     (if (assoc 1 edata)                  ; if value found
26       (progn
27         (setq att_value (cdr (assoc 1 edata))) ; get att value
28         (if (= att_value str1)
29           (repeat num_flashes
30             (command "select" blk_ent_name "")
31           ) ; endrepeat
32         ) ; endif
33       ) ; endprogn
34     ) ; endif
35     (setq e (entnext e)) ; Set e to next record in the database
36   ) ; endwhile
37   (setvar "cmdecho" old_cmdecho)
38   (princ)
39 ) ; end findatt
```

Loading & Running the Program

Create the program with an ASCII text editor and save it in a directory on your hard disk from which it is easy to load AutoLISP programs. Load the program into your editing session by typing at the Command prompt:

Type: `(load "find_att") <Return>`

After the program is loaded, invoke the program by typing the program name at the Command line as follows:

Type: `find_att <Return>`

The program will prompt you to enter the attribute text you wish to find.

After you enter the attribute text you wish to find, the program will prompt you to enter the number of times you wish to have the block flash to which the attribute text belongs.

The program will then scan the drawing database to find the attribute text you specified.

NOTE: This program will only find attribute text.

How the Program Works

Here's a line-by-line explanation of how the FIND_ATT.LSP program works.

Line 1

```
1  (defun C:FIND_ATT (/ strl e enttyp edata att_value)
```

The program will become a new AutoCAD command called **FIND_ATT**. The program's variables are listed behind the program name (function) definition name.

Lines 2–3

```
2    (setq old_cmdecho (getvar "cmdecho"))
3    (setvar "cmdecho" 0)                    ; turn cmdecho off
```

The **cmdecho** system variable is turned off to minimize commands being echoed to the screen during the selection process.

Lines 4–9

```
4     (setq str1
5       (strcase (getstring "\nEnter exact string to search for: "))
6     ) ; endsetq
7     (setq num_flashes
8       (getint "\nEnter number of times to flash block/text: ")
9     ) ; endsetq
```

The program prompts the user to enter the text string to be found. Then the user is prompted to enter the number of times the block and text (if it's visible) should flash. The function used to get the number of flashes specifies integer input.

Line 10

```
10    (setq e (entnext))            ; start at beginning of database
```

The **(entnext** function, when given with no arguments, begins searching at the beginning of the database.

Line 11

```
11    (while e                       ; loop... look at every entity
```

As long as entities are found, the program will continue to run through the **(while** loop.

Line 12

```
12      (setq enttyp (cdr (assoc 0 (entget e)))) ; Save entity type
```

The entity data is found with the **(entget** function. The **(assoc** function trims the data down to just the association list with the entity type. The **(cdr** function reads only the last part of the list which contains the actual entity type. Finally, the entity type is saved in the **enttyp** variable.

Lines 13–17

```
13      (if
14        (and
15          (equal enttyp "INSERT") ; If current entity is a Block
16          (equal (cdr (assoc 66 (entget e))) 1) ; & has attribute
17        ) ;endand
```

The **(if** function is used with the **(and** function to check two conditions. They look to see if the entity is a block and if it has an attribute. If both conditions are true, the next instruction is performed. If either is false, the matching parenthesis for the **(if** function is found and the next instruction beyond it is evaluated.

Lines 18–23

```
18        (progn                              ;Evaluate every list
19          (setq blk_ent_name e)             ; remember entity name
20          (setq e (entnext e))              ; next entity
21          (setq edata (entget e))           ; get data
22        ) ; endprogn
23      ) ; endif
```

The **(progn** function allows many functions to be included as a single group of functions when they are enclosed within its parentheses. The entity name is remembered so it can later be selected and flashed for visual purposes. The next entity is then found.

Line 24

```
24      (setq edata (entget e))
```

The entity data is recorded in the **edata** variable.

Lines 25–26

```
25      (if (assoc 1 edata)                 ; if value found
26        (progn
```

The **(if** function checks to see if an entity was found during the previous program instructions. The **(progn** function then allows several functions to be evaluated.

Line 27

```
27          (setq att_value (cdr (assoc 1 edata))) ; get att value
```

The attribute value is found.

Lines 28–32

```
28         (if (= att_value str1)
29           (repeat num_flashes
30             (command "select" blk_ent_name "")
31           ) ; endrepeat
32         ) ; endif
```

The **(if** and **(=** functions are used to compare the attribute value that was found with the string that the user typed at the beginning of the program. Then the **(repeat** function calls the AutoCAD **SELECT** command to select the block where the attribute text is located. The block is selected the number of times specified by the user.

Lines 33–36

```
33       ) ; endprogn
34     ) ; endif
35     (setq e (entnext e)) ; Set e to next record in the database
36   ) ; endwhile
```

When the **(entnext** function is called with the AutoCAD-assigned name as an argument, the function looks for the next entity in the database. This function is inside the **(while** function so the program will continue to run as long as there are entities to examine.

Lines 37–39

```
37   (setvar "cmdecho" old_cmdecho)
38   (princ)
39 ) ; end find_att
```

The **(setvar** function is used to read the setting of the **cmdecho** system variable as it was saved at the beginning of the program in the **old_cmdecho** variable. The function resets the variable back to its earlier state. The **(princ** function suppresses the "nil" message from the program.

Rapid Entry of Text Into Attributes

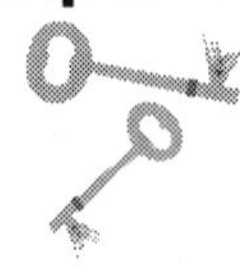

Typing has always been slow in any CAD system. One of the most popular ways people speed up the CAD text entry process is to have a fast typist prepare ASCII text with a text editor or text processor and to import the text into AutoCAD. Text is easily imported into AutoCAD by way of the ASCTEXT.LSP program that has been delivered with several AutoCAD releases. Once it's in the drawing, the text can be moved wherever the designer or drafter chooses. The drawback, however, is that the imported text is just "plain" text. None of it is converted to become assigned as attribute text.

The following program provides the additional step it takes to assign imported ASCII text to pre-defined attributes.

The C:FILL_ATT.LSP Program

The FILL_ATT.LSP program is written more specifically than the preceding programs because it uses a block with three attributes already defined. However, it's simple and straightforward to make changes to the program to fit your own circumstances.

The program asks you where to place the block that has the attributes. It then prompts you to digitize a line of imported text that you want to place into the first attribute location. After the first text is placed, the program goes on to ask for two other pieces of text.

Again, line numbers are for reference only, and words to the right of a semicolon are comments.

```
1  (defun C:FILL_ATT ()
2    (setq pt1 nil
3           enameblk nil
4           ename1 nil
5           edatablk1 nil
6           ename2 nil
7           edatablk2 nil
8           enameblk3 nil
9           edatablk3 nil
10          enameN nil
11          edataN nil
12          ename2 nil
13          edata2 nil
14          ename3 nil
```

```
15          edata3 nil
16          rept T
17    ) ; endsetq
18    (setvar "CMDECHO" 0)
19    (while rept
20      (setq pt1 (getpoint "\nDigitize location for block: "))
21      (if (not (equal pt1 nil))
22        (progn
23          (setvar "ATTREQ" 0)
24          (command "INSERT" "demo_blk" pt1 1 1 0)
25          (setq enameblk (entlast))
26          (setq ename1 (entnext enameblk))
27          (setq edatablk1 (entget ename1))
28          (setq ename2 (entnext ename1))
29          (setq edatablk2 (entget ename2))
30          (setq enameblk3 (entnext ename2))
31          (setq edatablk3 (entget enameblk3))
32          (setq ename1 (car (entsel "\nDig. str1 to convert: ")))
33          (setq ename2 (car (entsel "\nDig. str2 to convert: ")))
34          (setq ename3 (car (entsel "\nDig. str3 to convert: ")))
35          (if ename1
36            (progn
37              (setq edata1 (entget ename1))
38              (setq str1 (cdr (assoc 1 edata1)))
39            ) ; endprogn
40            (setq str1 "_")
41          ) ; endif
42          (if ename2
43            (progn
44              (setq edata2 (entget ename2))
45              (setq str2 (cdr (assoc 1 edata2)))
46            ) ; endprogn
47            (setq str2 "-")
48          ) ; endif
49          (if ename3
50            (progn
51              (setq edata3 (entget ename3))
52              (setq str3 (cdr (assoc 1 edata3)))
53            ) ; endprogn
54            (setq str3 "-")
```

```
55          ) ; endif
56          (setq edatablk1
57            (subst (cons 1 str1) (assoc 1 edatablk1) edatablk1)
58          ) ; place 1st text in first slot
59          (setq edatablk2
60            (subst (cons 1 str2) (assoc 1 edatablk2) edatablk2)
61          ) ; place 2nd text in second slot
62          (setq edatablk3
63            (subst (cons 1 str3) (assoc 1 edatablk3) edatablk3)
64          ) ; place 3rd text in third slot
65          (entmod edatablk1)
66          (entmod edatablk2)
67          (entmod edatablk3)
68          (entupd enameblk)
69          (if ename1
70            (entdel ename1)
71          ) ; endif
72          (if ename2
73            (entdel ename2)
74          ) ; endif
75          (if ename3
76            (entdel ename3)
77          ) ; endif
78          (setvar "highlight" 0)
79          (setq pt2 (getpoint "\nDig. new location for block: "))
80          (if (= pt2 nil)
81            (setq pt2 pt1)
82          ) ; endif
83          (command "MOVE" "L" "" pt1 pt2)
84          (setvar "highlight" 1)
85        ) ; endprogn
86        (setq rept nil) ; else, set repetition check to nil
87      ) ; endif
88    ) ; endwhile
89    (princ "\nDONE")
90    (princ)
91  ) ; endFILL_ATT
```

Loading & Running the Program

Before you can successfully run the FILL_ATT.LSP program you must create a block with three attributes. Figure 6-1 shows how the attributes should be defined. It's not important that you have a circle as part of the block. You can choose any graphics, or none at all. The example shows the attribute tags defined as: T1, T2 and T3, but you can define them with whatever tags you like. The block must be called DEMO_BLK.

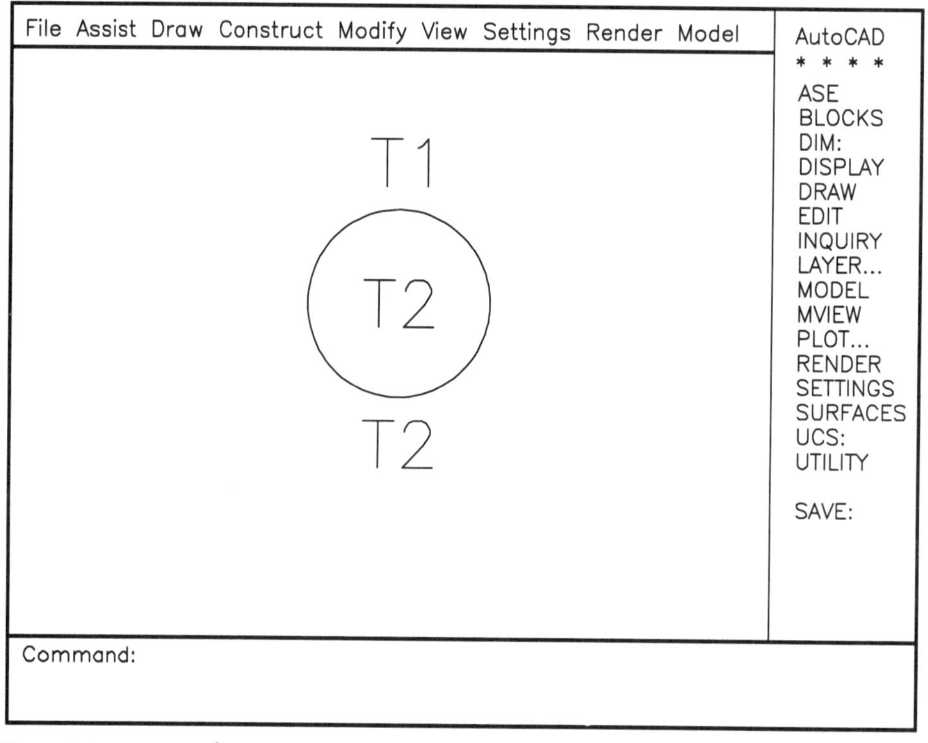

Figure 6-1: Block with attribute definitions for FILL_ATT.LSP

You must also place some text on your drawing by using the TEXT or DTEXT command (don't use attribute text). Place at least as many lines of text as you'll want to transfer to the attributes; i.e., the DEMO_BLK block has room for three lines of text, so for each block you'll add, have three lines of text ready to transfer to it.

If you don't have three lines for each block you add, you can hit the Return key for each blank line. For each blank line, a hyphen (-) will be placed where the text would have gone had you added it. Figure 6-2 shows the drawing editor with text added, ready to run the FILL_ATT.LSP program.

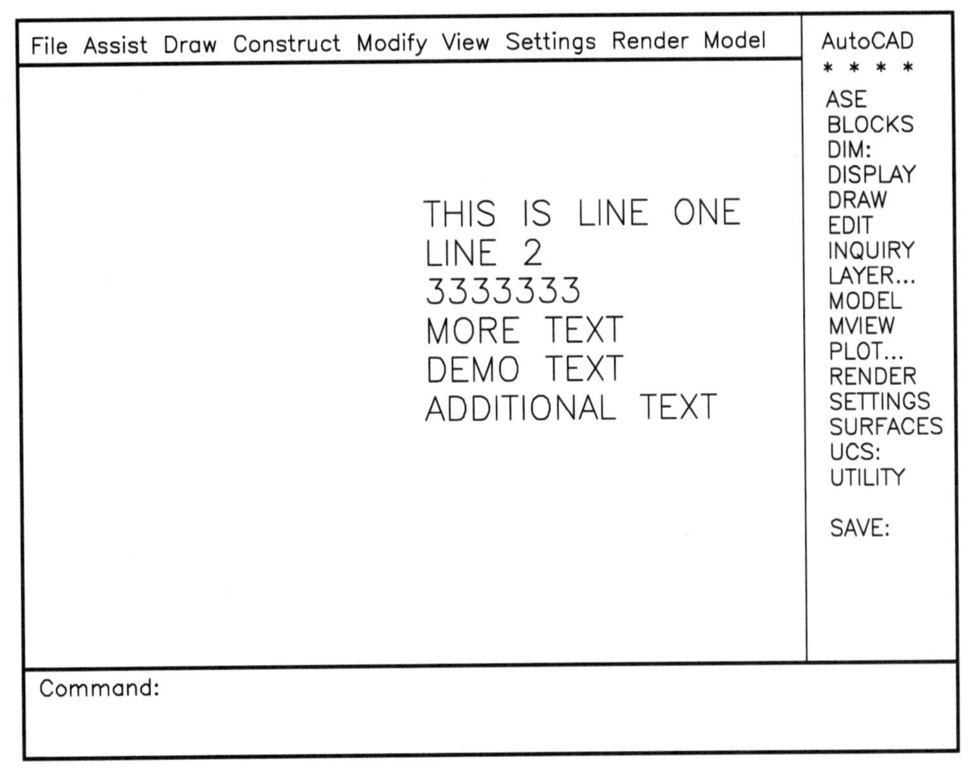

Figure 6-2: Drawing editor ready for FILL_ATT.LSP

Create the program with an ASCII text editor and save it in a directory on your hard disk from which it's easy to load AutoLISP programs. Load the program into your editing session by typing:

Type: `(load "Fill_att") <Return>`

After the program is loaded, call it by typing the program name at the Command line as follows:

Type: `Fill_att <Return>`

The program will prompt you to digitize an initial location for the DEMO_BLK block to be placed while you transfer the text into it.

After you digitize a location, the program will prompt you to digitize each text string to be transferred to the block.

The program will then prompt you to digitize the final location for the block. Figure 6-3 shows the final result, with all of the lines of text added to the blocks. Your results may look different, depending on the text you place in the drawing and depending how you place the blocks and pick the text to be added.

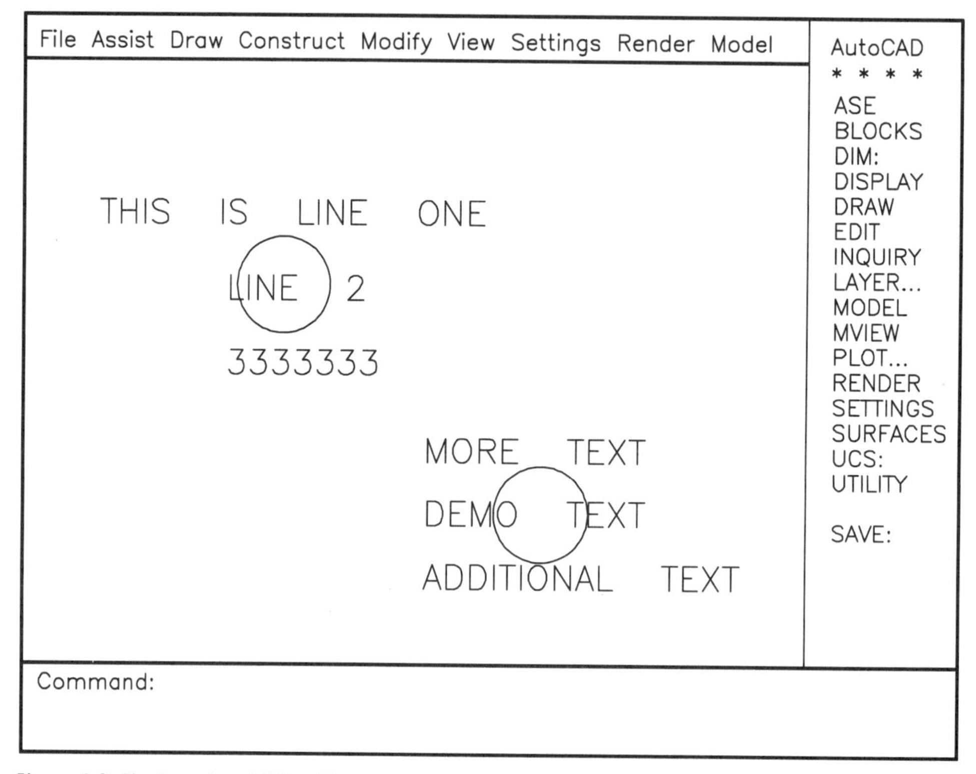

Figure 6-3: Final results of FILL_ATT.LSP

How the Program Works

Here's a line-by-line description of how the FILL_ATT.LSP program works.

Lines 1–17

```
1  (defun C:FILL_ATT ()
2    (setq pt1 nil
3          enameblk nil
```

```
4          ename1 nil
5          edatablk1 nil
6          ename2 nil
7          edatablk2 nil
8          enameblk3 nil
9          edatablk3 nil
10         enameN nil
11         edataN nil
12         ename2 nil
13         edata2 nil
14         ename3 nil
15         edata3 nil
16         rept T
17    ) ; endsetq
```

The program will become a new AutoCAD command called **FILL_ATT**. The program's variables are listed and initialized below the program name (function) definition name.

Line 18

```
18    (setvar "CMDECHO" 0)
```

The **CMDECHO** system variable is turned off to minimize commands being echoed to the screen during the selection process.

Line 19

```
19    (while rept
```

A variable is used to "flag" the program when to continue and when to stop.

Lines 20–22

```
20      (setq pt1 (getpoint "\nDigitize location for block: "))
21      (if (not (equal pt1 nil))
22        (progn
```

The program prompts the user to digitize a location where the DEMO_BLK block will be added. If no location is given, the program aborts.

Line 23

```
23          (setvar "ATTREQ" 0)
```

The system variable **ATTREQ** is turned off so the system won't prompt you to enter attribute values.

Line 24

```
24          (command "INSERT" "demo_blk" pt1 1 1 0)
```

The block is inserted at the digitized point at a scale of 1 and a rotation of zero.

Lines 25–31

```
25          (setq enameblk (entlast))
26          (setq ename1 (entnext enameblk))
27          (setq edatablk1 (entget ename1))
28          (setq ename2 (entnext ename1))
29          (setq edatablk2 (entget ename2))
30          (setq enameblk3 (entnext ename2))
31          (setq edatablk3 (entget enameblk3))
```

Entity names of the block and its attribute definitions are pulled from the database so that the text can be put into place.

Lines 32–34

```
32          (setq ename1 (car (entsel "\nDig. str1 to convert: ")))
33          (setq ename2 (car (entsel "\nDig. str2 to convert: ")))
34          (setq ename3 (car (entsel "\nDig. str3 to convert: ")))
```

The user is prompted to digitize the text that will be placed into the block.

Lines 35–55

```
35          (if ename1
36            (progn
37              (setq edata1 (entget ename1))
38              (setq str1 (cdr (assoc 1 edata1)))
39            ) ; endprogn
40            (setq str1 "_")
41          ) ; endif
```

```
42          (if ename2
43            (progn
44              (setq edata2 (entget ename2))
45              (setq str2 (cdr (assoc 1 edata2)))
46            ) ; endprogn
47            (setq str2 "-")
48          ) ; endif
49          (if ename3
50            (progn
51              (setq edata3 (entget ename3))
52              (setq str3 (cdr (assoc 1 edata3)))
53            ) ; endprogn
54            (setq str3 "-")
55          ) ; endif
```

Each user input is checked to see if any text was or was not digitized. If no text was digitized, a hyphen (–) will be placed into the attribute.

Lines 56–64

```
56          (setq edatablk1
57            (subst (cons 1 str1) (assoc 1 edatablk1) edatablk1)
58          ) ; place 1st text in first slot
59          (setq edatablk2
60            (subst (cons 1 str2) (assoc 1 edatablk2) edatablk2)
61          ) ; place 2nd text in second slot
62          (setq edatablk3
63            (subst (cons 1 str3) (assoc 1 edatablk3) edatablk3)
64          ) ; place 3rd text in third slot
```

Each digitized string of text is placed into the corresponding attribute.

Lines 65–68

```
65          (entmod edatablk1)
66          (entmod edatablk2)
67          (entmod edatablk3)
68          (entupd enameblk)
```

The changes are transferred into the block and the attribute entities, and the block is updated to show the changes.

Lines 69–77

```
69          (if ename1
70            (entdel ename1)
71          ) ; endif
72          (if ename2
73            (entdel ename2)
74          ) ; endif
75          (if ename3
76            (entdel ename3)
77          ) ; endif
```

Each string of text that was digitized is erased from the drawing.

Line 78

```
78          (setvar "highlight" 0)
```

The **highlight** system variable is turned off for the sake of appearances.

Lines 79–84

```
79          (setq pt2 (getpoint "\nDig. new location for block: "))
80          (if (= pt2 nil)
81            (setq pt2 pt1)
82          ) ; endif
83          (command "MOVE" "L" "" pt1 pt2)
84          (setvar "highlight" 1)
```

The program prompts you to digitize a final location for the block. If you don't give a location, the block stays where it is. Then the **highlight** system variable is turned back on.

Lines 85–91

```
85        ) ; endprogn
86        (setq rept nil) ; else, set repetition check to nil
87      ) ; endif
88    ) ; endwhile
89    (princ "\nDONE")
90    (princ)
91 ) ; endFILL_ATT
```

The continuation flag is cleared, causing the program to stop if no input was initially given. A message is printed on the screen to signal that the program is done, the CMDECHO variable is returned to its original setting, and the program ends.

Moving On

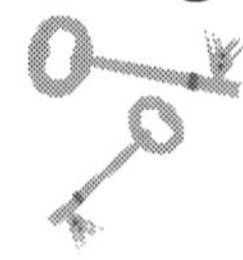

This chapter has presented some programs to assist you in using attributes. More importantly, concepts have been given that can be applied in many ways for the purpose of increasing your effective and productive use of attributes.

The next section, "AutoCAD for Windows," explores and explains the world of AutoCAD for Windows and will teach you the steps to using DDE—Dynamic Data Exchange—in the Windows environment. We'll discuss AutoCAD for Windows techniques, including how to prepare the AutoCAD for Windows toolbar and buttons for your own applications.

SECTION III

AutoCAD for Windows: Use and Customization

AutoCAD for Windows

This chapter provides an insight into the advantages and benefits of AutoCAD for Windows. Release 12's AutoCAD for Windows is even more efficient than the AutoCAD DOS 386 version.

You'll also learn about Dynamic Data Exchange (DDE) and how to use it to tie together graphic data from AutoCAD with data managed by other tools, such as a spreadsheet system.

The Benefits of Windows

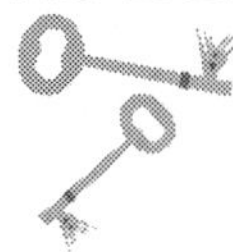

Clearly, the Windows user interface is now one of the most powerful and persuasive computer tools available. Powerful because it allows you to take better advantage of an application's capabilities; persuasive because it influences you to buy one software package over another, depending on which software runs better under the Windows environment.

Microsoft Windows has emerged as a popular solution for a friendly graphical interface that has been sought after ever since the introduction of personal computers. As Windows's popularity grows, more and more software manufacturers are offering their products as Windows applications.

Now AutoCAD, one of the newer software applications, has been given a Windows interface. But just because Windows is new to AutoCAD doesn't mean few people are using it. In fact, the already large number of Windows-based AutoCAD users continues to grow daily.

Why Use Windows?

You already know the answer to this question if you've ever had to learn DOS—the personal computer's "Disk Operating System." It contains a large variety of powerful commands but offers no menus; and only if you have version 5.0 is a help system available. DOS does exactly what you tell it to do—but you have to understand it to use it! And most new DOS users don't know how to make DOS perform even the simplest task.

Windows, on the other hand, is a collection of menus categorized by types of operations and by applications that are easily identified by pictures (icons). You just click on the pictures with the mouse instead of typing in arcane commands, as DOS requires.

Many DOS users would rather not be DOS users, but until Windows became available they had little choice. Today, many former DOS users are taking advantage of Windows's powerful and convenient features.

Loading & Using Special Applications

Loading an application into the Windows Graphical User Interface (GUI) usually takes nothing more than clicking the pointer on the File menu in the menu bar, clicking on the RUN command (see Figure 7-1) and then typing the diskette drive name followed by **setup** (see Figure 7-2).

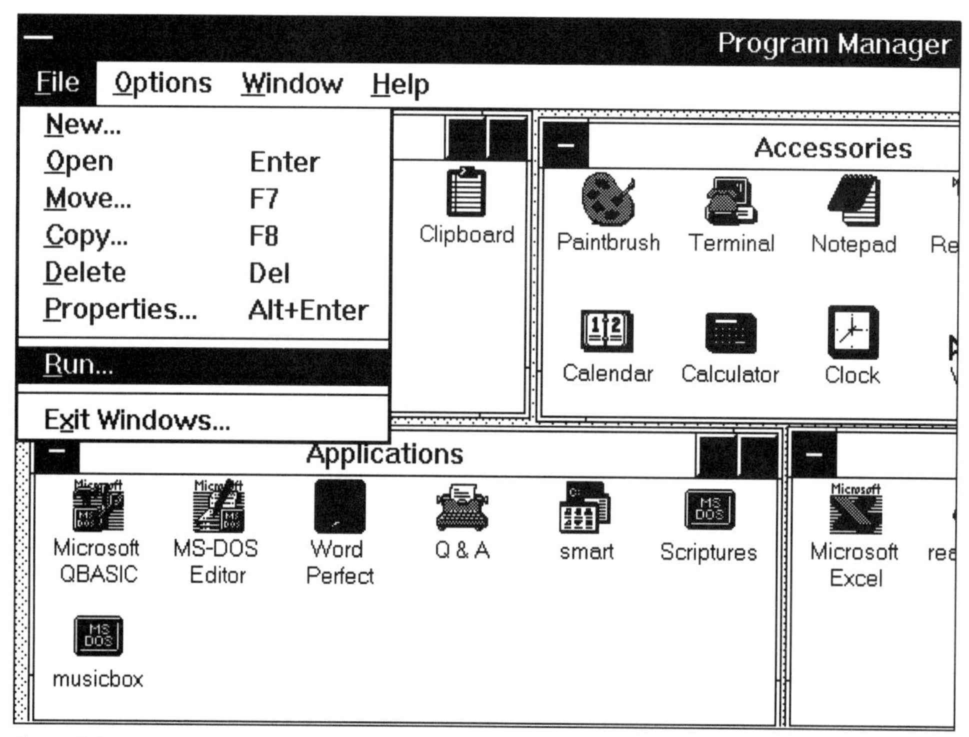

Figure 7-1: The Windows File menu

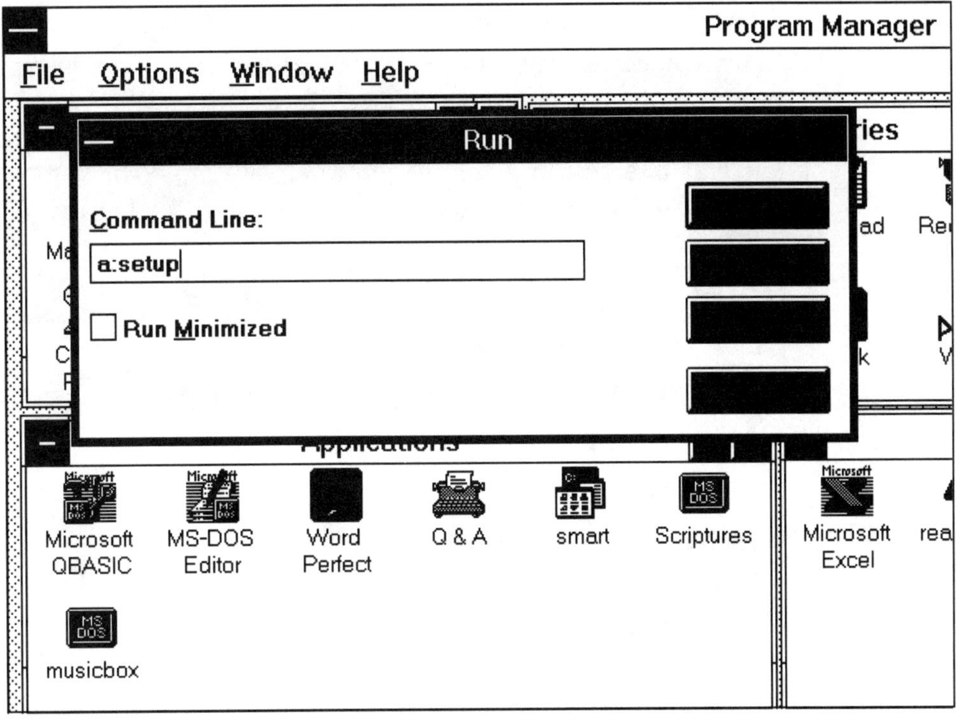

Figure 7-2: Loading a Windows application via setup

Most of the time, the application you're loading will prompt you for any extra information it needs. It will also provide most, if not all, of the other settings required by Windows and the application itself. You won't need to do any batch programming in DOS.

If the application is built for use within Windows, just click on its program icon to activate it. Each icon is a simple picture with a title below it that reminds you of the application it stands for.

Context-Sensitive Help

Many computer programs have context-sensitive help, but unless the programs share a common user interface such as Windows, each one will have its own method of getting you to its help screens. Windows has only one way to access any application's help system. What's more, the help system for each application looks very similar (see Figures 7-3 and 7-4).

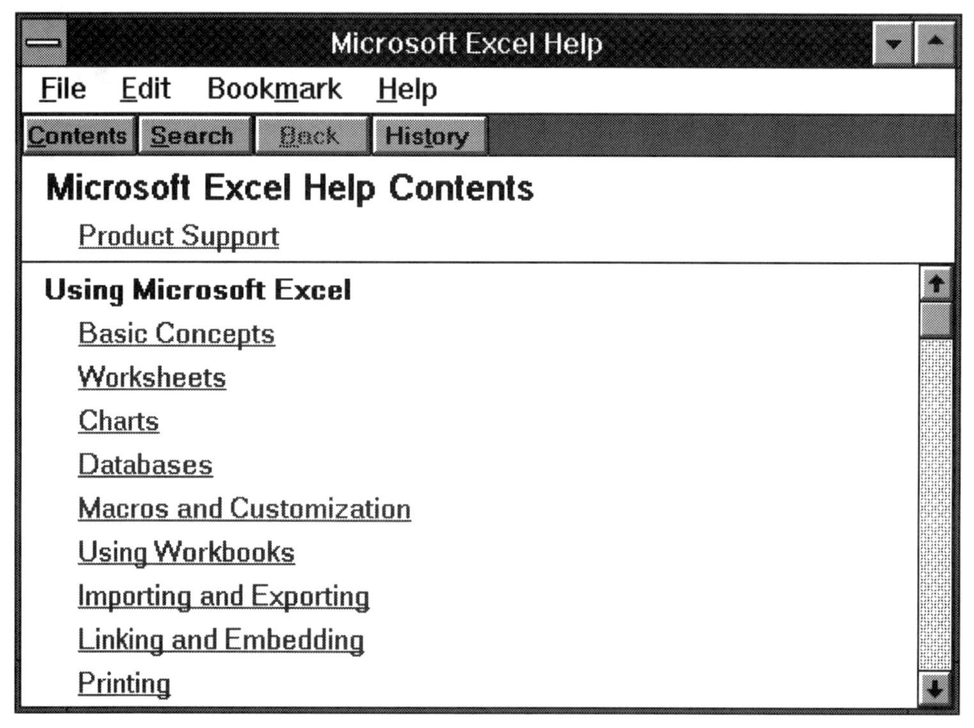

Figure 7-3: The Excel for Windows help system

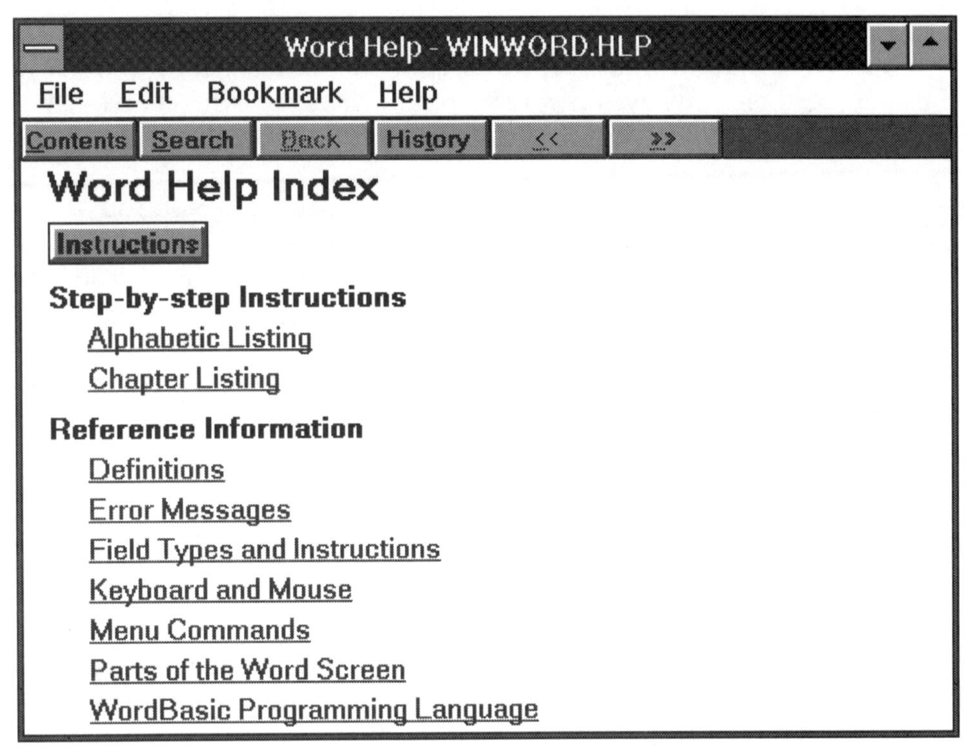

Figure 7-4: The Word for Windows help system

DOS Versus Windows

Let's look at some DOS frustrations.

Applications. DOS allows you to work with only one application at a time. If you want to switch from one application to another, you have to save your work, exit the current application and then load the other program.

Sharing Data. To move information from one application to a second application, you have to save the information in a file, exit the first application, start the second and then load the information you've saved—that is, if you can still remember the name of the file and which directory it's saved in!

Now, let's compare those DOS frustrations to Windows, which uses a completely different approach.

The Desktop. When you start Windows, a special graphical screen (the Windows *desktop*) appears, showing the icons for the applications and tools you have on your computer. You have direct access to any tool or application you want to use.

Tools. Windows tools include a Calendar, a Notepad, a Clock and a Calculator. You can work with one or more tools at a time, get more out as you need them and put away the ones you don't need. Windows has many of the same tools that you might have on your desk.

Sharing Data. Sharing information between the Notepad and the Calendar is one example of sharing data. To copy a note from your Notepad to your Calendar, select the note with the mouse, choose Copy from the pull-down menu, pick the location on the Calendar where the note will be copied and pick Paste from the Calendar pull-down menu.

Copying Data. Windows lets you move and copy many kinds of information easily. Translation routines can bridge the communication gap between programs that "speak" different languages. For example, Windows lets you copy a drawing (or a portion of a drawing) from AutoCAD and paste it into a Word for Windows document. All translation between AutoCAD and Word for Windows is done for you.

Storing Tools. Tools and other applications on your desktop can be sized to fit in the space you wish to give them. If your desktop is cluttered, you can put one or more tools or applications away by clicking on the command(s) that will automatically "shrink" them into a miniature icon for use at a future time.

Your Own Custom Menu

The purpose of a menu is to give you easy access to the programs and tools in your computer. DOS-based menus usually show the name of each command you can type, along with a short description of what the command will do.

Custom DOS menus are very difficult for new users to build. In fact, building the simplest DOS menu requires experience with a text editor, an understanding of how to write batch files and text files and, of course, an understanding of each application's requirements.

Preparing a custom Windows menu is easy. There's no batch programming involved and no creation of special text files. To create a custom menu in Windows, just place the desired program icons on your desktop, where you can select them at any time.

Shortening the Learning Curve

If you've used DOS, you know that each program has its own method of operation. Each time you install and begin using a new program, you have to go through a learning curve that includes getting the program up and running, operational techniques, input and output procedures and individual commands.

While Windows doesn't eliminate the learning process, it can shorten it. Many of the input and output techniques are similar across all Windows applications; once you're able to use one application, you can pretty much use any application.

Why AutoCAD for Windows?

Most PC users are starting to use Windows. If you're an engineer or a designer—and a Windows user—your Windows desktop would be incomplete without AutoCAD. Windows is a Graphical User Interface (GUI) and AutoCAD is a high performance graphics-based Computer Aided Design system. Placing AutoCAD into the Windows environment opens the world of Windows to you as an AutoCAD user.

We've looked at some of the reasons why you might use Windows instead of DOS. Now let's look at how Windows can contribute to your success in business and your ease of use with AutoCAD.

The Write Text Editor

It's no secret that text entry in any CAD system has long been a problem for CAD users. CAD systems were not designed to be text processors. The DOS text editor (EDLIN) has always left something to be desired, and the EDIT editor in DOS 5.0 is limited in the size of file it can edit. Windows, however, has an excellent text editor called Write.

Write has a good set of editing features that take advantage of many Windows capabilities. It can edit files of virtually any size, which makes it an excellent choice for editing very large menus and AutoLISP files. It is simple and, as such, is easy to use for entering large amounts of text that will be placed into your drawing.

You can easily create drawing notes, lists and other textual information with the Write editor. After you've created and saved the desired text into a file, you can retrieve it using Release 12's built-in text import feature (see Figure 7-5).

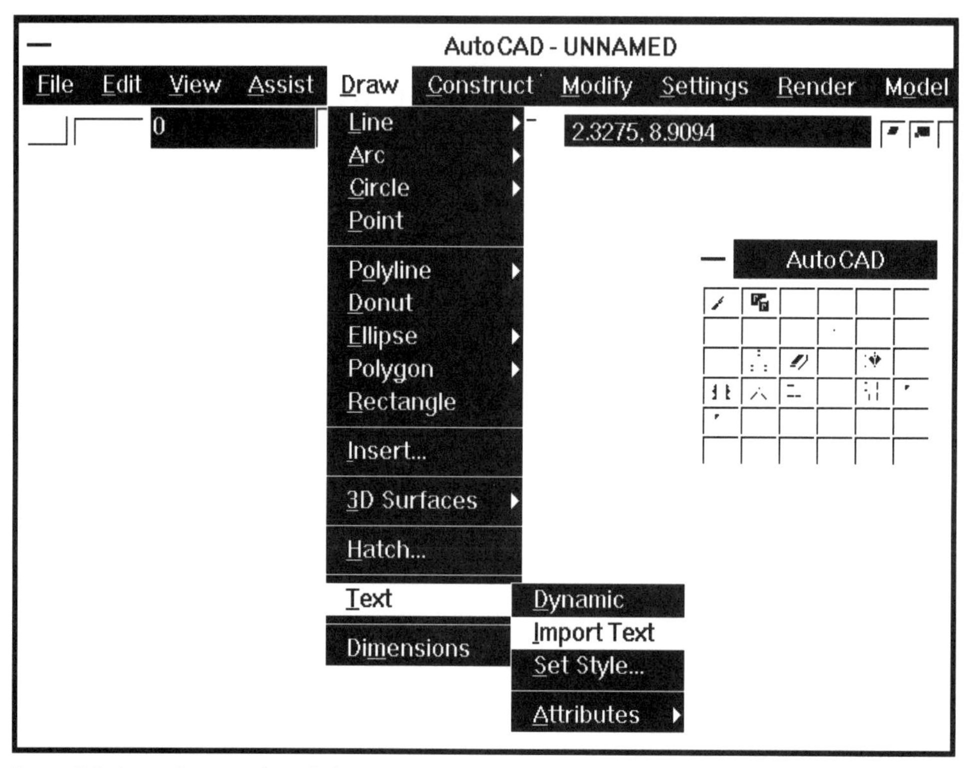

Figure 7-5: Importing text via pull-down menus

A major advantage of using a Windows-based text editor is that you can make the editor and your drawing visible at the same time (see Figure 7-6). You can easily create the text using the editor and then transfer the text to your drawing, watching each step as it takes place.

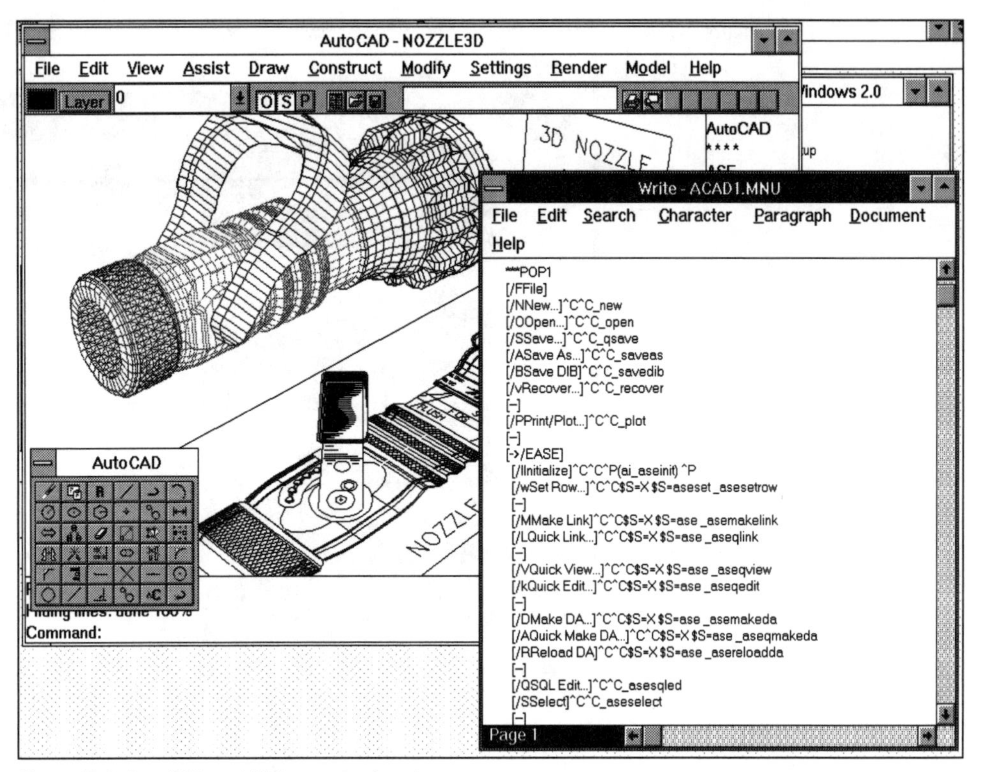

Figure 7-6: AutoCAD and Write—sharing the screen

Capturing the AutoCAD Screen

AutoCAD slides have always been a useful means of capturing particular views and other points of interest in a drawing file. But Windows adds another capability. The Edit pull-down menu, shown in Figure 7-7, contains selections that allow images, or parts of images, to be copied to the Windows Clipboard. The following methods will show you how to use this new feature.

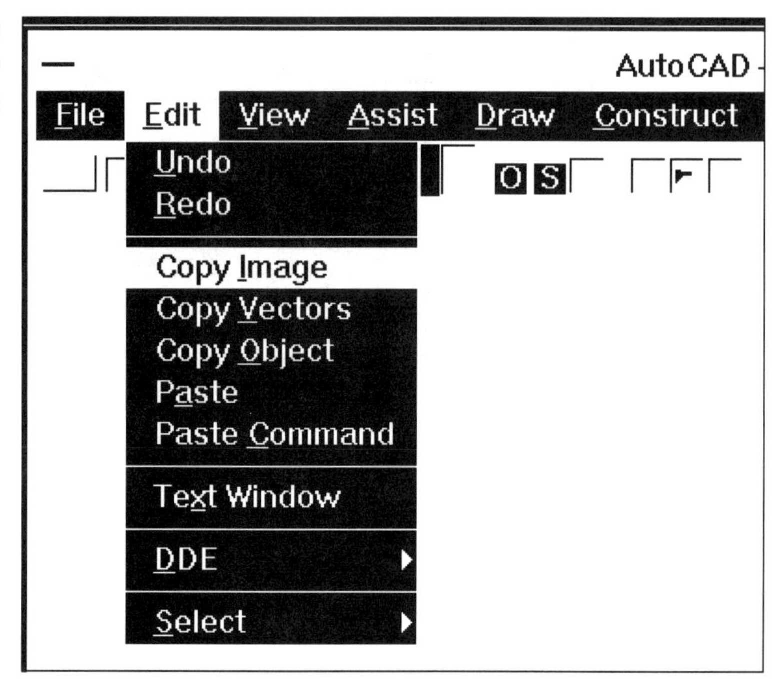

Figure 7-7: The AutoCAD for Windows Edit menu

To copy a raster screen image to the Clipboard, select the Copy Image option from the Edit menu. When you make the selection from the menu, the cursor will change shape, turning into a small cross. When the small cross appears, digitize the first corner of a window containing the information you wish to capture. Then drag the cursor to the other corner of the area you wish to capture and click the cursor again. After this final cursor click, the screen image that's inside the rectangle you've made will be captured and copied to the Clipboard. The captured information will be in Windows bitmap format. You can now transfer the picture that's in the Clipboard to other Windows applications, such as a word processor.

Windows also allows you to capture vector information in much the same way. After choosing the Copy Vectors menu option, you're prompted to select the vectors you wish to place onto the Clipboard.

You can capture AutoCAD or any Windows-environment screen by simply tapping the Print Screen key once. When you do, the current Windows screen is captured and placed onto the Clipboard. If you wish to edit the picture or convert it from BMP to PCX format, you can bring the image into the Windows Paint utility.

Paint lets you edit a bitmapped image by using tools to trim away unwanted portions, add and change color where desired and highlight areas of interest. You can then save the image as a BMP or PCX file.

Do the following to use Windows's screen capture capability and edit the image with Paint:

1. Press the Print Screen key to capture the image to the Clipboard.
2. Open the Paint utility.
3. Pick the View menu selection, then pick the Zoom Out selection that appears below it (see Figure 7-8).

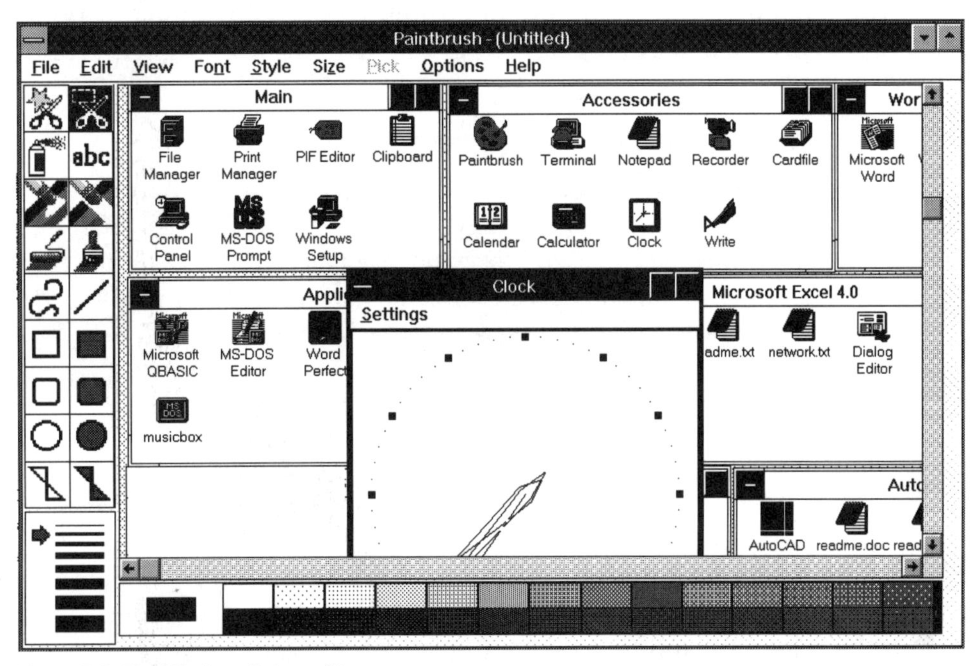

Figure 7-8: The Windows Paint utility

4. Pick the Edit menu (in the Windows Paint utility), then pick the Paste selection.
5. Repeat step 4 (yes, paste it one more time).
6. Pick the View menu selection, then pick the Zoom In selection that appears below it.

Upon completing step 6, the image you captured will be displayed in the Paint utility.

Other Desktop Tools

AutoCAD with Windows puts many other desktop tools at your fingertips. You have instant access to the Windows Calculator, Calendar and Clock. The File Manager is available to help you find, copy, move and delete files, and it can help you copy entire diskettes without going to DOS. For minor note-taking, you can use the Notepad text editor. And even more tools are available.

If you have a modem, the Terminal selection gives you access to online information services, bulletin boards and other computers. And, of course, any Windows application you've added to your Windows environment becomes accessible when you're working with AutoCAD.

Windows-based AutoCAD Help

Few computer users like to carry a set of user manuals with them. There are times, however, when you simply need help. AutoCAD for Windows includes the *AutoCAD Reference Manual* as an integral part of the program, providing fast on-screen information—from commands to system variables. And you don't have to carry the book around.

Dynamic Data Exchange

Dynamic Data Exchange (DDE) is probably the most powerful feature of AutoCAD for Windows: it lets you attach AutoCAD's graphic entities to an outside program. Such a dynamic link allows you to work through a conceptual design faster than ever before. And by working faster, you have more time to experiment with designs. The quality of your work goes up and so does your bottom-line profit.

You can use DDE in parametric applications to optimize a design, or you can use it in Bill of Materials (BOM) applications, Geographic Information Systems (GIS), Facility Management (FM) and environmental studies, to name only a few.

Moving On

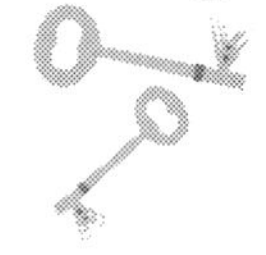

The next chapter, "Opportunities for Customization," includes hands-on examples of many of the concepts described in this chapter. You'll experience the many benefits of using AutoCAD for Windows. You'll probably want to do Windows from now on.

Opportunities for Customization

This chapter discusses the many ways you can increase your design productivity with AutoCAD for Windows. You'll see how to customize AutoCAD's Windows-based toolbar, toolbox and pull-down menus. In addition, you'll learn how the ACAD.INI file works and how to modify it to suit your needs. We'll also discuss how to use Object Linking and Embedding (OLE).

I'll assume that you have AutoCAD for Windows configured, loaded and running with a minimum of 8 Mb of RAM memory in your computer.

The Look & Feel of Windows

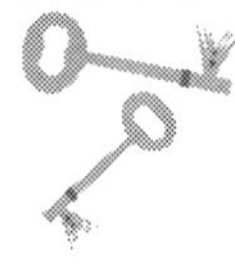

The familiar AutoCAD editor has a new look, partly because of Release 12 and partly because of the Windows Graphical User Interface (GUI). When you start AutoCAD from Windows, you'll first see the AutoCAD graphics window, an example of which is shown in Figure 8-1.

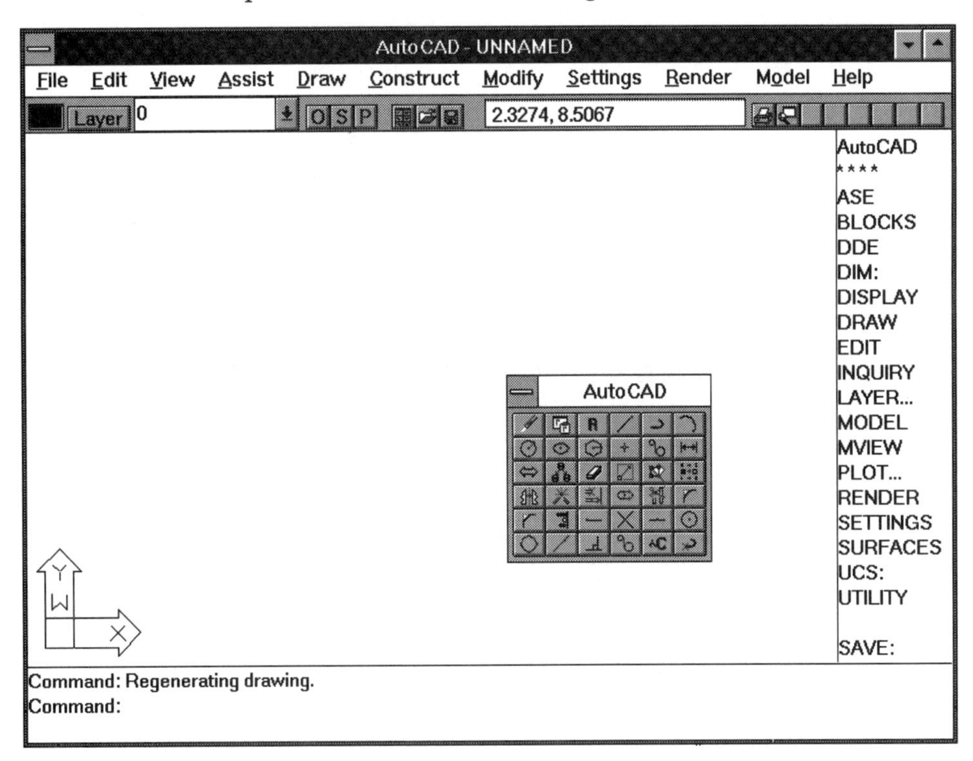

Figure 8-1: The AutoCAD graphics window

Along the top of the window, you'll see a collection of tools and information. The drawing's title is shown in the title bar. The menu bar, which is below the title bar, contains the pull-down menus. Just below the menu bar, you'll see the toolbar.

The toolbar contains information and buttons to control entity colors, layers, Osnap mode, Snap and Paper Space modes, programmable buttons and more. Notice the toolbox in the lower-right part of the screen. You can place it anywhere on the screen and easily and quickly program it.

Multiple AutoCAD Sessions

AutoCAD for Windows Release 12 lets you have up to three sessions of AutoCAD running at the same time. You'll need at least 8 Mb of RAM for the first session and about 4.5 Mb of RAM for each additional session that you intend to open.

Starting additional AutoCAD sessions is easy. After starting the first session, press the Alt and Esc keys at the same time to bring up the Windows Program Manager. Double-click on the AutoCAD icon to start an additional session.

Resizing Graphics Windows

If you don't want an AutoCAD graphics window to occupy the entire screen, you can resize it by moving the cursor to the edge or lower-right corner of the window until the cursor becomes a double arrow. Press and hold the first mouse button and drag the screen edge(s) until the window is the size you want. Then release the mouse button.

Resizing the AutoCAD graphics windows will let you see more than one AutoCAD session at once. You can also use this technique to make room for a spreadsheet, word processor or other application.

Introducing OLE

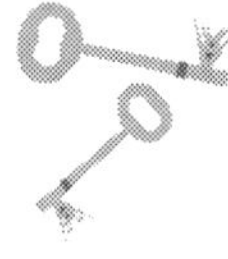

Object Linking and Embedding (OLE) is one of the biggest reasons for using AutoCAD for Windows Release 12. OLE lets you place a "live" AutoCAD drawing into another application, such as a word processing document. ("Live" means that when you make a change to the drawing, you can update the drawing in the document simply by pushing a button.) And you can place your drawing into many documents as easily as placing it into a single document. The update procedure is the same for each document. Here's a simple example using AutoCAD for Windows and Word for Windows.

An OLE Example

Creating accurate documentation is an integral part of the engineering design process. Word for Windows is one word processor that lets you easily place illustrations into your document so you can achieve the accuracy required for today's designs. But simply placing an illustration into a document doesn't guarantee that the picture will always match the AutoCAD drawing from which it came. That's where Object Linking and Embedding comes in.

Object Linking and Embedding lets you create an object (a drawing, graph, illustration, etc.) using one Windows tool and display the object in another. For instance, using OLE, you can create a drawing in AutoCAD and display it in a Word for Windows document. *Embedding* the drawing in the document causes a copy of the drawing to become a part of the document. *Linking* reserves a space in the document for the drawing to appear, then references the drawing from the hard disk.

To embed or link AutoCAD-created graphics into a Word for Windows document, start Word for Windows and begin a new document. Choose Insert from the pull-down menu bar. Choose Object... from the pull-down menu. Choose AutoCAD Drawing from the pop-up menu when it appears. Word for Windows automatically starts AutoCAD for Windows.

Create the graphics you wish to place into the Word for Windows document (or load the drawing containing it). From the Edit menu selection in the AutoCAD menu bar, choose Copy Object. The system will prompt you to select objects. Select the object(s) you wish to place into the Word for Windows document, then press Return.

NOTE: Choose only a few objects for your first attempt at this process.

Although it won't be apparent, the system responds by placing a copy of the objects you selected onto the Windows Clipboard. The objects can now be placed into your document. Exit AutoCAD, saving the drawing on the way out.

Return to your Word for Windows document. From the Edit pull-down menu, pick Paste. The graphics you selected in AutoCAD will be inserted into your Word for Windows document at the current cursor location.

Updating an Embedded Object

To edit a drawing that has been embedded into a Word for Windows document, start Word for Windows and open the document containing the drawing. Double-click on the drawing you wish to change. Word for Windows automatically starts AutoCAD for Windows and loads the drawing to be edited.

Make the desired changes you need to edit the drawing. From the AutoCAD File menu, choose Exit or Update. If you choose to exit, be sure to update on your way out (Update causes the changes you made to be copied to the Word for Windows document). When you return to Word for Windows, you'll see that the drawing in your document matches the updated AutoCAD drawing.

The Client/Server Concept

In the Object Linking and Embedding process, AutoCAD acts as the *server*, or source, of the application. That means AutoCAD is the source from which the drawing comes.

If you plan to embed or link an AutoCAD drawing into a Word for Windows document, the Word for Windows document becomes the client, or destination, application.

OLE rules you should remember:

- AutoCAD acts only as the source application. AutoCAD is always the server (source), never the client (destination).
- You can embed an AutoCAD drawing only into a Windows application that supports OLE as a server.

Comparing Linking & Embedding

Both linking and embedding let you place an AutoCAD drawing into another application and edit the drawing from inside that application. That's because when you place a drawing into a document that's outside AutoCAD, you create a link from the client document to the AutoCAD drawing. Thus when you edit the AutoCAD drawing and update the link from the external document, you see the changed drawing in your document.

If you want to place an AutoCAD drawing into several documents, it's best to link them all. When drawing changes are required, you can change the drawing once in AutoCAD, then update each document to see the changes.

When you *embed* a drawing into an external document, however, and update the drawing using AutoCAD, the original drawing remains unchanged. In other words, no active link is created when you embed a drawing in a document. If you plan to place a drawing into a single document and never change the original drawing, you should embed the drawing.

Updating Linked & Embedded Drawings

You can update a linked or embedded drawing using similar methods if you wish. That is, from within the client document, you can double-click on the drawing and your client application will start AutoCAD and load the drawing so it can be edited. When you finish editing the drawing, follow one of the methods below to update the drawing in the document.

For an embedded drawing, pull down the File menu and choose Update (you'll notice that the Save command has been replaced with the Update command.) When you return to the client document, you'll see the changes you made to the drawing.

The process is different for a linked drawing. After you've made the necessary changes to the drawing, choose Save from the File pull-down menu. It's important you save a linked drawing after a change is made so that all documents with links to the drawing can be updated.

When you bring up the client document, the application will know that a change has occurred to the linked drawing and will prompt you to update the link so that the changes will appear in the document.

Customization

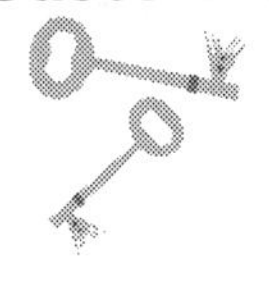

AutoCAD for Windows follows the same philosophy as traditional AutoCAD: a major key to productivity is open software design. When you start AutoCAD Release 12 for Windows, the AutoCAD graphics window appears, with a programmable toolbar at the top of the window and a programmable toolbox in the drawing area. Creating a custom toolbar and toolbox is fast and easy.

Creating a Custom Toolbar

Figure 8-2: The AutoCAD for Windows toolbar

NOTE: If your AutoCAD graphics window is small, the programmable toolbar buttons may not be visible. You may need to enlarge the graphics window so you can see them.

You can program most of the buttons in the toolbar. Only the Ortho mode, Snap mode, Paper Space and floating toolbox buttons are not programmable. Your screen resolution will also affect the number of visible programmable buttons: the lower the resolution, the fewer the buttons.

It's easy to program a button. Say you want to program a button to set your snap to 1/8 inch and set the grid to 2 times the snap setting. Begin by clicking with the right mouse button on the button you wish to program. The Toolbar Customization dialogue box appears (see Figure 8-3). Notice that the number of the button you're programming appears in the top of the dialogue box.

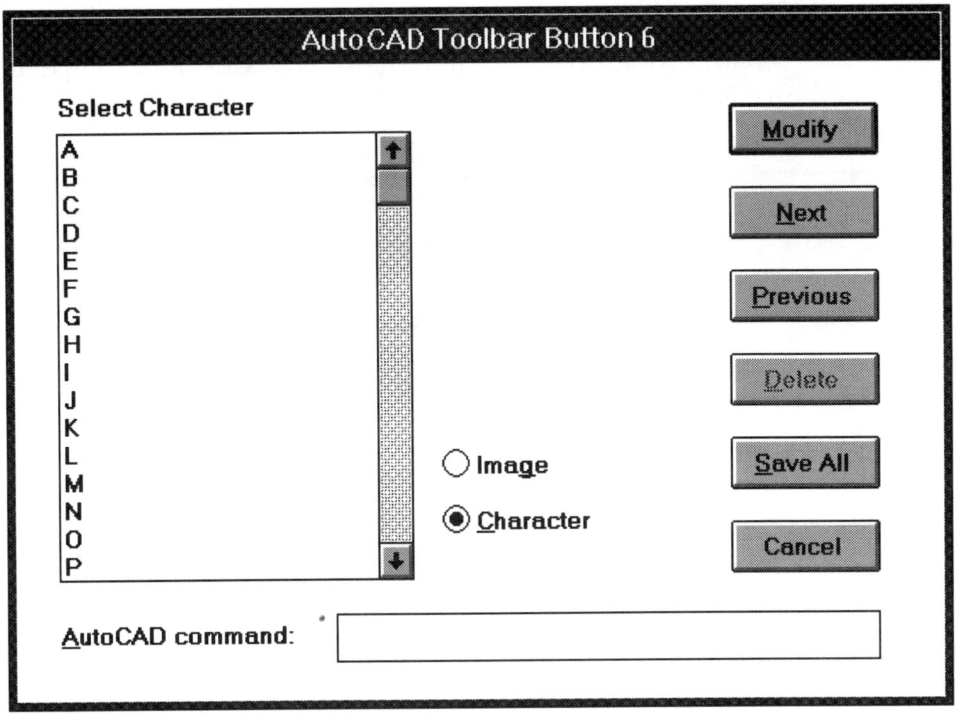

Figure 8-3: The Toolbar Customization dialogue box

In the AutoCAD command area,

Type: SNAP <Return>
.125 <Return>
GRID <Return>
2X <Return>

Choose an alphabetic character to be placed on the button (the buttons are in the Character ID area). Remember, if you click on the Bitmap Resource ID button, a list of icons appears in the Enter Character ID area. From this area, you can choose one of these icons. Click on the OK button. AutoCAD returns control to the AutoCAD graphics window.

NOTE: If you wish to save the button definition for use in future AutoCAD sessions, click on the Save All button before you click the OK button. The Save All button saves the definitions to the ACAD.INI file (discussed later in this chapter).

Other Buttons in the Toolbar Customization Dialogue Box

Four other buttons appear in the Toolbar Customization dialogue box. They are:

- Cancel—The Cancel button cancels the current operation and returns you to the normal drawing screen.
- Next—The Next button goes to the next programmable button on the toolbar.
- Previous—The Previous button goes to the previous programmable button on the toolbar.
- Delete—The Delete button deletes the definition of the current button.

Special Command Characters

Special characters are available for use in the AutoCAD Command area. The special characters are shown below. Remember, special characters are case sensitive:

- **\3** places a Ctrl-C in a command.
- **\t** places a tab character in a command.
- **\n** places a new line in a command.

You can place other ASCII characters in a command by using a backslash (\) followed by the ASCII decimal code. For instance, **\032** is a space.

Creating a Custom Toolbox

The toolbox comes with a set of commonly used commands. You're free to change any of the commands assigned to the buttons, change the size and shape of the toolbox and change the order in which the buttons appear. You customize the toolbox the same way you customized the toolbar.

The following example shows you another way to customize the toolbox—by modifying the ACAD.INI file (located in the \ACADWIN directory by default). Let's say that you want to program the upper-left Toolbox button surface to show an Array symbol and begin the ARRAY command.

Load the ACAD.INI file into an ASCII text editor. Find the part of the listing containing the toolbox definitions. It will look similar to the partial listing of the file below:

```
[AutoCAD Toolbox]
ToolBox1=undo ^UNDO^
ToolBox2=\3copyclip ^COPY_VECTORS^
ToolBox3=\3redraw ^REDRAW^
ToolBox4=\3line ^LINE^
ToolBox5=\3pline ^POLYLINE^
ToolBox6=\3arc ^ARC^
ToolBox7=\3circle ^CIRCLE^
ToolBox8=\3ellipse ^ELLIPSE^
ToolBox9=\3polygon ^POLYGON^
ToolBox10=\3point ^POINT^
ToolBox11=\3dtext ^TANGENT^
ToolBox12=\3ddim ^DIM^
ToolBox13=move ^MOVE^
ToolBox14=copy ^COPY^
ToolBox15=erase ^ERASE^
ToolBox16=scale ^SCALE^
ToolBox17=rotate ^ROTATE^
ToolBox18=change ^CHANGE^
ToolBox19=mirror ^MIRROR^
ToolBox20=\3break ^BREAK^
ToolBox21=\3extend ^EXTEND^
ToolBox22=stretch ^STRETCH^
ToolBox23=\3trim ^TRIM^
ToolBox24=fillet ^FILLET^
ToolBox25=chamfer ^CHAMFER^
ToolBox26=align ^ALIGN^
ToolBox27=endp ^ENDPOINT^
ToolBox28=int ^INTERSECTION^
ToolBox29=mid ^MIDPOINT^
ToolBox30=center ^CENTER^
ToolBox31=quad ^QUADRANT^
ToolBox32=near ^NEAREST^
ToolBox33=per ^PERPENDICULAR^
ToolBox34=tan ^TANGENT^
ToolBox35=\3\3 ^CANCEL^
```

```
ToolBox36=\3pedit ^PEDIT^
TBoxOption=1
TBoxWidth=6
TBoxStart=1
TBoxLocation=437 300
```

You'll find a listing of the entire ACAD.INI file in Appendix D.

Find the line containing **ToolBox1**. In this example, the line appears as follows:

```
ToolBox1=undo ^UNDO^
```

Now substitute the ARRAY command for the UNDO command and substitute ^ARRAY^ for ^UNDO^. In this example, ^ARRAY^ is the name of the icon that will be displayed on the surface of the button.

Save the ACAD.INI file and exit the text editor. The changes you've made will take effect the next time you start AutoCAD for Windows.

Customizing the Pull-Down Menus

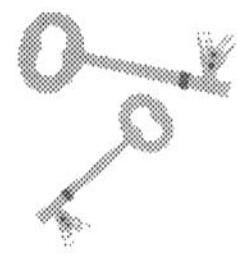

All you need to customize AutoCAD's pull-down menus is an ASCII text editor and a little knowledge about the menu. You can edit a single menu entry, add a few commands or build your own complete application. For this example, let's suppose you'd like a menu entry that would let you enter text and then drag it into the desired location.

Your first step is deciding whether to place the command under an existing pull-down menu heading or to create a new heading. Since a TEXT command is already available under the DRAW heading, we'll add our routine in that location.

We'll now go to the DOS prompt and make a copy of AutoCAD's standard Windows menu. It's important to keep the original menu file unchanged so it can always be used as a reference. Go to the DOS prompt by double-clicking on the DOS Prompt icon. Then, assuming your ACADWIN.MNU file is in the \ACADWIN\SUPPORT subdirectory:

Type: `copy \acadwin\support\acadwin.mnu acadwin\support\acad1.mnu <Return>`

Response: `1 file(s) copied`

You now have your own menu file to customize the way you want. Go back to Windows.

Type: `exit <Return>`

Load the ACAD1.MNU file into the Windows Write text editor. You'll find that any ASCII text editor will work as long as it has the capacity to load your ACAD1.MNU file. The Windows Write editor has no problem editing very large files.

Go to the Draw pull-down menu heading. The heading and some of its definitions appear as follows:

```
***POP5
**p5text
[/DDraw]
[->/LLine]
  [/SSegments]^C^C_line
  [/11 Segment]^C^C_line;\\;
  [/DDouble Lines]^C^C_dline
  [--]
```

Be careful, there are two **[/DDraw]** areas. Make sure you're in the one that has ****p5text** above it.

Now go down and position your cursor at the end of the line that looks like the following:

```
[->/TText]
```

Press Return to insert a blank line.

Now type the following (two spaces precede your routine):

Type: `[/PDrag into Place]^c^c_text (getvar "viewctr") ;;\move last ;@`

Your routine should fit into the pull-down menu routine and look like the following:

```
[--]
[->/TText]
  [/PDrag into Place]^c^c_text (getvar "viewctr") ;;\move last ;@
  [/DDynamic]^C^C_dtext
  [/IImport Text]^C^C_asctext
  [/SSet Style...]$I=icon_fonts1 $I=*
  [--]
```

Save the file, restart AutoCAD (if it's not already started) and load your menu by typing (at the Command prompt):

Type: `menu <Return>`

Response: `The Select Menu File dialogue box appears.`

Double-click on the ACAD1.MNU filename.

Response: `Loaded menu C:/ACADWIN/SUPPORT/ACAD1.MNX`

Now click on the Draw pull-down menu, go down and click on the Text menu selection, then click on your own routine: **Drag into Place.**

Response: `Enter Text:`

Type: `This is a test <Return>`

The text will be initially placed in the center of your screen and will then jump to the crosshairs, waiting to be dragged into place.

All you need do now is digitize the location where you want the text.

Pull-Down Menu Control Codes

Several special control codes are used in the AutoCAD for Windows menu. Some are used to underline certain characters in menu selections; some cause cascading menus to appear and disappear; others affect the appearance of menu selections in other ways.

Accelerator Keys

A slash (/) and an alpha character (such as an A, B, C, etc.) at the beginning of a menu definition causes the letter that follows it to be underlined in the menu selection. When a menu selection is underlined, it becomes an *accelerator key* that allows you to select it by pressing the Alt key and the underlined key. Observe the menu definition:

```
[/NNew]^C^C_new
```

In this example, a slash-N (**/N**) precedes the menu label and causes the first letter (**N**) of the menu selection to be underlined. If you wanted to underline the **e** in this example, you'd precede the menu selection with **/e**. Now, to select this routine from the keyboard, you can just press **Alt+N**.

Check Marks

A check mark beside a pull-down menu item means the item is a toggle and is turned on. When you program a menu key, you can add a check mark to its definition. Let's add a menu definition that turns the Grid on and off and displays a check mark by the command if it's on.

Load your ACAD1.MNU file into the Windows Write text editor and go down to the Settings pull-down menu heading. A portion of the menu definitions are shown below:

```
***POP8
**p8text
[/SSettings]
[/DDrawing Aids...]'_ddrmodes
[/LLayer Control...]'_ddlmodes
[/OObject Snap...]'_ddosnap
[--]
[/EEntity Modes...]'_ddemodes
[/PPoint Style...]'_ddptype
[--]
```

Again, be careful. Make sure you're in the **[/SSettings]** area that has ****p8text** above it.

Position your cursor at the end of the line that appears as follows:

```
[/OObject Snap...]'_ddosnap
```

Press the Return key to insert a blank line.

Now we'll place a separator bar into the pull-down menu to make it easy to find our definition when we look for it in AutoCAD.

Type: `[--] <Return>`

Two dashes enclosed in square brackets cause a separator bar to be placed into the pull-down menu. Now enter:

Type:

```
[$(if,$(getvar,gridmode),!.)/GGrid]^C^Cgridmode +
$M=$(if,$(getvar,gridmode),0,1)
```

You don't need a Return in the above definition because it would cause an unwanted blank line to appear in your pull-down menu.

NOTE: The plus sign in the above text indicates that the code should be typed as one single line.

The definition will appear unfamiliar to you if you haven't used AutoCAD's DIESEL (Direct Interpretively Evaluated String Expression Language). I used DIESEL because it's commonly used throughout the AutoCAD for Windows menus.

Here's a short explanation of the above definition. The text inside the brackets—[and]—will be the title of the pull-down menu selection. In this definition, the **$(if** begins an IF statement that will examine a condition. The **$(getvar,gridmode)** gets the value of the GRIDMODE system variable. If the variable is on, the **,!.)** instruction is executed, which displays a check mark at the beginning of the menu selection title. If the variable is off, nothing is displayed because the right paren **)** closes the IF statement.

Following the DIESEL expression inside the square brackets is the title of the menu selection, **/GGrid**. The **G** in Grid is underlined.

The menu definition begins by issuing two CANCELs (**^C^C**), followed by the GRIDMODE command and a space. Another DIESEL expression follows. The expression begins with **$M=** because whenever a DIESEL expression is used in a menu definition, it must follow the format used to call a submenu (such as $S=submenuname). The **$(if** begins an IF statement that will examine a condition. The **$(getvar,gridmode)** gets the value of the GRIDMODE system variable. If the variable is on, the **,0** instruction turns it off (sets it to zero). If it is off, the **,1)** instruction turns it on (sets it to 1) and closes the expression.

Now save the file and return to AutoCAD. Then, at the AutoCAD Command prompt, type:

Type: `menu <Return>`

The Select Menu File dialogue box appears. Double-click on the ACAD1.MNU filename.

Response: `Loaded menu C:/ACADWIN/SUPPORT/ACAD1.MNX`

Now click on the Settings pull-down menu. The Settings pull-down menu will appear with the modification you've made (see Figure 8-4).

Figure 8-4: The Settings pull-down menu (modified)

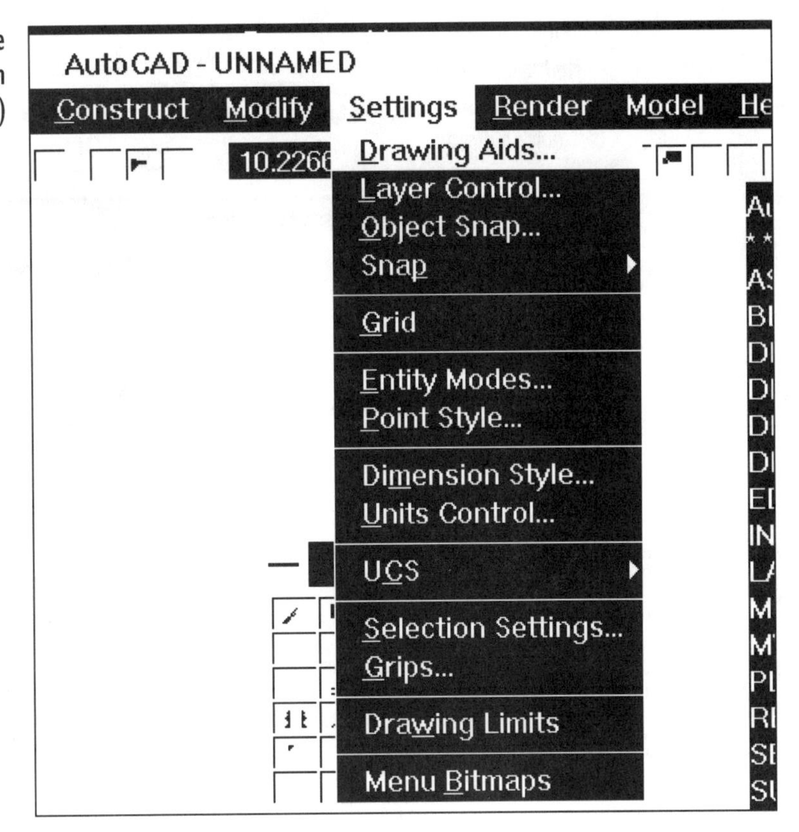

Now, go down and click on the Grid menu selection. The grid will be turned on.

Click on the Settings pull-down menu again and notice that a check mark appears next to the Grid menu selection (see Figure 8-5), indicating that the grid is on.

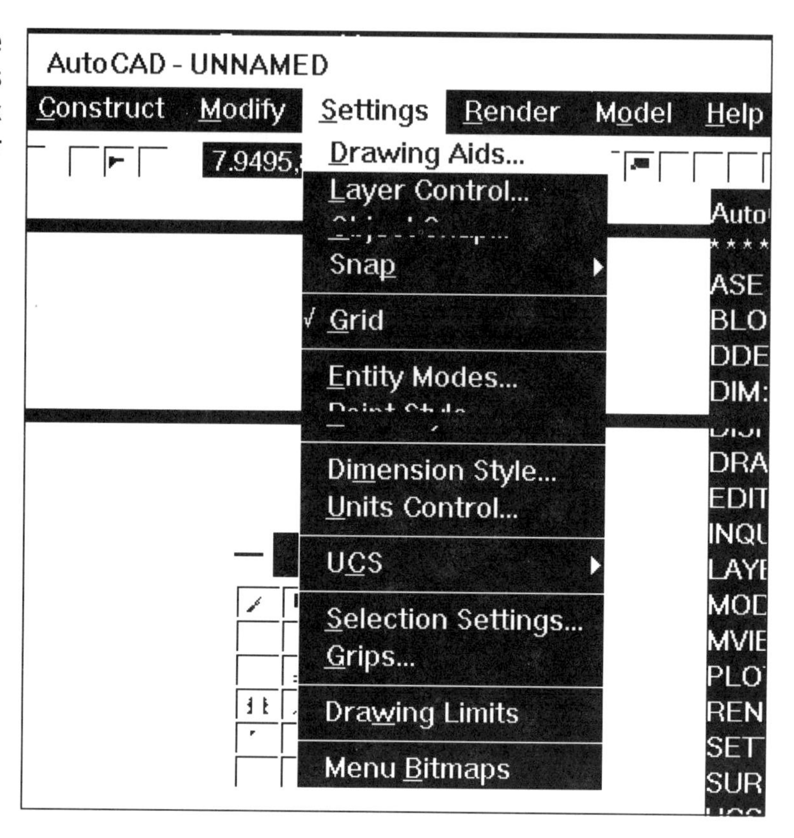

Figure 8-5: The Modified Settings menu with check mark indicator

Each time you click on the Grid menu selection, the check mark will toggle on and off with the grid.

Graying-out a Menu Item

A menu selection can be grayed-out when you don't want it to be available for execution. To gray out an item, place a tilde (~) character as the first character in the menu item's title. For instance, if you wanted to gray out a Line menu item, you'd construct it as follows:

Type:
```
[~LINE]^C^Cline
```

The tilde (~) causes the **LINE** title to be grayed-out and prevents the menu definition from being executed.

Creating a Cascading Menu

A cascading pull-down menu item has a right-pointing arrow (->) on the right edge of the item. When you pick the item, a submenu cascades to the right of the menu item you picked (it only cascades to the left if there's not enough room for it on the right). Let's say you want to create a menu for the SNAP command that cascades into a list of snap options.

Load the ACAD1.MNU file into the Windows Write editor and go to the Settings pull-down menu. Position your cursor to the right of the Object Snap menu definition and press Return. A blank line is created on which to place your new menu item.

Type the following (the cascading menu items are indented two spaces, and you don't need a Return after the last line):

Type:
```
[->/pSnap]
[/nOn]^C^CSnap on
[/fOff]^C^CSnap off
[/AAspect]^C^CSnap a
[/RRotate]^C^CSnap r
[/SSpacing]^C^CSnap
[<-/tStyle]^C^CSnap s
```

The first line contains a right-pointing arrow (->) made from the minus sign and the greater-than sign. This causes all the following menu items to cascade from this item until a left-pointing arrow (<-) is found. Notice that the last item in the list of menu items contains the left-pointing arrow.

If you want the last item (**Style**) to cascade into another menu, your menu items would appear as follows:

```
[->/pSnap]
  [/nOn]^C^CSnap on
  [/fOff]^C^CSnap off
  [/AAspect]^C^CSnap a
  [/RRotate]^C^CSnap r
  [/SSpacing]^C^CSnap
  [->/tStyle]^C^CSnap s
    [/IIsometric]i
    [<-<-/SStandard]s
```

Notice that the last menu item in this example has two left-pointing arrows (<-<-) to balance the total of the two right-pointing arrows above them.

When you finish editing the menu for this example (if you've chosen to create two cascading menus), your pull-down menu will look like the portion of the Settings pull-down menu shown below:

```
***POP8
**p8text
[/SSettings]
[/DDrawing Aids...]'_ddrmodes
[/LLayer Control...]'_ddlmodes
[/OObject Snap...]'_ddosnap
[->/pSnap]
  [/nOn]^C^CSnap on
  [/fOff]^C^CSnap off
  [/AAspect]^C^CSnap a
  [/RRotate]^C^CSnap r
  [/SSpacing]^C^CSnap
  [->/tStyle]^C^CSnap s
    [/IIsometric]i
    [<-<-/SStandard]s
[--]
```

Moving On

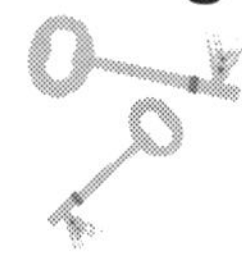

In this chapter, you've learned how to save time in AutoCAD and in the creation of external documents with Object Embedding and Linking (OLE). You've also learned how to customize the AutoCAD for Windows interface by programming the toolbar, the toolbox and pull-down menus.

The next chapter, "Using Dynamic Data Exchange," concentrates on AutoCAD for Windows's Dynamic Data Exchange (DDE) capability. With it, you'll be able to work inside the AutoCAD database—from outside AutoCAD!

Using Dynamic Data Exchange

This chapter will introduce you to Dynamic Data Exchange (DDE) and some of the advantages it offers. You'll learn how to export a drawing database to a spreadsheet and how to make changes to the drawing from outside AutoCAD by modifying values in the spreadsheet file.

DDE is one of the most powerful features of Windows. It's often used between text-based applications, such as spreadsheets and database management systems. But when DDE is used in support of Computer Aided Design applications, its potential is even greater because it gives you the flexibility to work parametrically with your graphic designs. So let's get started...

DDE Applications

The most well-known DDE application is the *shaft* example that comes with each AutoCAD for Windows package. It is an excellent illustration of the use of Dynamic Data Exchange for parametric programming.

The *shaft* is a mechanical part of a power transmission. Proper design of such a shaft requires precisely correct dimensions, proper material and a reasonable factor of safety.

DDE lets you work with these parameters in a spreadsheet before you begin the detailed graphic design process. When you're comfortable with a set of parameters, you simply give a command and the shaft is drawn in three dimensions in AutoCAD. When you modify a parameter in the spreadsheet, the shaft in AutoCAD shows the changes. If you make changes to the drawing, you can export the changes to the spreadsheet by a single AutoCAD menu selection.

Other Applications

Alternative applications are equally beneficial. Spreadsheets, for example, are perfectly suited to bill-of-materials reports. By placing in your drawing attributes that contain bill-of-materials information, you can use DDE to link that information to a spreadsheet file. When a change occurs in the drawing, a single command updates the bill-of-materials report in the spreadsheet file.

Exporting a Drawing

AutoCAD drawings that are exported using DDE are shown in DXF format in the spreadsheet. You can export a drawing by making a few preparations and following a few steps.

Make sure you have a spreadsheet system that supports DDE. The examples in this chapter use Microsoft Excel. You'll find that Excel and Lotus 1-2-3 are good choices because the AutoCAD system is already set up for using Excel or Lotus.

When you installed AutoCAD, you should have included ADS/DDE in the installation.

Now you're ready to try a DDE example. Activate AutoCAD in the Windows environment and draw a line, an arc and a circle anywhere on the screen.

Go to the Edit pull-down menu and pick DDE. The DDE cascading menu appears. Pick Export Drawing. The DDE Initiate Conversation dialogue box appears (see Figure 9-1).

NOTE: If Excel is not running, the Excel startup banner will appear before the dialogue box.

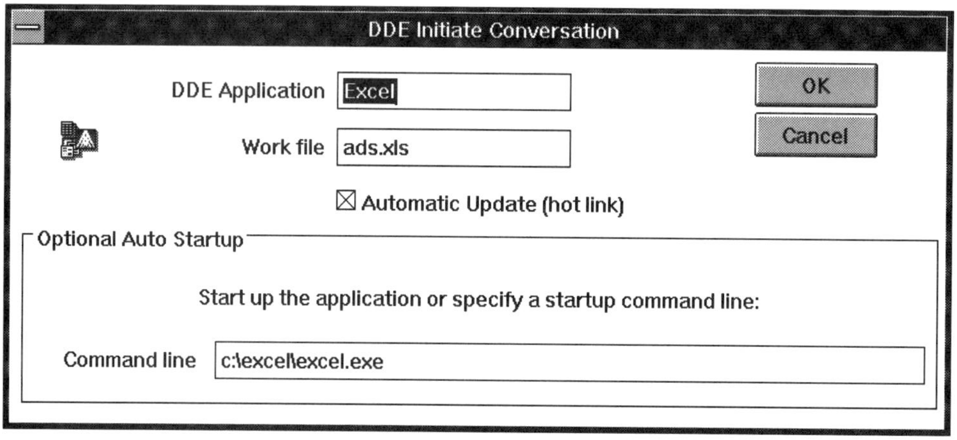

Figure 9-1: The DDE Initiate Conversation dialogue box

The DDE Application area contains the name of the application to which you'll be exporting data. Excel and Lotus 1-2-3 are the two standard applications that are supported.

The Work file area contains the name of the spreadsheet file you wish to edit. A *new* spreadsheet file can only be created by using your spreadsheet program.

The Automatic Update [hot link] box should be checked if you wish to have your drawing automatically updated to match changes you make to the spreadsheet file. If the box is left blank, you'll have to update the AutoCAD file by using a menu selection (explained below). Even when the box is checked, updates are only made automatically from the spreadsheet to AutoCAD. When you change your drawing, you can only update the spreadsheet by reissuing the export command you used originally.

The Optional Auto Startup area contains an edit box that can contain the path of the application you wish to automatically start up when you initiate DDE. The path should include the location and name of the application startup file. If you leave the edit box blank, the DDE Initiate Conversation dialogue box will be displayed when you initiate DDE.

Now, pick OK in the dialogue box. The Excel spreadsheet will appear with the DXF representation of your AutoCAD drawing (see Figure 9-2). Use the cursor to resize and position the spreadsheet so you can see the spreadsheet and your AutoCAD drawing.

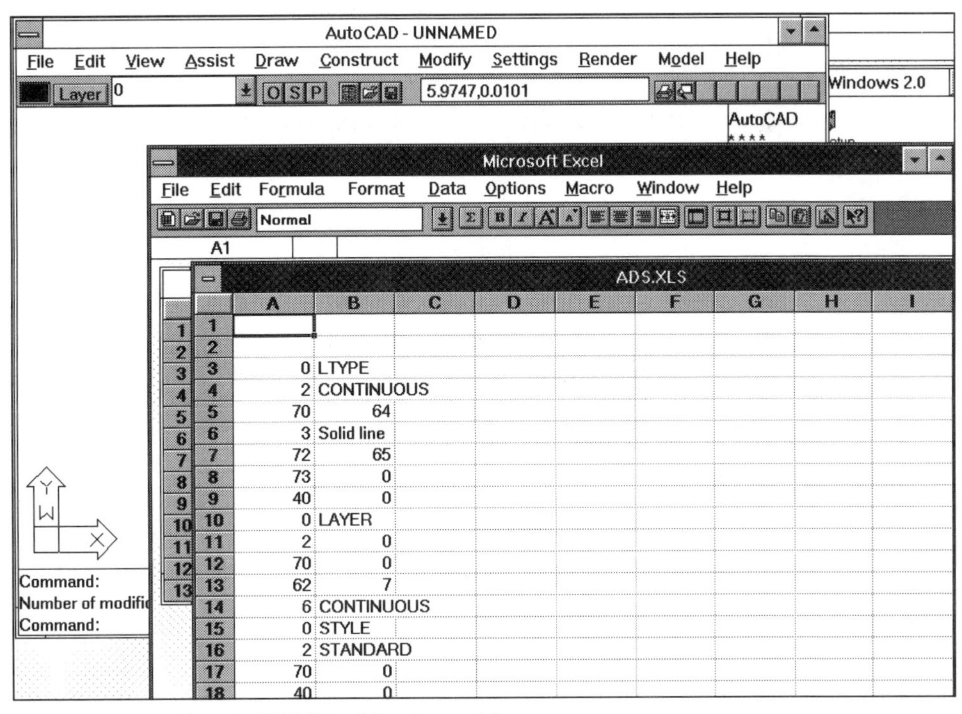

Figure 9-2: AutoCAD and a DDE-linked Excel spreadsheet

You can now experiment with the data in the spreadsheet. When you change a line's endpoint location in the spreadsheet, you can watch the corresponding endpoint move in your drawing. You can change the contents of a spreadsheet *cell* by clicking on the cell you wish to edit and typing in a new value for the cell.

NOTE: There are several cells you should not change. Do not change cells that are preceded by –1, 0 or 5, because those changes would be illegal database changes in AutoCAD.

Line endpoints are identified by DXF codes 10 and 11, and arc and circle centers and radii by codes 10 and 40, respectively. The DXF format codes are listed in Appendix C.

Go to your AutoCAD drawing and make a change or add a line or other entity. Notice that the spreadsheet did not change. Now go to the Edit pull-down menu, pick DDE and then Export Drawing. The DXF data in the spreadsheet is updated to match the drawing.

Shutting Down DDE

When you've finished experimenting with DDE, shut it down by going to the AutoCAD Edit menu, picking DDE and then Unload DDE. This gracefully turns off the DDE link between AutoCAD and the spreadsheet.

The DDE Menu Explained

The DDE menu appears as a submenu of the Edit pull-down menu (see Figure 9-3) and contains commands that let you control the output that goes to a spreadsheet. It also lets you import changes to the drawing from your spreadsheet.

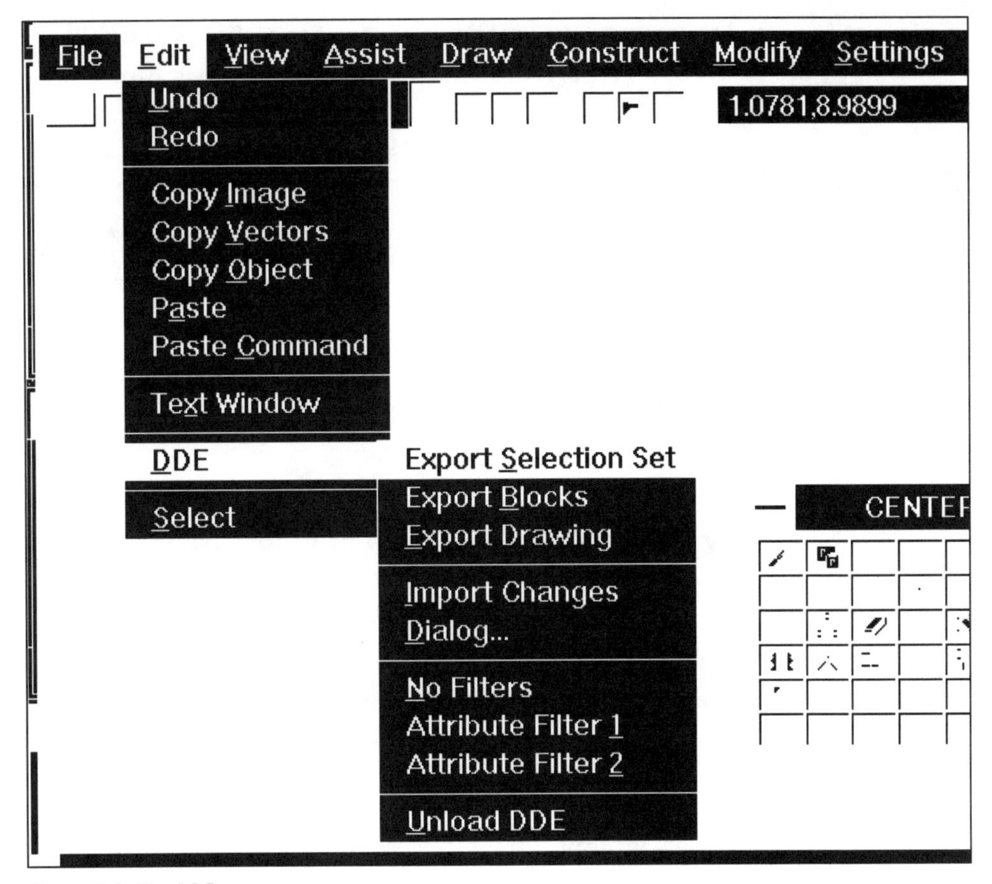

Figure 9-3: The DDE menu

An explanation of each menu selection is given below. All data that is exported is in DXF format that has been slightly modified for DDE applications.

- **Export Selection Set**—Exports the current selection set data to the specified spreadsheet.
- **Export Blocks**—Exports all data from the current block table to the specified spreadsheet.
- **Export Drawing**—Exports the entire drawing database to the spreadsheet.
- **Import Changes**—Updates your drawing by importing any changes that occurred in the spreadsheet since the last update. This selection can be used when the automatic update feature (in the Initiate Conversation dialogue box) is not in use.

- **Dialog...**—This selection causes the Initiate Conversation dialogue box to appear (refer back to Figure 9-1 to see this).
- **No Filters**—If this selection is active, the data you export to the spreadsheet will not be filtered. All data will be sent to the spreadsheet.
- **Attribute Filter 1**—If this selection is active, the data you export to the spreadsheet will be filtered to contain only attributes, attribute tags and entity handles.
- **Attribute Filter 2**—If this selection is active, the data you export to the spreadsheet will be filtered to contain only attributes and entity handles.
- **Unload DDE**—This selection terminates the DDE link between AutoCAD and your spreadsheet program and file.

DDE via AutoLISP

By providing you a set of DDE commands in a pull-down menu, AutoCAD for Windows gives you a fast and easy way to begin using DDE. To give you added flexibility and a quick way to begin building your own DDE applications, an AutoLISP-based set of DDE commands is also available.

The file containing the DDE commands and functions is DDE.LSP. You'll find the file in the \ACADWIN\SUPPORT directory (if you've done a standard AutoCAD for Windows installation). The DDE.LSP program is an excellent place to begin learning how DDE for AutoCAD really works, because the AutoLISP DDE program contains each function that sets up, runs and shuts down the DDE link.

Running the program is easy. Before you start it up, however, make sure that no DDE links are active (you should have unloaded DDE in the previous example). Make sure you have a few entities on your AutoCAD screen, create a line, an arc and a circle (as mentioned before) and load DDE.LSP by typing:

Type: `(load "dde") <Return>`

DDE.LSP and DDELISP.EXE are loaded (DDE.LSP automatically loads DDELISP.EXE).

You now have the same functionality as you have with the pull-down menus. Why have both? Because with an AutoLISP-based program, you're free to modify it to suit your own individual needs. The program is written to work with Excel or Lotus 1-2-3. (If you have Lotus 1-2-3, you'll have to change a number at the beginning of the program to indicate that you're using Lotus. You can make the change with any ASCII text editor.)

With a single command, you can now start up your spreadsheet and load your drawing data into it.

Type: `send <Return>`

Your spreadsheet application will be loaded, a spreadsheet file will be opened and a copy of your drawing data will be sent to the open spreadsheet file. This example will display your drawing data in the spreadsheet file, just as in the previous example, because the default settings for the filter modes are identical in each example. If you wish to change the filter mode settings in this example, at the AutoCAD Command prompt:

Type:	**Explanation:**
(setddeformat 0) <Return>	sends all data, uses entity names
(setddeformat 1) <Return>	sends all data, uses entity handles
(setddeformat 2) <Return>	sends entity handle, attribute & tag
(setddeformat 3) <Return>	sends decimal and hex handle, attribute and tag

NOTE: If you wish to try using more than one of the above modes, you should erase the data in your spreadsheet before you send new data using another mode. Your spreadsheet will not automatically erase any previous data.

Export Modes in Detail

When you export a drawing or drawing data to a spreadsheet, you can send the entire set of drawing data or you can filter the data so only a subset of the drawing data is sent.

The above examples give you methods of setting the export mode to achieve that control. Each mode is explained below:

Entity Name Mode—This is a filter that can only be set under program control (it's not available in the pull-down menu). When this filter is set, your drawing data will be exported and identified in the spreadsheet by entity name. Be aware that entity names are assigned at the beginning of each edit session and can change with each session. This means that you cannot depend on linking any other data to the entity name because the name changes.

Entity Handle Mode—When this mode is in effect, no filter is active. All entities from your entire drawing will be output based on their handle number (you'll see the handle number for each entity in the spreadsheet). You can pick No Filters in the pull-down menu to set this mode, or type:

Type: `(setddeformat 1) <Return>`

at the Command prompt to set it when you're using DDE.LSP.

Attribute Mode—This filter causes only blocks with attributes to be output to the spreadsheet. Attribute tags are also output. This filter is often used when exporting information that will be used as a bill of materials. You can set this mode by picking Attribute Filter 1 from the DDE pull-down menu, or type:

Type: `(setddeformat 2) <Return>`

at the Command prompt when you're using DDE.LSP.

Attribute Mode 2—The result of using this filter is the same as the Attribute mode, as you saw earlier, except this filter does not export attribute tags. It is set in the DDE pull-down menu by picking Attribute Filter 2, or you can set it at the Command prompt when you're using DDE.LSP by typing:

Type: `(setddeformat 3) <Return>`

Shut-down via DDE.LSP

When you're ready to shut down the DDE link from AutoCAD to your spreadsheet, enter as below (remember to include the parentheses):

Type: `(ddedone) <Return>`

The **(ddedone** function returns the handle of the last channel (communications link) that was closed.

Additional DDE.LSP Information

As you become more familiar with Dynamic Data Exchange, you'll become more comfortable with building your own application links. As you delve into DDE, AutoLISP is an excellent way to experiment with DDE's capabilities because it's an easy language to work with. It's forgiving when you make mistakes, and you can use it to quickly build prototype and test programs.

This chapter explains only a few of the AutoLISP functions that are available for use with DDE. The AutoCAD Release 12 *Using AutoCAD for Windows* manual contains listings and explanations of all DDE AutoLISP functions, along with terms and definitions that are used in DDE applications. When you become familiar with these functions and how they are applied in the DDE.LSP file, you'll be at an intermediate stage of DDE usage and programming.

More Customization

If you tried the shaft example mentioned at the beginning of this chapter, you know that a spreadsheet that's linked to a drawing can have a "finished" professional look. As you work with spreadsheet programs, you'll become familiar with many ways to customize the spreadsheet to fit your application. You can place your own titles, headings, labels and formulas into the spreadsheet to give it functionality and a custom look that fits your application.

Moving On

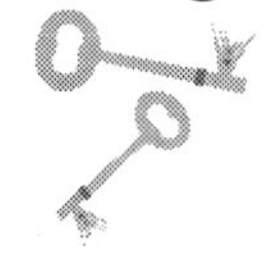

This section has explored AutoCAD for Windows and has shown you how to customize your own AutoCAD for Windows system—from toolbars and menus to OLE and Dynamic Data Exchange. Now we're ready to move on to ASE, the AutoCAD Sequel Extension.

The next section, "ASE," will introduce you to this powerful AutoCAD tool that you can combine with databases for managing a variety of database applications.

SECTION IV

ASE:
Building AutoCAD and DBMS Applications

CHAPTER 10

Overview

You can utilize the full power of any computer tool only if you know its capabilities. This chapter will introduce you to the AutoCAD SQL Extension (ASE) by describing what it is and the needs it can fill. If you wonder how you can use SQL, this chapter will present some example applications to help you recognize its potential in your own business. After reading this introduction to ASE, you'll be eager to learn how to put it to work!

ASE: The AutoCAD Sequel Extension

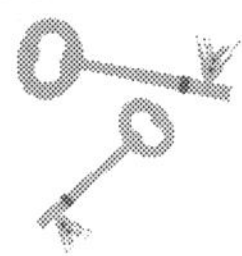

A myriad of third-party programs have been written to enhance AutoCAD's capability to manage and utilize the drawing database. Originally designed as a computer-aided design and drafting system, AutoCAD has taken the lead in its field, successfully serving as a mechanical, electrical and architectural design tool to name only a few. In the past few years, the use of CAD has grown beyond design to include facility planning and management, mapping, highway planning, forecasting and much more. Many traditional database tasks are now done from computer-aided design systems. Users demanded database management from a CAD system and CAD from a database management system.

To answer this major demand, Autodesk introduced *ASE,* the *AutoCAD SQL Extension.* ASE gives you all of AutoCAD's powerful graphics tools as well as full access outside of AutoCAD to SQL-structured (Structured Query Language) databases. All AutoCAD and SQL tools are literally at your fingertips.

A Review of Database Basics

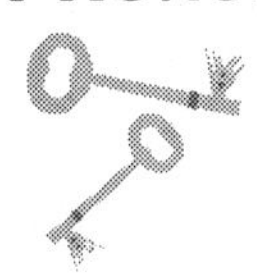

A *database* is an organized collection of information that is stored in such a way that it's easy to use. A *database program* or *database system* is a program you use to work with a database. It lets you quickly construct your database, look up and retrieve related information, create reports and even send related information to other programs such as spreadsheet systems.

A *relational database* contains information that is organized into tables. Because the data is in table format, it is especially easy to relate one piece of information to another piece that is in the same or in a different table.

You can combine information together to generate reports or to perform calculations on groups of data.

One example of a relational database application would be a list of employees with each person's employee number, position title, organization name and telephone number. If you organized these items into a table, the table might appear like the following:

Last Name	First Name	Empl. No.	Title	Org.	Phone
Green	Martha	2313	Sales Manager	Advertising	X-2313
Hendricks	Joseph	1025	Engineer	Engineering	X-4100
Jones	Susan	1997	Engineer	Engineering	X-1820
Murdock	Teri	5112	Programmer	Comp Science	X-1245
Matthews	Glenn	3229	Programmer	Comp Science	X-1280

As you look at the above table, you see that it's tabulated into rows and columns.

Rows: Each row of information in the above table is a *record.* A record contains related information about a subject; in this case, the subject is a person.

Columns: Each column in the table is a *field.* As you'll notice, each piece of information resides in a field.

Designing a Database

When you design a database, you can assign each field to contain a certain kind of data. For instance, you would assign the Last Name field to contain *alphabetic* characters while the Empl. No. field would contain *numeric* data. Other types of field type assignments are also possible, such as phone numbers, dates and currency fields.

If a field can contain only a date, it is a *date field,* whereas an *alphanumeric field* can contain one or more alphabetic characters, numbers and many other ASCII characters.

Tables can also be related to each other if they share a common item of information. In other words, if you have a table like the one above that shows employees and another table that contains office locations for each employee, you can relate the two tables together if each table contains a common field, such as the employee number.

This means that you can fill many of your database needs with one collection of data that you can organize and retrieve in various types of formats.

SQL—What Is It?

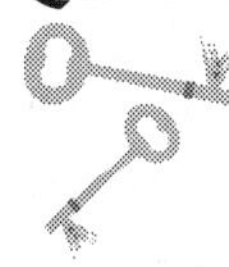

SQL allows a non-procedural language that provides for data definition, database queries and database updates. SQL (often pronounced "sequel") stands for Structured Query Language. SQL is a standard that was developed to allow common access to relational database systems and files.

A large number of relational database software packages are on the market, most with their own file format. But because many companies wanted to tie their software to one or more relational databases, a standard was needed. So SQL was developed. Several database system vendors now offer SQL compatibility. Oracle, Paradox, dBASE and Informix are some of the systems that support SQL.

The formal standard that defines SQL is ANSI X3.135-1989. ASE adheres to this standard but also adds a few of its own features. The portion of the standard that is used by ASE is listed with SQL syntax rules in the *AutoCAD SQL Extension Reference Manual.*

The SQL language is simple to learn, yet some AutoCAD users balk at diving into it because it's new and unlike the familiar AutoCAD commands. But you don't have to learn SQL to use ASE. One of ASE's best features is that it constructs many SQL commands for you.

ASE gives you a dialogue box that assists you in creating SQL queries, and after you've used it a few times, you'll find yourself constructing a few SQL queries without ASE's help. The dialogue box is like a built-in SQL tutor that works for real applications.

Why Combine SQL & AutoCAD?

Why would you want to combine SQL and AutoCAD? Imagine, for example, a facility management application. You have a building floor plan showing offices, furniture and office equipment. In AutoCAD you can easily design, draw and maintain each office. You can attach attributes to furniture, file cabinets, phones and computers and extract the information to create inventory lists.

Simple AutoLISP programs can help you locate any person or item of interest in the drawing (see Chapter 3, "The Power of Selection Sets," for an example). You can calculate square footage easily and run "what-if" exercises to optimize office and equipment layouts. And these are only a few of the ways you can use AutoCAD to improve facility management tasks. Dollars and time are both kept to a minimum while accuracy and quality are maximized. So what's to be gained by "marrying" AutoCAD to a database? Here's why...

AutoCAD was engineered to be a powerful and flexible design tool that can be used in almost any design application, from simple sketches to complex maps. You can customize AutoCAD to fit the business in which it is used. Graphics-oriented design and editing are AutoCAD's cup of tea. And while AutoCAD can also handle textual information, it's well known that you can't easily put large amounts of text into a drawing because they are a burden to graphics processing speed.

But database systems handle text like AutoCAD handles graphics. They organize data into relational tables. They support decision-making by sorting, retrieving and reporting information almost any way you want. A database manages events and the data surrounding them while a CAD system manages objects. Combining the strengths of both gives you an integrated tool that helps you work effectively with projects represented by objects and events.

What's ASE?

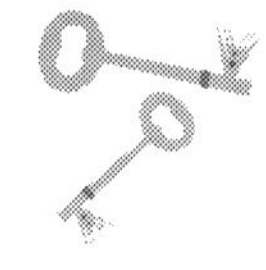

The AutoCAD SQL Extension gives you a complete set of tools for accessing an SQL database from inside of AutoCAD. Because of ASE, you don't need to overload your drawing with textual data. AutoCAD places a unique *handle* (a permanent AutoCAD-assigned code) on every entity in the drawing. ASE uses the handles with special database drivers (programs) to create a *link* between your drawing and an SQL database, giving you real-time access to the database from the drawing. Thus, the database can contain most of the text-based information, leaving mostly graphical data for AutoCAD.

ASE was created with a tool called ASI, the AutoCAD SQL Interface. ASI is a special programming interface you can use to create ADS (AutoCAD Development System) applications that work with databases outside AutoCAD.

ASE is made up of a collection of commands you use to work with links to an outside database. You can specify the type of database management system (DBMS) and the database name, open communication with the database, work with the database tables, export AutoCAD information to the database and perform many other operations using ASE commands. A complete ASE command listing is included in Chapter 11, "Learning & Applying ASE Commands."

Applications for ASE

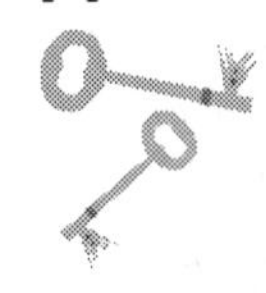

Following are several useful applications for ASE. As you learn the ASE commands, you'll discover even more uses.

Bill of Materials: Some applications come naturally to ASE. Bill of materials generation has traditionally been done using attributes, but AutoCAD's efficiency is increased when attribute information is moved to a database and managed via ASE.

Cost Estimates: While parametric design can be enhanced and improved through the use of DDE (see Chapter 7, "AutoCAD for Windows") and Windows, it's also an excellent candidate for estimate generation using ASE. Let's look at a few simple scenarios.

A friend of mine works at a company that combines parametric design capabilities and estimate generation in a custom valve design business. A customer requests a cost estimate on a custom valve meeting certain specifications and design criteria. The data is entered into their CAD system, and moments later they have a plot of a parametrically designed valve and an estimate ready to fax to their customer.

ASE is a natural for estimating applications as in this example. A database contains all parts information, including catalog and manufacturer numbers, cost, parts descriptions and so forth. During the design process, accessing the database from AutoCAD to obtain one or more pieces of design information becomes an easy step.

Schedule Creation: A common need of residential or commercial architects is the ability to generate schedules. And schedules are a classic database application. A common door schedule that accompanies a set of house plans shows door size, manufacturer, part number, cost and number required. All of this information is included for each type of door included in the plans. Windows also have a schedule, as do other components in the design.

All of this information should reside in a database that you can access from AutoCAD through ASE. If a supplier of standard architectural items offers listings in database form for all of its products, you don't even have to build the database yourself; you just place the information into the database file you'll use.

Catalog Access: Engineers use pre-designed components whenever possible in their design tasks. The expense is far less to use standard components than to design and manufacture special parts. The challenge comes in knowing where to go to find the part you want. While veteran engineers have learned the sources to check for the items they want, new designers must gain this type of experience a little at a time. But just as in architectural engineering applications, mechanical and electrical parts catalogs are becoming available on disk and can be accessed via database programs.

Mapping Applications: Real estate development is a valuable ASE mapping application. Housing subdivision site development maps include survey information for each piece of property, electrical, gas and telephone utility data, owners' names, project development dates and more.

The real estate development project is graphically planned and designed using AutoCAD, and all the supporting information is managed using a related database outside of AutoCAD. As design decisions must be made, all information to assist in the decisions is on-line and immediately available.

Municipal Services: Some city governments are now using AutoCAD and ASE to enhance services they provide to their citizens. One service that has been improved through graphic and database automation is garbage collection. Each household and business that requires garbage pickup service is listed by name and address in a city computer in database form. The number and type of containers are also included in the database, along with the monthly cost for each customer.

An AutoCAD drawing shows each customer address with symbols representing the type and number of garbage containers at each customer location. When it comes time to pick up the garbage, AutoCAD-generated maps are given to each worker. If a customer adds or removes a garbage container, the worker notes the change on the map. Back at the city office, employees easily make updates in AutoCAD or in the database. Macro routines update the drawing or database as needed. Then when billing time comes, the costs are always accurately assigned to each customer.

Inventory Tracking: One of the most popular ASE applications, automated inventory tracking with AutoCAD and databases keeps you up-to-date on all components in a building, office or other location. You can easily plan upgrades to your inventory, play "what-if" games with office layouts and track configurations from planning stages through final setup.

Safety Management & Emergency Preparedness: Adherence to safety standards is a growing need in companies throughout the world. CAD-generated floor plans show fire suppression system controls and fixtures and other safety-related devices that must always be kept in reliable working condition.

For such situations, ASE lets you use AutoCAD to keep all facility drawings and all maintenance records current for all safety equipment. If a piece of equipment is scheduled for maintenance, ASE provides a means to highlight that equipment on the AutoCAD screen.

ASE in Your Own Business: Perhaps you've identified some ASE applications for your own business from the above list. Almost every business that uses computer-aided design can effectively and profitably use ASE. If you find yourself keeping design, graphics or other records in manual or computerized databases, you should consider ASE as a way to save time and money in your business. Besides the applications described above, other business areas that can benefit from CAD-to-database connections include the following:

- Interior design
- Medical technology
- GIS applications
- Highway design
- Piping design
- Automotive research

...and the list continues.

Moving On

In this chapter you learned about the benefits and applications of the AutoCAD SQL Extension, including many real-world applications for ASE. The next chapter explains each ASE command and then goes on to describe how to use ASE from AutoCAD's pull-down menu system so you can immediately begin to use this powerful capability....

CHAPTER 11

Learning & Applying ASE Commands

ASE commands are the means AutoCAD gives you to establish communications between your drawing and a database outside of AutoCAD. After you've made the link, you can use ASE commands to control how you use the information in the database. You can access the commands from the pull-down menus as well as directly from the keyboard. This chapter will serve as a reference as you prepare to use ASE in your own applications because the purpose and use of each command is explained in detail.

ASE Commands

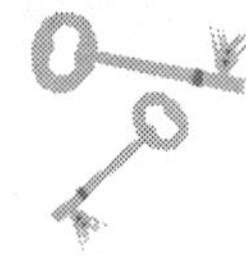

ASE commands are database tools that assist you in accessing and using databases that are outside AutoCAD. By using ASE, you can execute from inside AutoCAD the database operations that you would normally perform using a database management system (DBMS). ASE's big advantage is that you can modify your drawing and the external database associated with it at the same time.

NOTE: These commands obey all of the permission requirements that exist in your database. You can use all of these commands to work with your database within the rules of the database.

The four categories of ASE commands are

- Administrative commands
- Utility commands
- Link commands
- Manipulative commands

You can access some commands by picking ASE from the File pull-down menu (see Figure 11-1).

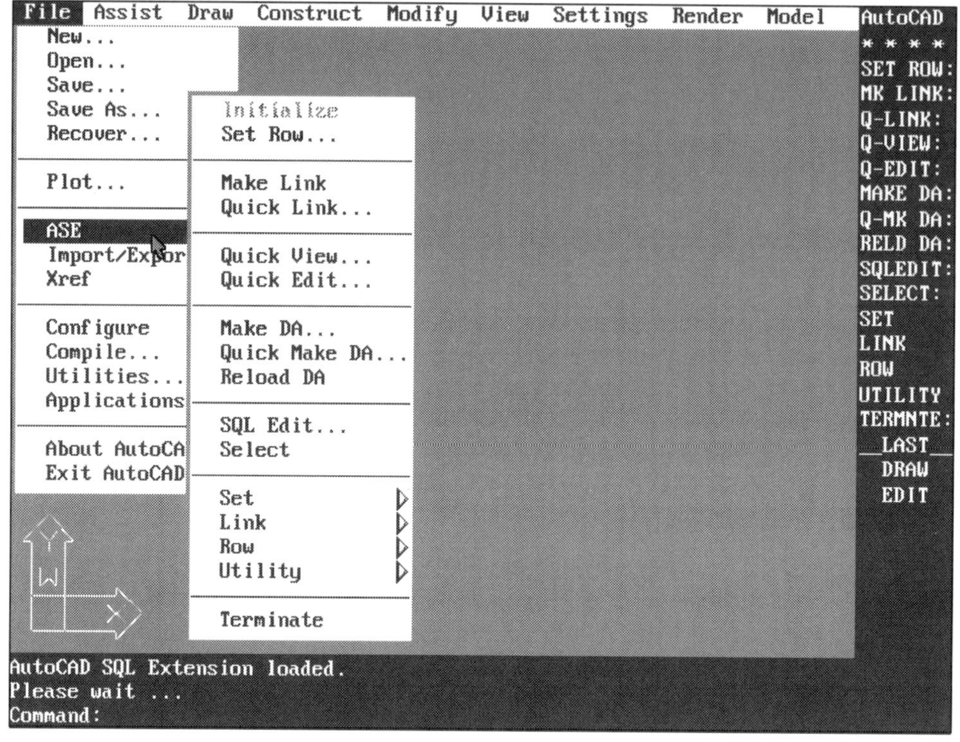

Figure 11-1: The ASE pull-down menu

For the purposes of this chapter, the commands are described with dialogue boxes active (CMDDIA ON). If you choose not to use dialogue boxes (CMDDIA OFF), all input and output will be given at the AutoCAD command prompt. You'll find detailed command descriptions for typed ASE commands in the *AutoCAD SQL Extension Reference Manual.*

NOTE: Your dialogue box appearance may vary from the ones illustrated in this chapter, depending on the type of database you're using.

Administrative Commands

Administrative commands activate, deactivate and set modes for ASE commands. Following is a complete list of administrative commands:

ASECLOSEDB: This command closes an open database. A dialogue box that lists each open database will appear (see Figure 11-2). You can select the database(s) to close. After you choose a database, ASE requires that you confirm the action before closing the database.

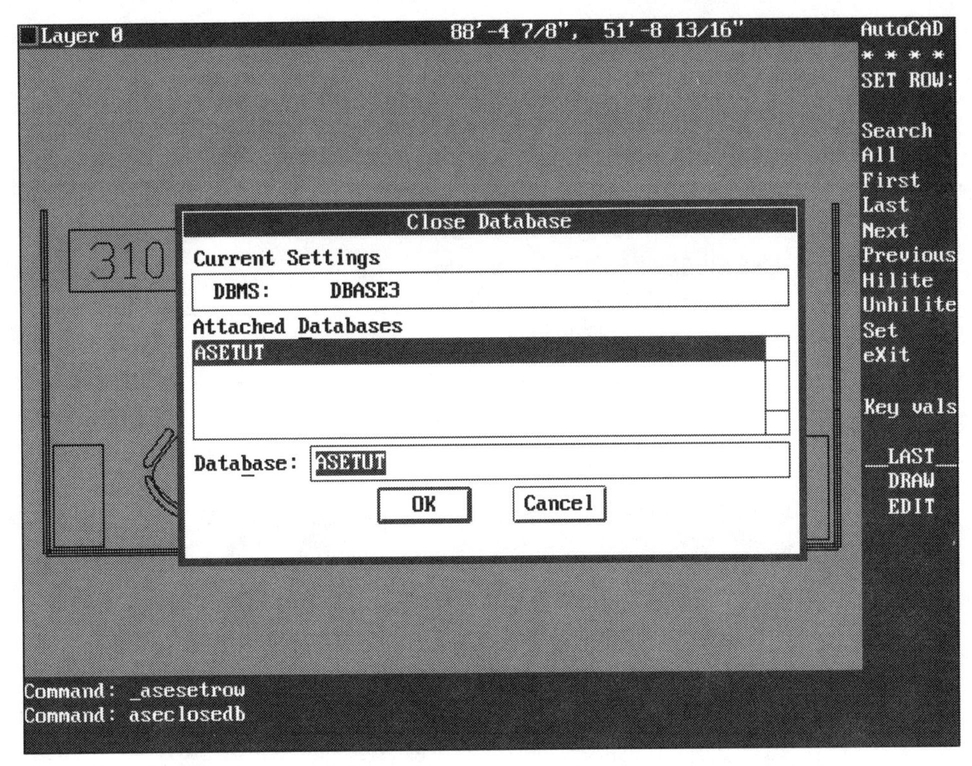

Figure 11-2: The Close Database dialogue box

ASEERASEALL: This command erases the control database. The control database is created and saved as part of the drawing database and contains DBMS names, database names, tables and link information between AutoCAD and outside databases.

NOTE: Use with caution! When you execute this command, all information that is in the control database is permanently erased! You cannot undo the effects of this command.

When you execute this command, ASE closes all open databases, unloads DBMS drivers, erases all references to active DBMSs, deletes all active links and erases displayable attributes from the screen. ASE is not terminated. You'll be required to confirm the action before the control database is erased.

ASEERASEDB: This command closes the specified database and causes all references to the specified database to be erased from the control database. All links to the database are also deleted, and any displayable attributes are erased. A dialogue box will give you a list of databases you can erase. You'll be required to confirm the operation before it takes place.

NOTE: Use with caution! When you execute this command, you permanently lose any links to the specified database. You cannot undo the effects of this command.

ASEERASEDBMS: This command closes all databases assigned by the specified DBMS, erases all references to the specified DBMS from the control database and unloads the DBMS driver. All links to the files associated with the specified DBMS are deleted, and any displayable attributes are erased. The Erase DBMS Driver dialogue box will appear (see Figure 11-3). You'll be required to confirm the action before it takes place.

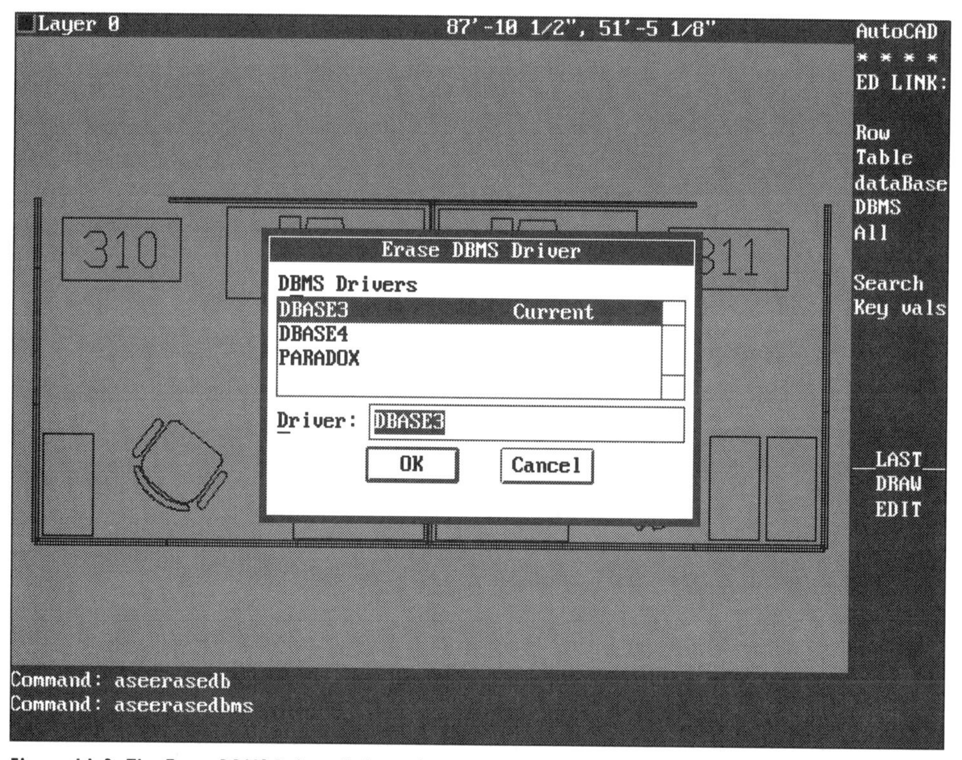

Figure 11-3: The Erase DBMS Driver dialogue box

NOTE: Use with caution! When you execute this command, you permanently lose information from the control database! You cannot undo the effects of this command.

You can erase DBMS drivers that are listed in the dialogue box by doing the following:

Double-click on the DBMS driver you wish to erase.

or

Pick the DBMS driver you wish to erase and then pick OK or press the Return key.

or

Type the name of the DBMS driver in the Driver Edit box and then pick OK or press the Return key.

or

If the DBMS driver you wish to erase is already highlighted, you can pick OK or press the Return key.

ASEERASETABLE: This command erases the specified table from the control database, deletes all links associated with the table and erases any displayable attributes from the screen. You'll be required to confirm the action before it takes place.

NOTE: Use with caution! When you execute this command, you permanently lose information from the control database! You cannot undo the effects of this command.

If you attached tables since you initiated ASE, they will be listed in the Erase Table dialogue box. You can erase any of the tables listed in the dialogue box by doing the following:

Double-click on the table you wish to erase.

or

Pick the table you wish to erase and then pick OK or press the Return key.

or

Type the name of the table in the Driver Edit box and then pick OK or press the Return key.

or

If the table you wish to erase is already highlighted, you can pick OK or press the Return key.

ASEINIT: This command initializes ASE. It is the first command you give when preparing to use ASE. To access the command, pick the File pull-down menu, then the ASE menu selection and finally the Initialize selection (see Figure 11-4).

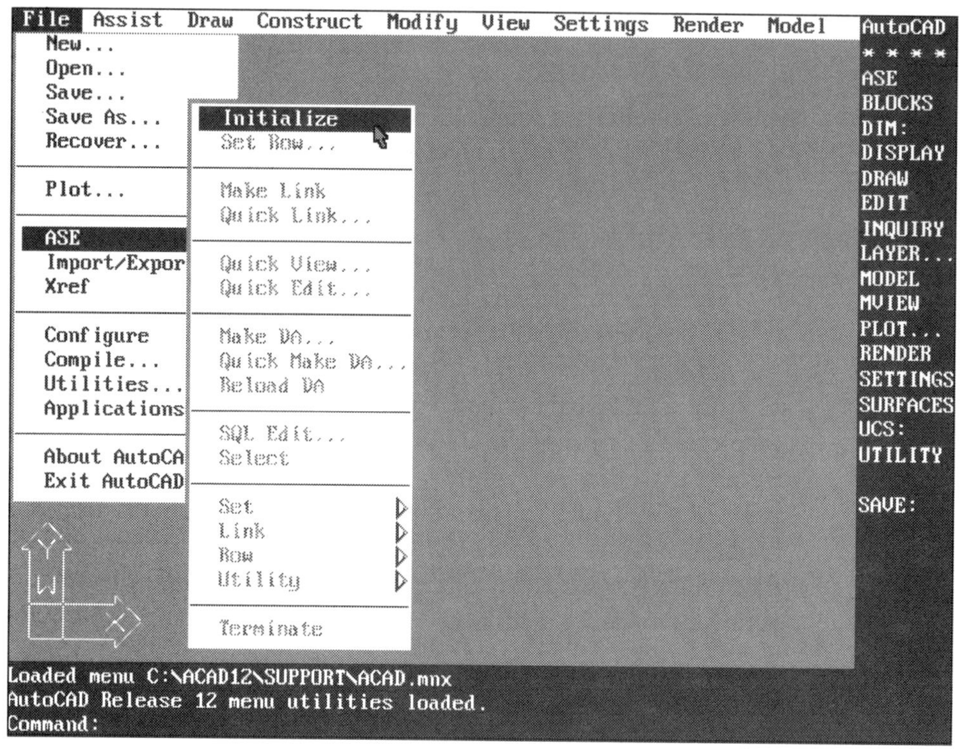

Figure 11-4: Initializing ASE via the pull-down menu

To initialize ASE from the command prompt, do the following:

Type: `(xload "ase") <Return>`

Response: `"ase"`

Type: `(load "ase") <Return>`

The command prompt is given at this point.

Type: `ASEINIT <Return>`

Response: `Please wait...`

Then the command prompt is given.

The ASEINIT command creates the control database that contains the information AutoCAD uses to link entities in your drawing to an external database. The control database is placed on a special layer (ACADASE) of your drawing.

NOTE: Do not change any part of the ACADASE layer. If you make any changes to this layer by any means other than the AutoCAD SQL Extension, links between your drawing and the outside database will be lost.

ASESETDB: This command lets you select the name of the database file you wish to make current. If you haven't yet chosen a DBMS type, this command will automatically invoke the ASESETDBMS command so you can choose a database type. After you give this command, the Set Current Database dialogue box appears (see Figure 11-5).

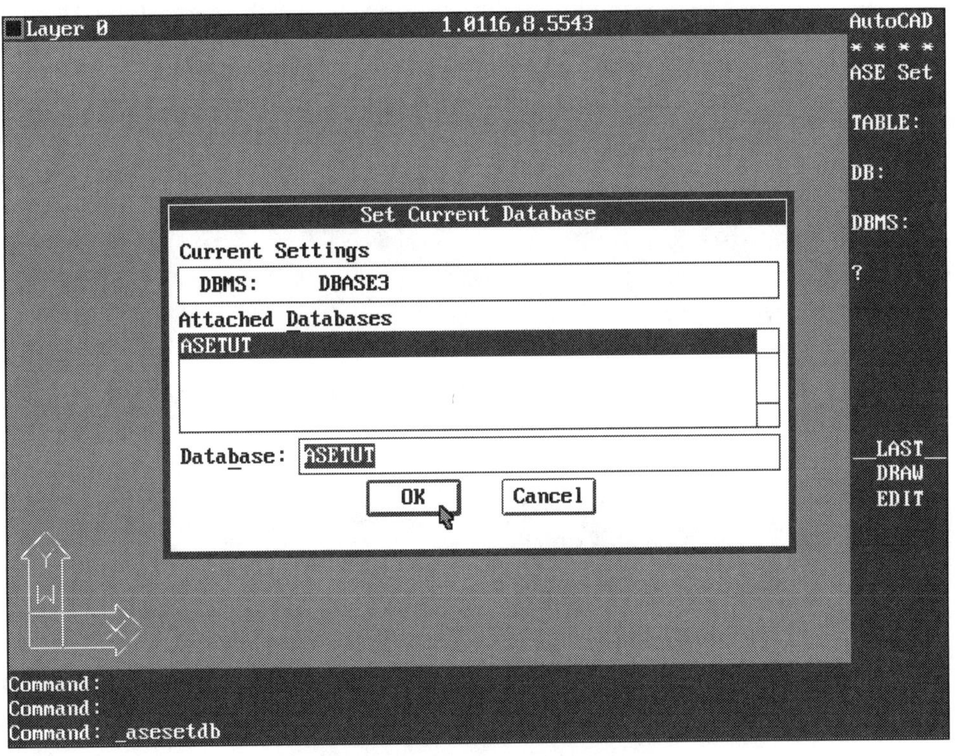

Figure 11-5: The Set Current Database dialogue box

If one or more database file names are listed in the dialogue box, you can pick one as the current database by doing the following:

Double-click on one of the database names.

or

Type the name of the database you wish to make current and press the Return key.

If no database file name is present, type the name of the database you wish to make current and press the Return key. A dialogue box will appear, requesting a username and password. If the database you have specified requires a username and password, enter it here.

ASESETDBMS: ASE has built-in drivers for certain database management systems, such as dBASE III and Paradox. This command lets you choose which DBMS driver you will use. The available drivers will be listed in the Set DBMS Driver dialogue box (see Figure 11-6).

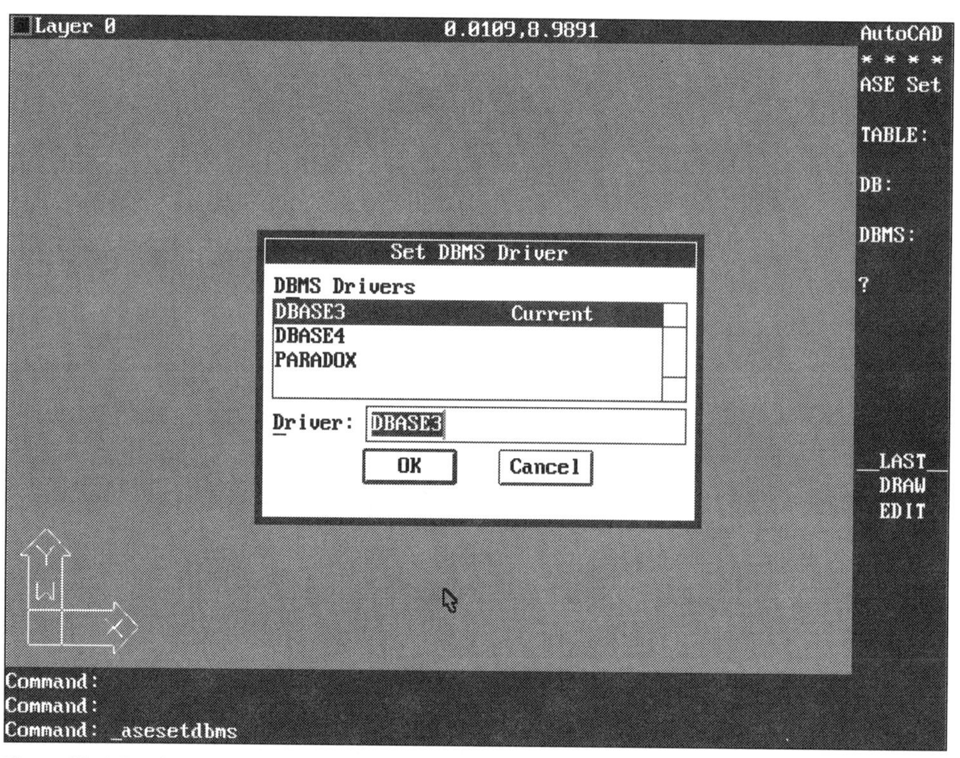

Figure 11-6: The Set DBMS Driver dialogue box

The Set DBMS Driver dialogue box displays the status of each DBMS beside each DBMS name. The status can be *current*, *loaded* or *attached*. An attached DBMS is stored in the control database but is not loaded into memory. A loaded database is loaded into memory but is not running. A current database is loaded into memory and is running.

To choose a DBMS, do the following:

Double-click on the DBMS name you wish to use.

or

Type the name of the DBMS you want and then press the Return key.

If you can't see all DBMS names due to the size of the dialogue box, use the scroll bars to make the desired DBMS name visible.

ASESETROW: This command sets a row in the current table. If you try to select a row before selecting a DBMS type and a database, ASE will prompt you through that selection process. To select a row, you can pick one of the following options in the Set Row Options dialogue box (see Figure 11-7):

Key...: Specify one or more key values.

Search...: Use an SQL WHERE clause to request a row.

Graphical <: Pick an entity in your drawing that is linked to the desired row.

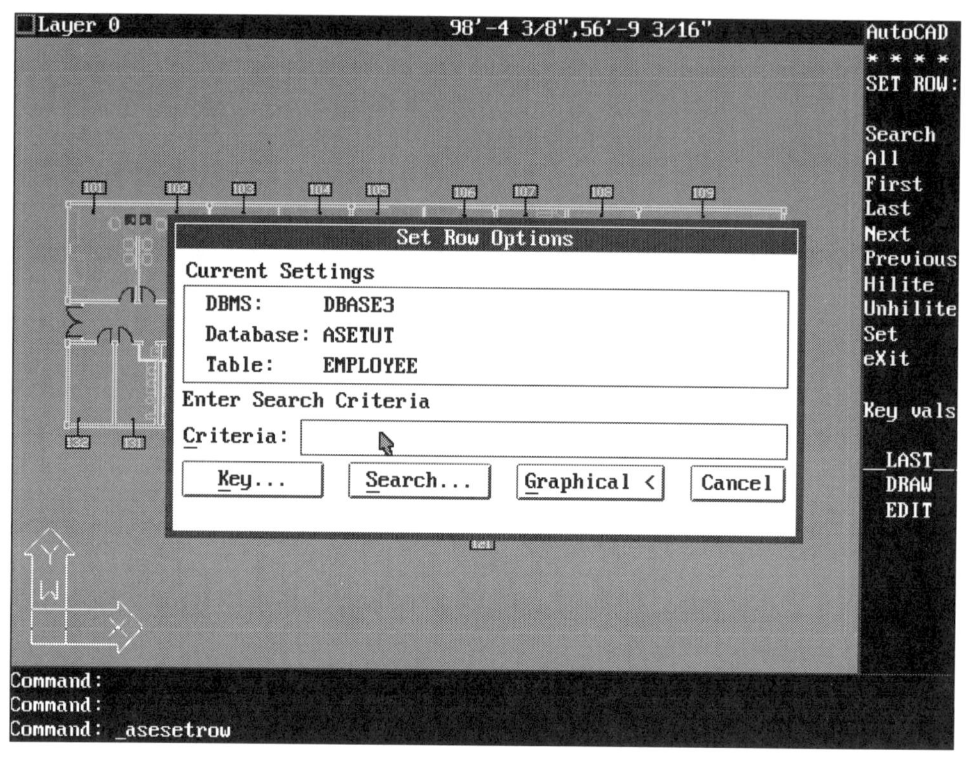

Figure 11-7: The Set Row Options dialogue box

If you specify a row by Key... values, the Set Current Row by Key Values dialogue box appears (see Figure 11-8).

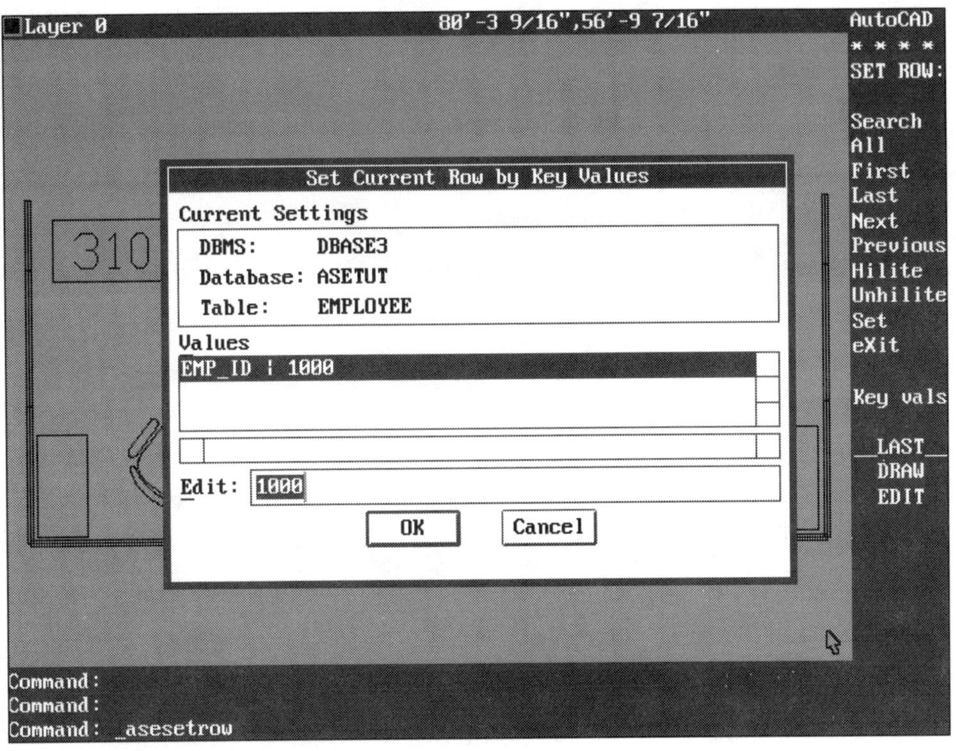

Figure 11-8: The Set Current Row by Key Values dialogue box

To use this dialogue box, first type the value you wish to search for in the Edit box and then press the Return key. If more than one column name is listed, pick each one on the list and enter a search value for each. Then pick OK when you've finished entering search values.

If you use the Search... option, first type a search string in the Edit box and then pick Search... or press the Return key. An example search string might be **LASTNAME='McDonald'**. Be sure you choose a search string that will be satisfied by only a few rows, at most. If you pick Search... without typing any search string in the Edit box, all rows in the entire table will be selected and will be displayed in the Set Current Row by Search Criteria dialogue box (see Figure 11-9).

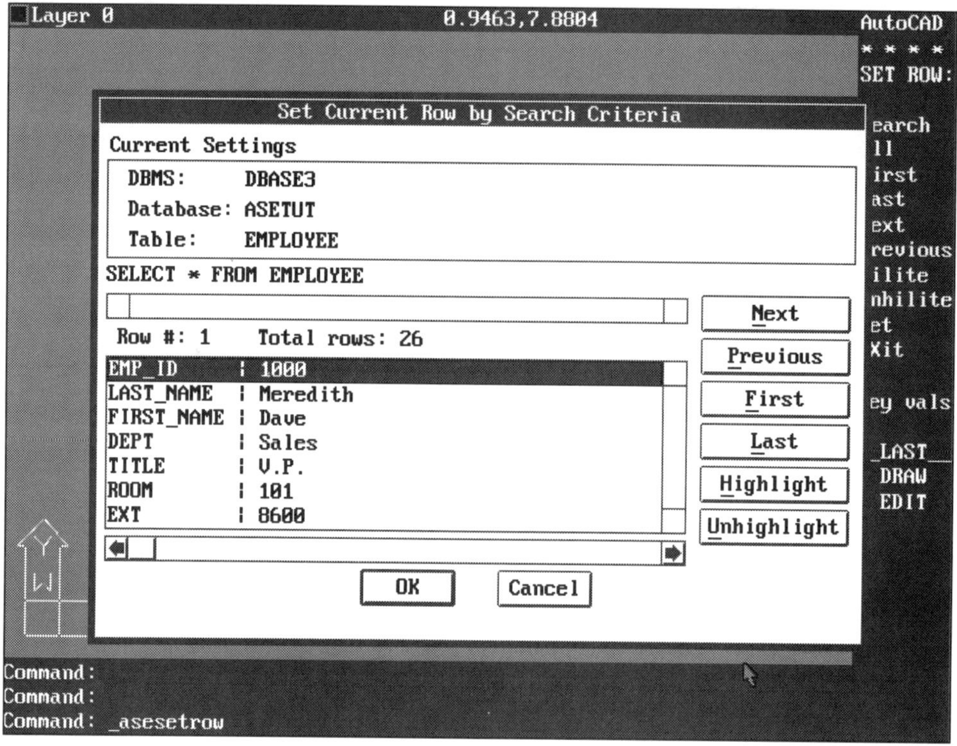

Figure 11-9: Set Current Row by Search Criteria dialogue box

This dialogue box displays the applicable SQL select statement, the current row, the total number of rows in the table and all column names and values for the current row.

- The Next button displays the next row that matches the selection set.
- The Previous button displays the previous row that matches the selection set.
- The First button displays the first row that matches the selection set.
- The Last button displays the last row that matches the selection set.
- The Highlight button causes the entities that are linked to the displayed row to be highlighted (highlighting is dependent on your system display).
- The Unhighlight button causes linked highlighted entities to be unhighlighted.

After you've selected the desired row, pick the OK button to set the row.

If you choose to set a row by picking an AutoCAD entity, pick Graphical... and then pick the entity that is linked to the row you wish to set as the current row. If you choose a drawing entity that is linked to more than one row, the Selection Link dialogue box appears, in which you can choose the row you desire. To set a row, highlight the row and then pick OK.

ASESETTABLE: This command displays the Set Current Table dialogue box (see Figure 11-10) so you can specify the table you wish to use for database operations. The table you specify will be attached to the drawing. The first time you specify a table, you're prompted to specify the key columns in the table.

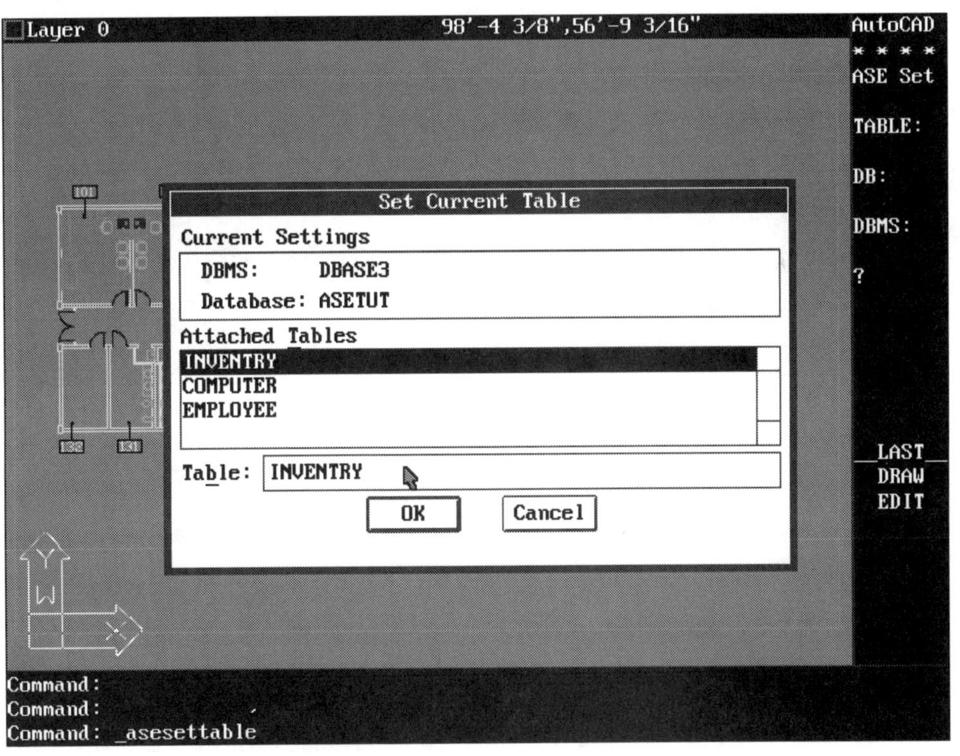

Figure 11-10: Set Current Table dialogue box

If the table you wish to specify is listed as an Attached Table, you can specify it as the current table by double-clicking on its name. If it is not listed, type the name of the table in the Table box and click the OK button or press the Return key.

If the selected table has not been set during the current ASE session, the Select Key Columns dialogue box appears (see Figure 11-11).

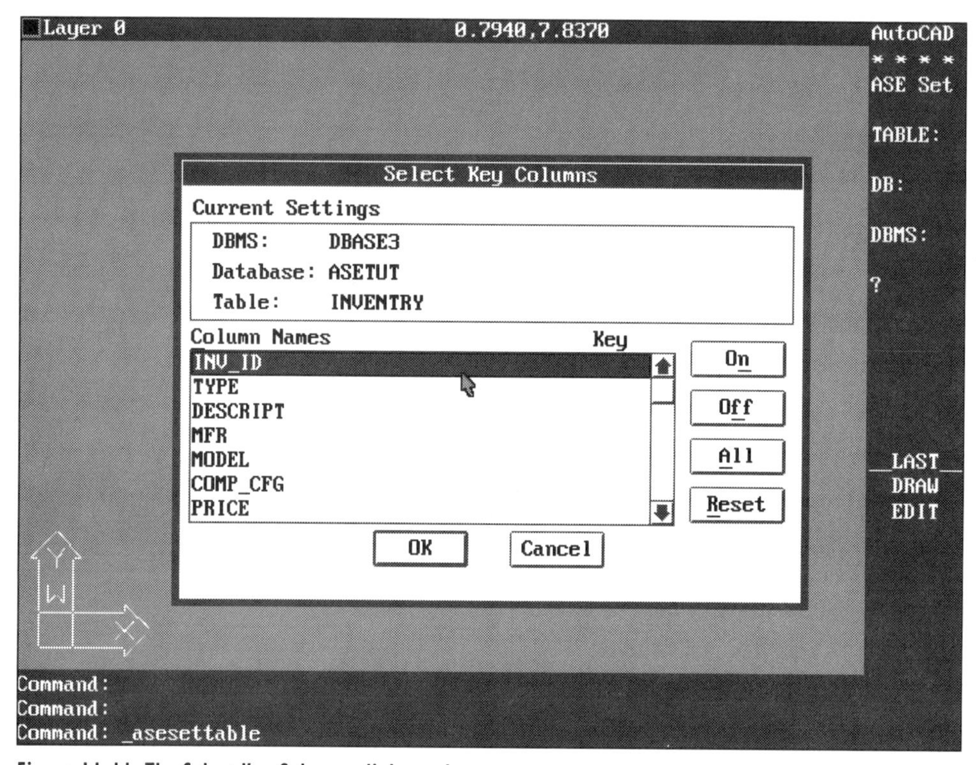

Figure 11-11: The Select Key Columns dialogue box

In this dialogue box, you'll find the following buttons:

- The On button causes the highlighted column name to be selected.
- The Off button causes the highlighted column name to be unselected.
- The All button selects all columns as key columns.
- The Reset button causes all columns to be unselected.

ASETERM: This command terminates ASE. All databases are closed, all database drivers are deactivated, the control database is saved in the drawing database, and ASE commands are no longer active. A dialogue box will appear, requiring you to confirm ASE termination.

NOTE: You should issue a COMMIT command before issuing the ASETERM command so that any changes you've made to the database tables will be saved.

ASETERMDBMS: This command terminates use of a selected DBMS. It is useful for freeing memory when the DBMS is not in use. The Terminate DBMS Driver dialogue box in Figure 11-12 appears when you issue the ASETERMDBMS command.

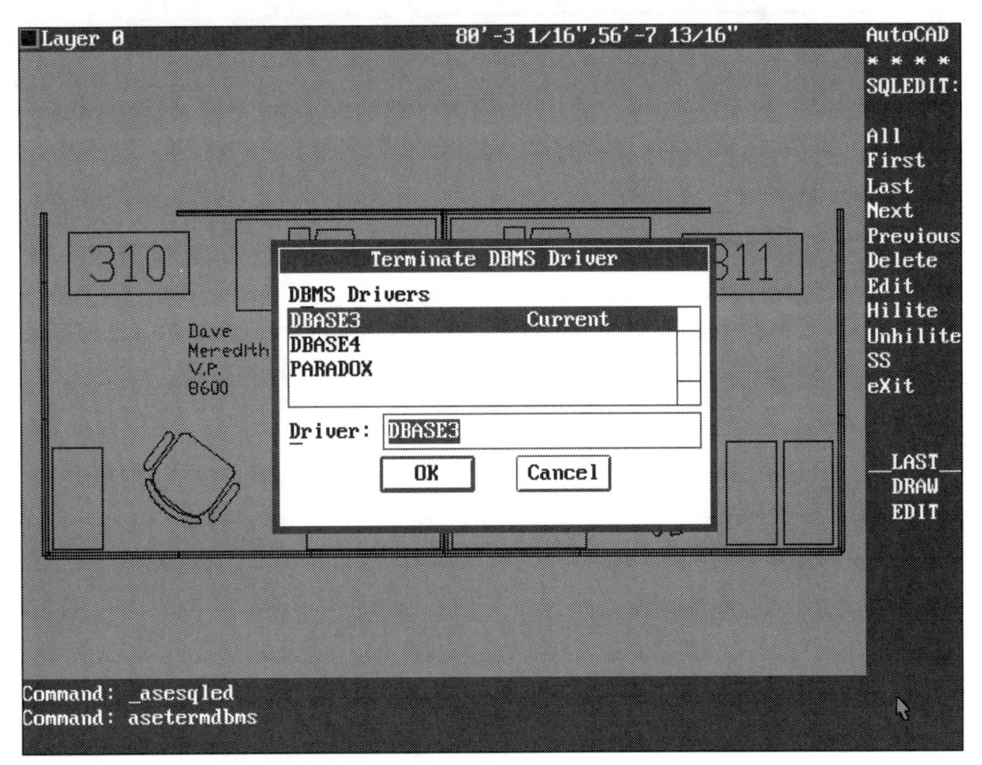

Figure 11-12: The Terminate DBMS Driver dialogue box

You can terminate a DBMS driver by double-clicking on the DBMS name, or by typing the DBMS name and picking OK or pressing the Return key.

Utility Commands

Utility commands perform utility operations such as creating reports, exporting link information and resolving link conflicts between the drawing and the external database. Following is a list of these commands:

ASEEXPORT: This command creates text files by exporting link information for selected entities. No dialogue box is associated with this command; you are prompted through its options.

When you give the ASEEXPORT command, you are prompted to select objects by specifying all links to selected entities, all links associated with a DBMS, selected entities only or a table. You can create one file per table. You then specify the name of the file you will create (don't specify an extension yet).

After specifying the name of the file, you're asked to choose the type of file to be created. Your choices include *SDF* (Space Delimited Format), *CDF* (Comma Delimited Format) or *Native* format. Your choice will determine the filename extension. In an SDF file, each field of information is separated by one or more spaces. In a CDF file, each field of information is enclosed by quotation marks and is separated from other fields by a comma (Chapter 5, "Attribute Extraction," gives a detailed explanation of CDF and SDF formats). If you choose Native format, ASE will create a file in the format of the database type you've chosen. The file you create will contain link information including a key column value for an item, along with the entity handle.

The primary purpose of this command is to let you export link information to applications other than your database for reporting purposes.

ASEMAKEREP: The ASEMAKEREP command lets you use your database management system's report generation utilities to generate a report. This command displays the ASE Make Report dialogue box, as shown in Figure 11-13.

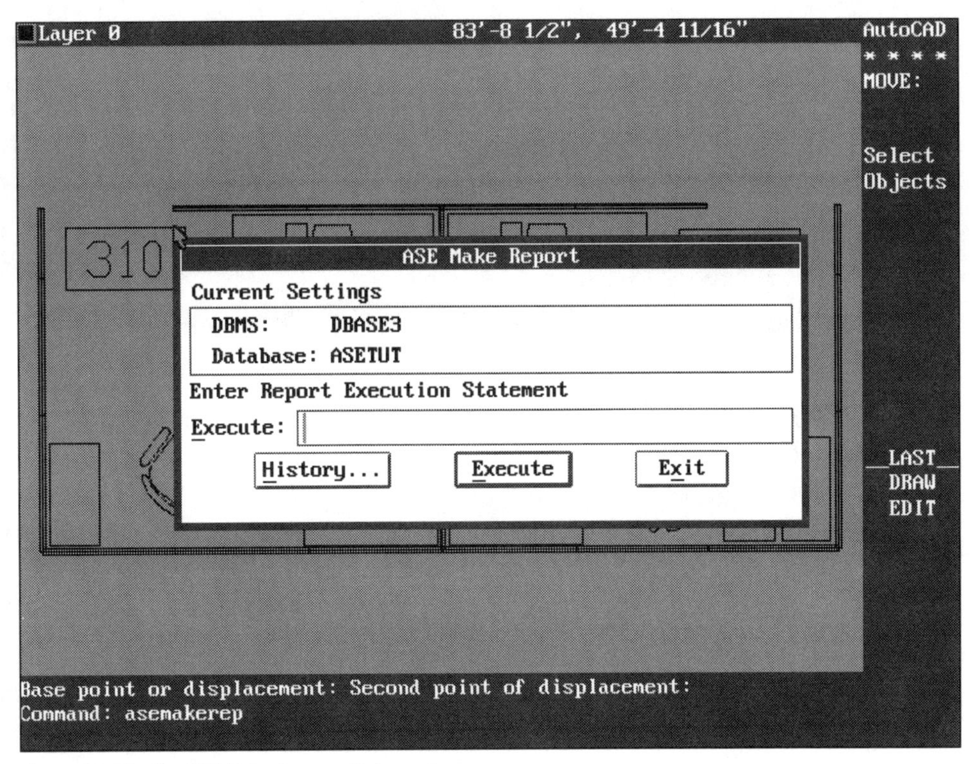

Figure 11-13: The ASE Make Report dialogue box

To use the dialogue box, type the name of the DBMS's report generation program in the Execute box (include the full path to the program) and then pick the Execute button to run the report generation utility. The output will be printed to your text screen. Switch to the text screen to see the report. An example of a report generator is dBASE III Plus' FLT_INFO.PRG program. Instructions for using your DBMS's report generator are included with your DBMS software package.

If you pick the History button, the ASE Make Report History dialogue box, which contains a list of the report generation commands you've given during the drawing session, will appear (see Figure 11-14).

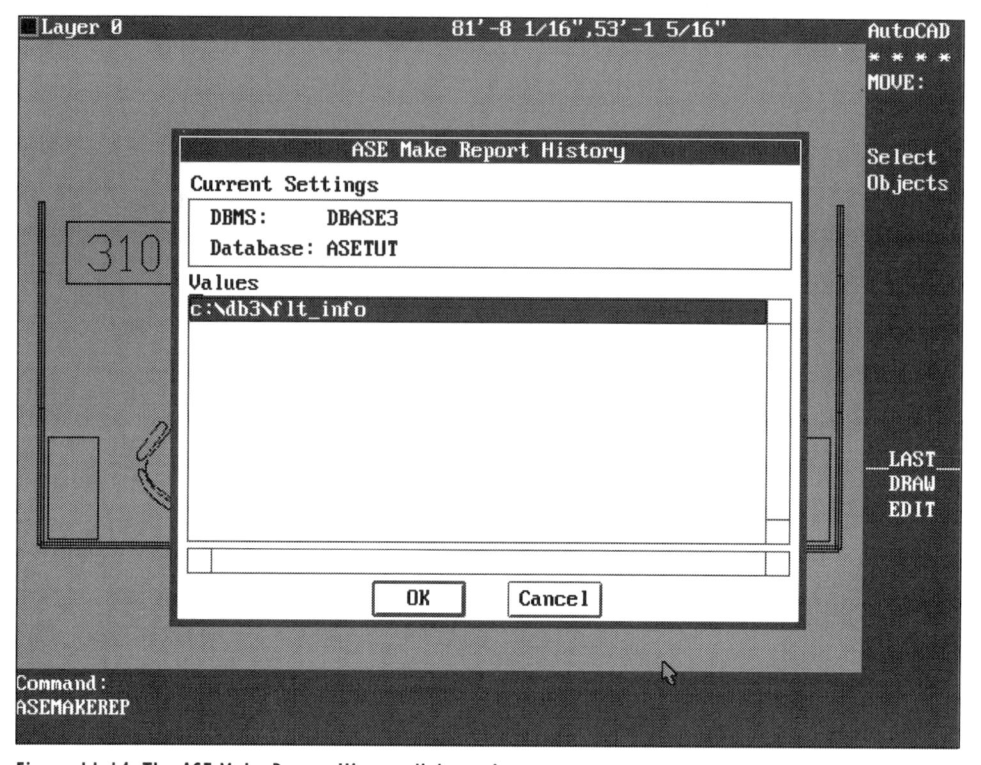

Figure 11-14: The ASE Make Report History dialogue box

ASEPOST: This command lets you find conflicts between your AutoCAD drawing and the database file. Conflicts are created when you make changes to the database from the DBMS or by some means other than with AutoCAD, or by changing the drawing without having ASE active. If you include an *R* argument after the command name, conflicts will only be reported. An *F* argument fixes conflicts but causes a confirmation dialogue box to appear before fixing any conflicts. If you choose the Fix option, no drawing entities will be affected. Only the database will be changed to match the current condition.

ASESELECT: This command creates entity selection sets by combining selected entities with database information. You can use three operations to combine selection set data: Intersection, Subtraction and Union. No dialogue box accompanies this command. At the command prompt, do the following:

Type: `ASESELECT <Return>`

Response: `Export/<Selection Set>`

Following are the options for this command:

E (Export): Exports data to an external database (see the explanation for ASEEXPORT in this chapter).

S (Selection Set): Creates a selection set based on your response to the next part of the command.

If you choose Selection Set, you'll be given the following options:

Intersection: Creates a selection set consisting of the selected entities that are referenced by links to the database.

Subtraction: Creates a selection set by subtracting all database search criteria from the selected entities or by subtracting the selected entities from the database search criteria. Your answer to the next set of options determines the order of subtraction.

Union: Creates a selection set that includes all selected entities and all entities linked to the database search criteria.

If you choose Subtraction, you'll be given the following options:

G (Graphical): Prompts you to select graphic drawing entities.

T (Textual): Prompts you to enter a database search instruction, such as **employee_name="McDonald"**.

ASESQLED: This command displays the SQL Editor dialogue box (see Figure 11-15) so you can give SQL commands by typing each command or by giving the name of an ASCII text file that contains one or more SQL commands.

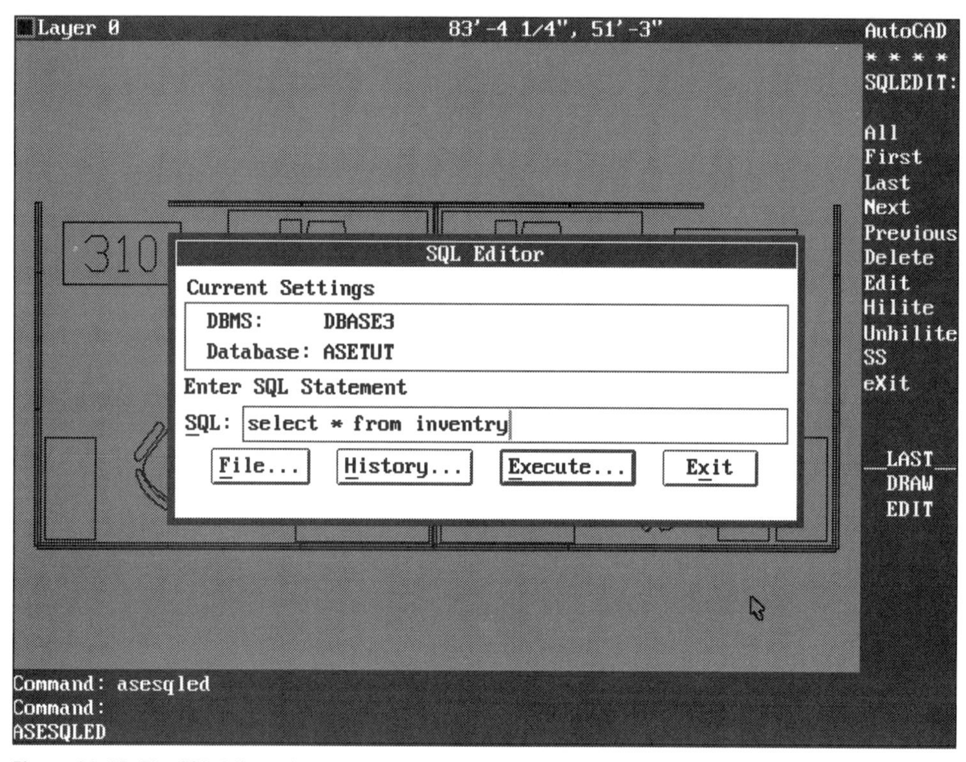

Figure 11-15: The SQL Editor dialogue box

To enter a single command from the dialogue box, type the SQL command in the SQL box in the dialogue box and pick Execute.... If you enter an SQL SELECT statement, the Edit SQL Selection Set dialogue box will be displayed (see Figure 11-16).

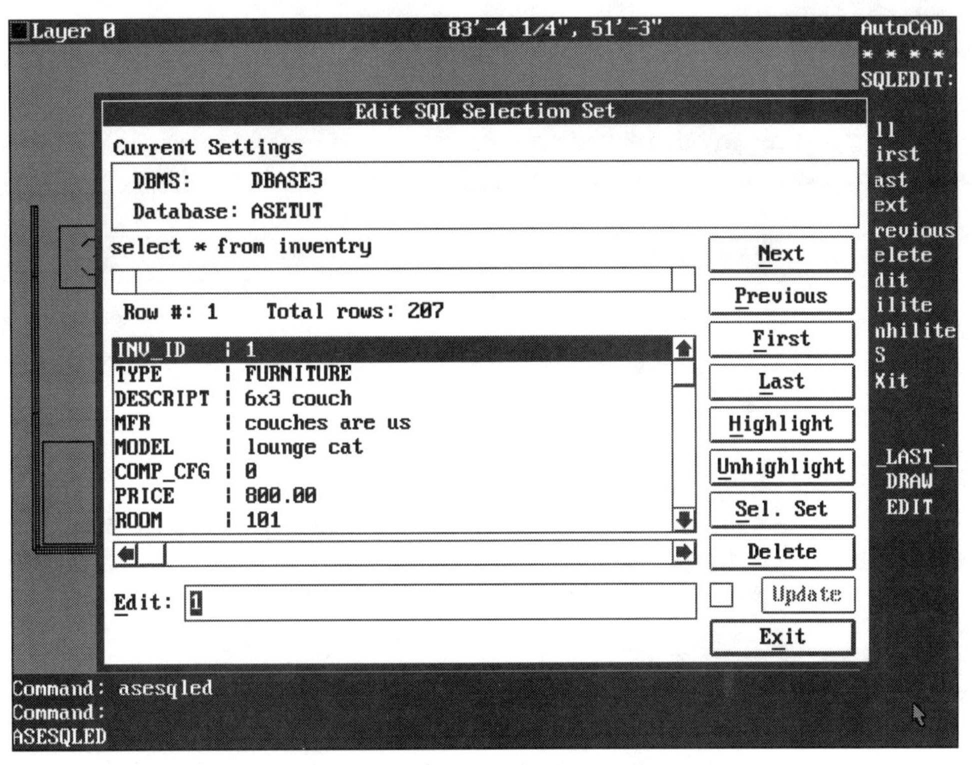

Figure 11-16: The SQL Selection Set dialogue box

This dialogue box gives you the following navigation buttons to move through the table rows:

- The Highlight and Unhighlight buttons let you designate an entity that is linked to a displayed row.
- The Sel Set button adds entities to the selection set that are linked to the displayed row.
- The Delete button performs an SQL DELETE to remove a row from the table (it does not perform an ASE delete). It does not remove database links.
- The Update button has a checkbox next to it that determines how the update functions. If the checkbox has an *X* in it, you must pick the Update button to update any edited columns in the database table. If the box is not marked, updates occur when you press the Return key after filling in the Edit box.

If you picked the History... button in the SQL Editor dialogue box, the History of SQL Statements dialogue box appears (see Figure 11-17), showing a history of previously executed commands. If you double-click on any displayed command, that command is placed into the SQL Editor dialogue box. To execute the command, press the Return key.

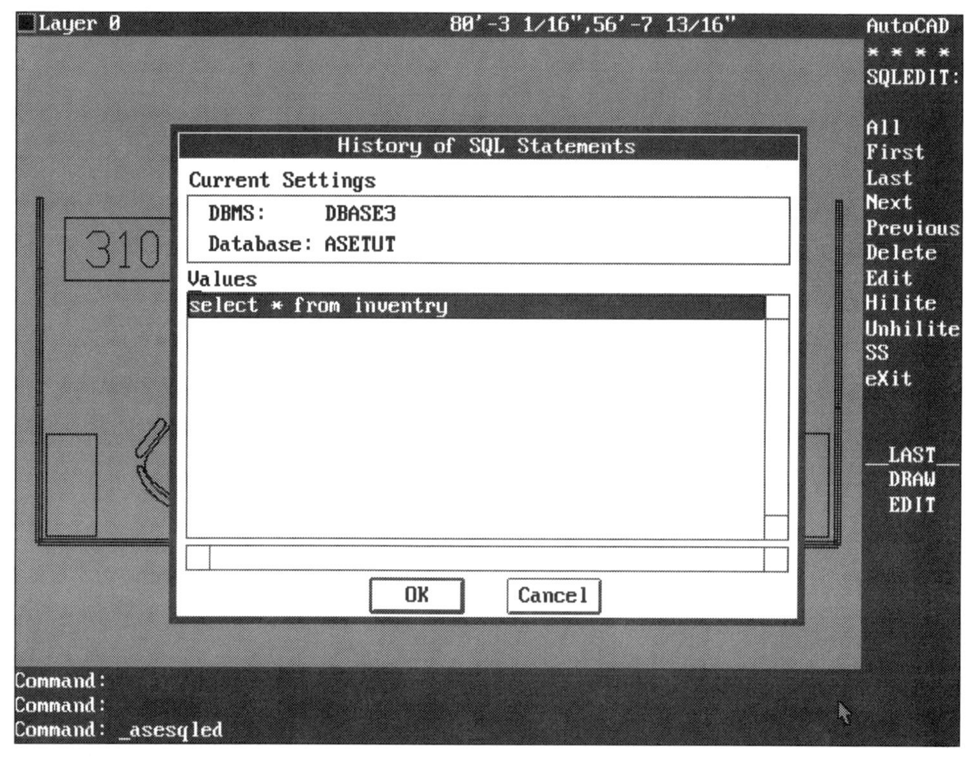

Figure 11-17: The History of SQL statements dialogue box

If you picked the File... button in the SQL Editor dialogue box, the SQL Filename dialogue box appears (see Figure 11-18), showing the names of *.txt files. If a file contains SQL statements you wish to execute, double-click on the filename.

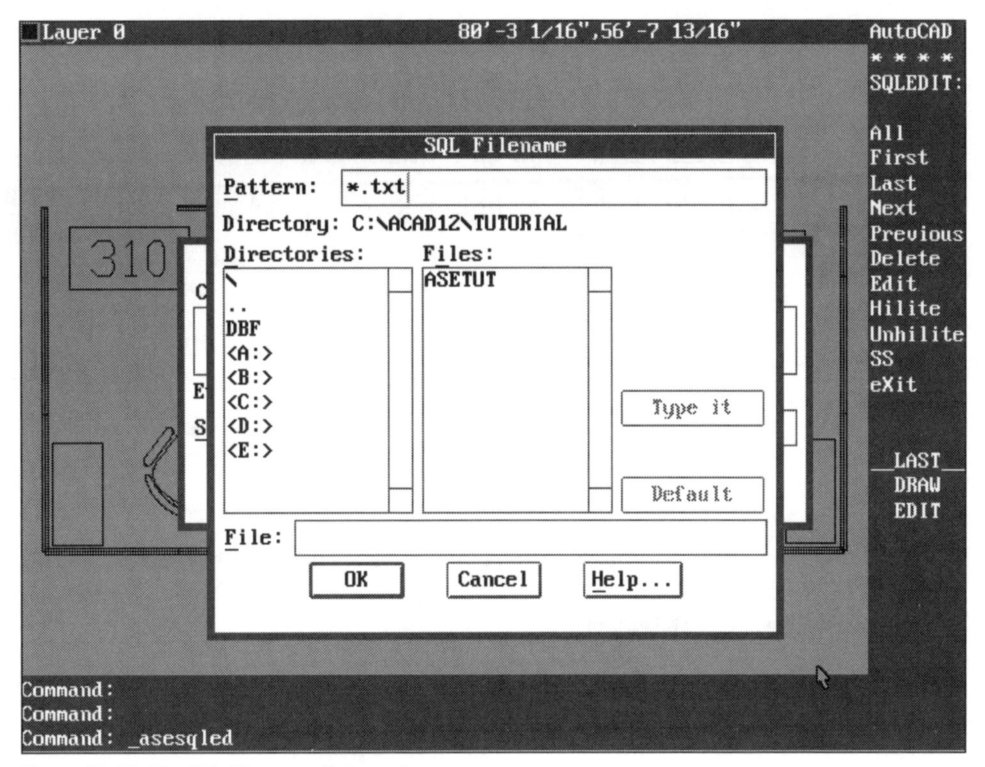

Figure 11-18: The SQL Filename dialogue box

Link Commands

Link commands create, edit, view and delete links and perform other link operations. Following is a list of link commands:

ASEDELLINK: This command deletes links belonging to selected entities. You can delete links from selected entities to the current row, table, database, DBMS or to all DBMSs. Deleting a link doesn't affect the database element or entity to which it belongs. If the entity is a displayable attribute entity (created with ASEMAKEDA), however, the entity is erased.

NOTE: Use with caution! You cannot recover a deleted link!

Before you can give the ASEDELLINK command, you must make sure the affected row (or table, database or DBMS) is current. You give the ASEDELLINK command at the command prompt, as follows:

Type: `ASEDELLINK <Return>`

The following argument options are given:

ALL: Deletes all links attached to the selected entities.

DBMS: Deletes all links between all selected entities and the current DBMS.

Database: Deletes all links between all selected entities and the current database.

Table: Deletes all links between all selected entities and the current table.

Row: Deletes all links between all selected entities and the current row.

Type one of the above arguments and press the Return key.

Response: `Select objects:`

After selecting the desired entities, press the Return key. Then a dialogue box is displayed requiring you to confirm the action.

ASEEDITLINK: This command edits links belonging to an entity. For example, this command lets you change a link's association so it is attached to a different row.

Before you can give the ASEEDITLINK command, you must make sure the affected row (table, database or DBMS) is current. If the selected entity has links, the Edit Link dialogue box will be displayed upon giving the ASEDELLINK command (see Figure 11-19).

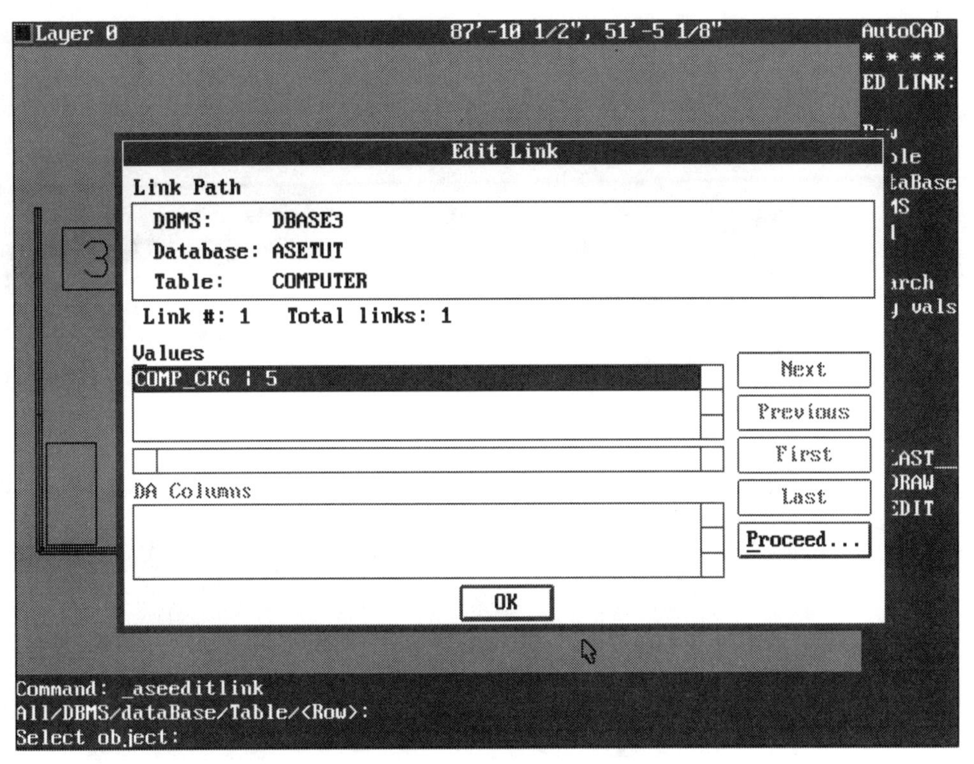

Figure 11-19: The Edit Link dialogue box

All links associated with the selected entity will be displayed in the dialogue box. You can scan through the links by clicking on the Next, Previous, First and Last buttons in the box. You can select a link by clicking on it. If a displayable attribute is shown in the DA Columns, you also can select it by clicking on it.

After selecting a link and clicking the Proceed button, the Edit Link Options dialogue box will be displayed (see Figure 11-20).

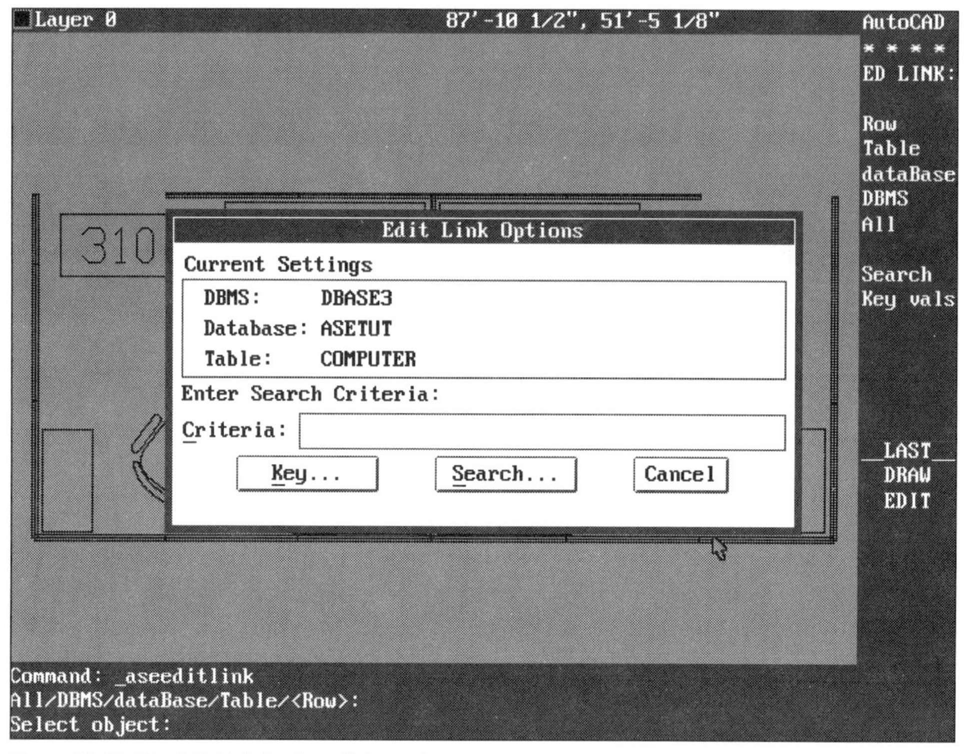

Figure 11-20: The Edit Link Options dialogue box

In the Edit Link Options dialogue box, you can select a row by picking one of the following two options:

Key...: Specify one or more key values.

Search...: Use an SQL WHERE clause to request a row.

If you select Key..., the Edit Link Key Values dialogue box appears (see Figure 11-21).

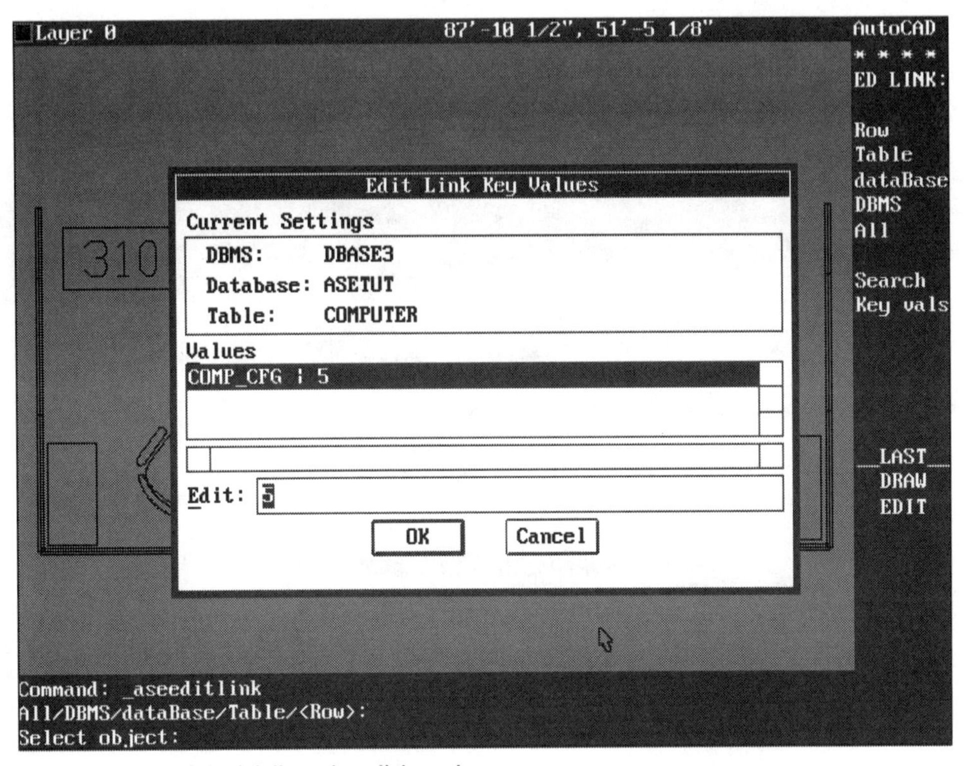

Figure 11-21: The Edit Link Key values dialogue box

To use this dialogue box, pick the desired column and then pick in the Edit box and type the column value for the row of the new link. Then press the Return key. Now pick the next column name and type the column value in the Edit box again. When you're finished, click the OK button or press the Return key.

If you select Search..., the Set Row Options dialogue box appears (refer to Figure 11-7 again). Follow the instructions given for the ASESETROW command to fill in this box.

ASEMAKEDA: This command makes a displayable attribute by printing selected current row text fields on the screen. Give this command as follows:

Type: `ASEMAKEDA <Return>`

You are prompted to pick a location in your drawing for the displayable attribute text. Now go ahead and pick the location for the displayable attribute text. Then the Make Displayable Attribute dialogue box appears (see Figure 11-22).

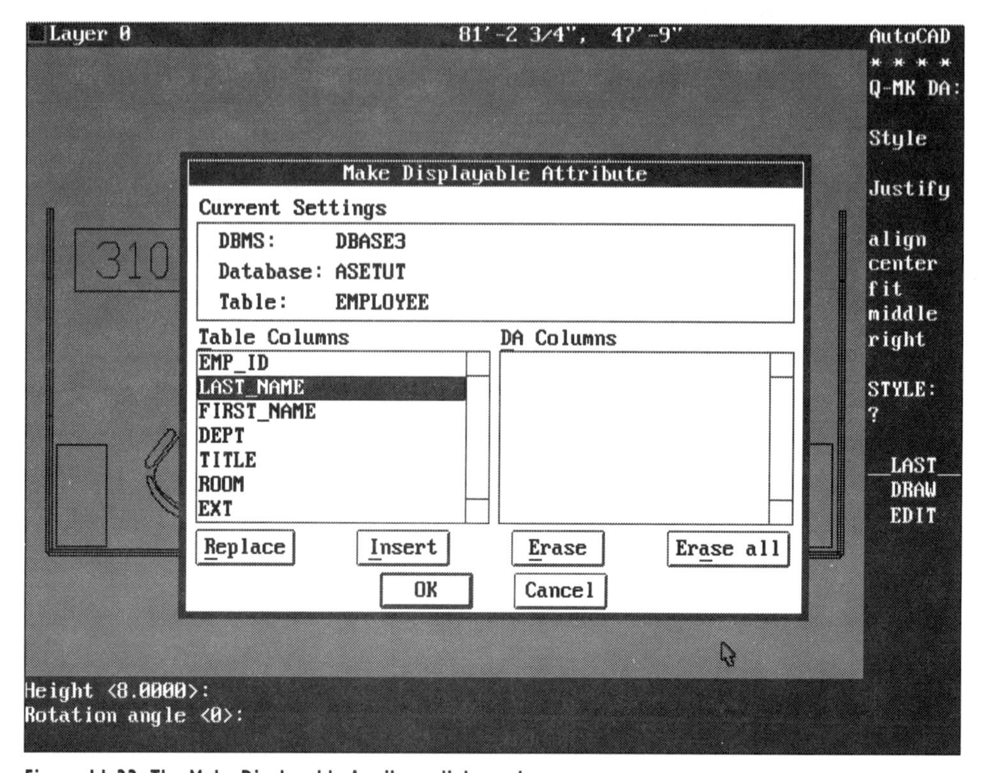

Figure 11-22: The Make Displayable Attribute dialogue box

The table columns are listed in the Table Columns area (the left half) of the dialogue box. You can choose any of these entries to display in your drawing by doing the following:

Double-click on each entry you wish to display.

or

Click once on an entry you wish to display and then click on the Insert button.

When you select an entry using one of these methods, a copy of the entry appears in the DA Columns area (right half) of the dialogue box.

- If you click on the Replace button, the highlighted Table Columns entry will replace the highlighted DA Columns entry.
- The Erase button erases the highlighted DA Columns entry.
- The Erase all button erases all the entries in the DA Columns area.
- Pick the OK button or press the Return key to complete the command.

The displayable attributes will be placed at the location you chose when you gave the ASEMAKEDA command (the displayable attributes will appear as text but will not be text entities).

ASEMAKELINK: This command creates a link that connects the selected entity to the current row. When an entity is linked to a row, you can select the entity and display the information in the row to which it is linked.

Before you use this command, you should first use ASESETROW to set the row to which you'll link the entity. Use ASEMAKELINK to select the entities to be linked to the current row. The ASEQLINK (ASE Quick Link) command is also available and combines these two steps.

ASEQLINK: This command combines the ASESETROW and ASE-MAKELINK process into one command. It lets you set the current row and link it to an entity while using only one command.

ASEQMAKEDA: This command combines ASESETROW (Graphical option) and ASEMAKEDA into one command. This command is useful if you want to make a displayable attribute for a row already linked to an entity.

ASERELOADDA: This command updates displayable attributes with current data from the external database(s). If you've edited a row, you can use this command to cause the displayable attributes to show the current values as you have modified them.

ASEVIEWLINK: This command displays all the links for a selected entity in the View Link dialogue box (see Figure 11-23).

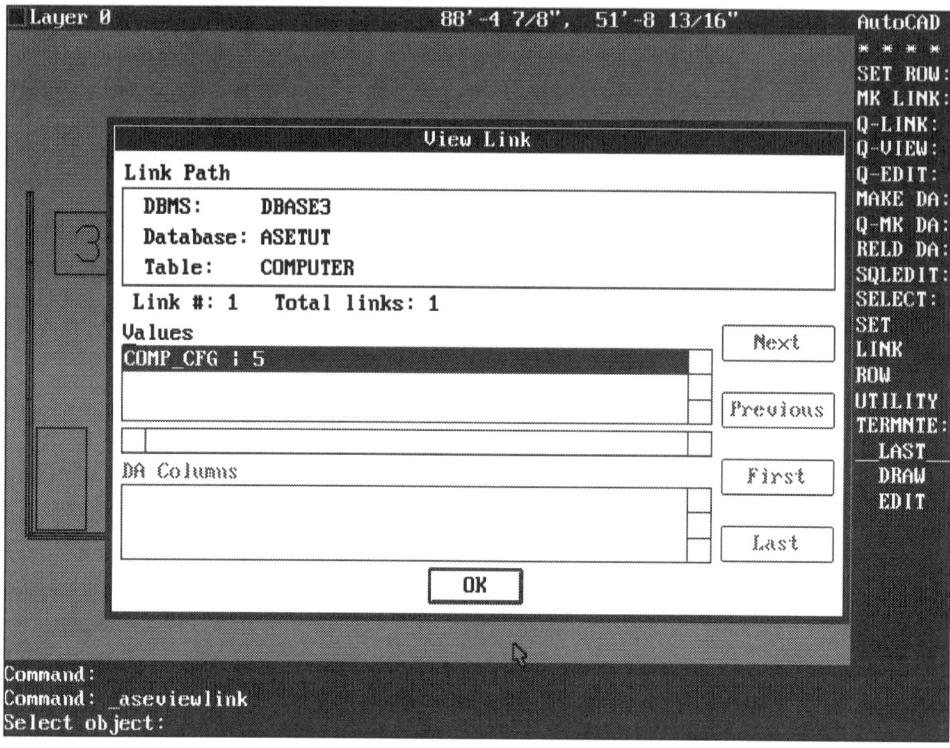

Figure 11-23: The View Link dialogue box

The Next, Previous, First and Last buttons in the dialogue box let you scan through the list of links if several are displayed. If you select a value with a displayable attribute, its displayable attribute column value appears in the DA Columns area.

Manipulative Commands

Manipulative commands work directly with the database by adding, editing, deleting and performing other row and table operations. Following is a complete list:

ASEADDROW: This command adds a row to the current table. Before you can use this command, you must have already set a current DBMS, database or table. When you give the ASEADDROW command, the Add Row dialogue box is displayed with the values for the current row (see Figure 11-24).

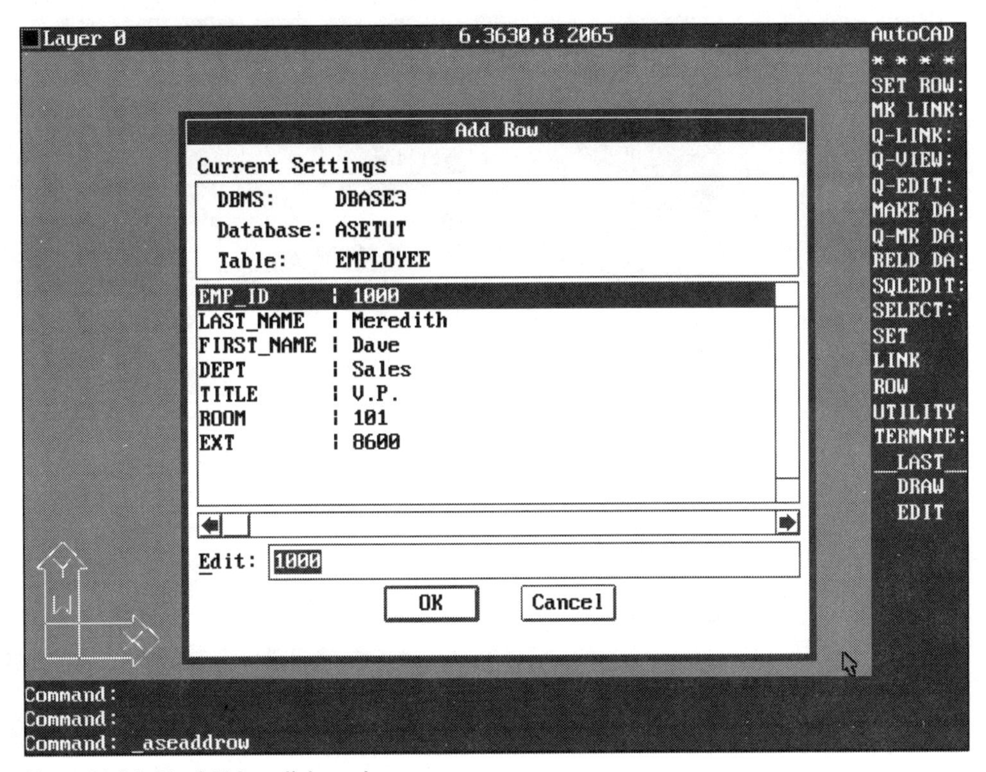

Figure 11-24: The Add Row dialogue box

To use the dialogue box, highlight the column field whose row value you wish to change or add. Then, in the Edit box, type the value you desire and press the Return key. Repeat these steps for each column as you desire. If more columns are listed than can be displayed, use the scroll bars in the dialogue box to display them. When you're finished editing the values, pick OK to accept the data.

ASEDELROW: This command deletes the current row from the current table. When ASEDELROW deletes a row, all links to the row as well as associated displayable attributes are removed from the control database. A dialogue box will be displayed requiring you to confirm the action.

NOTE: ASEDELROW will delete all rows with the same key value!

ASEEDITROW: This command edits the current row in the current table. The Edit Row dialogue box (see Figure 11-25) will assist you in editing the current row.

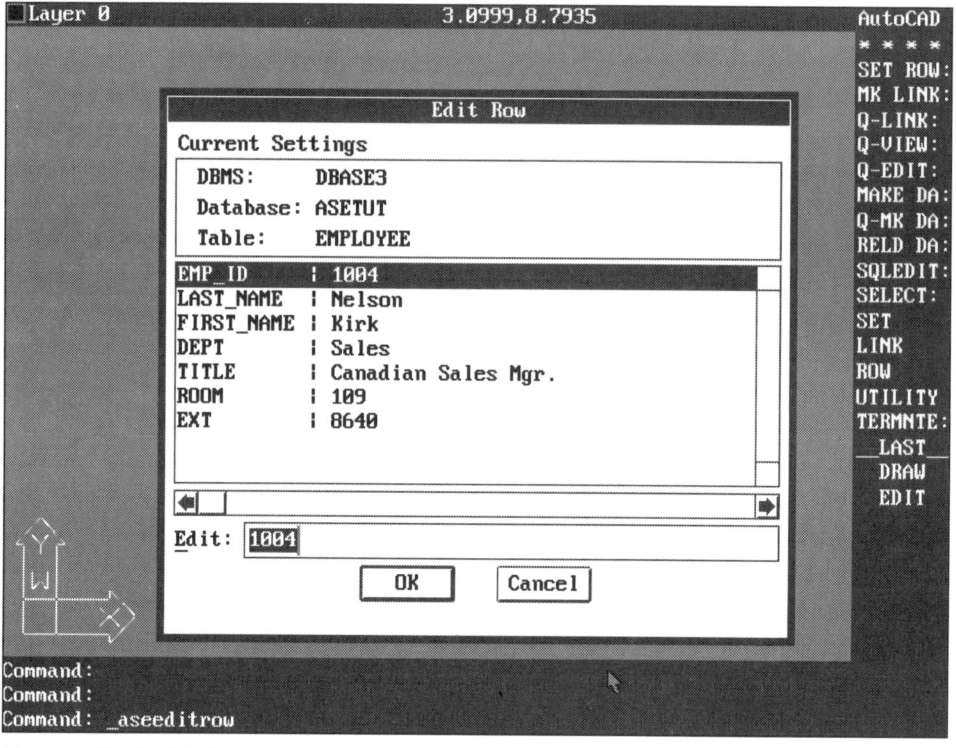

Figure 11-25: The Edit Row dialogue box

The dialogue box displays the current row. To edit a column, first pick the column in the dialogue box and press the Return key. The value will appear in the Edit box. Then type the new value for the column and press the Return key again. Now the new value appears next to the column. Repeat these steps for each value you wish to edit.

When you've finished editing the row, pick OK to accept the changes. If you edited a key field, you'll be prompted to confirm the changes.

NOTE: If you change a key value, any links to that row will become invalid. ASEPOST will report such a problem. You can use ASEEDITLINK to change a link's key value.

ASEEDITROW performs various checks on the data before it is passed to the database. Type checking is done after you complete all entries in the dialogue box. This command does not check for unique keys; that is done when the entire row is passed to the DBMS driver. If multiple rows have the same key values, this command will update these rows with the values from the edited row.

ASEQEDIT: This command combines ASESETROW (Graphical option) and ASEEDITROW into one command. You can use this command to edit an entity's linked attribute. If you want to edit a row that is not current but is linked to an entity in the drawing, give this command and then pick the entity. You can set the row as you would when using the ASESETROW command. The ASEEDITROW command operates the same here as when used by itself.

ASEQVIEW: This command combines ASESETROW (Graphical option) and ASEVIEWROW into one command. Use this command to view a row that is not current but is linked to an entity in the drawing. Give the command and then pick the entity. Operate the command as you would the ASESETROW and ASEVIEWROW commands.

ASEVIEWROW: This command lets you view the current row in the View Row dialogue box (see Figure 11-26). You can scan through the information in the dialogue box by using the scroll bars.

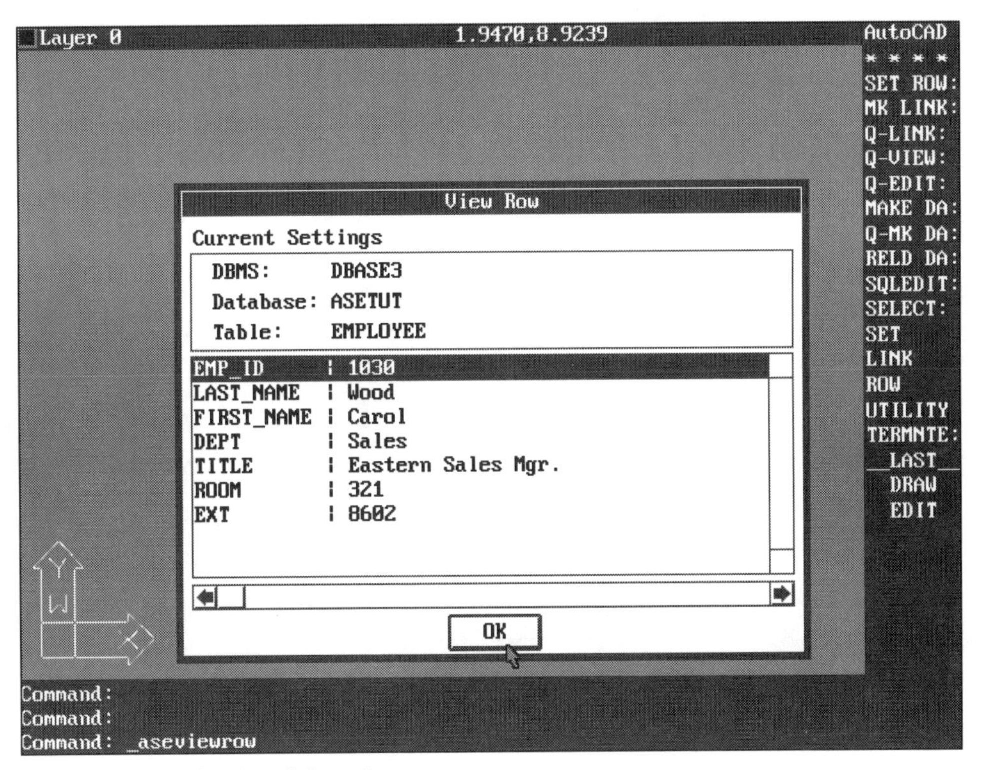

Figure 11-26: The View Row dialogue box

Moving On

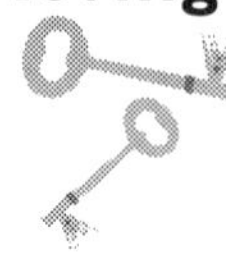

In this chapter you've learned the administrative, utility, link and manipulative ASE commands. You can use this chapter as a reference as you develop ways to use ASE with your drawings. In the next chapter, "A Hands-on Example," we'll use AutoCAD's tutorial database files with our own drawing to demonstrate the use of ASE....

ASE: A Hands-On Example

This hands-on chapter will focus on how to apply ASE. It begins with an explanation of how the Chapter database example is structured and then, according to how you specified the structure, it moves into using ASE to work with the data assigned in the database.

For your convenience, you'll build the example on three database files packaged with AutoCAD Release 12. In this hands-on example, you'll create your own OFFICE drawing and then use ASE to work with the drawing and the external database. The example application will relate to facility management and involve employees, computers and other office inventory. As an end-product you're actually going to link the graphic entities in the OFFICE drawing to the data in the database that describes each entity.

Creating a Sample Drawing

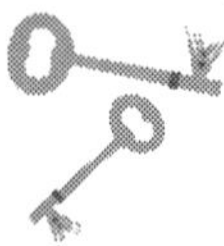

If you have the *Outside AutoCAD Companion Diskette,* OPEN the drawing called OFFICE. Figure 12-1 shows the office layout example that you'll be using. If you need to create the drawing, build each item that is included in the following list.

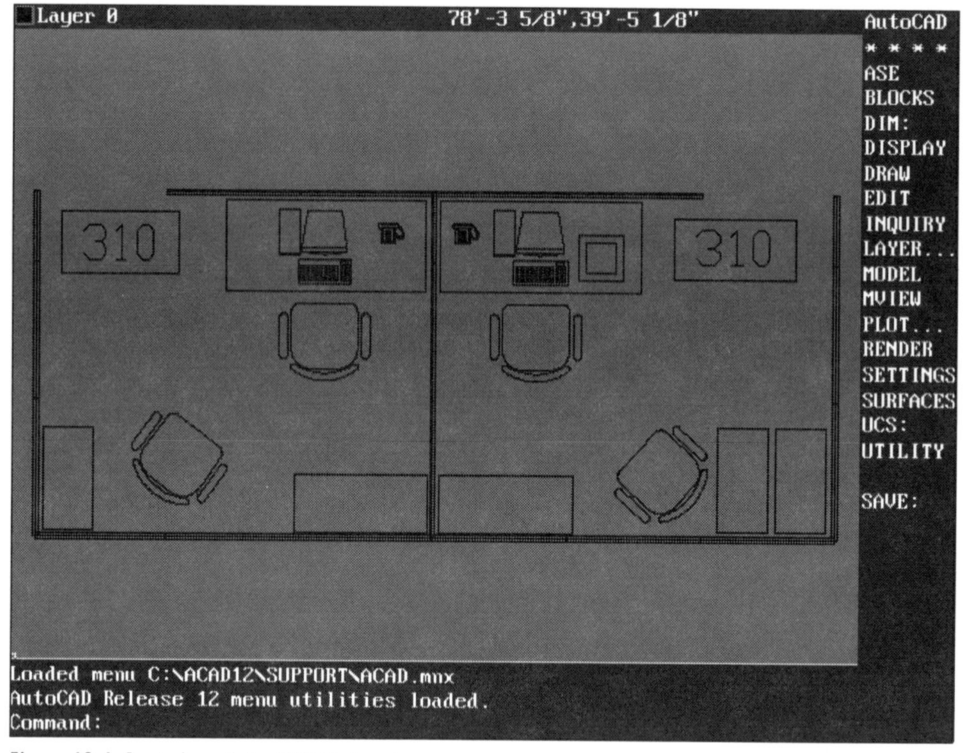

Figure 12-1: Part view of the OFFICE drawing

Create separate layers for the furniture, the panels, the office equipment (file cabinet, shelf and phone), the computer equipment (PC and graphics tablet) and the ROOM_NUM block.

Layer Name	Description
FURNITURE	For chair, desk
PANELS	For pnl2x5, pnl4x5—wall panels
OFF_EQUIP	For file cabinet, shelf, phone
COMP_EQUIP	For personal computer, graphics tablet
ROOM_NUM	For placing office numbers

Each block name with its description is shown below:

Block Name	Description
CHAIR	Office chair
DESK	Office desk
FILECAB	File cabinet
PC	Personal Computer
PHONE	Telephone
PNL2X5	2' x 5' wall panel
PNL4X5	4' x 5' wall panel
ROOM_NUM	Box with an office number
SHELF	Bookshelf
TABLET	Graphics tablet

When you OPEN the OFFICE drawing, note that it contains no attributes. The text you see inside the ROOM_NUM block is not part of the block and is not attached to it in any way. It is plain text created with the TEXT or DTEXT command. The size of the objects is not important.

Database Requirements

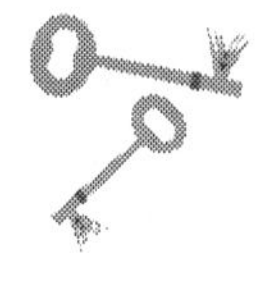

Each database management system (DBMS) has its own requirements for establishing access to its databases. Before you start using a DBMS, you should become familiar with your DBMS's setup requirements. You can find most DBMS setup requirements in the DBMS documentation under a heading similar to "Setup and Installation." For this example, use dBASE III as your DBMS.

Preparing the DOS Environment

The *DOS environment* is like a message board inside your computer. It's similar to a message board in your office. If you're leaving the office but want to leave instructions for a coworker regarding how to do a certain job, you would leave the instruction on a message board where your coworker would see it. When your coworker arrives, he or she will read the message and know how to perform the job.

In your computer, you can also leave messages for programs you'll run. The location for your messages is the DOS environment and, by default, holds 128 characters (your DOS manual will show you how to increase the amount of space in the environment by using the SHELL instruction in your CONFIG.SYS file).

When programs start up and begin to run, they check the message board for special instructions. The message that you'll leave for ASE will be the name of your database. For this example, your database will be called FACILITY and consist of three files: INVENTRY.DBF, COMPUTER.DBF and EMPLOYEE.DBF. If you installed AutoCAD on your C: drive using the installation defaults, locate the files in your \ACAD\TUTORIAL\DBF subdirectory. Now, let's use the DOS environment to tell ASE the name of your database and where to find it.

You may place your message in the AUTOEXEC.BAT file so it will always be in the DOS environment or in the batch file you use to start AutoCAD. If you use your computer primarily for AutoCAD, the AUTOEXEC.BAT file is a good location. But if you use your system to run a variety of applications (as most people do), you can conserve space in the DOS environment by placing your message in the ACADR12.BAT batch file you use to start AutoCAD. The line you'll place into your file looks like the following:

```
SET FACILITY=C:\ACAD\TUTORIAL\DBF
```

NOTE: The above line has only one space in it—right after the SET command.

Now, when ASE begins running, it will look in the environment and find the name of the database (which is an alias for the directory containing the database files).

The FACILITY Database Structure

Even before you start using any database management system, it's important that you organize your data so it's stored efficiently and so you can easily use it for look-up and reporting purposes.

The FACILITY database consists of three tables, or files. The structure of each table is shown on page 199:

INVENTRY

Column Name	Field Type	Number of Characters	Description
INV_ID	N	12.0	Item Number
TYPE	C	20.0	Item Type
DESCRIPT	C	40.0	Item Description
MFR	C	40.0	Manufacturer
MODEL	C	15.0	Item Model Number
COMP_CFG	N	12.0	Computer Configuration No.
PRICE	N	10.2	Price of Item
ROOM	C	5.0	Room Location of Item
EMP_ID	N	12.0	Identification of employee to whom item is assigned

COMPUTER

Column Name	Field Type	Number of Characters	Description
COMP_CFG	N	12.0	Computer Configuration Number
CPU	C	10.0	Type of Computer CPU
HDRIVE	C	10.0	Type of Hard Drive
RAM	C	5.0	Amount of Main Memory
GRAPHICS	C	10.0	Type of Graphics Board
INPUT	C	15.0	Type of Input Device

EMPLOYEE

Column Name	Field Type	Number of Characters	Description
EMP_ID	N	12.0	Employee Identification No.
LAST_NAME	C	25.0	Employee's Last Name
FIRST_NAME	C	15.0	Employee's First Name
DEPT	C	40.0	Employee's Department No.
TITLE	C	25.0	Employee's Position Title
ROOM	C	5.0	Employee's Room Assignment
EXT	C	6.0	Employee's Phone Extension

Let's take a brief look at how the data is set up. The table structure on the previous page describes the data that you'll place into each table. For example, the COMPUTER table will have six columns. The first column is called COMP_CFG and contains a number (hence, the N, for Numeric). It can hold a maximum of 12 numbers, which represent a computer configuration number. We'll assume that this database is used in a company that has several standard computer configurations.

The second column in the COMPUTER table is the CPU column. Note that it's a character field and can contain a maximum of 10 letters, numbers or a combination of letters and numbers. The data contained in this field will describe the type of CPU (286, 386, 486, Sparc, etc.) belonging to the computer system.

Notice also that some column names appear in more than one table. This convention helps tie the information in the tables together—when you wish to pull information from more than one table at a time.

A Sample Data Set

When you're trying to picture a database structure, it's sometimes helpful to look at a set of sample data that will fit into the database. The data that fits into the COMPUTER table is shown below:

486/33	300Mb	8Mb	Super VGA	Digitizer
286/12	60Mb	640K	VGA	Mouse
MACIILC	40Mb	2Mb	Standard	Mouse
386SX/16	80Mb	4Mb	VGA	Mouse
386/33	300Mb	6Mb	VGA	Mouse
SPARC2	600Mb	16Mb	Standard	Mouse

Each row in the above listing is a description for a computer configuration. From left to right, the first item in each row is the CPU type. The hard disk type (size) is next, followed by the size of the main memory, the type of display board (or adapter) and then the input device type. ASE will keep track of this part of the data. Notice that this set of data does not contain the computer configuration number. That's because that number belongs to another file. When you define your table structure, you can see this item in the inventory table or in the computer table.

The database files are already created for you in this example, but you can create your own files for other applications using your DBMS. After you've created the database files, you're ready to use ASE to work with the data as it relates to your drawing.

NOTE: Before going any further in this example, make a copy of each of the database files because ASE will change the files with the .DBF extensions. At the DOS prompt, you can copy the files as follows:

Type: CD \ACAD\TUTORIAL\DBF <Return>

Type: COPY *.DBF *.BKU <Return>

You now have a copy of each database file, each with the .BKU extension. You can copy any or all of these files back to their original names for further practice with this example. If you don't make a .BKU (backup) copy of these files, you'll have to reload them from your original AutoCAD installation disks.

The ACADASE Layer

When you initialize ASE, it creates in your drawing a special layer called ACADASE that ASE uses to store database information as you save and end the drawing. As you reload the drawing and reinitialize ASE, ASE looks for the ACADASE layer to reestablish the database information that was there in the previous editing session.

NOTE: Do not change the ACADASE layer in any way! If you make any changes to it, you risk losing the links between your drawing and the external database.

Dialogue Box Usage

ASE's dialogue boxes are powerful tools that will guide you in your use of ASE. Each dialogue box gives you a graphical interface that assists you in building your database application. You also can run ASE directly from the command prompt, which is also a powerful feature when building macros or automated routines that bypass the dialogue boxes.

For your example, to utilize AutoCAD's dialogue boxes, turn on the dialogue boxes by doing the following:

Type: CMDDIA <Return>

Response: New value for CMDDIA <...>:

Type: 1 <Return>

NOTE: If CMMDIA is already set to 1, don't change it.

Initializing ASE

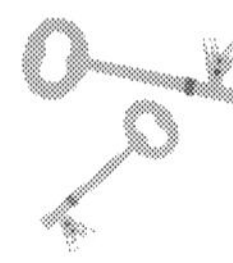

After bringing up your drawing, start ASE by picking Initialize from the ASE pull-down menu selection. See Figure 12-2, which shows the Initialize heading of the ASE pull-down menu.

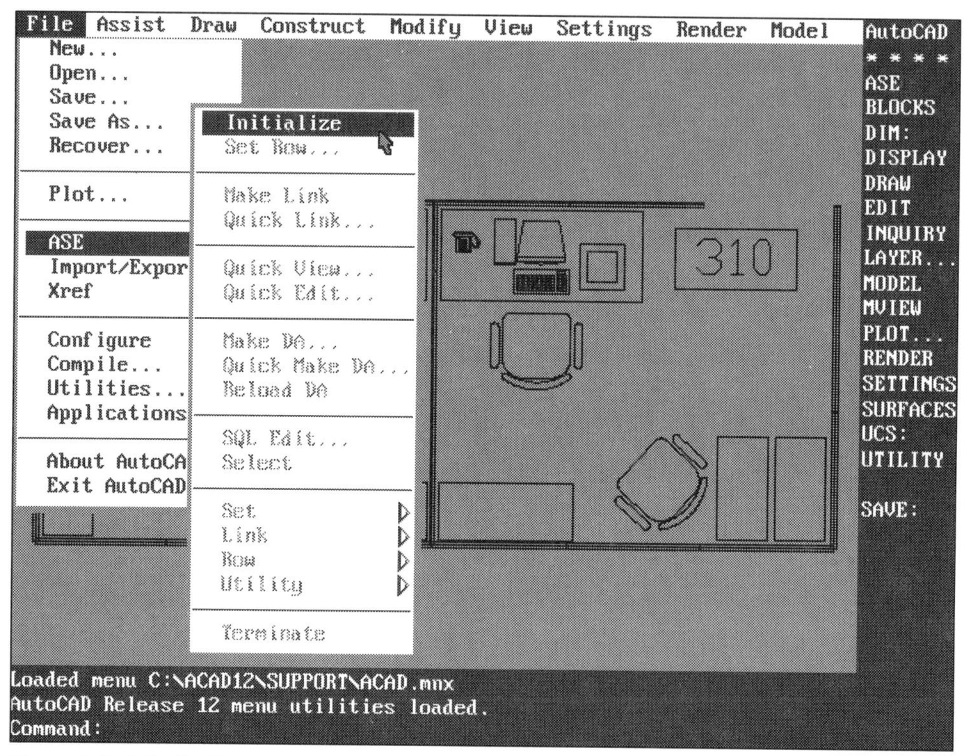

Figure 12-2: ASE Initialize menu selection

This procedure creates the ACADASE layer in your drawing that serves as the *control database.* If you have previously initialized ASE for a drawing and load the drawing to edit it, reinitializing the drawing will cause ASE to reestablish the relationships between the drawing entities and the external database that were made when the drawing was ended in the last editing session (as long as the database was not changed in the meantime).

Setting the DBMS Driver

The next step is to set the database management system (DBMS) driver that you'll be using. Pick the Set option and the DBMS... menu selection, as shown in Figure 12-3. The Set DBMS Driver dialogue box will appear. See Figure 12-4, which shows the Driver box and dBASE3 highlighted.

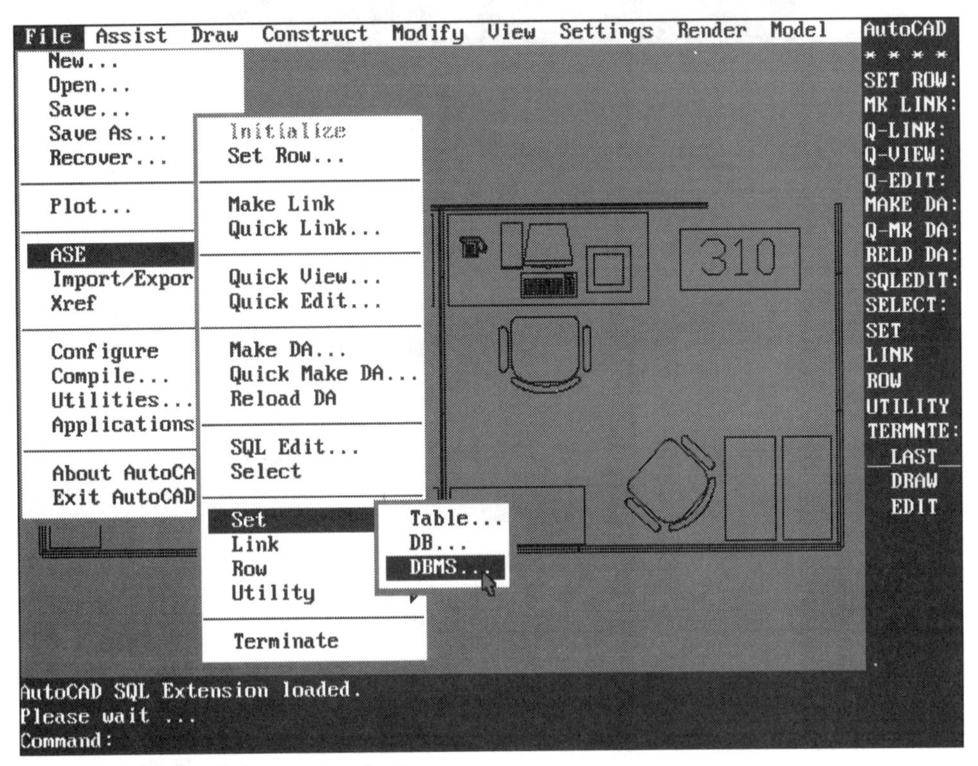

Figure 12-3: DBMS pull-down menu selection

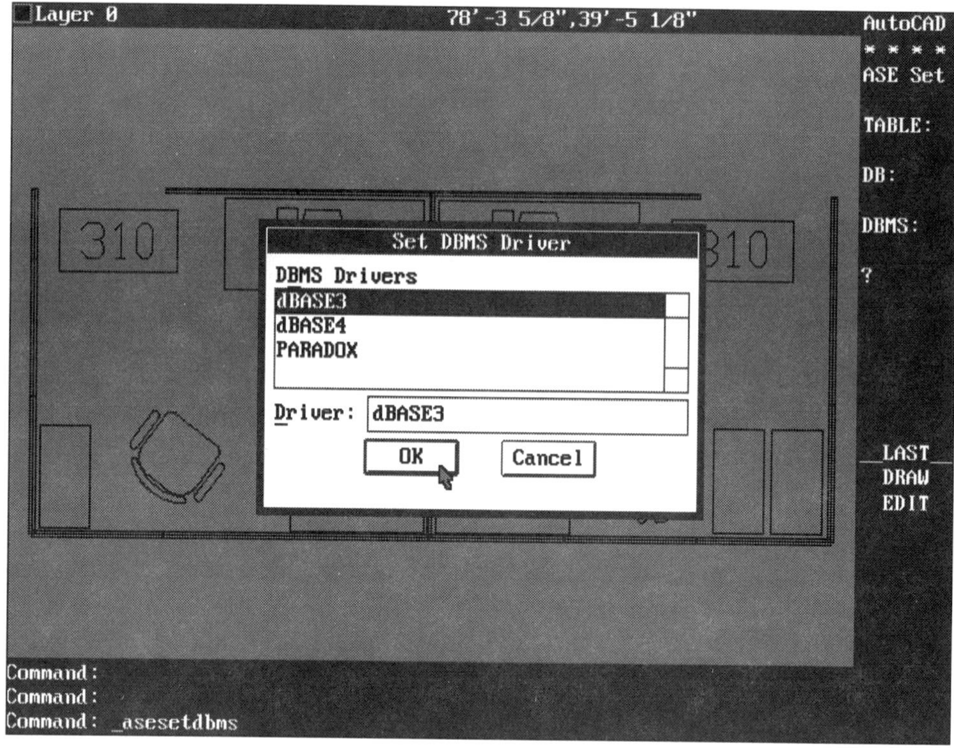

Figure 12-4: Set DBMS Driver dialogue box

For your example, use the dBASE3 DBMS driver. Pick the dBASE3 driver by double-clicking on the name or by clicking once on the name and then picking the OK box. dBASE3 is now the current DBMS driver.

Setting the Current Database

Set the database by first picking the DB... pull-down menu selection, as shown in Figure 12-5. The Set Current Database dialogue box will appear, as shown in Figure 12-6.

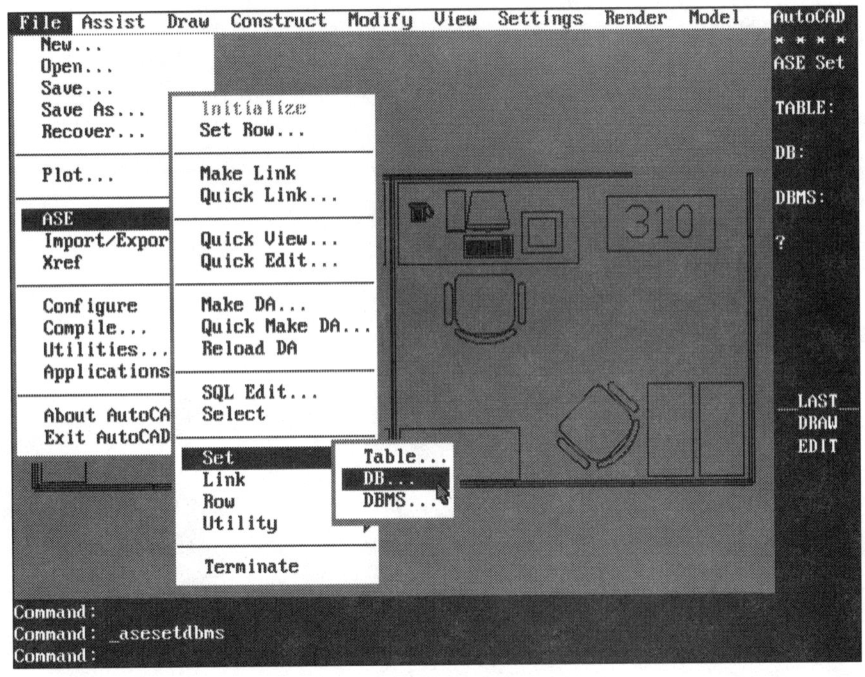

Figure 12-5: The DB... pull-down menu selection

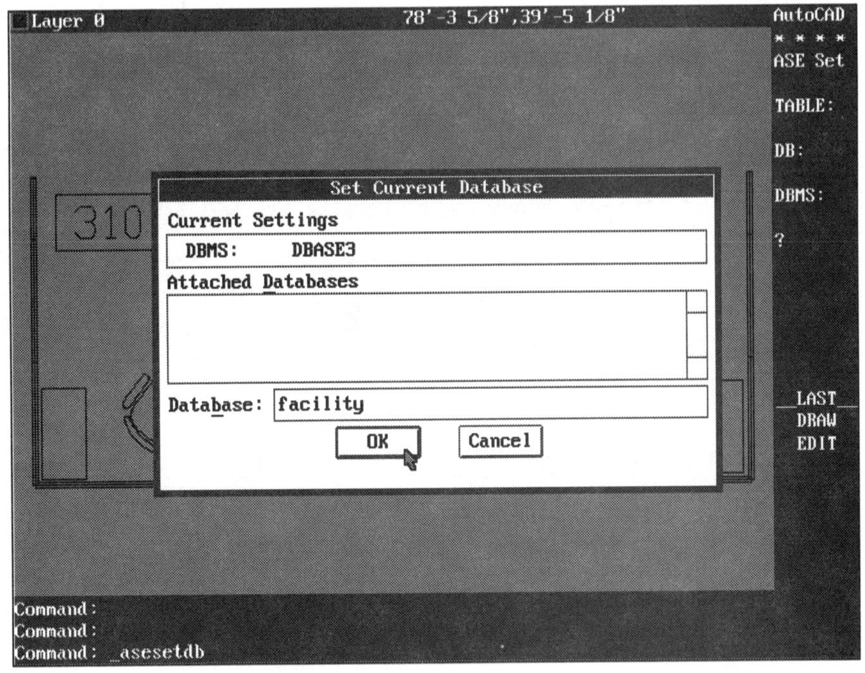

Figure 12-6: The Set Current Database dialogue box

Click in the Database box (so you can type in the box) and type the name of the database you wish to make current. Remember, the name of the database we saved in the DOS environment is FACILITY.

Type: `facility`

Then pick the OK button.

When you pick the OK button, the Set Database Please Enter dialogue box appears, prompting you to enter your username and password. Figure 12-7 shows this dialogue box.

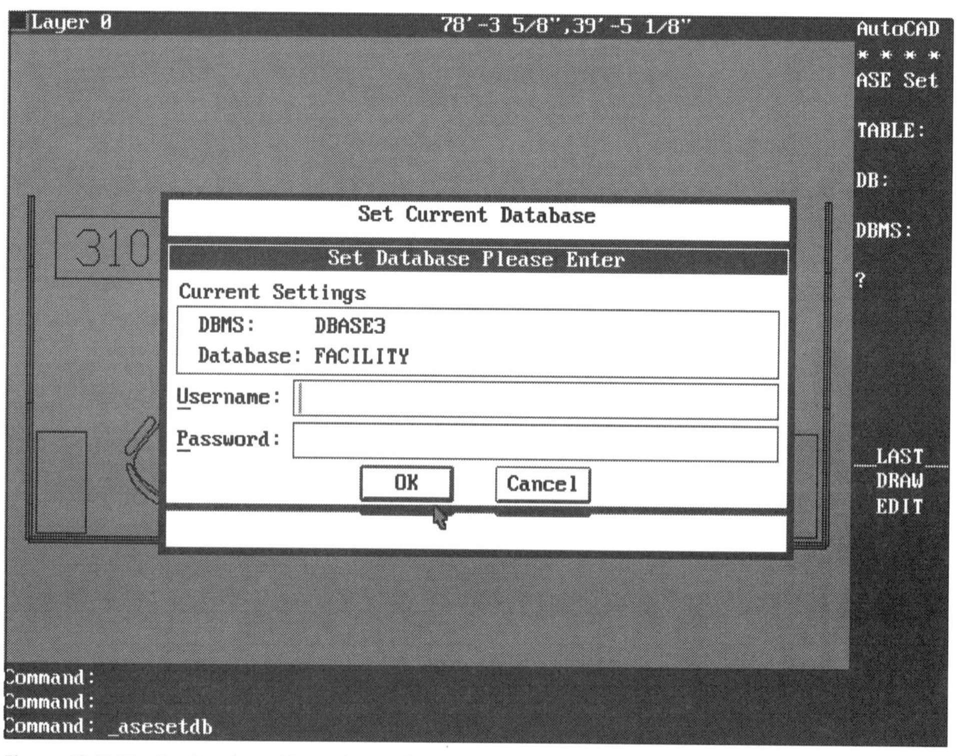

Figure 12-7: The Set Database Please Enter dialogue box

If your database requires a username and a password, you can enter them here. The example does not require a username or password, so bypass this dialogue box by clicking the OK button.

Setting the Current Table

You can now choose the tables that you'll use. We will make three tables available for use, and we'll make one of the three the current table (only one table can be current at a time). Pick the Table... pull-down menu selection, as shown in Figure 12-8. When you do, the Set Current Table dialogue box will appear, as shown in Figure 12-9.

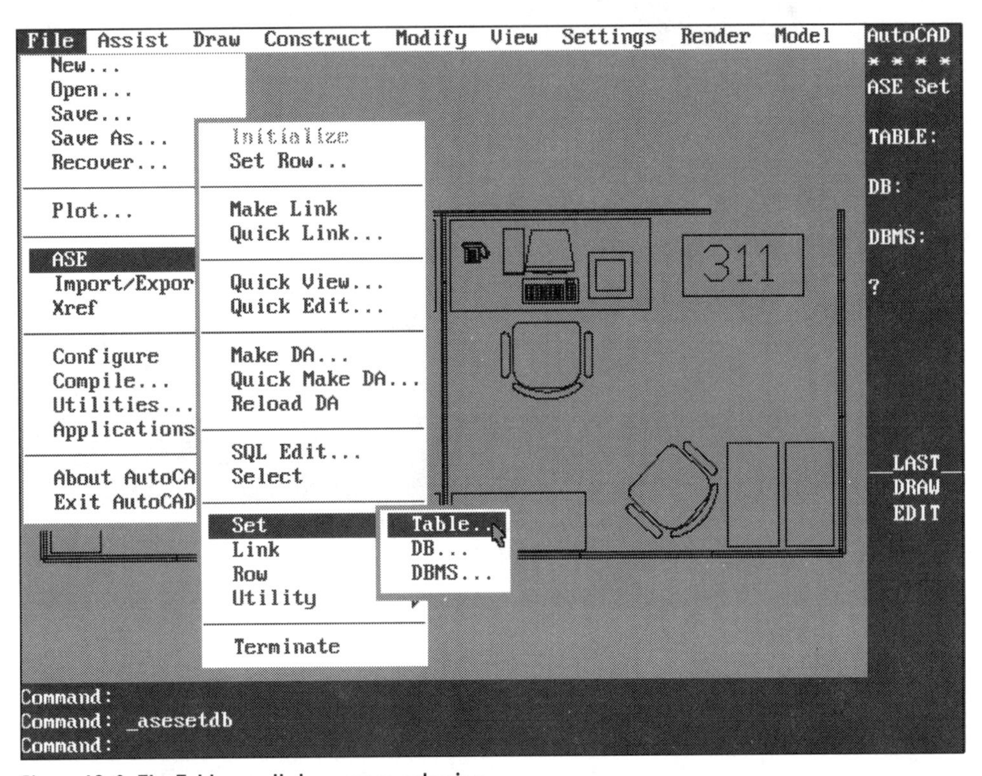

Figure 12-8: The Table... pull-down menu selection

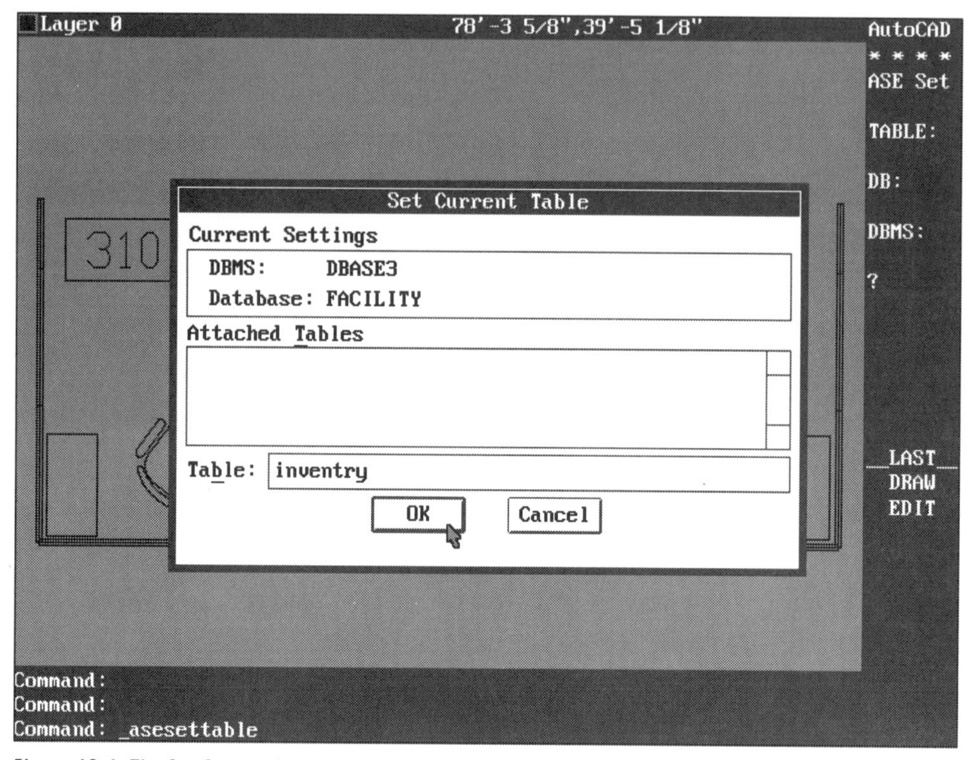

Figure 12-9: The Set Current Table dialogue box

Click in the Table box (near the bottom of the dialogue box) and then do the following:

Type: `inventry`

Then click the OK button. The Select Key Columns dialogue box will appear, as shown in Figure 12-10.

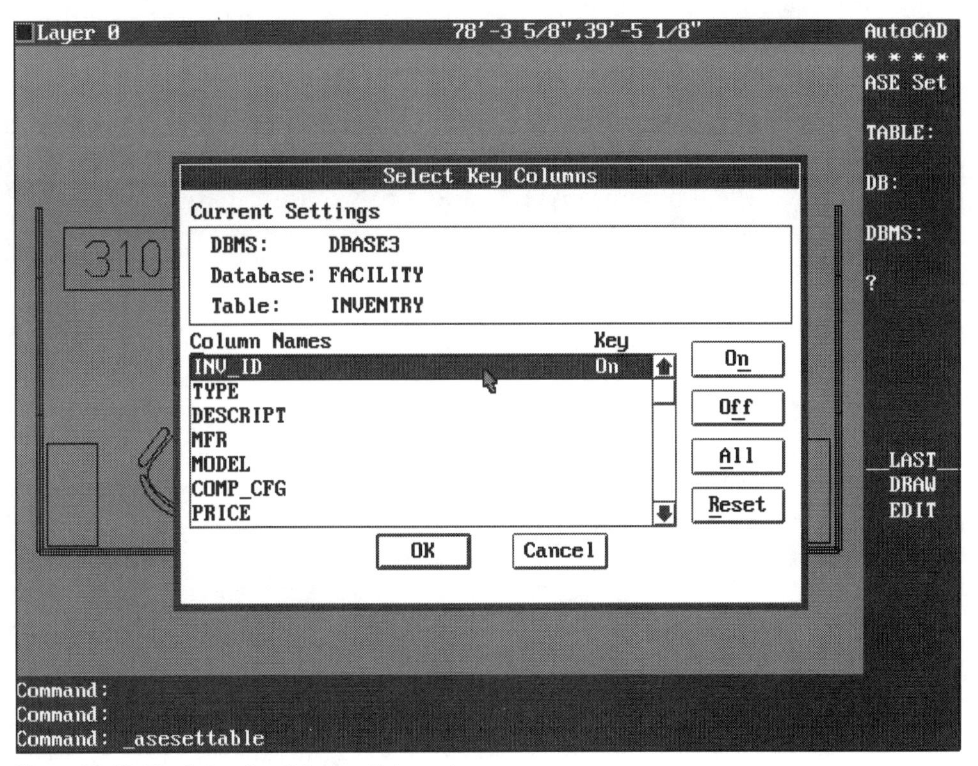

Figure 12-10: The Select Key Columns dialogue box

Designate the INV_ID column as a Key value by double-clicking on that column name. You'll know it has been designated as a Key column because the word *On* will appear to the right of the INV_ID column name. Look at Figure 12-10 to see this feature. Pick the OK button to close the dialogue box. As you'll note from Figure 12-10, the Key identifies a specific row in the table as a unique selection. In some database applications, more than one Key is sometimes necessary to achieve this effect.

The INVENTRY table is now available and current. Now make the COMPUTER table available and current, just as you did the INVENTRY table. In the COMPUTER table, choose the COMP_CFG column name as the Key. Finally, make the EMPLOYEE table available and current. Choose the EMP_ID column name as the Key.

When you've finished making tables available, all the tables will be available, but only the last table you chose will be the current table (you can make any table current by setting it as the current table at any time).

ASE's Viewing & Editing Tools

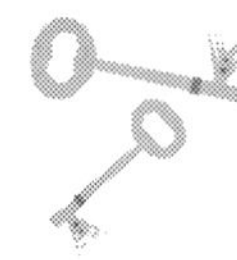

ASE lets you view and edit the current database. As you already know, your database consists of three files: INVENTRY.DBF, COMPUTER.DBF and EMPLOYEE.DBF. The database name is FACILITY.

We'll now use ASE to add a row of information to the EMPLOYEE table of the database. First, we'll set a row as the current row so we can use it as a template for creating a new row. Pick Set Row... from the pull-down menu, as shown in Figure 12-11. The Set Row Options dialogue box will appear, as shown in Figure 12-12.

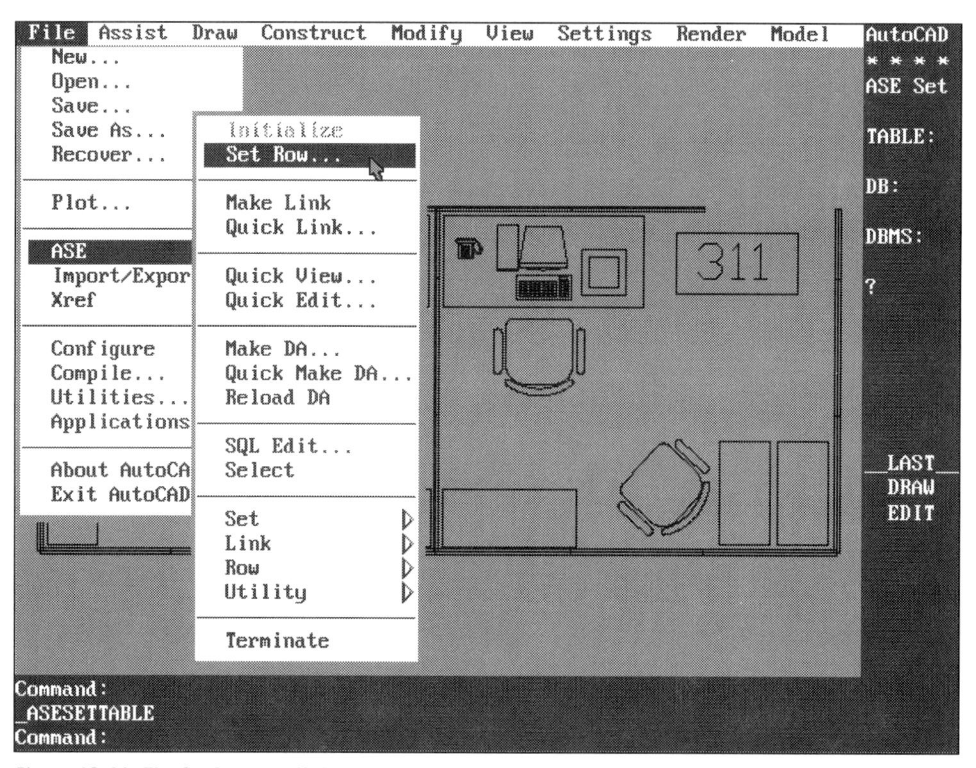

Figure 12-11: The Set Row... pull-down menu selection

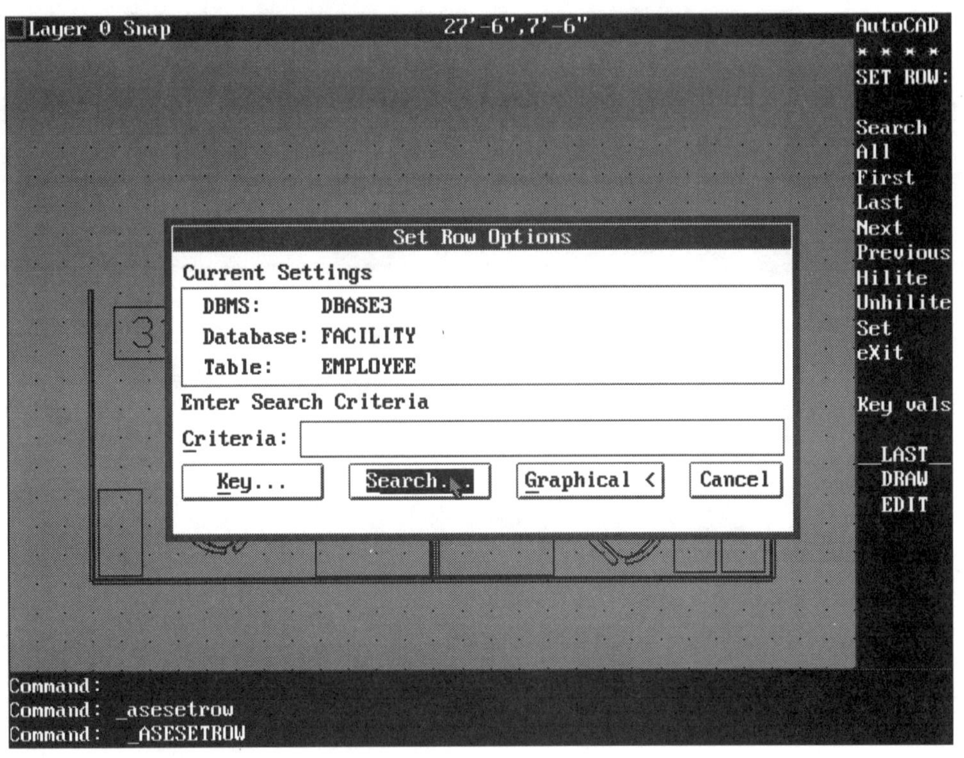

Figure 12-12: The Set Row Options dialogue box

Because you may not be sure which row to pick as a template, let's look at all the rows available. On the dialogue box, pick the Search... button. Now the Set Current Row by Search Criteria dialogue box appears. You see a view of it in Figure 12-13.

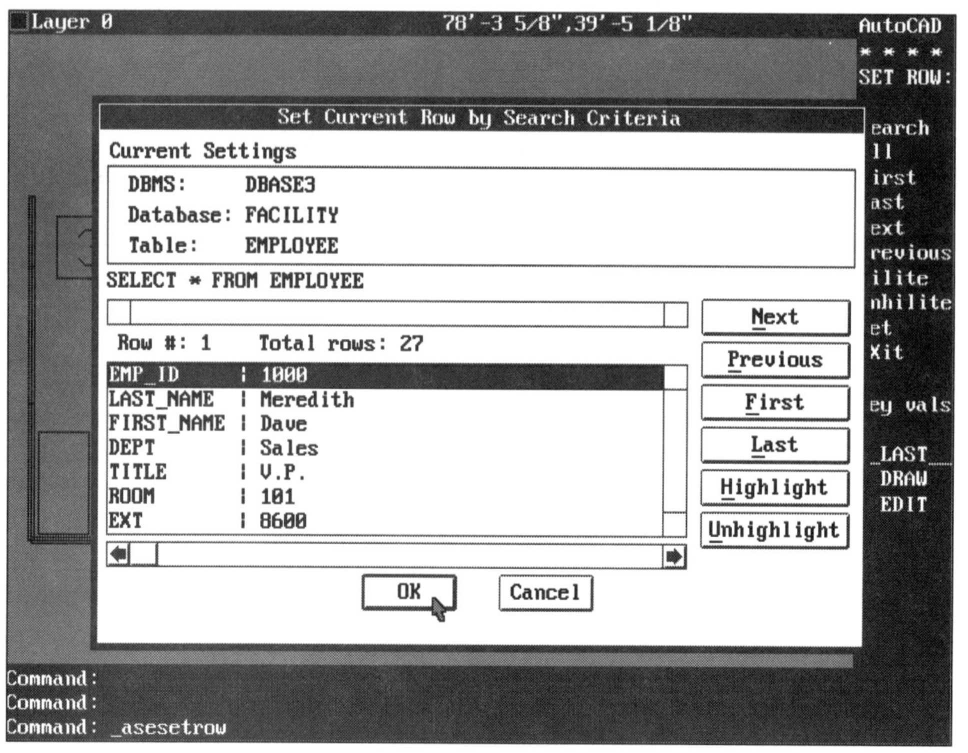

Figure 12-13: The Set Current Row by Search Criteria dialogue box

This dialogue box contains each row from the EMPLOYEE table. Each row consists of the employee ID (EMP_ID), the employee's last and first name, the department, position title, room number and telephone extension. You can look at each row in the table by picking the navigation buttons (Next, Previous, First, Last) on the right-hand side of the dialogue box. Pick the First button to set the first row as the current row. Then pick the OK button to accept your choice.

Adding a Row to the EMPLOYEE Table

You're now ready to add a new row to the EMPLOYEE table. By adding a new row, you add an additional employee to the table. Pick Add... from the pull-down menu, as shown in Figure 12-14. The Add Row dialogue box will appear, as shown in Figure 12-15.

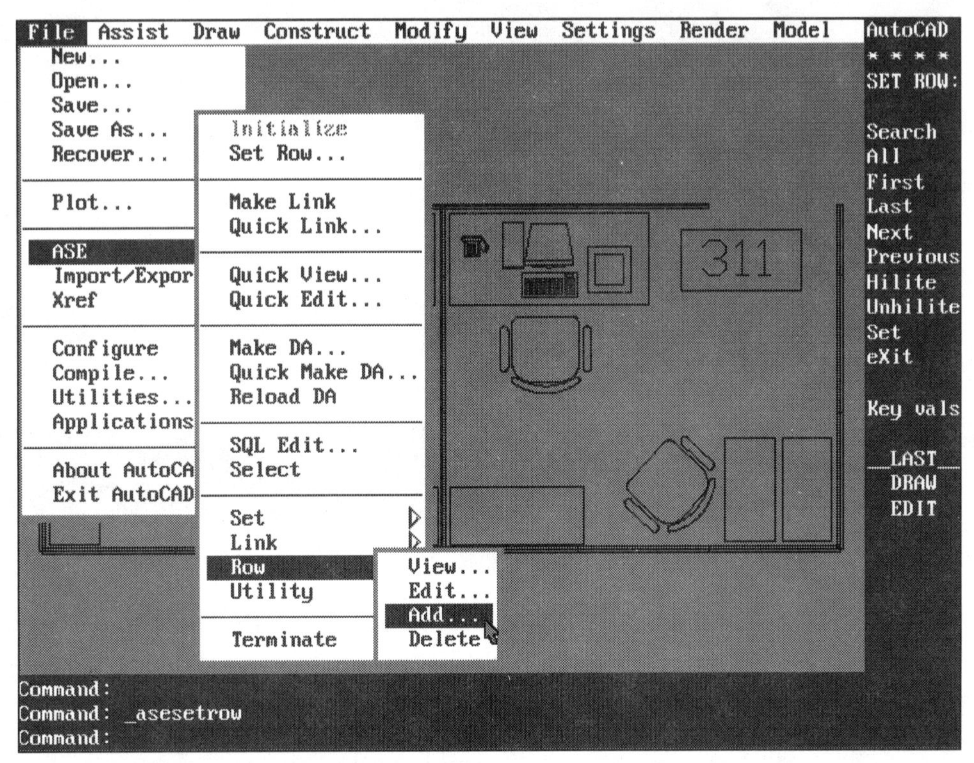

Figure 12-14: The Add... pull-down menu selection

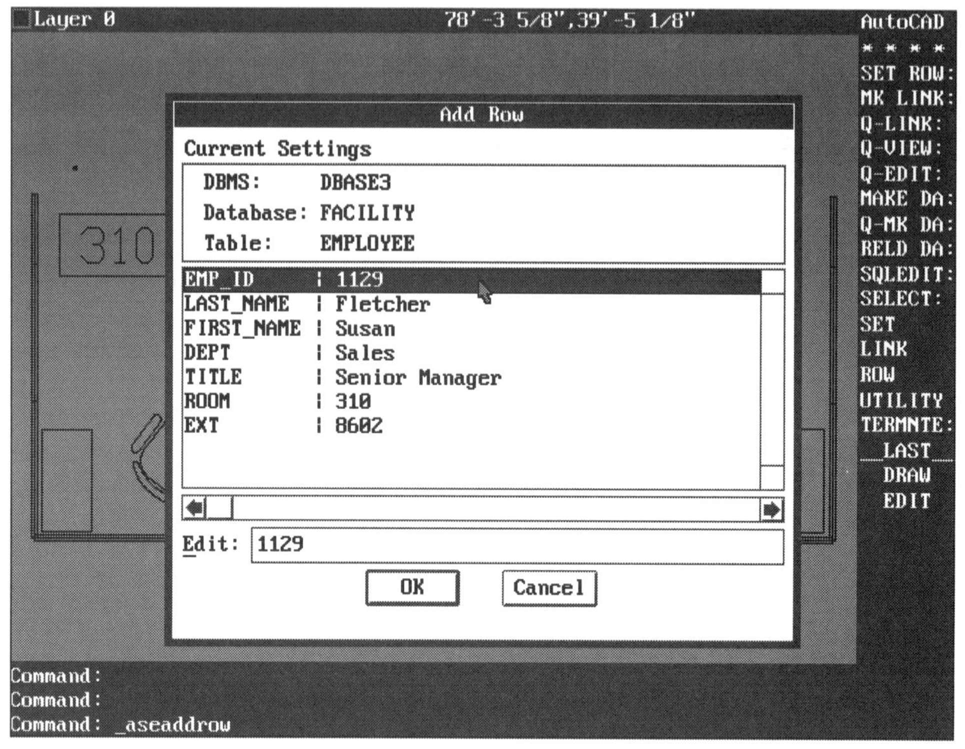

Figure 12-15: The Add Row dialogue box

Your dialogue box will contain information for Dave Meredith. The information you see in your dialogue box is a template you use as you add an additional row. Double-click on the EMP_ID data. Double-clicking will cause the employee identification number to appear highlighted in the Edit box. Then type the new ID number as it's shown in Figure 12-15 and press the Return key to update the column data.

Now double-click on the LAST_NAME data, type the new employee name (**Fletcher**) and press the Return key. Do the same for each item that must be changed. The DEPT data is already correct, so you won't need to change it.

When you're finished making changes, pick the OK button to accept your work. The new employee has now been added to the EMPLOYEE table in the database. If you want to look at the new row as you have added it, you can see it in the View Row dialogue box by picking the View option from the Row pull-down menu selection or by typing **ASEVIEWROW** at the command prompt.

Setting a Row by Key Value

Let's now make a change to a row by selecting it by Key Values and then change it by using the Edit Row menu selection. Pick Set Row... from the pull-down menu (as you did earlier in the example) and then pick Key... from the Set Row Options dialogue box, as shown in Figure 12-16.

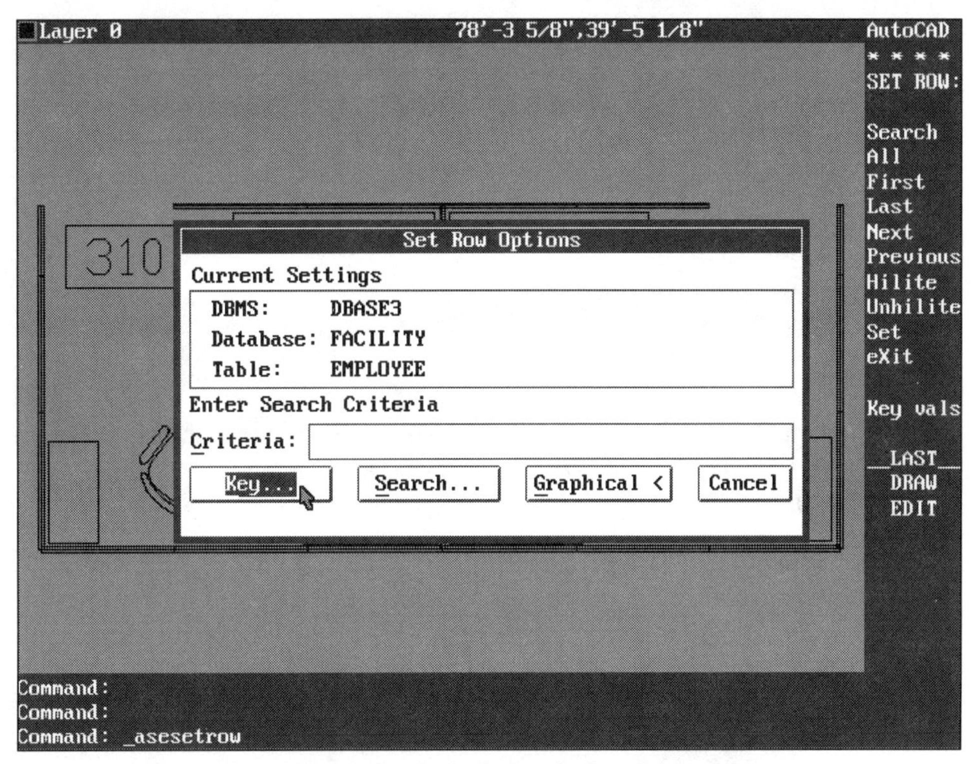

Figure 12-16: The highlighted Key... button in the Set Row Options dialogue box

When the Set Current Row by Key Values dialogue box appears, (see Figure 12-17), type **1004** in the Edit box and press the Return key or accept your choice by picking the OK button.

Pick Edit... from the Row —> Edit... pull-down menu, as shown in Figure 12-18. The Edit Row dialogue box will appear, as shown in Figure 12-19.

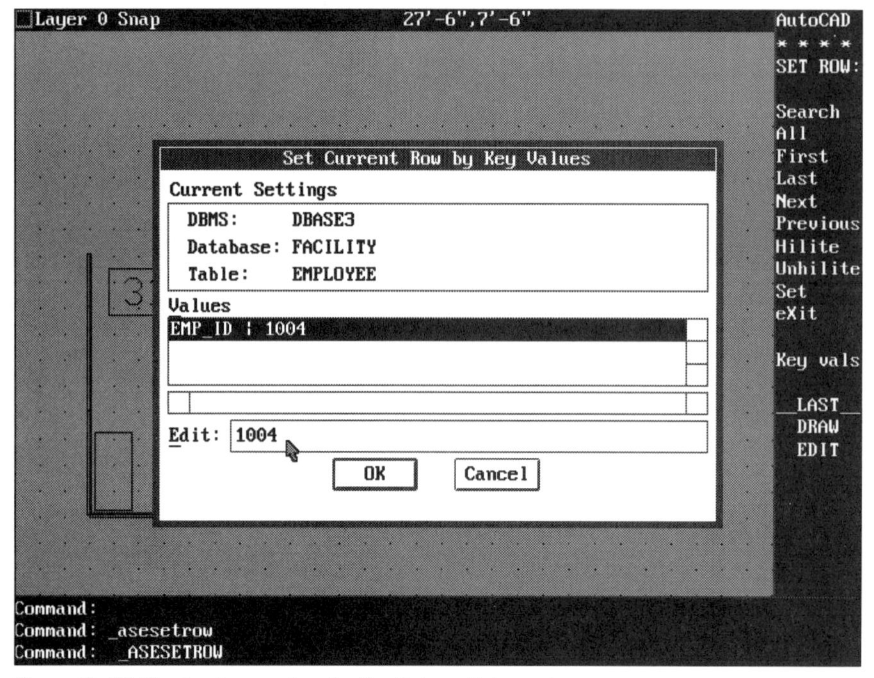

Figure 12-17: The Set Current Row by Key Values dialogue box

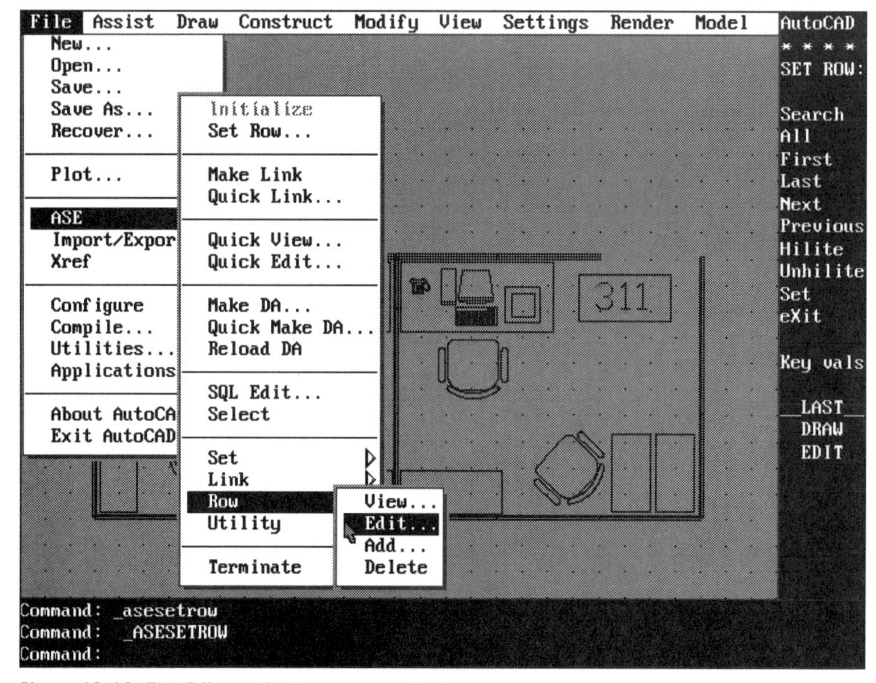

Figure 12-18: The Edit... pull-down menu selection

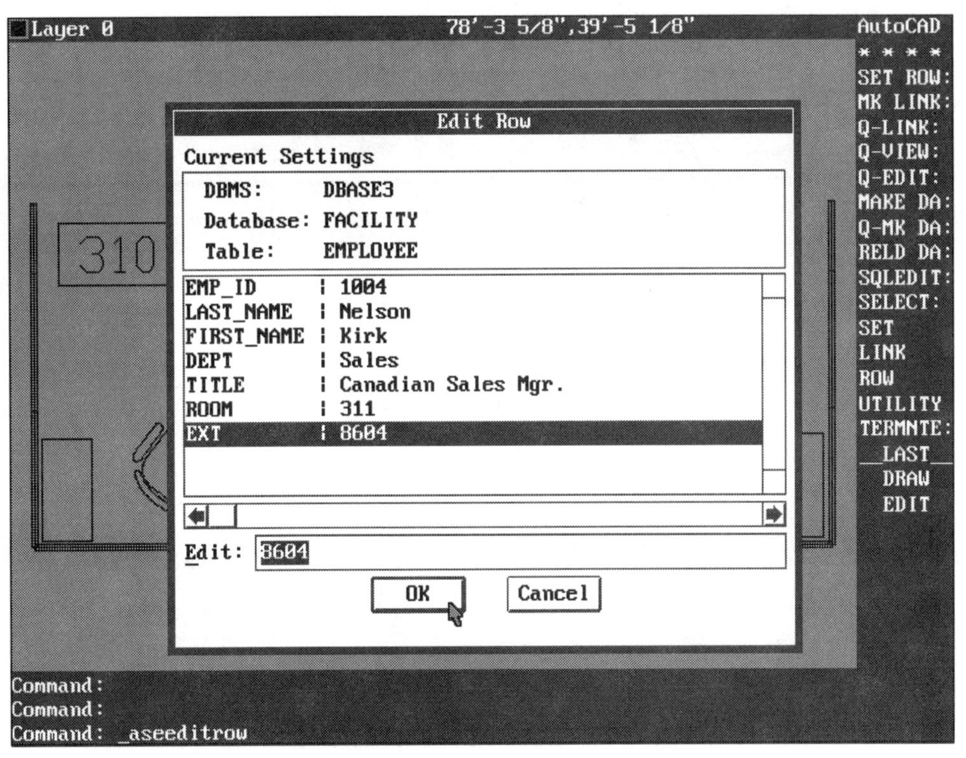

Figure 12-19: The Edit Row dialogue box

Double-click on the data to be changed and then change the room number to 311 and the phone extension to 8604. (Remember to press the Return key after making each change.) Then pick the OK button to accept your changes. These changes have now been written to the external database.

Deleting a Row in a Table

If an employee leaves the company, you can delete his or her name and accompanying information by setting his or her row as the current row and then giving the ASEDELROW command. For your example, set the current row belonging to Frank Thompson by using search criteria. See Figure 12-20. Pick Set Row... from the pull-down menu, pick in the Criteria box and then do the following:

Type: `first_name='Frank' and last_name='Thompson' <Return>`

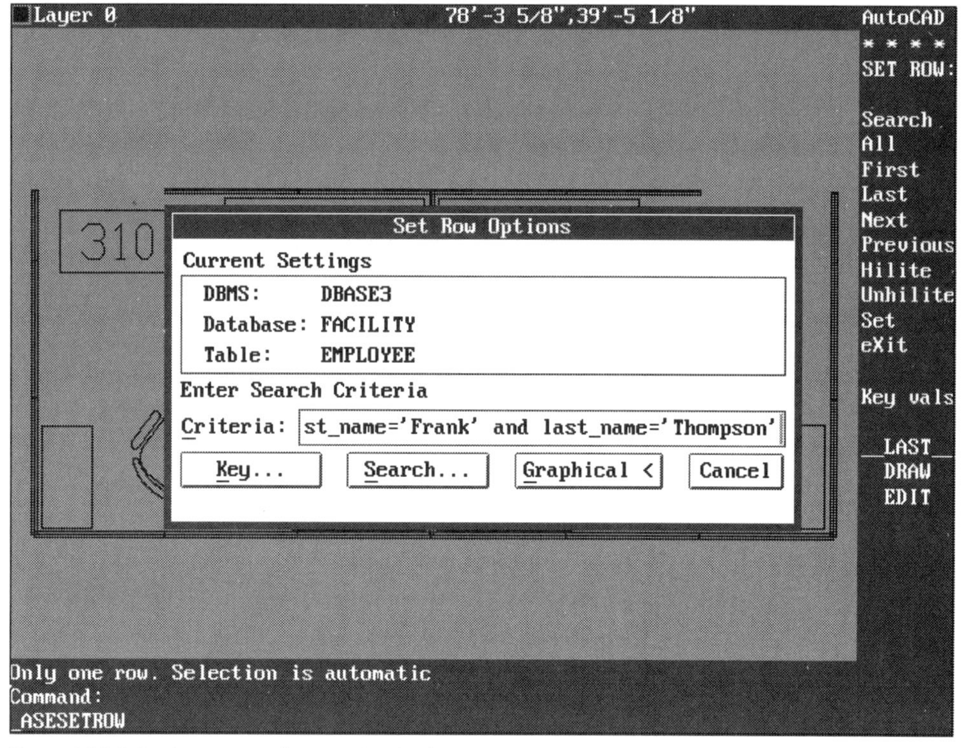

Figure 12-20: Setting a row using search criteria

The row containing the above information is set as the current row. Now, at the command prompt, do the following:

Type: `ASEDELROW <Return>`

You will be prompted by an ASE Confirmation dialogue box with a Delete current row? message highlighted. To confirm the deletion of the current row, pick the Yes button.

NOTE: Although the row appears to have been deleted, dBASE requires you to PACK the database from the dBASE program before the row is actually deleted.

Linking Your Drawing to the Database

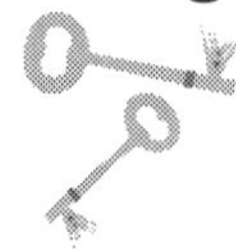

Even though you've been able to make changes to the external database using ASE, the entities in your drawing are not yet linked to any part of the database. Let's begin by linking the chairs in office 310 to a row in the database. Each chair in the database has a unique identification number (INV_ID), so each chair in the drawing will be linked to a separate row.

Set the current table to INVENTRY, then pick Set Row... and set the current row by using search criteria (pick Search... from the Set Current Row dialogue box, without typing any criteria in the box). Use the Next navigation button on the right side of the Set Current Row by Search Criteria dialogue box to move to row number 2 (see Figure 12-21). Pick OK to accept row 2 as the current row.

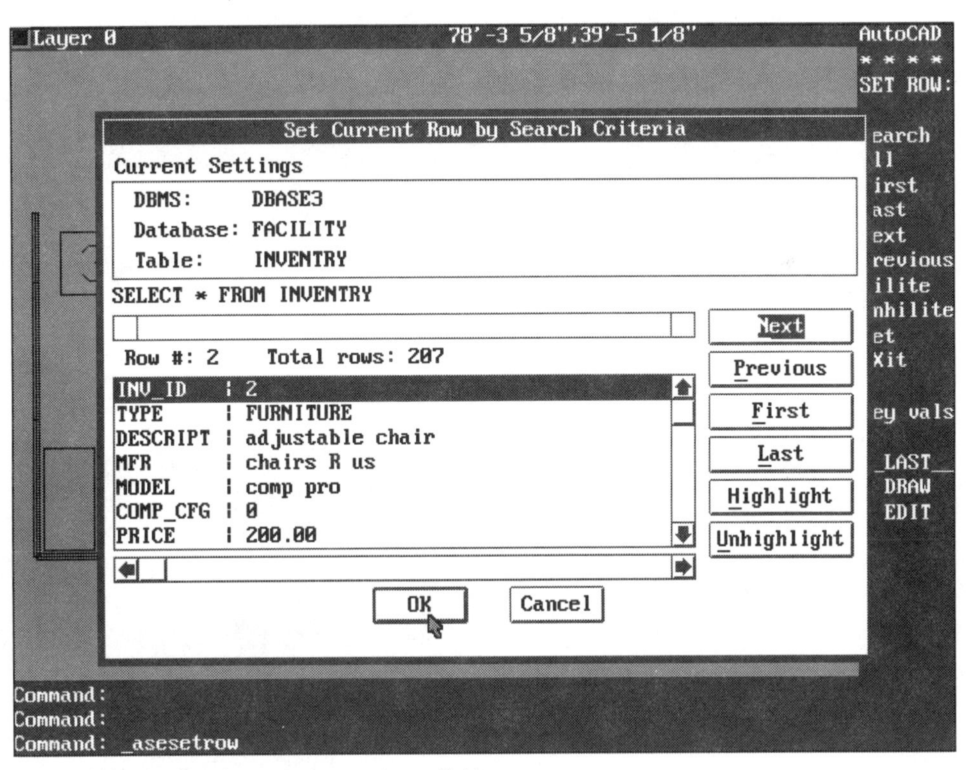

Figure 12-21: Setting the current row prior to linking

Now change the ownership of the chair by editing the current row, just as you edited the row for Frank Thompson. Pick Row —> Edit... and then change the room number to 310 and the employee identification number (EMP_ID) to 1129. See Figure 12-22. Pick OK to accept your changes.

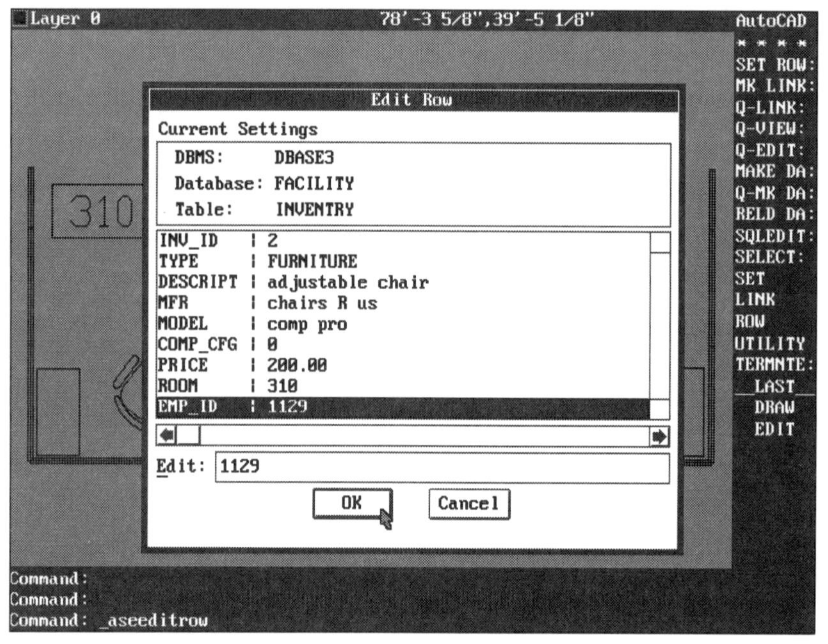

Figure 12-22: Changing ownership of the chair by editing a row

You can now link the chair entity in the drawing to the current row in the table. Pick Make Link from the pull-down menu, as shown in Figure 12-23.

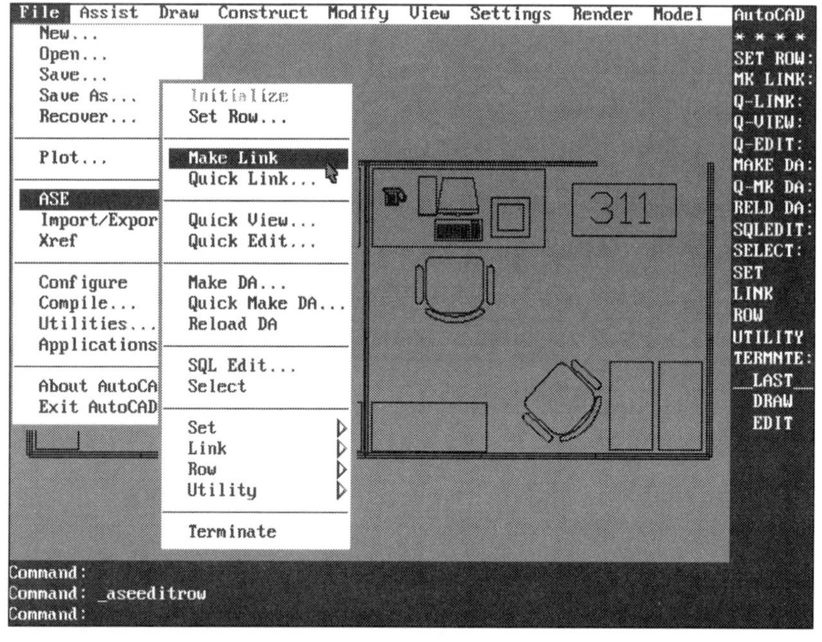

Figure 12-23: The Make Link pull-down menu selection

Response: `Select object(s):`

Select the chair at the desk in room 310 and press the Return key. The link from the chair to the current row in the database has now been made! You can view the link by typing **ASEVIEWLINK** at the command prompt.

Type: `aseviewlink <Return>`

Response: `Select object:`

Pick the chair and the dialogue box will appear. Figure 12-24 shows the View Link dialogue box you've just picked.

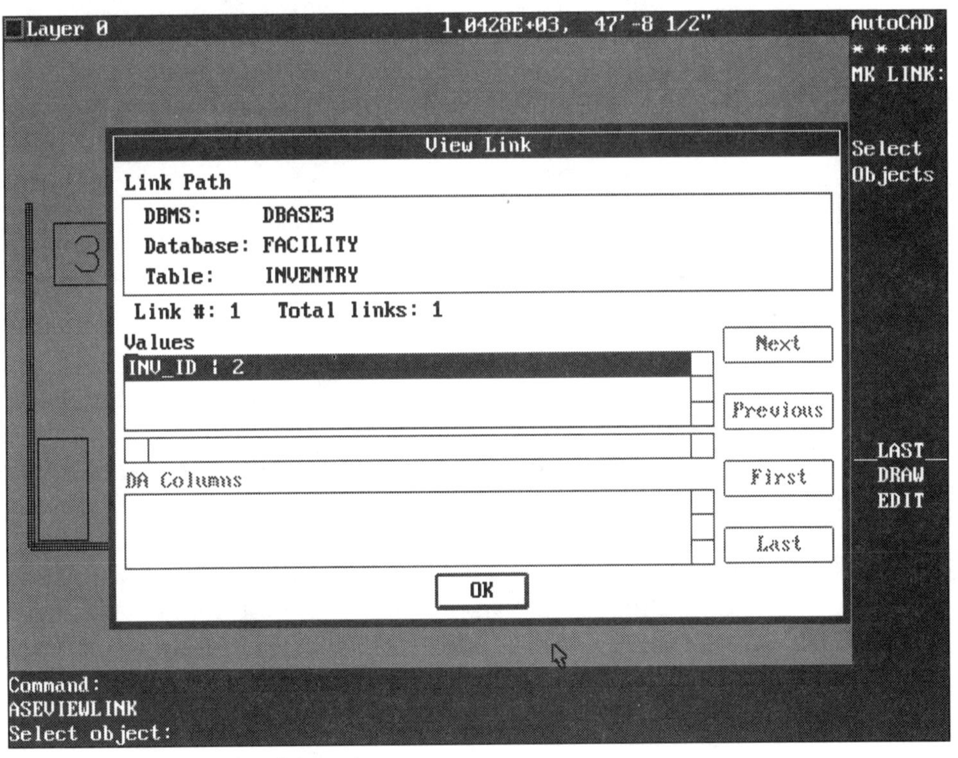

Figure 12-24: The View Link dialogue box

Linking with Quick Link (ASEQLINK)

Now let's link the other chair in office number 310, but this time we'll use ASE's Quick Link feature. Pick Quick Link... from the pull-down menu, as shown in Figure 12-25.

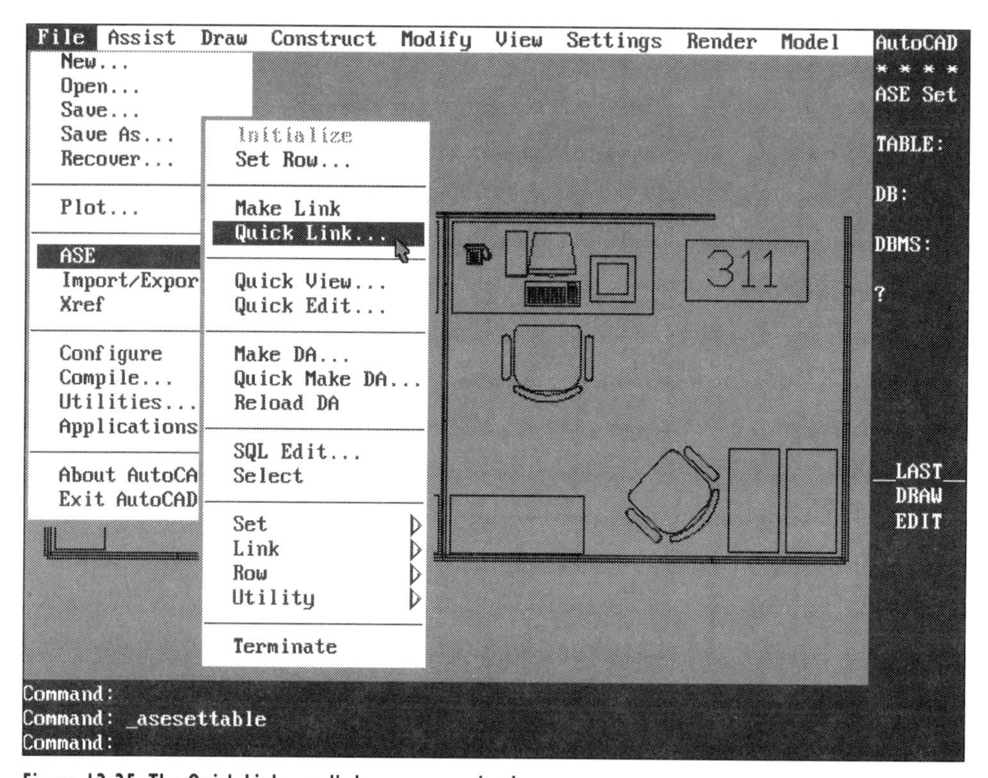

Figure 12-25: The Quick Link... pull-down menu selection

The Quick Link capability will let you set the row (choose the row with *(INV_ID=3)*) and pick the chair as one continuous operation. After linking the chair, edit the row so that the second chair is owned by the same employee (Susan Fletcher) as the first chair.

Linking to Two or More Rows

Now let's link the computer in room 310 with its proper row in the COMPUTER table and also with another row that you'll create in the INVENTRY table. You'll use the Quick Link feature to link the computer to the COMPUTER table. First, set the current database, choose Set —> Table... for the Computer table and then use Quick Link.... Then link the computer with the row as shown in Figure 12-26. Then pick Set Row..., then Search... and pick Next until you get to row 5, as shown in Figure 12-26.

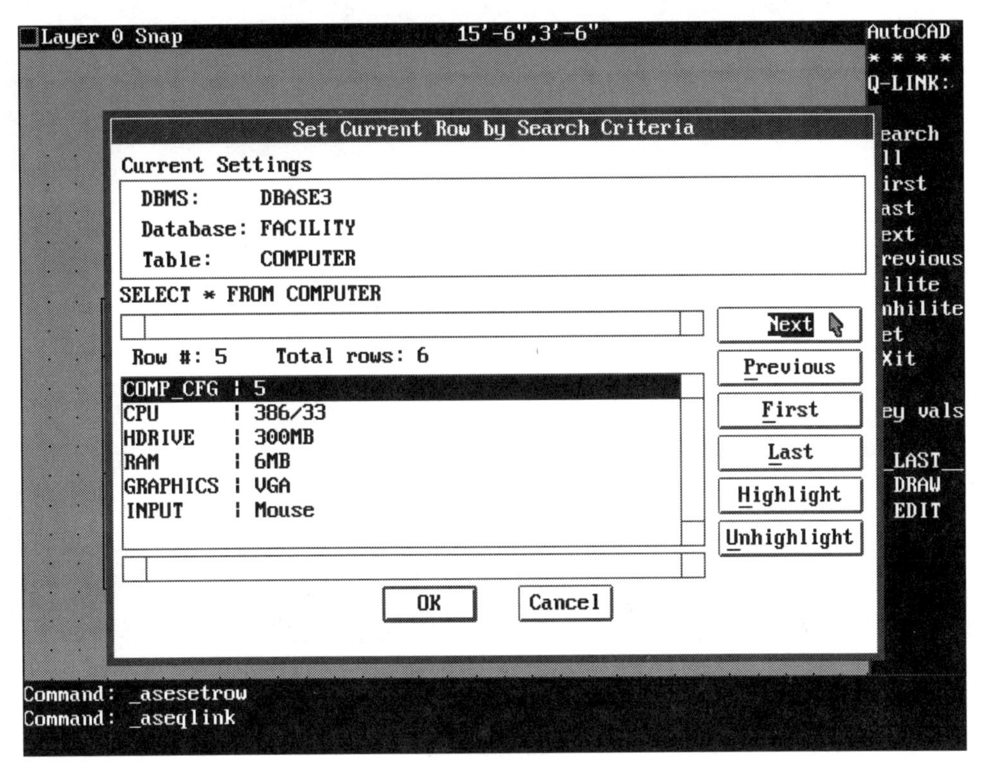

Figure 12-26: Preparing to link to row 5 in the COMPUTER table

Now that you've linked the computer in room 310 with a row in the COMPUTER table, you're almost ready to link it with a row in the INVENTRY table, but first you'll need to add a row to the INVENTRY table. Set the INVENTRY table as the current table using the ASESETTABLE command or by picking Set and then Table... from the pull-down menu.

Next, in the INVENTRY table, set a row that will work well as a template. Figure 12-27 shows a row from the INVENTRY table that will serve as a good template.

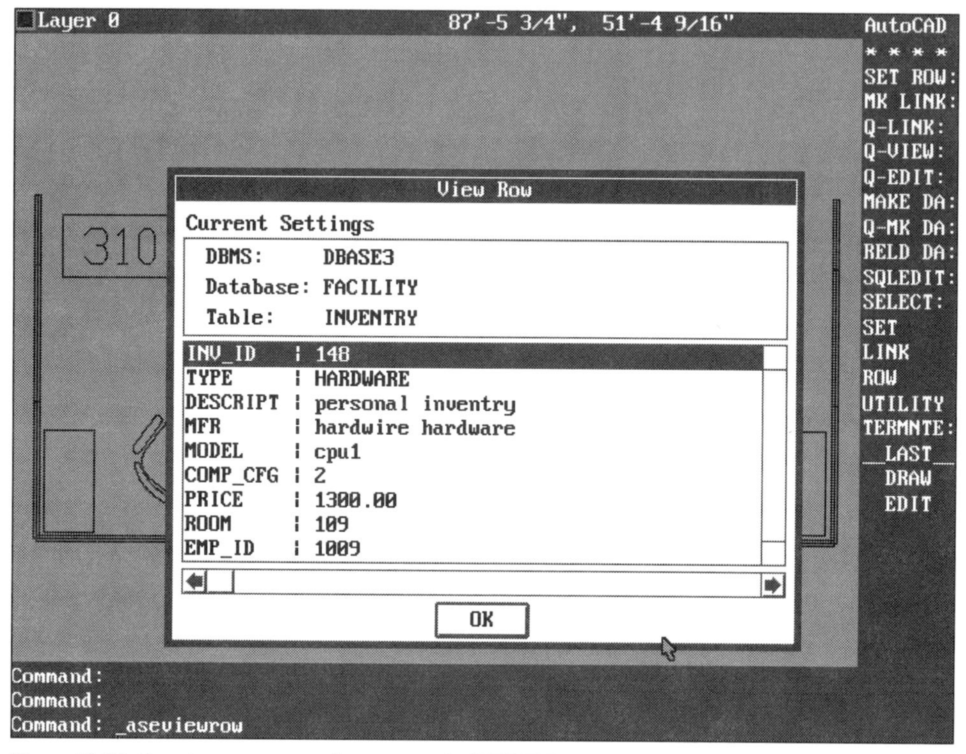

Figure 12-27: Template row to use for new row in INVENTRY table

You can set this row by Key value (the easiest way) or by using the Search method. The Search method will also be easy if you specify the inventory ID. If you search without any search criteria, you'll have to navigate through the table until you come to INV_ID=148 so that you can choose it for the current row.

After setting the template row as being current, use the ASEADDROW command or the Row —> Add... pull-down menu selection to add a row to the INVENTRY table. Remember to use the template to save time in filling in the new information for the new row. The row you add should look like the one in Figure 12-28.

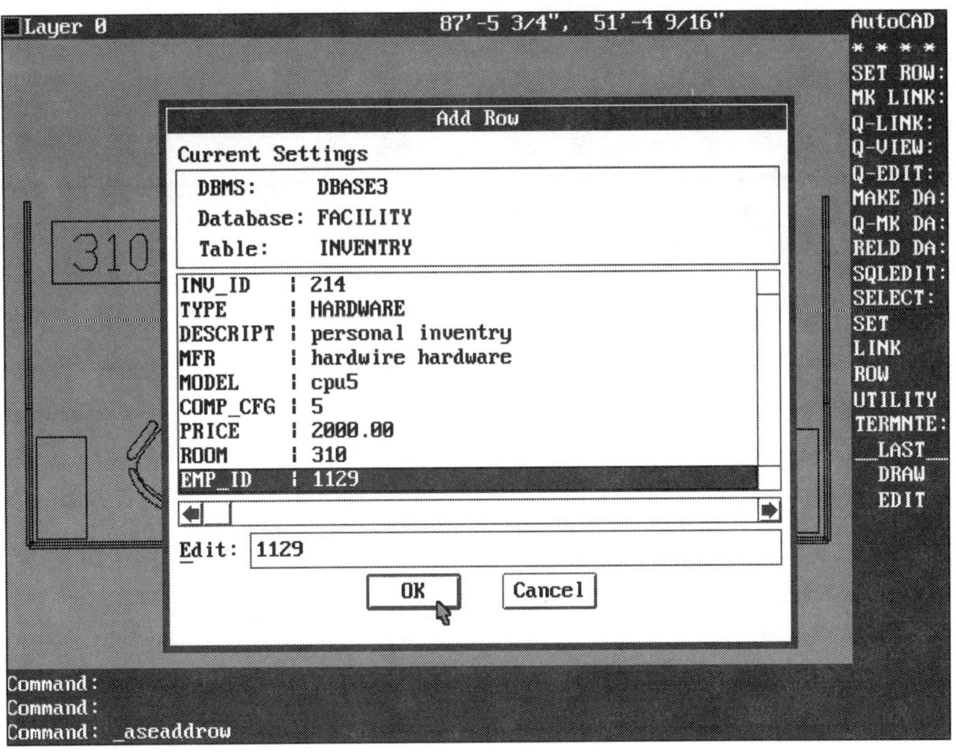

Figure 12-28: Using Add Row to add a row to the INVENTRY table

Now that you've added the new row and because it is still the current row, use ASEMAKELINK to link the computer to the new row.

NOTE: You could have used the Quick Link feature, but you may have had some difficulty because the computer is already linked to the COMPUTER table.

You can use the Quick View... feature (on the pull-down menu) to view the links associated with the computer. See Figure 12-29. One link is shown, and to move to the other link, pick the Next or Previous buttons.

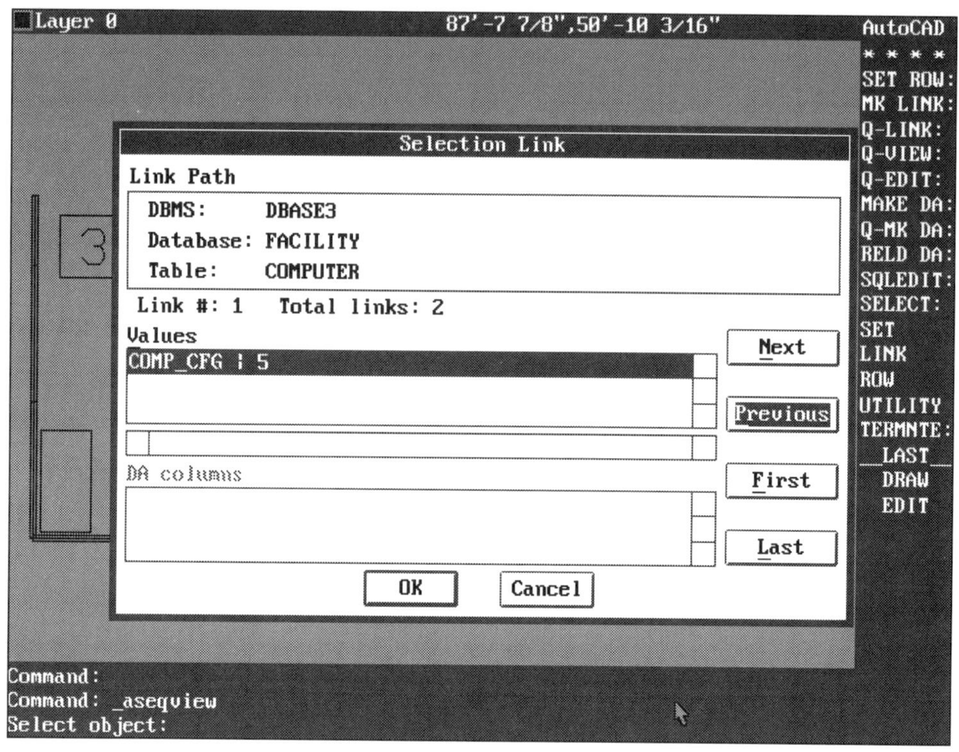

Figure 12-29: The Selection Link dialogue box

Linking Occupants to the Offices

Finally, let's link an employee name to office number 310. Set the EMPLOYEE table as the current table; then use Quick Link... to set the row and make the link. Choose the row containing Susan Fletcher, shown in Figure 12-30. When prompted to select objects, pick the box that surrounds the room number and then press the Return key. The box will be linked to the row containing the new employee's data in the EMPLOYEE table.

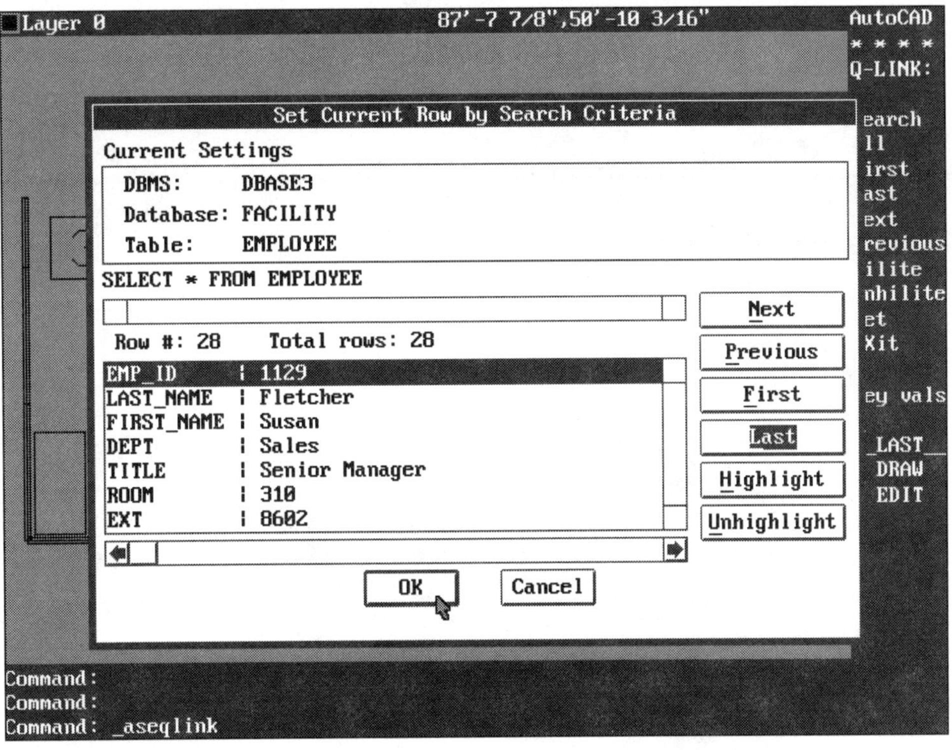

Figure 12-30: Preparing to link employee data to the drawing

Now that you've created several links, you can display some of your database information by using Displayable Attributes.

Displayable Attributes

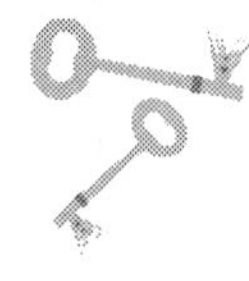

Displayable Attributes (DAs) have no relation to the familiar AutoCAD drawing attributes. DAs are the means whereby you can see portions of the external database in your AutoCAD drawing. A link allows an entity to be tied to the outside database, and DAs allow you to see a portion of that database. The portion of the database you see is user definable. Let's go ahead and make a displayable attribute.

The first step is to decide what table to get the displayable attribute data from. For this example, let's use the EMPLOYEE table and display the name of the employee who works in office number 310.

The next step is to create a link from the entity in the drawing whose table data will be displayed. You can create the link as you have in earlier examples in this chapter by using the ASESETROW and ASEMAKELINK commands or by using the ASEQLINK command. You've already established a link for the employee in office 310, so let's move on to the next step.

After establishing the link from the entity to the table, you can make the displayable attribute. You can either use the ASESETROW and ASEMAKEDA commands, or you can use the ASEQMAKEDA command. Let's use the pull-down menu to pick the ASEQMAKEDA command by picking the Make DA... pull-down menu selection. This selection causes the Make Displayable Attribute dialogue box to appear, as shown in Figure 12-31. (You'll have to pick a location <Start point>: and a height and a rotation angle.)

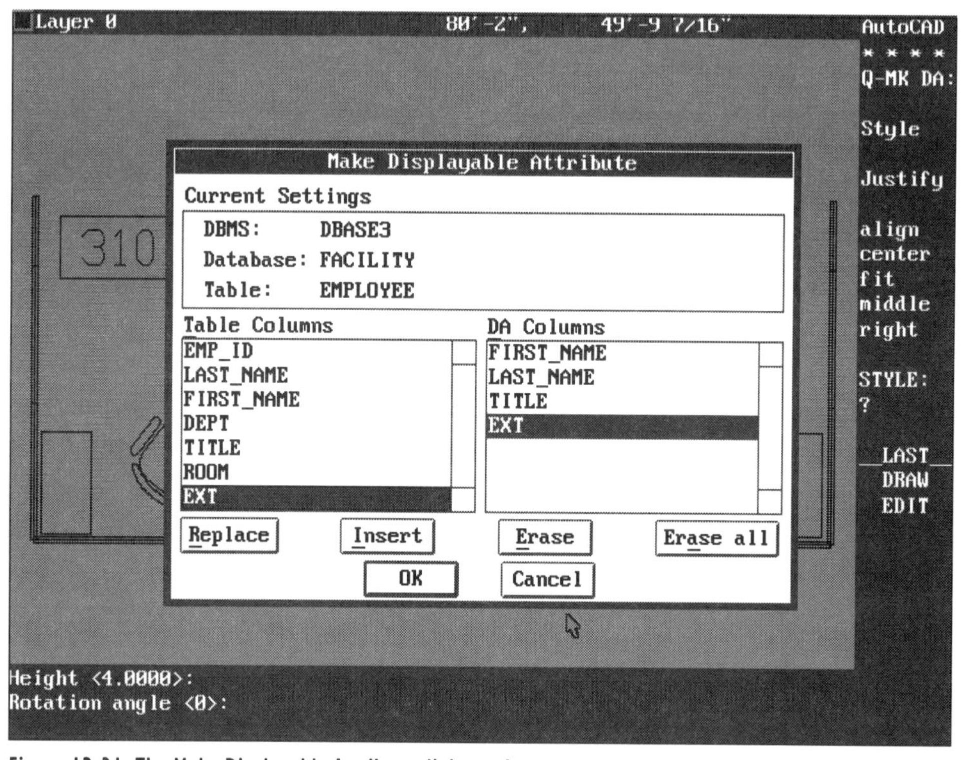

Figure 12-31: The Make Displayable Attribute dialogue box

Select the Table Columns items you wish to include as displayable attributes by double-clicking each desired item. Or you can single-click an item and then pick the Insert button. Each item you select is placed in the DA Columns area of the dialogue box. If you mistakenly place an item in the DA Columns area, select the item you wish to remove and pick Erase.

When you are finished selecting items, pick OK to accept your choices.

ASE will prompt you to select objects. Select the box that contains the office number 310 (don't select the number, just the box) and press the Return key. Remember, you'll be prompted to digitize a location for the DA and asked to specify a text height. If the AutoCAD coordinate display is on, you can use it to assist you in picking a text height. You'll also be prompted to enter the text rotation angle. After you enter this information, the displayable attribute will be placed into the drawing at the location you specified, as in Figure 12-32.

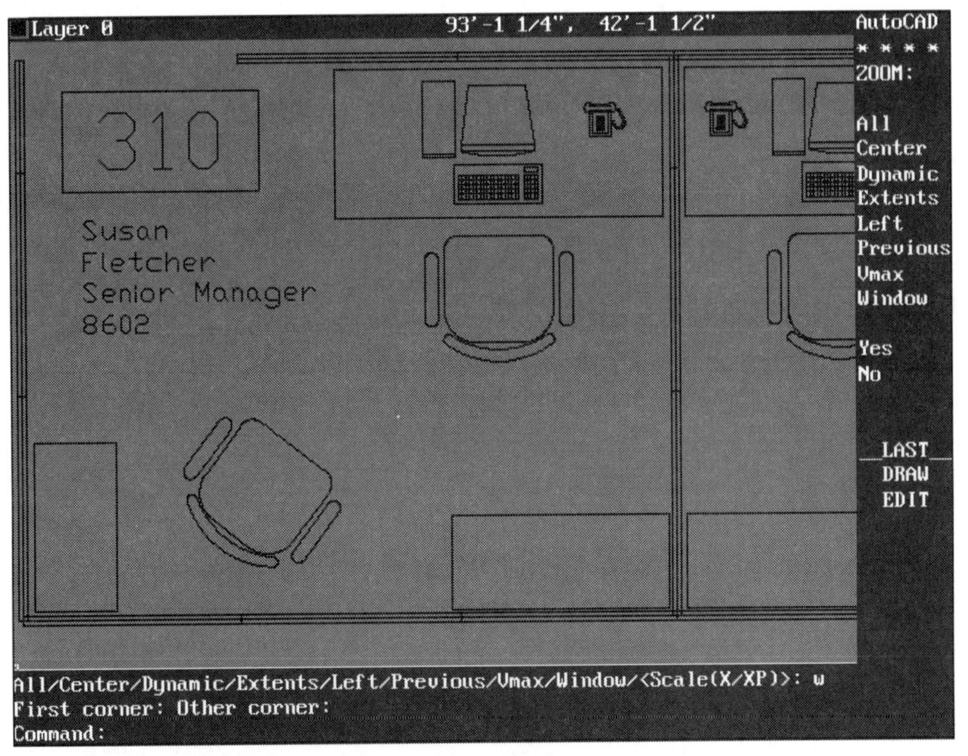

Figure 12-32: A displayable attribute in the OFFICE drawing

Now that part of the database is displayed within the drawing, you can readily refer to it. If an employee's information changes, you can easily see that you need to update the database. For instance, if an employee's title changes, you can use the ASEEDITROW command or the ASEQEDIT command to edit the employee's title in the appropriate table.

NOTE: Changing data in the table will not update the displayable attribute. You have to give the ASEUPDATE command to update the DAs.

Selection Using ASE

One of ASE's most powerful features is its capability to select graphic information based on non-graphic data. Say you want to find and highlight all of the employees who belong to a particular organization. You can use the ASESELECT command or pick the command from the menu. You can specify that you want to select only the employees who belong to that organization. A selection set is created that you can use in later operations.

Using SQL and the SQL Editor

SQL lets you do many of the operations you've read about in this chapter, and you can choose whether you wish to use dialogue boxes. From the pull-down menu, pick SQL Edit.... See Figure 12-33 for its location in the pull-down menu. The SQL Editor dialogue box will appear, as shown in Figure 12-34.

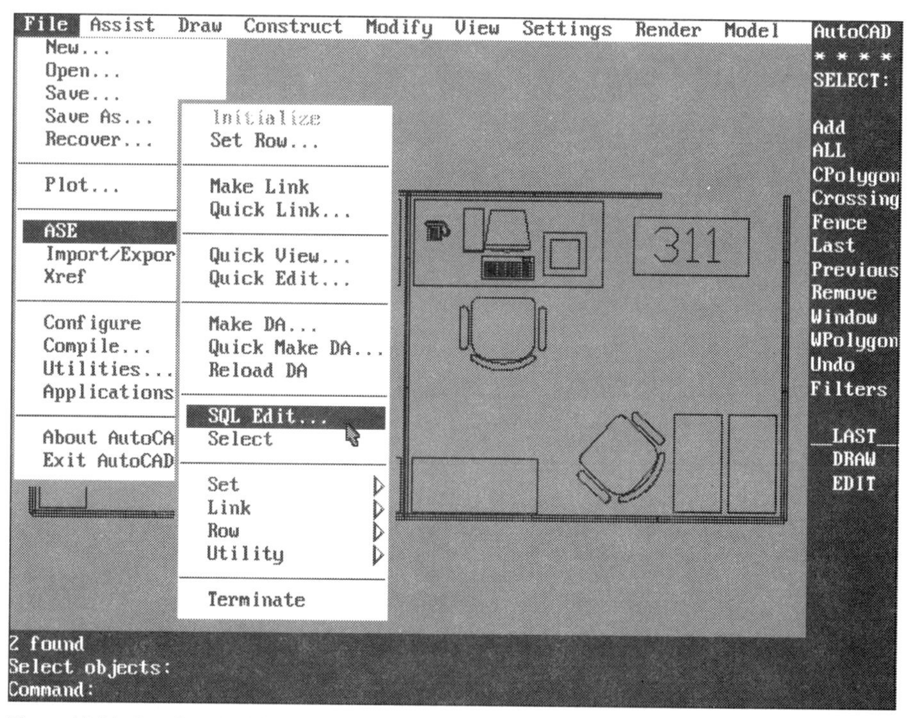

Figure 12-33: Starting the SQL Editor

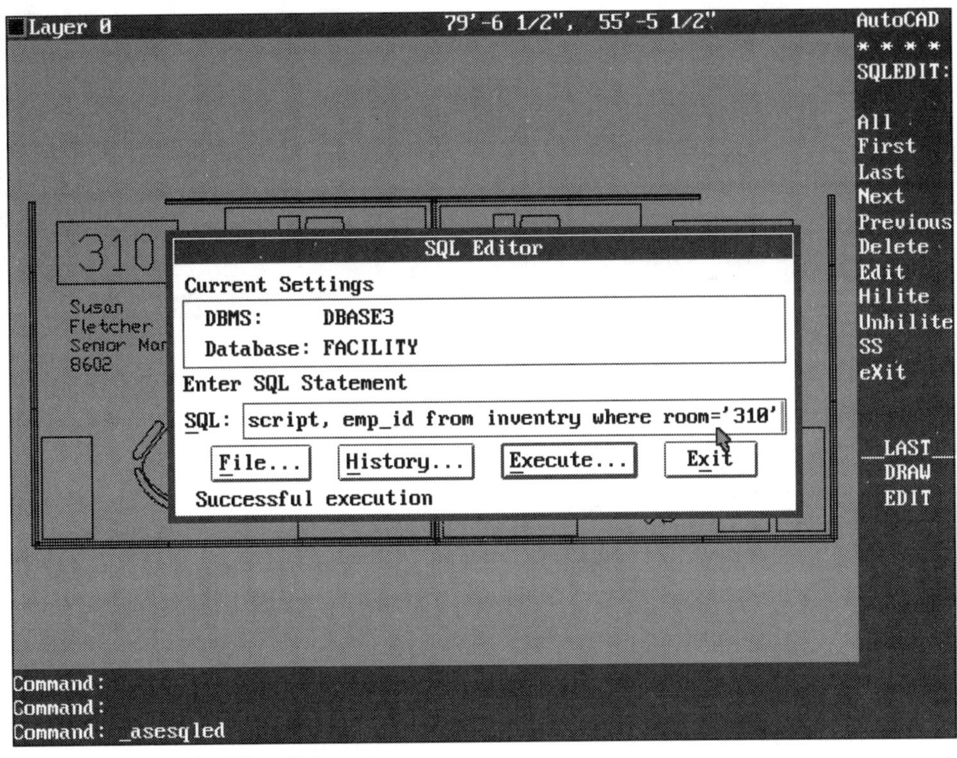

Figure 12-34: The SQL Editor dialogue box

The SQL Editor lets you type an SQL command and then execute it from the dialogue box. It also keeps a history of the SQL commands you've given so that you can give them again.

In the SQL Editor dialogue box, do the following:

Type: `select description, emp_id from inventry where room='310' <Return>`

When you pick the Execute... button, this command selects all rows in the INVENTRY table that have the room number equal to 310. Only the description and EMP_ID will be selected.

You can reissue a command by picking the History... button and then picking the SQL statement from the History of SQL Statements dialogue box. This dialogue box is shown in Figure 12-35.

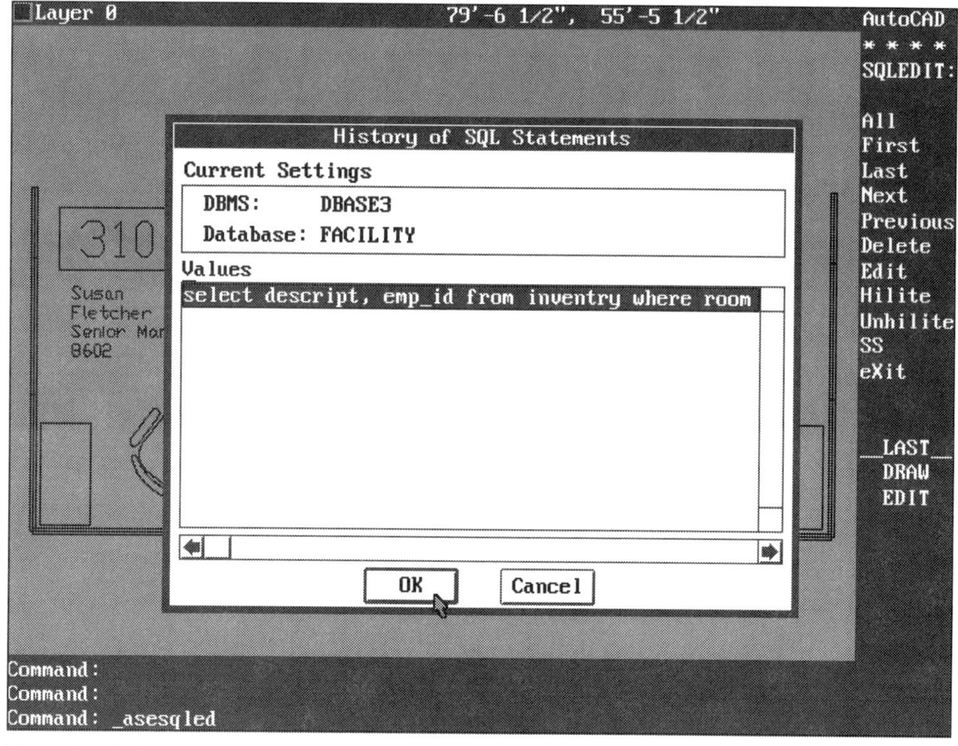

Figure 12-35: The History of SQL Statements dialogue box

SQL can save you a great deal of time by letting you operate on several rows at the same time. Say you want to update all inventory information associated with one employee. SQL lets you make the changes all at once. You'll find a list of SQL commands in Appendix D.

Exporting Your Data

Although ASE doesn't have a report generation capability, it will allow you to export your data to a file on your disk. Two commands are available:

ASEEXPORT: This command lets you export selected data in CDF, SDF and Native formats.

ASEMAKEREP: This command lets you use the report generation capabilities of your DBMS.

For more information on these commands, refer to Chapter 11, "Learning & Applying ASE Commands."

Moving On

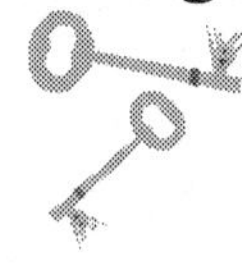

As you've learned in this chapter, ASE gives you the best of AutoCAD and your database management system. You can work with your drawing and your database using AutoCAD and DBMS tools. In the next section we'll look at the AutoCAD Development System (ADS) and how it can boost your AutoCAD productivity in ways you can choose yourself....

SECTION V

The AutoCAD Development System: Creating Your Own ADS Applications

CHAPTER 13

ADS—Is It for You?

If ever you've wondered what ADS is, you'll find this section invaluable. Section V, "ADS," introduces you to the AutoCAD Development System. You'll learn how to start using ADS and how it benefits you. And without buying an expensive set of programming tools, you'll also complete an exercise in ADS programming.

Let's first look at the benefits of using ADS in third-party AutoCAD applications.

- It raises the productivity of its users by increasing speed.
- It improves product design methods.
- It streamlines the AutoCAD user interface.

But what can ADS do for the everyday user who'd like to create an ADS application? Why not use AutoLISP? Do you have a choice? This chapter will answer these questions and others, by exploring ADS purposes and benefits.

ADS—What Is It?

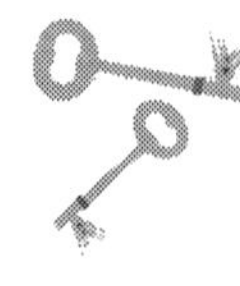

The AutoCAD Development System is an interface that allows externally written and compiled programs to work with AutoCAD and its database. The ADS interface is made up of programming libraries that give your program the capability to work with AutoCAD drawings from outside AutoCAD.

Until ADS was introduced, custom programming was limited to AutoLISP (that is, unless you knew the secrets of AutoCAD's proprietary program code).

How Do I Use It?

Most ADS applications are integrated with AutoCAD so well that you won't know you're using them. In fact, much of AutoCAD Release 12 was developed using ADS. Many third-party applications are developed using ADS and run by dialogue boxes and pull-down menus.

AutoCAD comes with several ADS-written demonstration programs that you can practice with as you learn about ADS. You'll recognize them because of their *.EXP* file extension. The demonstration programs are located in your \ACAD\ADS directory if you installed AutoCAD using the installation default directories. One such program is MAGNETS.EXP. The MAGNETS program simulates a pendulum swinging through several magnetic fields. As it runs, it shows you the position of the magnets and the pendulum path. You can run this program by using the APPLOAD command to load it, or you can follow the instructions below. Start with a new, empty drawing and type the following at the command prompt:

Type: `(xload "magnets") <Return>`

Response: `"magnets"`

NOTE: If the program does not load, find the MAGNETS.EXP program and copy it to your drawing directory. Then try loading it again.

To start the MAGNETS program, do the following:

Type: `demo <Return>`

The program responds by drawing the magnets and pendulum location, as shown in Figure 13-1.

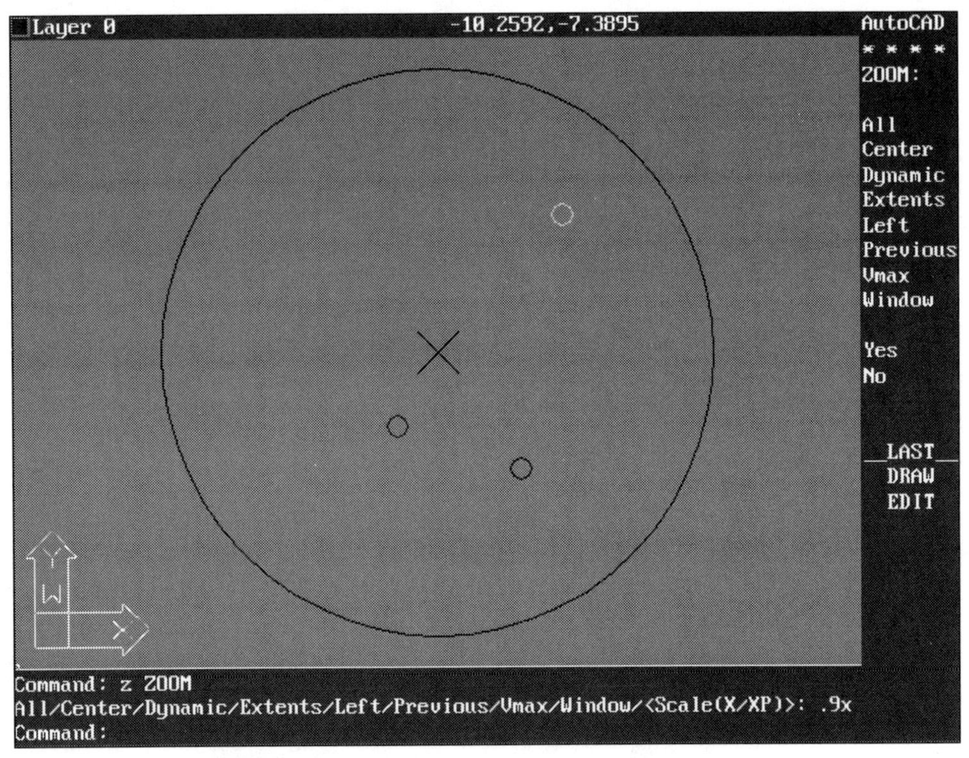

Figure 13-1: The MAGNETS.EXP opening screen

The following commands control the program characteristics. You can run the program using default values, or you can set new values by typing these commands before running the program.

magnet: Creates a new magnet and prompts you to enter the magnet's strength and location. You can specify positive or negative strength.

magedit: Lets you change a magnet's strength.

reset: Erases the pendulum paths and resets the program back to its initial state.

setmag: Lets you set several variables that control the operating parameters of the program.

Run the program from the command prompt by doing the following:

Type: `run <Return>`

Response: `Steps or (– simulated seconds):<3000>`

You can change the number of steps (the default is 3000) or type a negative value to indicate the number of simulated seconds you want the program to run. For this exercise, use the default.

Type: `<Return>`

Response: `Pendulum start position:`

Digitize the location where the pendulum will be released.

See Figure 13-2 for a sample view of the program. The figure displays the path of the pendulum as it passes through the magnetic fields.

NOTE: The pendulum path, by default, is drawn with temporary vectors, not lines. Use the REDRAW command to remove the path from the display.

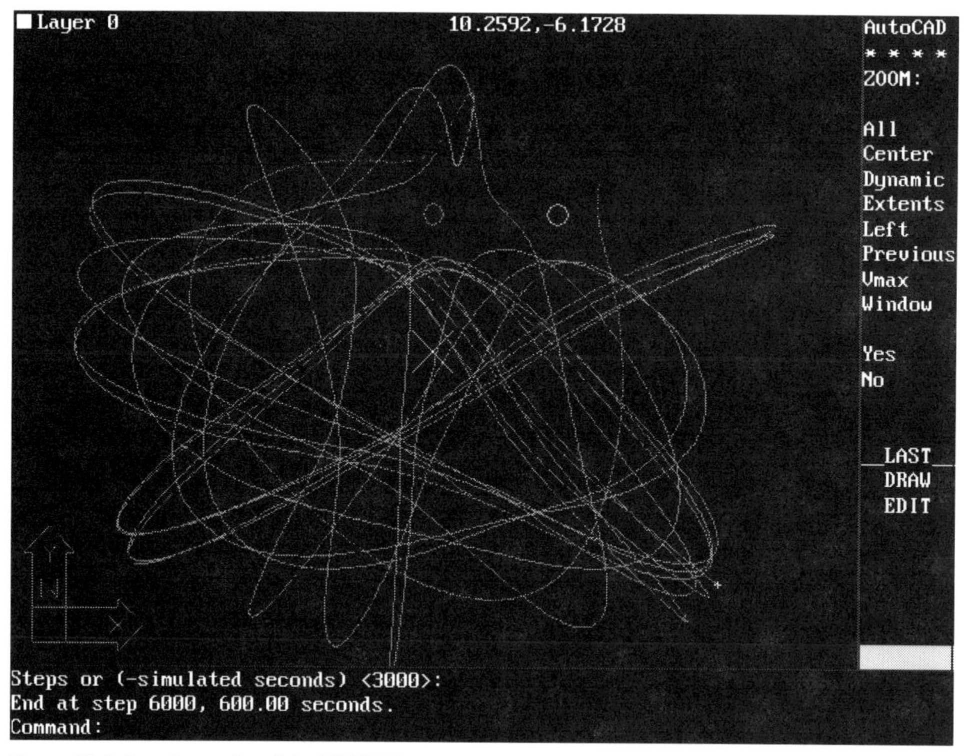

Figure 13-2: Sample results of the MAGNETS program

More sample ADS programs are located in the \ACAD\ADS directory and are explained in the *AutoCAD Development System Programmer's*

Reference Manual. You can become more comfortable with ADS programs by experimenting with these programs.

Is ADS a Programming Language?

ADS is not a programming language. ADS is a means of letting AutoCAD communicate with a program you've written and compiled. Most ADS programs are written in the C programming language. Autodesk programmers have written a library of routines in C that are the heart of ADS. These library modules, together with a special program *header* (the first section of a program), give you access to AutoCAD.

Do You Have to Use C?

You don't have to use C to program in ADS—although it's advisable. But many AutoCAD users aren't programmers and are especially not familiar with the C language. Therefore, Autodesk has made it possible for you to write an ADS application in other languages that can be understood by ADS. In fact, special library routines are available for writing ADS applications in BASIC and in a language called ATLAST.

In Chapter 14, "ADS—Getting Involved," we'll look at a BASIC program written to run under ADS. We won't work with the ATLAST language, but you can learn about it from the *Autodesk Software Developer's Kit* (SDK), version 2.0. The SDK is available directly from Autodesk for a $150 fee. Or you can download it from the Autodesk forum in CompuServe at no charge (other than your connect time).

Why Use ADS? Why Not AutoLISP?

You may wonder why you should use ADS and not AutoLISP. You'll be able to answer these questions yourself by learning the strengths and weaknesses of both approaches. ADS was never intended to replace AutoLISP. In fact, all ADS applications communicate with AutoCAD through AutoLISP. By understanding the strengths of each approach, you'll be able to decide what tools to use for your own applications.

Let's look at the strengths of using AutoLISP in third-party AutoCAD applications.

Prototyping: One of AutoLISP's biggest strengths is its excellent prototyping capability. You can write an AutoLISP program a little at a time and test each line by typing it at the command prompt. You can stay in your AutoCAD drawing and look at values of variables and make changes to your program on the fly. AutoLISP also has good response for interactive code development.

Portability: You can write an AutoLISP program and run it on any AutoCAD hardware platform. No conversion is needed.

Cost: AutoLISP comes with AutoCAD. You don't have to buy any development tools (compilers, debuggers, linkers, memory extenders). Your only investment is the time it takes to learn the language.

Complexity: Although you can write very complex code with AutoLISP, it can also be very simple because it is a stand-alone system in AutoCAD. Because AutoLISP requires no compilation or linking, you can write a small program and have it running in a very small amount of time.

No Risk: It's very unlikely that your AutoLISP program will corrupt your AutoCAD program or your current AutoCAD drawing because AutoCAD doesn't allow it to work directly with the AutoCAD drawing database. AutoLISP must work through the AutoCAD program code to get to the drawing.

Uniqueness: Because AutoLISP is an evaluated language, it can "learn" from itself. During execution, an AutoLISP program can learn from its environment and modify its own code.

Now let's look at the weaknesses of using AutoLISP in third-party AutoCAD applications.

Performance: AutoLISP programs have gained the reputation of having slow computational capabilities. Because AutoLISP is an *evaluated* (not compiled) language, it takes longer to run than compiled code.

Memory Limits: AutoLISP programs cannot run in protected mode (to make efficient use of memory) like ADS applications.

File I/O: AutoLISP is slow when reading and writing external files. And it can read and write only ASCII files (it cannot read nor write binary files).

No Risk: While AutoLISP won't corrupt a drawing, the payment for "no risk" is its inability to work directly with a drawing. AutoLISP must go through the AutoCAD program code to get to the drawing database. This restriction limits your ability to write some applications.

Let's look at the strengths of using ADS in third-party AutoCAD applications.

Performance: ADS is well known for its computational performance. If your application has large computational requirements, an ADS application will perform them in compiled code outside AutoCAD in a fraction of the time AutoLISP would take.

Memory: You can write ADS applications to run in and take advantage of DOS's protected mode.

File I/O: Because ADS applications consist of compiled code, they can quickly read and write files on disk. What's more, they can read and write ASCII and binary files.

Risk: With ADS, the door to working directly with AutoCAD's drawing code is open. This means you can easily get and change almost anything in the drawing from your ADS application code.

Integration: ADS programs are already outside AutoCAD, so integrating other programs is possible. ASE (see Section IV, "ASE") is one example of integrating outside programs with AutoCAD.

(continued)

Protection: Because ADS programs are compiled, they are protected from being changed by the user to a much greater degree than AutoLiSP programs. A compiled program is also more difficult for a competitor to copy, if you are a developer.

Debug Tools: While creating ADS applications, you have your programming language tools available to assist you in debugging your program.

Now let's look at the weaknesses of using ADS in third-party AutoCAD applications.

Cost: Writing protected-mode ADS applications can be expensive because of the tools you must purchase before you can create your programs. A compiler and other programming tools will be required. And if your ADS application is to run on more than one hardware platform, you'll need a set of tools for each platform. You'll also invest a great amount of learning time in writing ADS applications.

Portability: ADS applications are not portable to all AutoCAD platforms. You'll have to port them to each platform on which they'll run.

Debugging: Although you have debugging tools for your programming language, an ADS application usually requires more debugging than an AutoLISP application.

Inexpensive ADS Development

Although tools for writing protected-mode programs can cost over $1000, you can also write programs to run in *real mode.* That means you can use cheaper tools (a QuickC or QuickBasic compiler costs less than $100). The ADS library routines and header mentioned earlier in this chapter also work under real mode. And if you want to write an ADS program in BASIC, a set of library routines and a header—all written in BASIC—are included in the *Autodesk Software Developer's Kit.*

Moving On

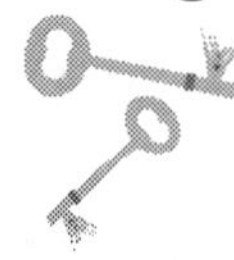

In this chapter you learned about ADS and why you should use it. You also learned about the strengths and weaknesses of ADS and AutoLISP. In the next chapter we'll use Microsoft QuickBasic and tools from the *Software Developer's Kit* to build a real mode ADS program. You'll see how the header, ADS library and your program all fit together to create your application.

CHAPTER 14

ADS—Getting Involved

This chapter will focus on another hands-on approach to get you further involved with the AutoCAD Development System, or ADS. As you learned in the preceding chapter, "ADS—Is It for You?" ADS is an interface you use to allow externally written and compiled programs to work with AutoCAD and its internal database. In that chapter you also used a MAGNETS.EXP program in protected mode. In this chapter you create a DRW_CIR.EXE as a real mode application.

But before you get into the hands-on example, let's lay some groundwork by looking at ADS concepts you'll find helpful. Then let's dive into building an AutoCAD Development System program in real mode.

The ADS Concept

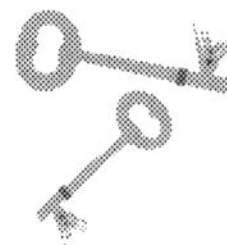

The *main* concept behind using ADS is to make AutoCAD think it's running an AutoLISP application. Let's look first at a few other reasons behind using ADS concepts, however.

- ADS applications can run well in AutoCAD because of the ADS tie to AutoCAD through AutoLISP.
- ADS functions to AutoCAD; that is, ADS looks and responds like AutoLISP because AutoLISP is used to load and call every ADS application.
- All the routines used to communicate between ADS and AutoLISP are in the ADS libraries.

But remember: The main concept behind using ADS is to make AutoCAD think it's running another AutoLISP application. Also, the application of protected mode (.EXP) or real mode (.EXE) is basically one of how the program is compiled, linked and run. When you remember these points, it will make it easier for you to decide either to write your application in ADS or write it in AutoLISP. (You'll find the strengths and weaknesses to both ADS and AutoLISP listed in Chapter 13.)

How Much ADS Do You Need to Know?

Before you consider how much ADS you need to know, just reflect on the areas you should have some knowledge in, or at least be aware of the areas you should be aiming to acquire expertise in. These areas include AutoCAD, AutoLISP, the C language and BASIC.

It stands to reason that at first you'll need a good working knowledge of AutoCAD. You should also be familiar with AutoLISP because of its close ties and similarity with the ADS library.

If you plan to do any programming in C, you should have a good understanding of the C programming language (if you're new to C, start with a small program). One of the best ways to learn C is to do sample programs, and the *Autodesk Software Developer's Kit (SDK)* is an excellent place to get sample programs for sharpening your C programming skills. See Chapter 13 for information on getting a copy of SDK from Autodesk.

You also can write ADS applications in BASIC. The SDK includes a BASIC ADS library and header so you can get started using BASIC for ADS right away. And although you don't need a lot of ADS experience to get started using it, you should at least read the introduction and Chapter 1 of the *AutoCAD Development System Programmer's Reference Manual.*

Creating an ADS Application in BASIC

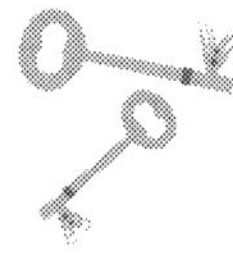

The following information will help you prepare to write your own ADS application in BASIC. I recommend you use Microsoft's QuickBasic compiler, version 4.5, as you do your BASIC ADS development. This compiler was used to develop the BASIC ADS library, header and sample code in the SDK.

An ADS application must contain a few particular elements to enable it to function. The first element in any ADS application program is the ADS main function. Its purpose is to allow the ADS application to communicate with AutoLISP. You must place the main routine at the beginning of the ADS code.

The ADS code itself must begin by initializing communication with AutoLISP. As you'll see below, the ADSINIT function performs the initialization.

ADS always remains inactive until AutoLISP requests it to perform an operation. Then, while ADS is responding, AutoLISP and AutoCAD wait for its answer. Because AutoCAD, AutoLISP and ADS communicate in this way, the main function should include a *dispatch loop*, which handles the requests from AutoLISP and the responses from ADS.

The following piece of code **(Courtesy of Autodesk, Inc.)** appears in the SDK and is a sample main routine written in BASIC.

NOTE: Where you see an ' (apostrophe) in the code, whatever appears after the apostrophe is an explanation comment only.

```
' MAIN — the main routine
DIM SHARED argc AS INTEGER    ' Number of arguments used to invoke
DIM SHARED argv AS LONG       ' Far address of invocation arguments
stat% = 0                     ' Status of the link to AutoLISP
scode% = RSRSLT               ' This is the default return code
rc% = 0                       ' Result code
 rc% = ADSINIT%(argc, argv)   ' Initialize the interface
WHILE 1                       ' Note the loop condition
    stat% = ADSLINK%(scode%)  ' Send status to AutoCAD and get
    IF stat% < 0 THEN         ' request from AutoLISP
        PRINT "TEMPLATE: bad status from ADSLINK = ", stat%
        END 1
    END IF
    scode% = RSRSLT           ' Reset default return code
                              ' Process the AutoLisp request
    SELECT CASE stat%
        CASE RQXLOAD          ' Register our function names
            rc% = loadfuncs%  ' Defined by this application
            IF rc% = GOOD THEN
                scode% = RSRSLT
            ELSE
                scode% = RSERR
            END IF
        CASE RQSUBR           ' Execute registered function
            rc% = dofun%      ' Defined by this application
        IF rc% = GOOD THEN
            scode% = RSRSLT
        ELSE
            scode% = RSERR
        END IF
        CASE RQXUNLD, RQSAVE, RQEND, RQQUIT
                              ' Normally these cases don't require
```

```
                                          ' special handling - just return
                                          ' RSRSLT
        CASE ELSE
                                          ' ALWAYS do nothing (return RSRSLT)
                                          ' for an unrecognized result code
    END SELECT
WEND
                                         ' End of main routine
```

As you write ADS applications, you can use this main routine to make sure that you successfully establish communications between ADS and AutoLISP.

NOTE: It's imperative that the main routine calls ADSINIT as one of its first operations, as shown in the above example. The ADSINIT function requires an integer (argc) and a long integer (argv) argument. The values of these two variables are set by the ADSINIT function. Any other ADS library function preceding ADSINIT can cause unpredictable and disastrous results!

After you compile your ADS program, you must link the BASIC ADS library (BADS.LIB) and the Real Mode ADS library (RADS.LIB) to it. Also, the BADS.INC include file declares the functions in the BASIC ADS library. You must include it in your ADS application in a command line, as follows:

```
$INCLUDE: 'bads.inc'
```

Besides the above requirements of BADS.LIB, RADS.LIB and BADS.INC, your ADS application must include at least two other functions: loadfuncs and dofun. The loadfuncs routine defines your application's AutoLISP external functions and calls the ADSDEFUN routine once for each external function in your application. The dofun routine executes the external functions.

The following example shows how you might construct the loadfuncs routine:

```
 ' LOADFUNCS - Define external functions
FUNCTION loadfuncs% STATIC
    rc% = ADSDEFUN%("sample", 0)    ' The function ID is 0
    IF rc% = RTNORM THEN
        loadfuncs% = GOOD
```

```
        ELSE
            loadfuncs% = BAD
        END IF
    END FUNCTION
```

A reference list of the BASIC ADS library subroutines included in the BADS.LIB file are included in Appendix D. Complete subroutine listings are included in the *Autodesk Software Developer's Kit*, version 2.0.

Creating a Sample ADS Application

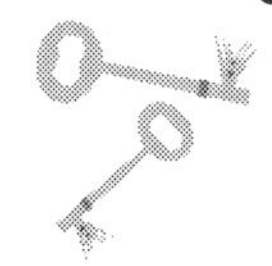

Now let's build an ADS application. You'll begin by using pre-written, tested code. Your sample ADS application solves a puzzle called the Tower of Hanoi. The puzzle consists of three pegs, one of which has a stack of disks of ascending size; the other two disks are empty. The smallest disk is on the top of the stack, and the largest is on the bottom. You see a view of the Tower of Hanoi Puzzle in Figure 14-1.

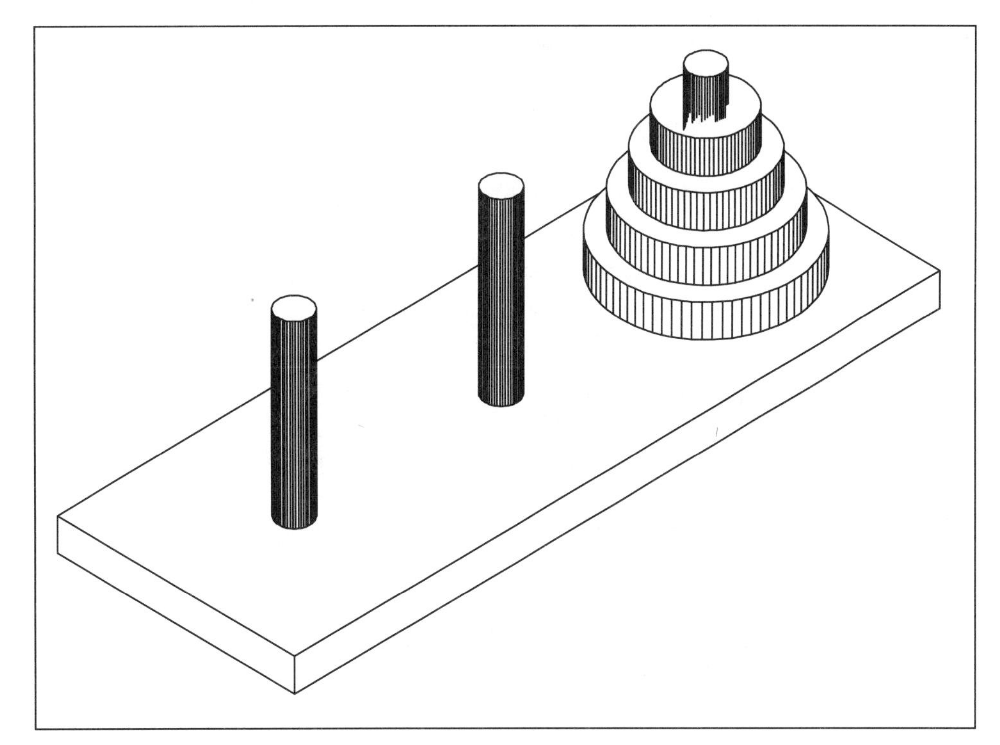

Figure 14-1: The Tower of Hanoi Puzzle

To solve the puzzle, you must move the stack of disks from their peg onto the adjacent peg. You may move only one disk at a time, and you can't place a disk on top of a smaller one. You can use the extra peg to help you restack the disks.

The program, BTOWER.BAS, has been written in BASIC as a real mode ADS application. The source code for this program is included in the Software Developer's Kit. A compiled version of the program, BTOWER.OBJ **(Courtesy of Autodesk, Inc.)**, is included as a bonus file on the *Outside AutoCAD Companion Diskette.*

To create a file that your ADS system can use, you must *compile* the source code and *link* it with the necessary files to produce an executable (.EXE) file.

You can compile BASIC ADS applications using the Microsoft QuickBasic compiler, version 4.5 or later.

NOTE: The BASIC ADS library supplied with SDK 2.0 was compiled with QuickBasic, version 4.5 (BADS.LIB).

Compiling the Source (.BAS) Code

If you have the BTOWER.BAS source code, you must begin by compiling the source code into *object* code. If you installed your QuickBasic compiler using default installation parameters, go to DOS and copy your BTOWER.BAS source code file into your \QB45 directory (QuickBasic 4.5). Then compile the source code as follows. Make careful note of the two spaces and forward slash:

Type: `bc /o btower.bas; <Return>`

If the source code compiles successfully, you'll receive the following message:

Response:
```
0 Warning Errors
0 Severe Errors
```

Let's look at the elements in the above instruction:

- **bc** is the QuickBasic command that compiles the BTOWER.BAS file and creates the BTOWER.OBJ object file.
- **/o** is an option switch that tells the compiler to use QuickBasic's stand-alone library.
- **btower.bas** is the name of the file containing the source code.

Linking Files

The next step is to link the necessary files using the Microsoft linker. Copy your BADS.LIB, RADS.LIB and BADS.INC files from their respective directories into your \QB45 directory.

Then go to your \QB45 directory and type the following all on one line:

Type:
```
link btower.obj, btower.exe,, bads.lib rads.lib /F /NOE /+
stack:32767 <Return>
```

Make sure you type the commas and spaces exactly as they are shown above. If your application links successfully, you will receive no messages. Only the DOS prompt will be redisplayed.

NOTE: The above instruction creates an executable (.EXE) file. If you attempt to execute the file outside of AutoCAD, the .EXE program will be placed into your computer's memory and will stay there until you reboot your computer.

Let's look at the elements in the above instruction:

- **btower.obj** is the name of the object file.
- **btower.exe** is the name of the executable file you'll create.
- **bads.lib** is the BASIC ADS library.
- **rads.lib** is the Real Mode ADS library.
- **/F** optimizes far calls.
- **/NOE** ignores the extended dictionary.
- **/stack:32767** sets stack size to 32,767 bytes.

If you create complex applications, you should learn to compile and link your programs through the use of a *make* file. A make file compiles and links in one step. It also helps you keep your source files organized and up to date. The *makefile* utility and instructions on using it are included in the Microsoft QuickBasic compiler software package.

Running a Real Mode ADS Application

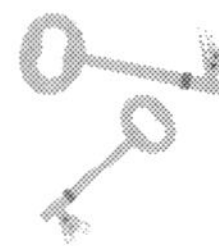

All ADS applications talk to AutoCAD through AutoLISP. A real mode application must communicate to AutoLISP through a special protected mode ADS application called *PWEDGE.EXP.* It is important you use the PWEDGE.EXP program. The PWEDGE protected mode application contains the functions you must use to load and unload your real mode application. (You cannot run a real mode application without it.) The PWEDGE.EXP file is included in the SDK.

For your convenience in running the examples in this chapter, a copy of PWEDGE.EXP **(Courtesy of Autodesk, Inc.)** is also included in the *Outside AutoCAD Companion Diskette.* Be sure to copy the PWEDGE.EXP file to your working directory on your hard disk.

Notice the differences below when loading. You *(xload)* the PWEDGE.EXP (protected mode), but you *(rload)* the TEST.EXE (real mode) file. When you are ready to load your real mode application, you must do the following at the command line.

First, enter your protected mode ADS application:

Type: `(xload "pwedge") <Return>`

Response: `"pwedge"`

Second, enter your real mode ADS application:

Type: `(rload "btower") <Return>`

Response: `"btower"`

NOTE: An ADS real or protected mode application stays loaded in memory, even if you save a drawing and open a new drawing. For example, if you load your ADS application while editing a drawing and then open another drawing, the ADS application will still be loaded, whereas you must reload an AutoLISP file for every drawing that is opened.

You can now run the BTOWER ADS application. See details in Chapter 13 for running the program.

Writing a Real Mode ADS Application

The following code is a simple example of a real mode ADS application written in QuickBasic. You can create the program yourself by typing it into an ASCII text editor exactly as it's written below and saving it under the name DRW_CIR.BAS in your \QB45 directory. Or, if you have the *Outside AutoCAD Companion Diskette,* you can copy it from the diskette into your \QB45 directory on your hard disk.

NOTE: Make sure your library and include files are also in the \QB45 directory.

Program Listing:

```
' Drw_cir.bas
' Copyright 1993 by Dale Evans.
' This simple ADS program draws a circle and then
' performs a ZOOM Extents.
' $INCLUDE: 'bads.inc'
'


DECLARE FUNCTION outputll% (linklist AS ANY)
DECLARE FUNCTION dofun% ()
DECLARE FUNCTION loadfuncs% ()

DIM SHARED result AS llhandletype
DIM SHARED NULL AS llhandletype     ' This llhandle should
                                    ' never be written to
DIM SHARED argv AS LONG             ' Far address to argv
DIM SHARED argc AS INTEGER          ' Number of arguments passed
                                    ' to the program


FUNCTION drawcir% STATIC
   DIM cmdlist AS llhandletype
   rc% = ApndStringNode%(cmdlist, "circle")
   rc% = ApndStringNode%(cmdlist, "0,0")
   rc% = ApndStringNode%(cmdlist, "5.0")
   rc% = ApndStringNode%(cmdlist, "zoom")
   rc% = ApndStringNode%(cmdlist, "e")

   rc% = ADSCMD%(cmdlist)
   rc% = DelLL%(cmdlist)
```

```
    rc% = ADSRETVOID%
    drawcir% = 1

END FUNCTION

FUNCTION dofun% STATIC
    id% = 0
                                            ' Get the function id
    id% = ADSGETFUNCODE%
    IF id < 0 THEN
       dofun% = 0
       EXIT FUNCTION
    END IF

                                            ' No arguments are passed as
                                            ' a part of C:XXX functions

    IF drawcir% = 0 THEN
      dofun% = 0
      EXIT FUNCTION
    END IF

    dofun% = 1

END FUNCTION

' LOADFUNCS - Define external functions
FUNCTION loadfuncs% STATIC
   rc% = ADSDEFUN%("C:DRAWCIR", 0)    ' drawcir command has id 0

   IF rc% = 0 THEN
         loadfuncs% = 0
         EXIT FUNCTION
   END IF
   rc = ADSPRINTF%("Type DRAWCIR to do demo...")

   loadfuncs% = 1
END FUNCTION
```

```
' MAIN - the main routine
stat% = 0                          ' Status of link to AutoLISP.
scode% = RSRSLT                    ' The default return code
rc% = 0                            ' Result code.
rc% = ADSINIT%(argc, argv)         ' Initialize the interface
WHILE 1                            ' Note the loop condition.
     stat% = ADSLINK%(scode%)      ' Send status to AutoCAD and
     IF stat% < 0 THEN             ' get request from AutoLISP.
          PRINT "TEMPLATE: bad status from ADSLINK = ", stat%
          rescode% = ADSEXIT%(1)
     END IF
     scode% = RSRSLT               ' Reset default return code
     ' Process the AutoLisp request
     SELECT CASE stat%
          CASE RQXLOAD             ' Register our function names
               rc% = loadfuncs%    ' Defined by this application
               IF rc% = GOOD THEN
                    scode% = RSRSLT
                ELSE
                    scode% = RSERR
               END IF
          CASE RQSUBR              ' Execute registered function
               rc% = dofun%        ' Defined by this application
          IF rc% = GOOD THEN
               scode% = RSRSLT
          ELSE
               scode% = RSERR
          END IF
          CASE RQXUNLD, RQSAVE, RQEND, RQQUIT
                                   ' Normally these cases don't
                                   ' require special handling
                                   ' - just return - RSRSLT.
          CASE ELSE
                                   ' ALWAYS do nothing
                                   ' (return RSRSLT) for an
                                   ' unrecognized result code
     END SELECT
WEND
                                   ' End of main routine
```

Now compile the DRW_CIR.BAS source code by doing the following:

Type: `bc /o drw_cir.bas; <Return>`

If your code compiles successfully, you'll receive a message to that effect.

Now link the object code with the libraries by typing the following all on one line:

Type:
```
link drw_cir.obj, drw_cir.exe,, bads.lib rads.lib /F /NOE /+
stack:32767 <Return>
```

If no error messages appear, you've built your .EXE file successfully.

NOTE: You may wish to place a copy of your executable file (DRW_CIR.EXE) into your drawing directory.

Running DRW_CIR.EXE

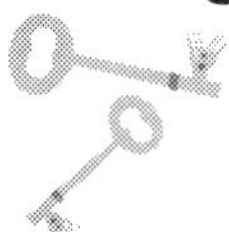

To run your real mode ADS application, start AutoCAD and bring up a NEW drawing (use no prototype). At the command prompt, do the following:

Type: `(xload "pwedge") <Return>`

Response: `"pwedge"`

Now you can load your ADS application. At the command prompt, do the following:

Type: `(rload "drw_cir") <Return>`

Response: `Type DRAWCIR to do demo...`

To run your ADS application, do the following:

Type: `DRAWCIR <Return>`

At this point the circle will be drawn, and the system will perform a ZOOM Extents.

You also can unload your ADS application from memory by doing the following at the command prompt:

Type: `(runload "drw_cir") <Return>`

All real mode ADS programs that are currently in memory will be listed when you do the following:

Type: `(rads) <Return>`

NOTE: You must load the PWEDGE.EXP protected mode ADS application for the (runload and (rads commands to function.

Moving On

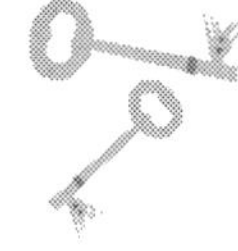

In this chapter you've learned how to create your own real mode ADS programs with only minimal investment. In the next section, "Proteus," you'll learn how to design and create your own Proteus dialogue boxes!

SECTION VI

Proteus: Creating Your Own Interface with Programmable Dialogue Boxes

CHAPTER 15

Proteus—The Fundamentals

You can achieve higher productivity via Proteus, AutoCAD's programmable dialogue system. This chapter, therefore, is a hands-on approach to help you understand it. In this chapter you'll review Proteus basics, and you'll learn how to design and create your own Proteus dialogue boxes.

Let's look at some of the objectives for this chapter:

- You'll build an understanding of Proteus concepts and gain hands-on experience using Proteus.
- You'll learn Proteus terms and how they apply to a dialogue box.
- You'll be introduced to Proteus with a small application that you can program yourself to help you learn Proteus concepts.

Introducing Proteus

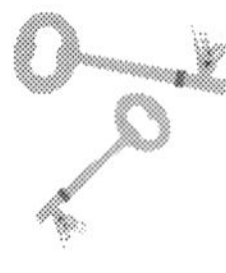

Proteus is the name of AutoCAD's user-programmable dialogue system. Why the name Proteus? Proteus was a Greek god who could change his appearance while retaining his basic identity. Like the Greek god, Proteus dialogue boxes change their appearance, depending on the GUI (Graphical User Interface) in which they are used. They always look like their surroundings. If you design a set of dialogue boxes in the DOS environment and then move them to a Windows environment, they will automatically take on a Windows look. In fact, Proteus dialogue boxes will automatically take on the look of any platform in which they appear. Even their size and function layout are automatically adjusted to match their GUI environment.

Languages Behind the Buttons

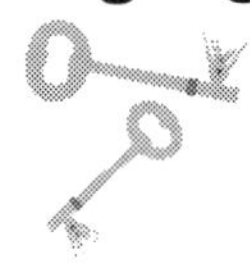

You use two programming languages to create a dialogue box. The first language is the *Dialogue Control Language* (DCL). DCL does just what its name says: it controls the dialogue of the dialogue box. You write DCL in ASCII, and you don't compile it.

The other language can be AutoLISP or an ADS application written in C language. In this chapter you'll work with AutoLISP, but the concepts used will apply to AutoLISP or C; even the library function names are nearly identical.

DCL

A Proteus dialogue box can contain a great variety of components, including buttons, tiles, edit boxes and list boxes—just to name a few. Use DCL to choose which components go into your dialogue box and where those components appear. You also use DCL to label each component and assign instructions to each control component. The following DCL code defines the simple dialogue box shown in Figure 15-1. Create SAMPLE.DCL through your DOS editor.

```
sample : dialog {
       label = "Little Dialogue Box";
       : text {
         alignment     = centered;
         label         = "This is a test";
       }
       : button {
          key          = "accept";
          label        = "All Right!";
          fixed_width = true;
          alignment    = centered;
          is_default   = true;
       }
}
```

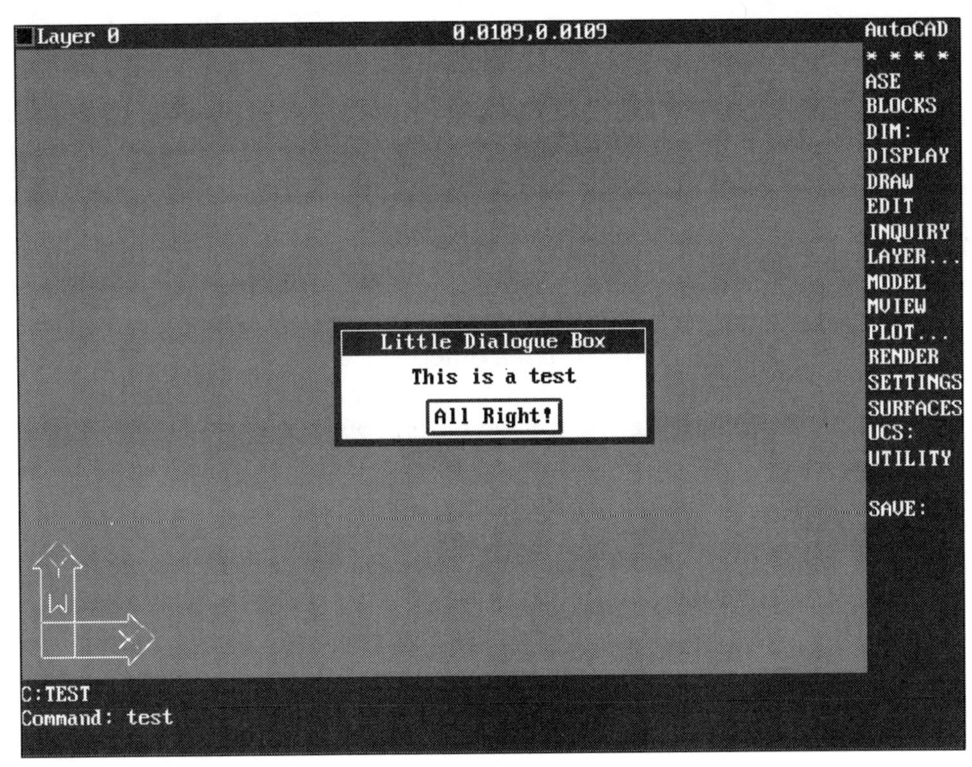

Figure 15-1: Sample dialogue box

Let's look at the code line by line to learn how the Sample dialogue box functions.

The name of this dialogue box appears at the beginning of the DCL program and is *sample.* The label function then places the text that appears at the top of the dialogue box.

The next component to be placed into the dialogue box is text. The alignment attribute is set to centered, causing the text to be centered in the dialogue box. The label attribute just below the text function shows what text will be in the text component.

The next component is a button. The button contains the attributes that are listed below it inside the curly braces { }. The key attribute gives the button a name ("accept"). This dialogue box gives you no chance to do anything else because there are no other controls.

The next attribute is another label, this one containing the text that will appear on the button. Following the label attribute is a fixed_width attribute. Because it is set to true, the button will be just large enough to accommodate its label text. This text is also centered in the dialogue box because of the alignment attribute.

The last attribute is the is_default instruction. Because its condition is set to true, this attribute tells the dialogue box that this key is the default key for the dialogue box.

AutoLISP/ADS

You can use AutoLISP or an ADS application to display and run this Sample dialogue box. In other words, DCL defines it, and AutoLISP or ADS runs it. The following program, written in AutoLISP, runs the above DCL definition, displaying it on your screen.

```
;; Copyright 1993 Dale Evans.
;; Test.lsp is a program to create a small dialogue box
;; it is used in conjunction with... Sample : dialogue {
;; for Chapter 15 of Outside AutoCAD...
;;
(defun c:test ()
  (setq id (load_dialog "sample"))
  (new_dialog "sample" id)
  (action_tile "accept" "(done_dialog)" )
  (start_dialog)
  (term_dialog)
  (princ)
)
```

The above program uses the (load_dialog function to load the SAMPLE.DCL file. The (new_dialog function initializes the dialogue box and displays it. The (action_tile function associates the key named "accept" with the (done_dialog function, which terminates the dialog box and stops displaying it. The (start_dialog function begins accepting user input. And finally, the (term_dialog function cancels the display of the dialogue box.

Building the Sample

Now that you've looked at this example, try building it! Use an ASCII text editor to create two files: SAMPLE.DCL and TEST.LSP. Place each file in your working drawing directory to load it. Start AutoCAD, and after it's fully loaded, load the TEST.LSP file as follows:

Type: `(load "test") <Return>`

Now display your new dialogue box by doing the following:

Type: `test <Return>`

Your dialogue box will be displayed. Notice how the text and the button are centered in the box.

Changing Dialogue Attributes

Now edit the SAMPLE.DCL file by removing the attribute (alignment) that centers the button. Your edited file should look like the following:

```
sample : dialog {
       label = "Little Dialogue Box";
       : text {
         alignment    = centered;
         label        = "This is a test";
       }
       : button {
          key         = "accept";
          label       = "All Right!";
          fixed_width = true;
          is_default  = true;
       }
}
```

Save the edited file and give the test command again (as you did in the preceding section). See the difference in the button location?

You can experiment with the DCL file by removing other attributes to see the effect each attribute has on the dialogue box definition.

In a moment I'll give you some guidelines that will help you as you design your own dialogue boxes. But first, let's take a moment to learn about tiles.

A *tile* is a component of a dialogue box. The commonly used tiles, such as momentary buttons, radio buttons and sliders, have already been defined in the BASE.DCL file, usually located in your \ACAD\SUPPORT directory. You'll find examples of each type of tile in Chapter 9 of the *AutoCAD Customization Manual.*

Each tile can have attributes that control its functionality and positioning. The SAMPLE.DCL file has attributes that are assigned a string value ("All Right!"). Other attributes are assigned *reserved words* (true). You also can assign integer values and real values to attributes, but if the value is less than one, you must write the number with a leading zero. For example, twenty-five hundredths must be represented by the number *0.25.*

NOTE: Attribute values are case-sensitive. Lowercase is used most often.

Some Helpful Dialogue Box Guidelines

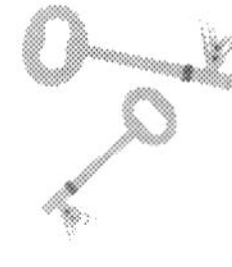

The following guidelines will assist you in making your dialogue boxes look as much as possible like those that come with AutoCAD. If you use these guidelines, the dialogue boxes will then be easier to create and maintain.

Text: Capitalize dialogue box text as you would the title to a report. When you place a prompt or message in a dialogue box, write the prompt as a normal sentence.

Abbreviations: Try not to abbreviate anything. It's much easier to understand the meaning of a dialogue box item with no abbreviations.

Layout: When you lay out a dialog box, try to group items together that will be used together. Align items in the dialogue box vertically and horizontally (the items are easier to notice and pick).

Size: A small dialogue box is best because it's easy to see and quick to get around in. If your dialogue box is too big, try rearranging the tiles, or better still, reevaluate if you really need all the tiles.

Nesting: You can "nest" dialogue boxes up to eight deep, but try not to nest them more than three deep. Also, try to make the size of a nested dialogue box smaller than its parent box (for appearance's sake).

Defaults: You should set a default value whenever you can for a dialogue box.

Portability: If you plan to use the dialogue boxes with AutoCAD on a type of computer that's different from the one you use to develop them, you should follow all the rules that will let your dialogue boxes be used on any hardware platform on which AutoCAD runs. If, for example, you plan to send your dialogue boxes to a foreign country, you should precede each of your AutoCAD commands by an underscore.

By following these guidelines, you will minimize mistakes and maximize the usability and friendliness of your dialogue boxes.

Moving On

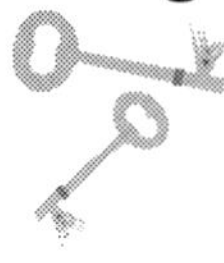

In this chapter you learned about the basic concepts of Proteus and learned how to create a Proteus dialogue box using a hands-on example. You also learned some basic guidelines for creating dialogue boxes. In the next chapter you'll take the next step in learning how to use Proteus. You'll learn techniques for designing and laying out a complex dialogue box.

CHAPTER 16

Putting Proteus to Work

This chapter will combine and focus what you learned in Chapter 15, "Proteus—The Fundamentals," with more advanced Proteus concepts. The concepts presented here allow you to plan and create dialogue boxes for your own applications. You'll learn these advanced Proteus concepts through a hands-on approach and actually plan and build your own dialogue box. But first you must plan your application....

Planning for Proteus

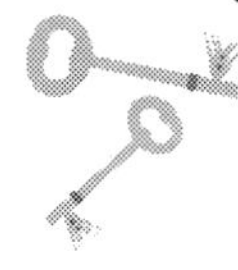

While simple dialogue boxes are easy to plan and program, larger, more complex ones take some forethought. If you take some time up front to plan your application, you'll save a great amount of time and avoid many problems in the long run.

Start planning your dialogue box (or system of dialogue boxes) by deciding what functions you wish your dialogue box to perform. First, take a close look at your application. What is the application intended to do? How do you want it to look? How will you program it—with AutoLISP or ADS?

The answer to these questions will be forthcoming as you design and build your own dialogue box. Let's begin....

Defining the Application

Let's assume you need a dialogue box that will help change the X and Y scale, the LAYER and the name of a BLOCK entity after it has been inserted. Thus, when a new block name is entered in the dialogue box, the new block will be substituted in place of the old block in your drawing.

Start defining your dialogue box layout by picturing it in your mind, or better yet, sketch it out on paper. Get an idea of how you want it to look. Figure 16-1 shows the Modify Block dialogue box that you'll define.

NOTE: The appearance of your finished dialogue box will be influenced by your hardware platform and GUI (Graphical User Interface). Your dialogue box for this example may differ slightly from the figures in this chapter.

Figure 16-1: Modify Block dialogue box

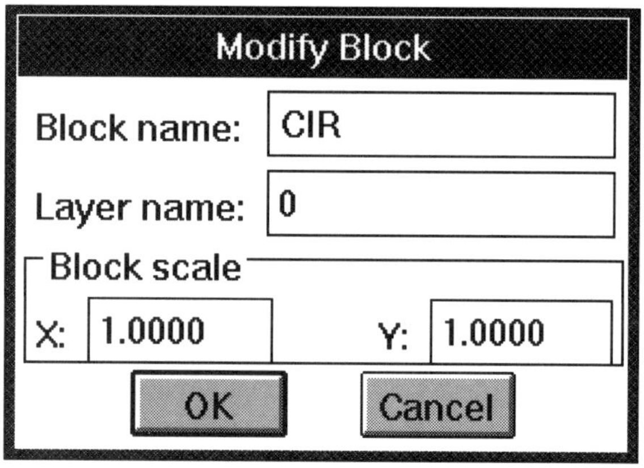

As you plan your dialogue box layout, you should consider several factors:

- Your dialogue box should look good. Keep it simple, yet functional. Color and Help facilities can add to the simplicity and functionality.
- Make your dialogue box easy to use. Group buttons with similar functions close together if possible. Remember to include OK and Cancel buttons when applicable. Remember also to use labels that are understandable so that the user doesn't have to look them up in a set of documentation.
- Integrate your dialogue boxes with those of standard AutoCAD Release 12. A user will already be familiar with standard dialogue boxes and will learn yours faster if they resemble the standard dialogue boxes.
- Try to give the user more than one way to operate the dialogue box. For example, the user might want to press the Return key instead of picking the OK button. Using keyboard mnemonics will enable you to press a key instead of picking a button.
- Write your applications so they will not "bomb" or cause AutoCAD to "hang" if the user makes a mistake. Provide feedback to the user and provide graceful exits (Cancel via Ctrl-C, for example) in case invalid data is entered.

Before you begin defining the layout, try to find pre-defined tiles to use. The more pre-defined tiles, the quicker you can define your dialogue box. In your advanced application, you'll start by using two edit_boxes: one for the block name and the other for the layer name on which the block has been placed. You'll combine two more edit boxes in a row tile where you'll place the X and Y scales. Below these you'll use the pre-defined ok_cancel buttons.

As you define the buttons in the DCL file, each will be given a default placement. Define the buttons from the top of the dialogue box to the bottom and then adjust the default placement so it will look the way you want. If the dialogue box is crowded because it contains too many tiles, you should have more than one dialogue box.

Controlling the DCL File

You can control the DCL file with AutoLISP or ADS. If you've never programmed an ADS application, you may wish to use AutoLISP until you're familiar with ADS. In making your decision, you should consider the calculations to be performed. ADS is an excellent choice if there will be many calculations. The example in this chapter will deal mostly with character data, so you'll use AutoLISP.

Writing & Examining the DCL File

A DCL file for this application is shown below. You can create this file using an ASCII text editor, or you can copy it to your drawing directory or \ACAD\SUPPORT directory from the *Outside AutoCAD Companion Diskette.* The name of the file is MB.DCL.

```
mb : dialog {
   label = "Modify Block";
   : edit_box {
       key = "blkname";
       label = "Block name:";
       allow_accept = true;
       edit_width = 16;
       edit_limit = 16;
   }
   : edit_box {
       key = "layrname";
```

```
            label = "Layer name:";
            allow_accept = true;
            edit_width = 16;
            edit_limit = 32;
        }
        : row {
            label = "Block scale";
            : edit_box {
                key = "x_scal";
                label = "X:";
                allow_accept = true;
                width = 10;
                fixed_width = true;
            }
            : edit_box {
                key = "y_scal";
                label = "Y:";
                allow_accept = true;
                width = 10;
                fixed_width = true;
            }
        }
        ok_cancel;
}
```

Let's look at the above DCL file in sections. The first section appears as follows:

```
mb : dialog {
   label = "Modify Block";
```

The first line gives the name of the dialogue box, mb. An open curly brace begins the definition of the mb dialogue box.

The second line is an attribute belonging to the main dialogue box. It causes a label (Modify Block) to appear at the top of the box. See Figure 16-2 for a view of the main dialogue box label.

Figure 16-2: Main dialogue box label

Modify Block

The next section, shown below, defines the edit box containing the block name.

```
: edit_box {
    key = "blkname";
    label = "Block name:";
    allow_accept = true;
    edit_width = 16;
    edit_limit = 16;
}
```

This section calls the pre-defined edit_box tile, followed by attributes that belong to the tile. All of the attributes are enclosed in the curly braces. The edit box enables you to enter or edit a single line of text. The first attribute, key, assigns a "key" name (blkname) to the edit_box tile so a controlling program can call it later on.

NOTE: Each tile must have a unique key name. You cannot assign the key name to more than one tile in the DCL file.

The label attribute lets you place a text label to the left of the edit box. In this instance, the label is Block name.

When the allow_accept attribute appears in a tile definition and is assigned the value true, you can press the Return key to accept your input into the dialogue box. (The normal way to accept input is to pick the OK button.)

The edit box is 16 characters wide, and it limits to no more than 16 the number of characters you can type. If the edit_limit is larger than the edit_width, the characters will scroll as you type or move back and forth with the arrow keys. Figure 16-3 shows the results of adding this section.

Figure 16-3: Block name edit box

Block name: CIR

The next section is almost identical to the section that defines the edit box for the block name. Differences include the unique key name (layrname) and the edit_limit of 32. Figure 16-4 shows the results of adding this section.

Figure 16-4: Layer name edit box

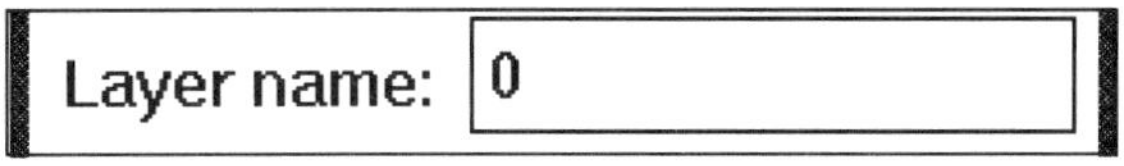

Layer name: 0

The next section defines the two edit boxes inside a row tile.

```
: row {
    label = "Block scale";
    : edit_box {
        key = "x_scal";
        label = "X:";
        allow_accept = true;
        width = 10;
        fixed_width = true;
    }
    : edit_box {
        key = "y_scal";
        label = "Y:";
        allow_accept = true;
        width = 10;
        fixed_width = true;
    }
}
```

The row tile has a label (Block scale) that appears just above the two edit boxes. Note how both edit box definitions are enclosed in the row definition's curly braces. The key value for the first edit box is "x_scal", followed by a label (X:) that appears on the left side of the edit box. The allow_accept attribute lets you press the Return key when you're in this edit box to accept all dialogue box values. The width is 10, and the fixed_width attribute causes the tile to always occupy only the number of characters specified in the width attribute. Figure 16-5 shows you the results of adding this definition.

Figure 16-5: Row definition with two edit boxes

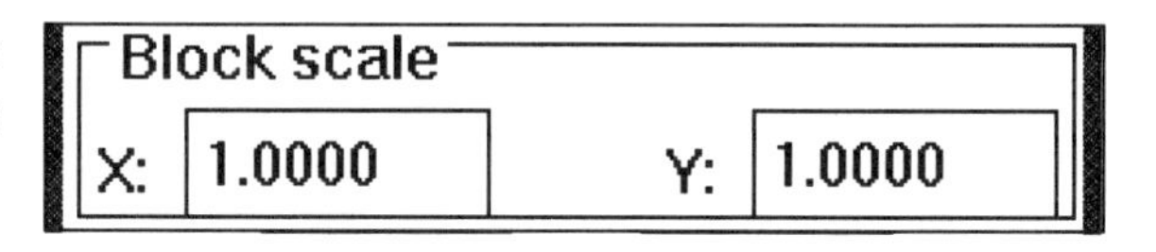

The last section in this DCL file is a single line:

```
ok_cancel;
```

The ok_cancel instruction calls the pre-defined tile containing an OK button and a Cancel button. Definitions for these buttons are contained in the BASE.DCL file, located in your \ACAD\SUPPORT directory. Key values for the OK and the Cancel buttons are accept and cancel, respectively. Figure 16-6 shows the results of this definition.

Figure 16-6: OK and Cancel buttons

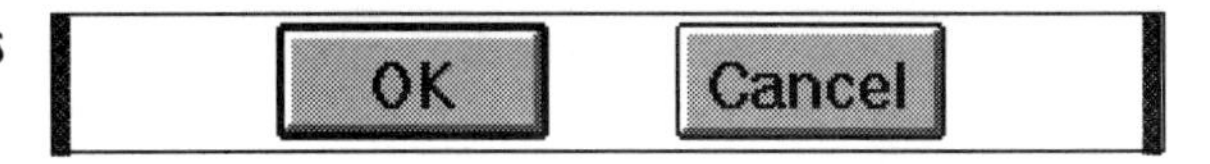

Displaying & Using the Dialogue Box

The following AutoLISP file (MOD_BLK.LSP) controls the display and use of the Modify Block dialogue box. If you have the *Outside AutoCAD Companion Diskette,* you can copy it to your hard disk; otherwise, create the file using an ASCII text editor.

```
;;; Mod_blk.lsp... Copyright 1993 Dale Evans...
;;; The program controls the display and use of a Modify Block
;;; dialogue for Outside AutoCAD.
;;; The program demonstrates how to control a PDB but does
;;; not include error checking, nor help facilities.
;;; These can be added as additional functions in the program.
 ;;;
;;; ********************
;;; error handler
;;;
(defun *error* (msg)
  (princ msg)
  (princ)
) ; end*error*
;;; ********************
;;; main program
;;;
(defun C:MOD_BLK ()
;;;
  (setq ename    nil                    ; initialize global variables
        edata    nil
        blk_name nil
        blk_layr nil
        x_scale  nil
```

```
          y_scale  nil
          newblk   nil
          newlayr  nil
          new_x    nil
          new_y    nil
          id       nil
    ) ; endsetq
   ;;
    (initget 1)                          ; disallow null input
    (setq ename (car (entsel "\nSelect Block: ")))
    ;; get entity data
    (setq edata (entget ename)
          blk_name (cdr (assoc 2 edata)) ; get block name
          blk_layr (cdr (assoc 8 edata)) ; get assigned layer
          x_scale (rtos (cdr (assoc 41 edata))) ; get x scale
          y_scale (rtos (cdr (assoc 42 edata))) ; get y scale
    ) ; endsetq
    (setq edata1 edata)                 ; remember initial edata setting
  ;;
     ;;; begin dialogue interaction
    (setq id (load_dialog "mb.dcl"))       ; load DCL file
    (if (not (new_dialog "mb" id)) (exit)) ; display dialogue box
     ;; initialize dialogue box
     ;; set initial conditions
    (set_tile "blkname" blk_name)  ; display block name in edit box
    (set_tile "layrname" blk_layr) ; display layer name in edit box
    (set_tile "x_scal" x_scale)    ; assign initial x value
    (set_tile "y_scal" y_scale)    ; assign initial y value
     ;; set actions for when tile is activated
    (action_tile "blkname" "(setq newblk $value)")   ; new blk name
    (action_tile "layrname" "(setq newlayr $value)") ; new layer name
    (action_tile "x_scal" "(setq new_x (atof $value))") ; new x scale
    (action_tile "y_scal" "(setq new_y (atof $value))") ; new y scale
  ;;
    (action_tile "accept" "(done_dialog)") ; OK, modify block
    (action_tile "cancel"                  ; cancel and exit
      (strcat "(progn (done_dialog) (exit))")
    ) ; endaction
  ;;
```

```
  (start_dialog)                         ; give control to dialog box
  (unload_dialog id)                     ; unload DCL file
;;
   ;; modify block if it has changed
  (if newblk                             ; if new block was entered
   ;; substitute new block name
    (setq edata
      (subst (cons 2 newblk) (assoc 2 edata) edata)
    ) ; endsetq
  ) ; endif
  (if newlayr                            ; if new layer was entered
   ;; substitute new layer name
     (setq edata
      (subst (cons 8 newlayr) (assoc 8 edata) edata)
    ) ; endsetq
  ) ; endif
  (if new_x                              ; if new x scale was entered
    ;; substitute new x scale
    (setq edata
      (subst (cons 41 new_x) (assoc 41 edata) edata)
    ) ; endsetq
  ) ; endif
  (if new_y                              ; if new y scale was entered
    ;; substitute new y scale
    (setq edata
      (subst (cons 42 new_y) (assoc 42 edata) edata)
    ) ; endsetq
  ) ; endif
  (if (not (equal edata edata1))         ; if any changes were made
    (entmod edata)                       ; apply all changes
  ) ; endif
  (princ)
) ; endMOD_BLK
```

MOD_BLK.LSP Explained

The MOD_BLK.LSP file begins with an optional error handler. This one is simple; it only captures the error and prints a short message. After the global variables are initialized, you are asked to select the block you wish to modify.

Immediately following the ;; get entity data line, the block name, layer name and X,Y scales are obtained from the selected block. The (setq edata1 edata) instruction saves the original block data settings in the edata1 variable. This variable will be used later in the program.

Following the ;;; begin dialogue interaction line, the DCL file—MB.DCL—is opened. The dialogue box called mb is then displayed. If the file was never opened, the (exit function is called, aborting the entire program.

Below the ;;; initialize dialogue box line, the initial conditions for each element of the dialogue box are set. The (set_tile function works as follows:

```
(set_tile "blkname" blk_name)
```

Here, (set_tile is the function name, "blkname" is the name of the specified file, and blk_name is the value given to the specified file.

In this example, the name of the block is saved in the tile called blkname. The name of the block was obtained when the data was obtained from the selected block.

The action_tile function is activated when you choose the tile by clicking on it or by typing information into it. It works as follows:

```
(action_tile "blkname" "(setq newblk $value)")
```

Here, (action_tile is the function name, "blkname" is the name of the specified tile, and "setq neweblk $value)" is the operation to be performed by the specified tile.

In this example, the blkname tile will perform the function (setq newblk $value) when you type information into the edit box. The $value gets the value from the keyboard. The value is then saved in the newblk variable. Notice how the operation to be performed is an AutoLISP expression surrounded by quotation marks. The quotation marks allow the entire AutoLISP expression to be assigned to the tile so that when the tile is activated, the entire AutoLISP command will be executed. Because the scales are numeric values, they must be converted to strings before they can be assigned to their tiles.

NOTE: The above initialization sets up only the values of the tiles.

When you select the accept tile (the OK button), the (done_dialog function is called, which terminates the dialogue box and stops displaying it. Control then moves to the (unload function.

When you select the cancel tile (the Cancel button), the (done_dialog and (exit functions are both called because they are concatenated together by the (strcat function. The exit function terminates the entire program immediately.

The (start_dialog function turns control over to the dialogue box. You can now work with the dialogue box by picking buttons and filling in information in the edit boxes.

The (unload_dialog function unloads the DCL file specified by the identifier following the function name.

The remainder of the program performs the modifications on the specified block. The block is only modified by the (entmod function if the contents of the edata1 variable no longer equal the contents of the edata variable, which indicates that the block data has been changed. For more information on the functions used in the last portion of the program, refer to Section 1 of this book, "The AutoCAD Database."

Running the Program

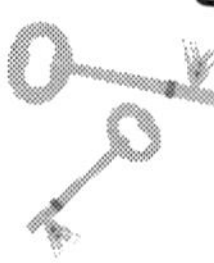

Using your new dialogue box is as easy as loading and running an AutoLISP program. Load the drawing called DIA_DEMO.DWG from the *Outside AutoCAD Companion Diskette*. Or, if you create your own drawing, it must include at least two blocks and several layers with color assignments so you can effectively test your dialogue box routines.

After loading the drawing file, make sure at least one block is visible on the screen. Then, at the command prompt, do the following:

Type: `(load "mod_blk") <Return>`

After the program is loaded, run the program as follows:

Type: `mod_blk <Return>`

Response: `Select object(s):`

Now select a block.

Your dialogue box will be displayed, as shown in Figure 16-1 (yours may have minor differences, depending on your hardware platform). You can now change one, several or all parameters that are listed in the dialogue box. When you have made the desired changes, pick the OK button, and the changes will be made!

Testing as You Program

While you're becoming familiar with programmable dialogue boxes (PDBs), don't start with complex problems. Instead, learn a little at a time by programming only a small portion of your application and then testing it. In the Modify Block example, start by defining only the main dialogue box in the DCL file. Your DCL file will look like the following:

```
mb : dialog {
   label = "Modify Block";
 }
```

Your AutoLISP file will look like the following:

```
(defun C:MOD_BLK ()
  (setq id (load_dialogue "mb.dcl"))
  (new_dialog "mb" id)
  (start_dialog)
  (unload_dialog id)
```

When you get that much of your program working, add a few more lines. If you follow this method, you'll be able to comprehend the purpose of each function and definition much faster.

On-line Resources: BASE.DCL & ACAD.DCL

The ACAD.DCL file is one of the most helpful tools you have for learning about DCL file structure. This file contains the definitions for all the dialogue boxes used throughout the standard AutoCAD Release 12 package. It's located in your \ACAD\SUPPORT directory.

The BASE.DCL file is also located in the \ACAD\SUPPORT directory. It contains the definitions of all the basic, pre-defined tiles and tile types.

WARNING: Never modify the BASE.DCL file. Modifying the BASE.DCL file will destroy the existing standard and custom dialogue boxes in AutoCAD.

Even though AutoCAD's Proteus PDBs are easy to use, their capabilities can become very complex. The *AutoCAD Customization Manual* contains detailed information on various ways to create DCL files as well as the AutoLISP and ADS programs that control the dialogue boxes. Appendix D of this book contains a list of PDB functions in AutoLISP.

Summary

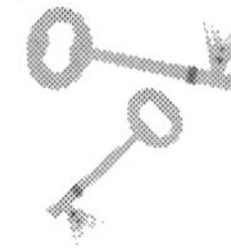

In this chapter you learned how to plan and create your own programmable dialogue boxes. You can use PDBs to enhance almost any AutoCAD application. They can be an interface to external databases and internal functions. Or you can use them as specialized menus. The possibilities are endless!

This chapter completes your set of *Outside AutoCAD* tools. Each section in *Outside AutoCAD* offers high-productivity tools and techniques that will let you apply AutoCAD more effectively in every design discipline. From AutoCAD's database to spreadsheets and SQL, this book lets you take full advantage of information that is inside...and *Outside AutoCAD!*

Fundamentals of AutoLISP

This first appendix section looks at more AutoLISP fundamentals and shows you how AutoLISP works. The section provides a listing of AutoLISP source code for each program plus guidance on the design of the program and its use. The AutoLISP ready-to-run programs outlined will become your Outside AutoCAD Database Toolkit.

The self-installing *Outside AutoCAD Companion Disk* is the quickest way to work with the Database Tool Kit, as it contains all the programs found in this appendix—plus they're ready to run. That way you don't have to debug your program code; you begin working with the programs instantly.

What follows is an overview of AutoLISP fundamentals to help you create your AutoLISP program files and load them in. The introduction to AutoLISP in Chapter 2, "AutoLISP as a Database Tool," provided the basics. If you are interested, further reading material is available from Ventana Press's *AutoLISP In Plain English.* It provides in-depth fundamentals about and good basic information about AutoLISP.

As you type the programs notice two fundamentals. First, note how the programs use indenting. For example, if a function cannot be completed on the same line where it starts, the lines that follow are still part of it, but they are indented by two spaces. Second, notice that the ending parenthesis is often on a line by itself and is aligned with the opening parenthesis of the function. (You may find an odd program where this does not occur such as DBTOOLS.LSP.)

Create your AutoLISP program as an as ordinary ASCII file. But note that for every program you create you must create a separate text file. If you see a + (plus) sign at the end of a line of code, it indicates that the line continues. You don't type the plus sign; it's there because the line of code wouldn't fit on a single line.

Remember, the text file uses the .LSP extension and has the same name as the name of the program. As to a type of editor, use the DOS 5.0 editor, Windows Write editor, NORTON editor or KETIV editor. Using your text editor, type in the program exactly as it appears in the book.

Database Toolkit Listing

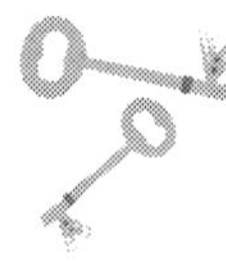

Although Chapters 2, 3, "The Power of Selection Sets," 4, "The Value of Attributes," and 6, "Attributes in the AutoCAD Database," gave you a complete program listing and directions on the use of each AutoLISP program, it's useful to have a concise review of each program.

Normally, you have to load each file individually. The first file called DBTOOLS.LSP in the Database Toolkit listing is a single file that loads all your files for you. You'll notice that all the database AutoLISP programs are included with a "load" line function within this file. Now all you have to do is to make sure that DBTOOLS.LSP is loaded, then you have access to all your programs from the AutoCAD command line.

The program descriptions are listed as follows...

DBTOOLS: Once DBTOOLS.LSP is loaded, all you have to do is type the name of the program you want to run. DBTOOLS will load and execute the program for you. You can add some of your own program files at the end of the file if you need them to be loaded automatically, but follow the same format as what's written.

LINE_MOD: The program of LINE_MOD.LSP uses the "entmod" function to modify the entity whose name appears at the beginning of the entity list. In this case, it's the line.

BLK_SCAL: To modify a block, use the BLK_SCAL.LSP. The program illustrates how you can scale a block entity independently in both the X and Y axes.

BLK_NAME: To substitute a block, you would use the BLK_NAME.LSP. The program is an illustration of how you can substitute block entities by name.

BLK_LIST: To search for facts on a blocks database within a drawing use the BLK_LIST.LSP. The program searches the database for block information.

FIND_BLK: The FIND_BLK.LSP program searches the drawing database for the block named by the user and reports the number of times it occurs in the drawing. It highlights the blocks found by using the AutoCAD SELECT command.

FIND_TXT: The FIND_TXT.LSP program works in a similar manner to the FIND_BLK program but finds user-specified text. When the text is found, it flashes a box around the text.

ATT_DEFF: The ATT_DEFF.LSP program creates attributes for the Resistor described in Chapter 4. It pauses to allow you to enter a start point for text, pauses to let you set a text height, then pauses again to allow you to set a text rotation value.

CA_STYLE: The CA_STYLE.LSP program finds each attribute occurrence from block names identified by you and substitutes the new text style for whatever style was there. For simplicity, this program works on a maximum of three attributes per block.

CH_LAYER: Use the CH_LAYER.LSP program if an attribute was defined on an incorrect layer setting to correct it. But remember the block must have only one attribute. It allows you to move the attribute text to a different layer.

FIND_ATT: The FIND_ATT.LSP program assists you through locating attribute text on your drawing. It flashes the block to which the text belongs.

FILL_ATT: The FILL_ATT.LSP program is written more specifically than the preceding programs because it uses a block with three attributes already defined. The program provides the additional step it takes to assign imported ASCII text to pre-defined attributes.

AutoLISP Tips & Tricks

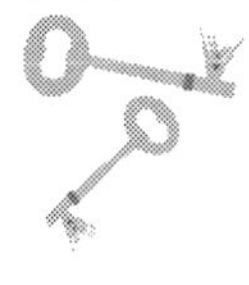

To a non-AutoLISP programmer, there are a number of small details that can go wrong when you try to type in and execute your home-typed programs. Purchasing the *Outside AutoCAD Companion Disk* stops these errors and, of course, it's easier.

A common error is to confuse lower case l (letter L) with number 1 (number one). O (upper case letter O) and 0 (zero) can also be misquoted.

Another common inaccuracy made when typing programs is an omission of a parenthesis or a quotation mark. When this occurs, the file will not load, and you can get a variety of error messages, such as null function error or missing parenthesis error.

A third fault is to omit double quotes when loading files or to place in the incorrect path of the files location when loading it. It's often easier to use the Release 12 APPLOAD command to load an application.

When you have to load multiple applications, you'll find that if you create the DBTOOLS.LSP file as shown you'll be able to load all the files at once instead of singly.

But first, let's look at tips on loading single AutoLISP files; then look further at tips about the ACAD.LSP and how a single file of DBTOOLS.LSP can automate loading your entire Database Toolkit programs. And finally we'll consider tips about finding and locating your AutoLISP programs.

Loading a Single AutoLISP File

Here's a tip on loading a single file: once your AutoLISP file is created, it must be loaded. Let's take the LINE_MOD.LSP program as an example. Normally, you would load a file from within the drawing editor by entering at the command line (**load "line_mod"**) without the extension. Remember, this only loads the file. To run it, you must type the name of the file as **line_mod.** But let's see how you have to create the file to do this.

You'll notice that the first line of each program begins with what is referred to as a (defun) statement. Here's how the (defun) statement works...

```
(defun C:Line_mod ()
```

Line_mod indicates the name of the above program. The **C:** in front of the **Line_mod** indicates to AutoCAD that this AutoLISP file is to be treated as a command level program. To you, that means the file can be typed in at the AutoCAD command line just as if it were an AutoCAD command. Remember, you'll create the LINE_MOD program as a file named LINE_MOD.LSP.

Once the file is created it is then loaded before it can be used. The **(load "line_mod")** second part of the AutoLISP file lets it load from inside your AutoCAD drawing. Thus, the statement of **(load "line_mod")** loads the LINE_MOD program automatically for you.

```
(load "line_mod")  <RETURN>
```

Remember that when you load the program the extension isn't included; then once the program is loaded, it's available as an ordinary AutoCAD command. Just type in its name and press Return.

Type: `line_mod  <RETURN>`

Finally, remember it's often easier to use the Release 12 APPLOAD command to load a single application.

Loading Multiple AutoLISP Files

Don't try to load files singly; you'll reduce your efficiency. If you're working with a number of AutoLISP programs or files, try to load them all at once. Here are a few tips to work around the problem of loading multiple files.

When you start AutoCAD, one of the files it loads is named ACAD.LSP. (It's located in your \ACAD\SUPPORT directory.) One answer would be to put all your programs into this file, then every time you OPEN a drawing all of the programs listed in it would load automatically. Yet using this file poses two dilemmas. The first is **speed** and the next that of **applications developers**. Let's outline these two problems one at-a-time and a bit more-in-depth.

Let's start with the speed problem. When you start a NEW drawing, or OPEN a drawing AutoCAD is already slow enough. If you place extra programs into the ACAD.LSP file it would add micro-seconds of time, particularly when you OPEN your existing drawing, so reducing your efficiency. It's also taking up valuable amounts of memory.

The second problem is that many third-party software developers require their own ACAD.LSP file. By adding your own programs to it, you may harm the file (so much that it may not load). Take LINE_MOD.LSP as an example; here's an improved way:

Place the following line-code in your ACAD.LSP file:

```
(defun C:LINE_MOD ()
  (load "LINE_MOD")
  (C:LINE_MOD)
)
```

LINE_MOD is now a loaded AutoLISP function, yet the function is not the real LINE_MOD program. (You've placed that either in the \ACAD\SUPPORT or a separate directory of your choice.) What you've done is to create a function by the same name that first loads LINE_MOD.LSP then executes the newly loaded LINE_MOD function. And you only used enough code required to load the larger file when the name of the file or command is called out by you at the command line as line_mod.

With this way, you don't need the entire file loaded at all times, and it saves time and memory. But every program you create has to be listed in the ACAD.LSP file in the same format as above, which again means the ACAD.LSP will slow you down every time you start a new drawing. Instead of placing these lines into your ACAD.LSP file, use a single file that can do it for you. It's called DBTOOLS.LSP. You'll find all the database AutoLISP programs are included with a "load" line within this file.

When you move into the DBTOOLS.LSP section in the next few pages, you'll see how this file works and how simple it is to create. DBTOOLS.LSP will quickly load all the files listed in it so there is no wait time before you begin your drawing. If you include the **(load "dbtools")** statement in your ACAD.LSP file the DBTOOLS.LSP file will be loaded automatically.

Alternatively, if you don't have access to your ACAD.LSP file because of a third-party program, add the above line to the end of the ACADR12.LSP file. It's found in the AutoCAD Release 12 Support directory. It does the same thing.

Finally, remember it's easy to use the Release 12 APPLOAD command to load a single file such as DBTOOLS for multiple applications.

Finding Your AutoLISP Files

Often when you try to load an AutoLISP file AutoCAD can't find it because of the directory it's in. Here are some tips you can use to overcome this.

You could place the AutoLISP files in the \ACAD\SUPPORT directory or directly in the \ACAD directory. This is not advisable. Your AutoLISP programs should be in their own directory, out of the way of AutoCAD itself. You should place all your AutoLISP programs in a subdirectory called \ACAD\DBTOOLS.

How do you get AutoCAD to know where your files are? Actually it's easy. AutoCAD Release 12 creates a batch file called ACADR12.BAT when it's installed. The first statement in the batch file is

```
SET ACAD=C:\ACAD\SUPPORT;C:\ACAD\FONTS;C:\ACAD\ADS
```

The SET ACAD= statement informs AutoCAD where to look for various files. Notice each drive and directory is separated by a semi-colon. You should use your text editor and add the following SET ACAD= statement to the end of the line.

```
;C:\ACAD\DBTOOLS
```

Your entire new line would now read

```
SET ACAD=C:\ACAD\SUPPORT;C:\ACAD\FONTS;C:\ACAD\ADS;C:\ACAD\DBTOOLS
```

This assumes that AutoCAD is installed on your C: drive and in the \ACAD directory. If your AutoCAD is installed on another drive or in another directory, your SET ACAD= line will, of course, reflect that.

The DBTOOLS.LSP File

This tip shows you how the the DBTOOLS.LSP file loads all your files at once. You'll notice there is one line in the file for each of the AutoLISP programs in the book. A complete listing of the file is found in this Appendix along with a complete listing of the other programs. But first, let's look at the first line in the program.

```
(defun C:Line_mod () (load "Line_mod") (C:Line_mod))
```

You'll notice the first line is a complete AutoLISP program in and of itself. Let's break it down. The name of the program is Line_mod, the same as the real program that is not yet loaded.

What the first Line_mod program does is load and execute the real LINE_MOD program...

```
(defun C:Line_mod ()
```

This next part defines the program...

```
(load "Line_mod")
```

And the last part loads the real LINE_MOD program file. Now the definition of the real LINE_MOD program has replaced our first one...

```
(C:Line_mod)
```

It executes the real program that is now in memory...

```
)
```

This final parenthesis closes the beginning (defun statement...)

Yet your program is still not running. It's just available. The first time you type in Line_mod and press Return, the real LINE_MOD program will be loaded and executed. You won't know it, but from then on each time you type Line_mod it doesn't have to reload because the real program has been placed in memory. Using this method, you're only loading the specific programs as you need them; and you're not taking up precious memory.

Here's a final tip. If you have other programs you can also add them to the DBTOOLS.LSP file for automatic loading. Make sure that your program is in a file of the same name as the program itself. Then follow the same format and add your program access line at the bottom of the DBTOOLS.LSP file.

DBTOOLS.LSP

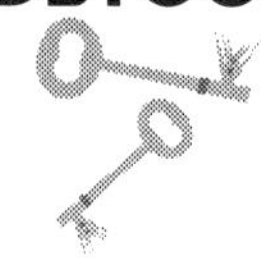

The DBTOOLS.LSP program controls all your AutoLISP files. This single file will load the file programs named within it. And as long as you follow the same format, you can place other files that you have made into the program. It will automatically load them for you. You may use the Release 12 APPLOAD command to load the DBTOOLS.LSP or do as follows:

Type: `(load "DBTOOLS") <Return>`

Because DBTOOLS loads all the files for you, you'll improve your functionality. Once you've loaded DBTOOLS.LSP, all you have to do then is type in the program name, press Return and execute the program.

Listing:

```
;; Copyright 1993 by Dale Evans.
;; This utility automatically loads any AutoLISP program listed
;; Each line of the program has two statements. The first
;; loads the program, the second executes the program.
;; Example: (load "Line_mod") first loads the program
;; then the second part (C:Line_mod) executes the program.
;;
(defun C:Line_mod ()(load "Line_mod")(C:Line_mod))
(defun C:Blk_scal ()(load "Blk_scal")(C:Blk_scal))
(defun C:Blk_name ()(load "Blk_name")(C:Blk_name))
(defun C:Blk_list ()(load "Blk_list")(C:Blk_list))
(defun C:Find_blk ()(load "Find_blk")(C:Find_blk))
(defun C:Find_txt ()(load "Find_txt")(C:Find_txt))
(defun C:Att_deff ()(load "Att_deff")(C:Att_deff))
(defun C:Ca_style ()(load "CA_style")(C:Ca_style))
```

```
(defun C:Ch_layer ()(load "Ch_layer")(C:Ch_layer))
(defun C:Find_att ()(load "Find_att")(C:Find_att))
(defun C:Fill_att ()(load "Fill_att")(C:Fill_att))
(princ "\n  ")
(princ "\n  ")
(princ "\nYour Dbase Lispkit is loaded")
(princ "\n  ")
(princ) ;; End of DBTOOLS
```

LINE_MOD.LSP

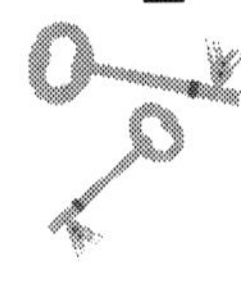

The LINE_MOD.LSP program located in Chapter 2 uses the (entmod function to modify the entity whose name appears at the beginning of the entity list. In this case, it's the line. When you've loaded the DBTOOLS.LSP file and the LINE_MOD command is typed, the data in the copy of the entity list takes the place of the data belonging to the entity itself.

Type: `Line_mod   <Return>`

You will see the endpoint of the line entity "move" from its original location to the new location, specified by the new x, same y and same z values.

Listing:

```
(defun C:LINE_MOD ()
;; Copyright 1993 by Dale Evans.
;; The program data in the copy of the entity list takes the
;; place of the data belonging to the entity itself. You will
;; see the endpoint of the line entity "move" from its original
;; location to the new location, specified by the new x,
;; same y and same z values.
;;
  (setq e (car (entsel "\nSelect entity: ")))
  (setq edata (entget e))
  (setq y_value (caddr (assoc 11 edata)))
  (setq z_value (cadddr (assoc 11 edata)))
  (setq edata (subst
```

```
    (cons 11 (List 8.0 y_value z_value)) (assoc 11 edata) edata)
  )
  (entmod edata)
  (princ)
) ;; End of LINE_MOD
```

BLK_SCAL.LSP

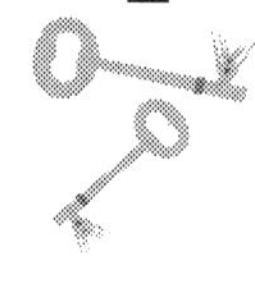

Use the BLK_SCAL program to scale a block. This program, also found in Chapter 2, is an illustration of how you can scale a block entity independently in the X and Y axes. When you've loaded the DBTOOLS.LSP file and the following command is typed, it will allow you to scale a block in both of the X and Y axes.

Type: `blk_scal <Return>`

It's actually a modification of the previous example of LINE_MOD.LSP. You can copy this program using your text editor and save it to your AutoCAD drawing directory.

Listing:

```
(defun C:BLK_SCAL ()
;; Copyright 1993 by Dale Evans.
;; This program is an illustration of how you can scale a
;; block entity independently in x and y axes.
;;
  (setq new_x_scal (getreal "\nEnter new x scale: "))
  (setq new_y_scal (getreal "\nEnter new y scale: "))
  (setq e (car (entsel "\nSelect block: ")))
  (setq edata (entget e))
  (setq edata
    (subst (cons 41 new_x_scal) (assoc 41 edata) edata)
  )
  (setq edata
    (subst (cons 42 new_y_scal) (assoc 42 edata) edata)
  )
  (entmod edata)
  (princ)
) ;; End of BLK_SCAL
```

BLK_NAME.LSP

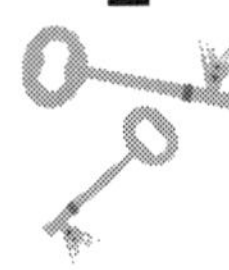

Use the BLK_NAME program to substitute one block for another. This Chapter 2 program is an illustration of how you can substitute a block entity. When you've loaded the DBTOOLS.LSP file and the following command is typed, it allows you to substitute one block for another by name.

Type: `blk_name <Return>`

It's a modification of the example of BLK_SCAL.LSP. You can copy this program using your text editor and save it to your AutoCAD drawing directory.

Listing:

```
(defun C:BLK_NAME ()
;; Copyright 1993 by Dale Evans.
;; This program is an illustration of how you
;; can substitute a block entity.
;;
  (setq new_bname (getstring "\nEnter new block name: "))
  (setq e (car (entsel "\nSelect block: ")))
  (setq edata (entget e))
  (setq edata
    (subst (cons 2 new_bname) (assoc 2 edata) edata)
  )
  (entmod edata)
  (princ)
) ;; End of BLK_NAME.
```

BLK_LIST.LSP

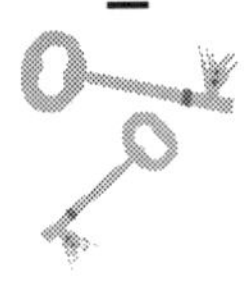

Use this program to search for blocks in the AutoCAD database. This program (found in Chapter 2) helps you search the database for block information. When you've loaded the DBTOOLS.LSP file and the following command is typed, it automatically searches a drawing for block information. Remember, it searches the whole database, so sit back and let it work if you have a large drawing.

Type: `blk_list <Return>`

The BLK_LIST.LSP file is an example of an AutoLISP-based database utility program. You can copy this program using your text editor and save it to your AutoCAD drawing directory.

Listing:

```
(defun C:BLK_LIST (/ e enttyp ename blkexist blkname blknum selset)
;; Copyright 1993 by Dale Evans.
;; This program is a database utility program that counts
;; and helps you search the database for block information.
;;
  (setq e (entnext))
  (while e
    (setq enttyp (cdr (assoc 0 (entget e))))
    (if (equal enttyp "INSERT")
      (progn
        (setq ename (cdr (assoc 2 (entget e))))
        (if (not (member ename blkexist))
            (setq blkexist (append blkexist (list ename)))
        )
      )
    )
    (setq e (entnext e))
  )
  (princ "\n")
  (princ "\n    Block    -    No.")
  (princ "\n    ---------------")
  (foreach blkname blkexist
    (setq selset
      (ssget "X" (list (cons 0 "INSERT") (cons 2 blkname)))
    )
    (setq blknum (sslength selset))
    (princ "\n    ")
    (princ blkname)
    (princ "     ")
    (princ blknum )
  )
  (princ)
) ;; End of BLK_LIST
```

FIND_BLK.LSP

This Chapter 3 program searches the drawing database for the block named by the user and reports the number of times it occurs in the drawing. It also highlights the blocks which are found by using the AutoCAD SELECT command. To use it, load the DBTOOLS.LSP file then enter:

Type: `find_blk <Return>`

The program will prompt you for the name of the block you wish to find. You can copy this program using your text editor and save it to your AutoCAD drawing directory.

Listing:

```
(defun C:FIND_BLK (/ blkname numberofblocks selset)
;; Copyright 1993 by Dale Evans.
;; The program searches the drawing database for any block named
;; by the user. It reports the number of times the named block
;; occurs in the drawing. It highlights the blocks found.
;;
  (setq blkname (getstring "\nEnter Block name: "))
    (setq blkname (strcase blkname))
    (setq selset
    (ssget "X" (list (cons 0 "INSERT") (cons 2 blkname)))
  )
  (if (equal selset nil)
    (setq selset 0)
    (progn
          (command "SELECT" selset "")
      (setq numberofblocks (sslength selset))
    )
  )
  (prompt "\nNumber of blocks named ") (princ blkname)
  (princ " = ") (princ numberofblocks) (princ)
) ;; End of FIND_BLK
```

FIND_TXT.LSP

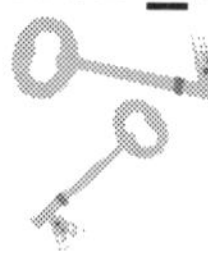

The program works in a similar manner to the FIND_BLK program but finds user-specified text. You'll find reference to it in Chapter 3. When the text is found, it flashes a box around the text. When you've loaded the DBTOOLS.LSP file and the following command is typed, it automatically searches a drawing files database for user-specified information.

Type: `find_txt <Return>`

The program is really two programs in one. The first, called "hilitebox", is what might be termed a "subroutine" that draws the flashing box around the text. The second program is the main program that finds the text and then tells the subroutine to flash the box around the text. You can copy this program using your text editor and save it to your AutoCAD drawing directory.

Listing:

```
;; Copyright 1993 by Dale Evans.
;; This program is really two programs in one.
;; The first program, called  "hilitebox", is a "subroutine"
;; it draws the flashing box around the text.
;; The second program is the main program, it finds the text
;; and tells the subroutine to flash the box around the text.
;;
(defun hilitebox (searchdata Yval1 Yval2)
  (setq counter 0)
  (setq dotX1 (- (cadr (assoc 10 searchdata)) 5.)
        dotX2 (+ dotX1 10.)
        dotY1 (- (caddr (assoc 10 searchdata)) Yval1)
        dotY2 (+ dotY1 Yval2)
        pt1 (list dotX1 dotY1)
        pt2 (list dotX2 dotY1)
        pt3 (list dotX2 dotY2)
        pt4 (list dotX1 dotY2)
  )
;;
;; This next section of the program draws a highlight box
;; color dark grey.
;;
```

```
  (while (<= counter 10)
    (grdraw pt1 pt2 8)
    (grdraw pt2 pt3 8)
    (grdraw pt3 pt4 8)
    (grdraw pt4 pt1 8)
    (setq counter1 0)
;;
;; This next section draws highlight box
;; color: white.
;;
    (while (< counter1 200)
      (setq counter1 (1+ counter1))
    ) ; delay
    (grdraw pt1 pt2 7)
    (grdraw pt2 pt3 7)
    (grdraw pt3 pt4 7)
    (grdraw pt4 pt1 7)
    (setq counter1 0)
    (while (< counter1 200)
      (setq counter1 (1+ counter1))
    )
    (setq counter (1+ counter))
  )
)
;;
;; end of hilitebox
;; This next section is the main function as you will
;; notice from the defun C: statement.
;;
(defun C:FINDTEXT ()
  (setq srchtxt
    (strcase (getstring "\nEnter string to search for: "))
  )
  (setq selset
    (ssget "X" (list (cons 0 "TEXT")))
  )
  (if (equal selset nil)
    (setq selset 0)
```

```
      (setq nfound (sslength selset))
    )
    (setq indx 0)
    (while (< indx (sslength selset))
      (setq ename (ssname selset indx))
      (if (equal srchtxt (cdr (assoc 1 (setq edata (entget ename)))))
        (progn
          (hilitebox edata 5 5)
          (setq look (strcase (getstring "\nKeep looking? y/n: ")))
            (if (= look "Y"))
              (setq indx (1+ indx))
              (setq indx (1+ (sslength selset)))
            )
          (setq indx (1+ indx)) ; else, increment index
        )
        (setq indx (1+ indx))
      )
    )
    (princ)
  ) ;; End of FIND_TXT.
```

ATT_DEFF.LSP

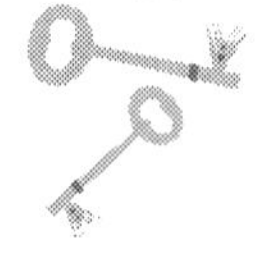

The program specifically creates attributes for the Resistor in Chapter 4. It will pause to allow you to enter a start point for text, then allow you to set a text height, then pause again to allow you to set a text rotation value. Use DBTOOLS.LSP to load the file, or Release 12 APPLOAD command, then type as follows:

Type:	`att_deff <Return>`	
Response:	`<Start point>:`	`Pick or digitize a point. <Return>`
Response:	`Height <2.0000>:`	`Enter a text height. <Return>`
Response:	`Rotation angle <0>:`	`Enter 0 (zero). <Return>`

The file pauses for an origin point, height and rotation value of your text. Once loaded and run, it will place both the attributes in at one pass.

You can modify the program to add more attributes. All you need to do then is BLOCK your Chapter 4 Resistor with the new attributes. You can copy this program using your text editor and save it to your AutoCAD drawing directory. Create the ATT_DEFF.LSP file as follows:

Listing:

```
(defun C:ATT_DEFF () (graphscr)
;; Copyright 1993 by Dale Evans.
;; The program creates attributes. It pauses to allow you
;; to enter a start point for text, set a text height,
;; set a text rotation value.
  (setq att_1 "REFERENCE")
  (setq att_1a "Enter Ref. Designation... ")
  (setq att_1b "R")
  (terpri)
  (setq att_2 "VALUE_IN_OHMS")
  (setq att_2a "Enter value in Ohms... ")
  (setq att_2b "Ohms")
  (terpri)
  (command "attdef" "" att_1 att_1a att_1b pause pause pause)
  (command "attdef" "" att_2 att_2a att_2b "")
 (princ)
) ;; End of ATT_DEFF
```

CA_STYLE.LSP

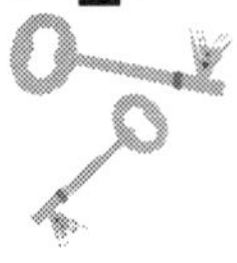

This Chapter 6 program finds each attribute occurrence from block names identified by you and substitutes the new text style for whatever style was there. To keep it simple, this program works on a maximum of three attributes per block.

Type:

```
ca_style <Return>
```

When the program prompts you, enter the name of the new (previously defined) text style, then type the name of the block that contains the text style you wish to be changed.

The program will look at every occurrence of the named block. If there is attribute text in the block, it will be assigned the new style you specified. You can copy this program using your text editor and save it to your AutoCAD drawing directory. Create the CA_STYLE.LSP file as follows:

Listing:

```
(defun C:CA_STYLE (/ new_style blk_name s_set indx +
                        e e_att1 edata1 e_att2 edata2 +
                        e_att3 edata3)
;; Copyright 1993 by Dale Evans.
;; You must have a previously defined text style.
;; At the program prompt enter the name of the new text style.
;; Type the name of the block containing the text style
;; you wish to be changed. The program looks at every
;; occurrence of the named block, if there is attribute text
;; in the block, it assigns the new style specified.
;;
;; Variable
;; Name          Description
;; =========     ===========
;; new_style     name of new text style
;; blk_name      name of blk whose attrib style will change
;; s_set         selection set containing all blks to change
;; indx          counter - counts number of blocks to change
;; e             AutoCAD-assigned entity name of block
;; e_att1        AutoCAD-assigned entity name of 1st attrib
;; edata1        entity data of 1st attribute
;; e_att2        AutoCAD-assigned entity name of 2nd attrib
;; edata2        entity data of 2nd attribute
;; e_att3        AutoCAD-assigned entity name of 3rd attrib
;; edata3        entity data of 3rd attribute
;;
   (setq new_style (getstring "\nEnter new text style name:  "))
   (setq blk_name (getstring "\nEnter block name:  "))
;; create selection set of specific blocks
   (setq s_set
     (ssget "X" (list (cons 2 blk_name)))
   ) ; endsetq
   (if s_set
```

```
      (progn
        (setq indx 0)
        (repeat (sslength s_set)
          (setq e (ssname s_set indx))
          (setq e_att1 (entnext e))
          (setq edata1 (entget e_att1))
        (setq edata1
            (subst (cons 7 new_style) (assoc 7 edata1) edata1)
          ) ; endsetq
          (entmod edata1)
          (setq e_att2 (entnext e_att1))
          (setq edata2 (entget e_att2))
          (setq edata2
            (subst (cons 7 new_style) (assoc 7 edata2) edata2)
          )
          (entmod edata2)
          (setq e_att3 (entnext e_att2))
          (setq edata3 (entget e_att3))
          (setq edata3
            (subst (cons 7 new_style) (assoc 7 edata3) edata3)
          )
          (entmod edata3)
          (entupd e)
          (setq indx (1+ indx))
        )
      )
      (princ "\nNo attributes found: ")
    )
    (princ)
  ) ; end of CA_STYLE
```

CH_LAYER.LSP

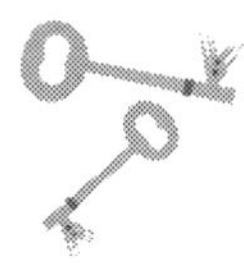

If an attribute was defined with an incorrect layer setting, this program will allow you to correct it. The block must have only one attribute. It then allows you to move the attribute text to a different layer, and the following Chapter 6 program allows you to easily make such a change.

Type: `ch_layer <Return>`

Remember, the program lets you change the layer assignment of a single piece of attribute text. You can copy this program using your text editor and save it to your AutoCAD drawing directory. Create the CA_LAYER.LSP file as follows:

Listing:

```
(defun C:CH_LAYER (/ newlayer blkname e edata el)
;; Copyright 1993 by Dale Evans.
;; The program lets you change the layer assignment
;; of a single piece of attribute text.
;;
  (setq newlayer
    (strcase (getstring "\nEnter name of new layer: "))
  )
  (setq blkname
   (strcase (getstring "\nEnter name of block to look at: "))
  )
  (setq e (entnext))
  (while e
    (setq edata (entget e))
    (if (and (= (cdr (assoc 0 edata)) "INSERT")
             (= (cdr (assoc 2 edata)) blkname)
        )
      (progn
        (setq el (entnext e))
        (setq edata (entget el))
        (setq edata
          (subst (cons 8 newlayer) (assoc 8 edata) edata)
        )
        (entmod edata)
        (entupd el)
      )
    )
  (setq e (entnext e))
  )
  (princ)
) ;; end of CH_LAYER
```

FIND_ATT.LSP

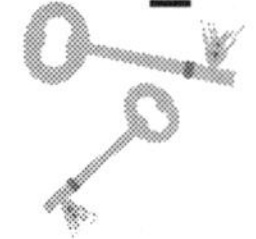

The program assists you in locating attribute text on your drawing by flashing the block to which the text belongs. You'll find it in Chapter 6.

Type: `find_att <Return>`

After starting the program, you enter the text string you wish to find. (The string is not case-sensitive.) Enter the number of times you wish the block to flash. You can copy this program using your text editor and save it to your AutoCAD drawing directory. Create the CA_LAYER.LSP file as follows:

Listing:

```
(defun C:FIND_ATT (/ str1 e enttyp edata att_value)
;; Copyright 1993 by Dale Evans.
;; The program assists you in locating attribute text on your
;; drawing, by flashing the block to which the text belongs.
;;
  (setq old_cmdecho (getvar "cmdecho"))
  (setvar "cmdecho" 0)
  (setq str1
    (strcase (getstring "\nEnter exact string to search for: "))
  )
  (setq num_flashes
    (getint "\nEnter number of times to flash block/text: ")
  )
  (setq e (entnext))
  (while e
    (setq enttyp (cdr (assoc 0 (entget e))))
    (if
      (and
        (equal enttyp "INSERT")
        (equal (cdr (assoc 66 (entget e))) 1)
      )
      (progn
        (setq blk_ent_name e)
        (setq e (entnext e))
        (setq edata (entget e))
      )
    )
```

```
      (setq edata (entget e))
      (if (assoc 1 edata)
        (progn
          (setq att_value (cdr (assoc 1 edata)))
          (if (= att_value str1)
            (repeat num_flashes
              (command "select" blk_ent_name "")
            )
          )
        )
      )
      (setq e (entnext e))
    )
    (setvar "cmdecho" old_cmdecho)
    (princ)
  ) ;; end of FIND_ATT
```

FILL_ATT.LSP

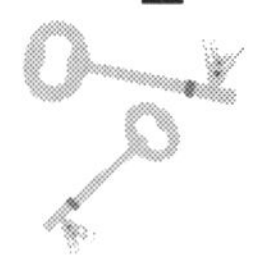

This Chapter 6 program provides the additional step it takes to assign imported ASCII text to pre-defined attributes. The FILL_ATT.LSP program is written more specifically than the preceding programs because it uses a block with three attributes already defined.

Type: `fill_att <Return>`

The program prompts you to digitize where the block that has the attributes should be placed. It also prompts you to digitize a line of imported text you want to place into the first attribute location. After the first text is in place, the program goes on to ask for two other pieces of text.

To run the FILL_ATT.LSP program successfully, first create a block with three attributes. Figure 6-1 shows how the attributes should be defined. You don't need a circle as part of the block. Choose any graphics, or none at all. The example shows the attribute tags defined as TAG1, TAG2 and TAG3. You can define the attributes with whatever tags you like. The block must be called DEMO_BLK. You can copy this program using your text editor and save it to your AutoCAD drawing directory. Create the FILL_ATT.LSP file as follows:

Listing:

```
(defun C:FILL_ATT ()
;; Copyright 1993 by Dale Evans.
;; The program asks where the block that has the attributes
;; should be placed. It prompts you to digitize a line of
;; imported text you want to place into the first attribute
;; location. After the first text is in place, the program
;; asks for two other pieces of text. You may choose any
;; graphics, or none at all. You can define the attributes
;; with whatever tags you like. The block is called "DEMO_BLK"
;;
(setq pt1 nil
      enameblk nil
      ename1 nil
      edatablk1 nil
      ename2 nil
      edatablk2 nil
      enameblk3 nil
      edatablk3 nil
      enameN nil
      edataN nil
      ename2 nil
      edata2 nil
      ename3 nil
      edata3 nil
      rept T
)
(setvar "CMDECHO" 0)
(while rept
  (setq pt1 (getpoint "\nDigitize location for block: "))
  (if (not (equal pt1 nil))
    (progn
      (setvar "ATTREQ" 0)
      (command "INSERT" "demo_blk" pt1 1 1 0)
      (setq enameblk (entlast))
      (setq ename1 (entnext enameblk))
      (setq edatablk1 (entget ename1))
      (setq ename2 (entnext ename1))
      (setq edatablk2 (entget ename2))
      (setq enameblk3 (entnext ename2))
```

```
(setq edatablk3 (entget enameblk3))
(setq ename1 (car (entsel "\nDig. str1 to convert: ")))
(setq ename2 (car (entsel "\nDig. str2 to convert: ")))
(setq ename3 (car (entsel "\nDig. str3 to convert: ")))
(if ename1
  (progn
    (setq edata1 (entget ename1))
    (setq str1 (cdr (assoc 1 edata1)))
  )
  (setq str1 "VACANT")
)
(if ename2
  (progn
    (setq edata2 (entget ename2))
    (setq str2 (cdr (assoc 1 edata2)))
  )
  (setq str2 "-")
)
(if ename3
  (progn
    (setq edata3 (entget ename3))
    (setq str3 (cdr (assoc 1 edata3)))
  )
  (setq str3 "-")
  )
(setq edatablk1
  (subst (cons 1 str1) (assoc 1 edatablk1) edatablk1)
)
(setq edatablk2
  (subst (cons 1 str2) (assoc 1 edatablk2) edatablk2)
)
(setq edatablk3
  (subst (cons 1 str3) (assoc 1 edatablk3) edatablk3)
)
(entmod edatablk1)
(entmod edatablk2)
(entmod edatablk3)
(entupd enameblk)
```

```
        (if ename1
          (entdel ename1)
        )
        (if ename2
          (entdel ename2)
        )
        (if ename3
          (entdel ename3)
        )
        (setvar "highlight" 0)
        (setq pt2 (getpoint "\nDig. new location for block: "))
        (if (= pt2 nil)
          (setq pt2 pt1)
        )
        (command "MOVE" "L" "" pt1 pt2)
        (setvar "highlight" 1)
      )
      (setq rept nil)
    )
  )
  (princ "\nDONE")
  (princ)
  ) ; end of FILL_ATT
```

Functionality

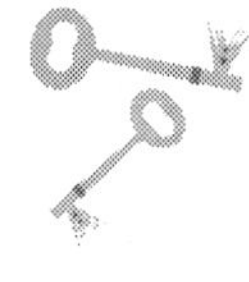

As with any AutoCAD command or AutoLISP program, its functionality is directly dependent on how it's used. You may feel you don't want to use the programs listed because they aren't part of your AutoCAD Release 12 core program. The truth is that most of the new features of Release 12 are not part of the core program.

Specifically, they are either AutoLISP programs or ADS programs written by Autodesk, and they're loaded and executed in a similar manner as the DBTOOLS.LSP file. By using the files, you'll inherently increase your database functionality and improve your knowledge of AutoCAD's database.

APPENDIX B

AutoLISP Function Listing

This appendix looks at more AutoLISP fundamentals and shows you AutoLISP functions and the AutoCAD database codes. The following AutoLISP functions are used in this book. Each is listed here with a brief description of its purpose and use. You can find complete definitions in the *AutoLISP Programmer's Reference Manual.*

(+ n1 n2 n3...) Adds n1, n2, n3...

(– n1 n2 n3...) Subtracts n2... from n1

(1+ num) Adds 1 to num

(< n1 n2) Returns T if n1 is less than n2

(<= n1 n2) Returns T if n1 is less than or equal to n2

(= n1 n2...) Returns T if n1, n2... are equal

(and a b) Returns T if a and b are both true

(append expr...) Appends any number of expressions together as one list

(assoc item aslist) Looks in the association list, aslist, to find item

(cadddr list) Returns the fourth item in list

(caddr list) Returns the third item in list

(cadr list) Returns the second item in list

(car list) Returns the first item in list

(cdr list) Returns all but first item in list

(command arguments) Calls AutoCAD command

(cons item list) Adds item to list to create new list

(defun funname () ... Defines AutoLISP function called funname

(entdel entname) Deletes entity called entname

(entget entname) Gets entity data from entname

(entlast)	Returns entity name of last entity in drawing database
(entmod entdata)	Updates drawing database for entity named in entdata
(entnext [entname])	Gets entity name of first entity past entname
(entsel)	Selects entity by digitizing it
(entupd entname)	Regenerates entity on-screen
(equal a b...)	Returns T if a, b... are equal
(exit)	Aborts AutoLISP program when encountered
(foreach item list expr...	For each item in list, do instructions in expr...
(getint)	Gets integer from keyboard
(getpoint)	Gets point from keyboard
(getreal)	Gets real number from keyboard
(getstring)	Gets string from keyboard
(getvar sysvar)	Gets system variable setting
(grdraw a b c [hl])	Draws temporary vector on screen from a to b in color c with optional highlighting, hl
(if expr a b)	If expr is true, do expression a; else, do expression b
(initget n)	Disallows input designated by n
(list a b c...)	Puts a, b, c... together in a list
(load "filename")	Loads AutoLISP file
(member expr list)	Searches list for expr expression
(not a)	Returns T if a evaluates to nil
(princ str)	Prints string str
(progn expr...)	Allows multiple expressions to be evaluated as one expression
(prompt str)	Prints str (string) in AutoCAD prompt area
(quote expr)	Same as 'expr, where expr is not evaluated

(rads)	Lists loaded real mode programs
(repeat n expr)	Repeats expr n times
(rload filename)	Loads real mode ADS application
(rtos n)	Converts real number n to a string
(runload ads_app)	Unloads real mode ADS application ads_app
(setq a b)	Sets a to the value of b
(setvar sysvar value)	Sets system variable sysvar to value
(ssget args)	Creates selection set according to arguments args
(sslength selset)	Returns number of entities in selection set selset
(ssname selset n)	Returns entity name of nth entity in selection set selset
(strcase str)	Converts string str to uppercase
(strcat str1 str2...)	Concatenates strings str1, str2... together into one string
(subst a b c)	Substitutes a for b in list c
(while condition expr...)	While condition is true, do expr...
(xload adsapp)	Loads protected mode ADS application

The AutoCAD Database Codes

Each AutoCAD entity is listed below. Each entity code is part of an association list that describes a specific feature belonging to an entity. The entity code is the "key" that identifies the feature.

EXAMPLE: Entity code 8 is the "key" part of the association list that contains the layer name for the entity.

Entity	Entity Code	Description/Contents Example (in bold)
LINE	–1	Entity name **(–1 . <Entity name: 60000014>)**
	0	Entity type **(0 . "LINE")**
	8	Layer name **(8 . "0")**
	6	If group code 6 appears, this is the linetype for this entity. **(6 . "DASHED")**
	62	If group code 62 appears, this is the color for this entity. **(62 . 1)**
	38	If group code 38 appears, this is the Z elevation for this entity. **(38 . 2.000000)**
	39	If group 39 exists in the list, then this entity has a Z thickness greater than zero. The second element in this list is the thickness. **(39 . 4.000000)**
	10	Starting x,y,z coordinates **(10 1.000000 1.000000 1.000000)**
	11	Ending x,y,z coordinates **(11 9.000000 9.000000 9.000000)**
POINT	–1	(same as LINE)
	0	Entity type **(0 . "POINT")**
	8	(same as LINE)
	10	x,y,z coordinates **(10 1.000000 1.000000 1.000000)**

Entity	Entity Code	Description/Contents Example (in bold)
CIRCLE	–1	(same as LINE)
	0	Entity type **(0 . "CIRCLE")**
	8	(same as LINE)
	10	Center x,y,z coordinates **(10 2.000000 3.000000 0.000000)**
	40	Radius **(40 . 2.000000)**
ARC	–1	(same as LINE)
	0	Entity type **(0 . "ARC")**
	8	(same as LINE)
	10	Center x,y,z coordinates **(10 5.000000 5.000000 5.000000)**
	40	Arc radius **(40 . 2.000000)**
	50	Starting angle in radians **(50 . 0.000000)**
	51	Ending angle in radians **(51 . 3.141593)**
SOLID	–1	(same as LINE)
	0	Entity type **(0 . "SOLID")**
	8	(same as LINE)
	10	First x,y,z coordinate for the base **(10 9.000000 1.000000 0.000000)**
	11	Second x,y,z coordinate for the base **(11 12.000000 1.000000 0.000000)**
	12	First x,y,z coordinate for the top **(12 9.000000 5.000000 0.000000)**

Entity	Entity Code	Description/Contents Example (in bold)
	13	Second x,y,z coordinate for the top. This group does not appear for triangular solids. **(13 12.000000 5.000000 0.000000)**
TEXT	–1	(same as LINE)
	0	Entity type **(0 . "TEXT")**
	8	(same as LINE)
	10	x,y,z Insertion point is always at the beginning of the text string. **(10 3.000000 4.000000 0.000000)**
	40	Text height **(40 . 0.180000)**
	1	Text string. Maximum length is 255 characters. **(0 . "This is text")**
	50	Text rotation angle in radians. This angle is always measured from the text insertion point (entity code 10). **(50 . 0.000000)**
	41	X scale factor **(41 . 1.000000)**
	51	Obliquing angle of the text in radians **(51 . 0.000000)**
	7	STYLE name. This name is not the name of the font file. **(7 . "STANDARD")**
	71	Text generation flag. You can set the second (2) and third (4) bits of this bit-coded flag. If both bits are 0, the text will appear normal. If the second bit (2) is set, the text will be mirrored in the X axis. If the third bit (4) is set, the text will be upside down. **(71 . 0)**

Entity	Entity Code	Description/Contents Example (in bold)
	72	Text justification type flag. This flag is not bit-coded. The value of this number determines how the text is justified. **(72 . 0)** <— left-justified **(72 . 1)** <— centered text **(72 . 2)** <— right-justified **(72 . 3)** <— aligned **(72 . 4)** <— middle-justified **(72 . 5)** <— fit
	11	Alignment point. This x,y,z coordinate point is where the text was inserted. If the text is LEFT-justified, the point where the text was inserted and the insertion point are the same. CENTERED text is centered on the alignment point. For RIGHT-justified text, this is the actual right insertion x,y,z coordinate of this text string. You pick this point for inserting the text after you pick the Right option in the TEXT command. For text to FIT, this point is halfway between the starting and ending points. For ROTATED text, this point is the x,y,z coordinate where the text was inserted. ALIGNED text is similar to Fit. MIDDLE-justified text is similar to Centered, except the alignment point is centered in both the X and Y axes. **(11 0.000000 0.000000 0.000000)**
BLOCK	–1	(same as LINE)
	0	Entity type **(0 . "INSERT")**
	8	(same as LINE)
	66	"Attributes Follow" flag. If set to 1, all following records will be attributes assigned to this block until a SEQEND occurs. If set to 0, no attributes are assigned to this block. **(66 . 0)**

Entity	Entity Code	Description/Contents Example (in bold)
	2	Block name. If the name starts with "*", then that block is an "unnamed" block such as a hatch pattern. **(2 . "DOOR")**
	10	x,y,z insertion point **(10 3.000000 4.000000)**
	41	X scale factor **(41 . 1.000000)**
	42	Y scale factor **(42 . 1.000000)**
	50	Rotation angle in radians **(50 . 0.000000)**
	43	Z scale factor **(43 . 1.000000)**
	70	Column count for MINSERT. If this or any of the next three entity codes have a value other than 0, then the MINSERT command is used. **(70 . 0)**
	71	MINSERT Row count **(71 . 0)**
	44	MINSERT Column spacing **(44 . 0.000000)**
	45	MINSERT Row spacing **(45 . 1.000000)**
ATTRIB	–1	(same as LINE)
	0	Entity type **(0 . "ATTRIB")**
	8	(same as LINE)
	10	x,y,z Insertion point. This is the starting location. **(10 4.000000 5.000000 0.000000)**

Entity	Entity Code	Description/Contents Example (in bold)
	40	Attribute text height **(40 . 0.180000)**
	1	The attribute value for this insertion of the attribute. The value of this entity code is linked to the attribute tag. **(1 . "Smith")**
	2	The attribute tag. **(2 . "NAME")**
	70	The attribute flag. You can set the first (1), second (2), third (4) and fourth (8) bits of this bit-coded flag. 0 0 0 1 = Invisible 0 0 1 0 = Constant 0 1 0 0 = Verification required 1 0 0 0 = Preset 0 0 0 0 = Visible, Variable, No verification, Not preset. You can set more than one bit at a time. **(70 . 0)**
	73	Field length (currently not usable) **(73 . 0)**
	50	Rotation angle in radians, for this attribute text **(50 . 0.000000)**
	41	X scale factor **(41 . 1.000000)**
	51	Obliquing angle in radians, for this attribute text **(51 . 0.000000)**
	7	Text style for this attribute **(7 . "STANDARD")**
	71	Text generation flag (same as entity code 71 for the TEXT entity) **(71 . 0)**

Entity	Entity Code	Description/Contents Example (in bold)
	72	Text justification type flag (same as entity code 72 for the TEXT entity) **(72 . 1)**
	11	Text insertion coordinate (same as entity code 11 for the TEXT entity) **(11 0.000000 0.000000 0.000000)**
SEQEND	–1	(same as LINE)
	0	Entity type **(0 . "SEQEND")**
	8	(same as LINE)
	–2	Entity name of the INSERT entity to which this SEQEND belongs **(–2 . <Entity name: 6000017C>)**
POLYLINE	–1	(same as LINE)
	0	Entity type **(0 . "POLYLINE")**
	8	(same as LINE)
	66	Vertex follows flag **(66 . 1)**
	70	Polyline flag (bit-coded). If the first bit (1) is not set, the polyline is open. If the bit is set, it's a closed polyline. If bit 2 (2) is set, the polyline has been curve fit. If bit 3 (4) is set, the polyline has been spline fit. **(70 . 1)**
	40	Default starting width. **(40 . 0.000000)**
	41	Default ending width. **(41 . 0.000000)**

Entity	Entity Code	Description/Contents Example (in bold)
VERTEX	–1	(same as LINE)
	0	Entity type **(0 . "VERTEX")**
	8	(same as LINE)
	10	x,y,z coordinates for this vertex **(10 10.000000 13.000000 0.000000)**
	40	Starting polyline width. **(40 . 0.000000)**
	41	Ending polyline width. **(41 . 0.000000)**
	42	Polyline bulge factor. This number is always 0 for a straight polyline. A bulge factor of 1 means that this polyline segment will be a semicircle. **(42 . 0.000000)**
	70	Vertex flag (bit-coded). If the first bit (1) is set, the next vertex record was added by AutoCAD to create a smoother curve. If the second bit (2) is set, a curve fit tangent has been defined. If the fourth bit (8) is set, this vertex is created by spline fitting. If the fifth bit (16) is set, this vertex is a spline frame control point. **(70 . 0)**
	50	Curve fit tangent direction in radians. This number is always 0, unless the second bit (2) flag in entity code 70 has been set. **(50 . 0.000000)**
TRACE	–1	(same as LINE)
	0	Entity type **(0 . "TRACE")**
	8	(same as LINE)

Entity	Entity Code	Description/Contents Example (in bold)
	10	First corner x,y,z location **(10 15.000000 2.100000)**
	11	Second corner x,y,z location **(11 15.000000 1.900000 0.000000)**
	12	Third corner x,y,z location **(12 16.900000 2.100000 0.000000)**
	13	Fourth corner x,y,z location **(13 17.100000 1.900000)**
3DFACE	–1	(same as LINE)
	0	Entity type **(0 . "3DFACE")**
	8	(same as LINE)
	10	First corner x,y,z location **(10 –6.000000 4.000000 3.000000)**
	11	Second corner x,y,z location **(11 –8.000000 5.000000 3.000000)**
	12	Third corner x,y,z location **(12 –6.000000 5.000000 1.500000)**
	13	Fourth corner x,y,z location. If the face is triangular, this will equal the third corner. **(13 –6.000000 4.000000 3.000000)**
DIMEN-SION	–1	(same as LINE)
	0	Entity type **(0 . "DIMENSION")**
	8	(same as LINE)
	2	Block name. The asterisk denotes an unnamed block, created by AutoCAD. D denotes an ASSOCIATIVE DIMENSION. The 3 is the unique block number for this dimension entity. **(2 . "*D3")**

Entity	Entity Code	Description/Contents Example (in bold)
	10	The dimension line DEFINING POINT. **(10 –6.000000 6.000000)**
	11	Middle point of the dimension text. **(11 –7.000000 6.000000)**
	12	Insertion points for CLONES of a dimension (for BASELINE or CONTINUE). **(12 0.000000 0.000000)**
	70	Dimension type (not bit-coded). The codes are as follows: 0 = Rotated, horizontal, vertical 1 = aligned 2 = angular 3 = diameter 4 = radius 5 = angular 3 point 6 = ordinate 64 = x-type ordinate at default location 192 = x-type ordinate at user-defined location **(70 . 0)**
	1	Dimension text string entered by the user. Two quotation marks means the dimension is associative and will be updated when stretched. **(1 . "")**
	13	Defining point for the starting point of the linear and angular dimensions **(13 –8.000000 –5.000000)**
	14	Defining point for the ending point of the linear and angular dimensions **(14 –6.000000 –5.000000)**
	15	Defining point for diameter, radius and angular dimensions. **(15 0.000000 0.000000)**
	16	Defining point for the dimension arc in angular dimensions. **(16 0.000000 0.000000)**

Entity	Entity Code	Description/Contents Example (in bold)
	40	Leader length for radius and diameter dimensions **(40 . 0.000000)**
	50	Angle of HORIZONTAL, VERTICAL or ROTATED dimensions **(50 . 0.000000)**

Drawing Interchange & File Formats (Release 12)

This appendix **(Courtesy of Autodesk, Inc.)** describes the AutoCAD DXF (Drawing Interchange File) format and the commands provided to read and write these files. DXF files are standard ASCII text files. They can easily be translated to the formats of other CAD systems or submitted to other programs for specialized analysis. AutoCAD can also produce or read a binary form of the full DXF file.

The DXF file contains technical information that you need only if you write your own programs to process DXF files or work with entity information obtained by certain AutoLISP and ADS functions.

It would probably be helpful to produce a DXF file from a small drawing, print it out and refer to it occasionally while reading the information presented next.

A Drawing Interchange File is simply an ASCII text file with a file type of .DXF and specially formatted text. The overall organization of a DXF file is as follows:

1. **HEADER section:** You can find general information about the drawing in this section of the DXF file. Each parameter has a variable name and an associated value (see Table C-3 for a list of the header variables).
2. **TABLES section:** This section of the file contains definitions of named items.
   - Linetype table (LTYPE)
   - Layer table (LAYER)
   - Text Style table (STYLE)
   - View table (VIEW)
   - User Coordinate System table (UCS)
   - Viewport configuration table (VPORT)
   - Dimension Style table (DIMSTYLE)
   - Application Identification table (APPID)

3. **BLOCKS section:** This section contains Block Definition entities describing the entities that make up each Block in the drawing.
4. **ENTITIES section:** This section contains the drawing entities, including any Block References.
5. **END OF FILE**

If you use DXFOUT's Entities option, the resulting DXF file contains only the ENTITIES section and the END OF FILE marker, and the ENTITIES section reflects only the objects you select for output.

NOTE: If you select an INSERT entity, the corresponding Block definition is not included in the output file.

The specific assignment of group codes depends on the item being described in the file. However, the type of the value this group supplies is derived from the group code, as shown in Table C-1.

Table C-1 **Group code ranges**

Group code range	Following value
0–9	String
10–59	Floating-point
60–79	Integer
140–147	Floating-point
170–175	Integer
210–239	Floating-point
999	Comment (string)
1010–1059	Floating-point
1060–1079	Integer
1000–1009	String

A program, therefore, can easily read the value following a group code without knowing the particular use of this group in an item in the file. The appearance of values in the DXF file is not affected by the setting of the UNITS command: coordinates are always represented as decimal (or possibly scientific notation if very large) numbers, and angles are always represented in decimal degrees with zero degrees to the east of origin.

Variables, table entries and entities are described by a group that introduces the item, giving its type and/or name, followed by multiple groups that supply the values associated with the item. In addition, special groups are used for file separators such as markers for the beginning and end of sections, tables and the file itself.

Entities, table entries and file separators are always introduced with a 0 group code that is followed by a name describing the item.

NOTE: The maximum DXF file string length is 256 characters. If your AutoCAD drawing contains strings that exceed this number, those strings are truncated during DXFOUT. If your DXF file contains strings that exceed this number, DXFIN will fail.

Group Codes

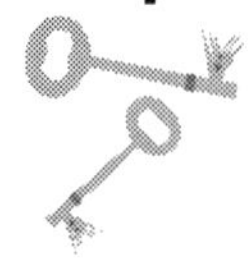

Group codes are used both to indicate the type of the value of the group, as explained earlier, and to indicate the general use of the group. The specific function of the group code depends on the actual variable, table item or entity description. Table C-2 indicates the general use of groups, noting as "(fixed)" any that always have the same function.

Table C-2. AutoCAD entity group codes (by number)

Group code	Value type
0	Identifies the start of an entity, table entry or file separator. The type of entity is given by the text value that follows this group.
1	The primary text value for an entity
2	A name: attribute tag, block name, and so on; also used to identify a DXF section or table name
3–4	Other textual or name values
5	Entity handle expressed as a hexadecimal string (fixed)
6	Line type name (fixed)
7	Text style name (fixed)
8	Layer name (fixed)

Group code	Value type
9	Variable name identifier (used only in HEADER section of the DXF file)
10	Primary X coordinate (start point of a line or text entity, center of a circle, etc.)
11–18	Other X coordinates
20	Primary Y coordinate. 2n values always correspond to 1n values and immediately follow them in the file.
21–28	Other Y coordinates
30	Primary Z coordinate. 3n values always correspond to 1n and 2n values and immediately follow them in the file.
31–37	Other Z coordinates
38	This entity's elevation if nonzero (fixed); exists only in output from versions prior to R11
39	This entity's thickness if nonzero (fixed)
40–48	Floating-point values (text height, scale factors, etc.)
49	Repeated value. Multiple 49 groups may appear in one entity for variable length tables (such as the dash lengths in the LTYPE table). A 7x group always appears before the first 49 group to specify the table length.
50–58	Angles
62	Color number (fixed)
66	"Entities follow" flag (fixed)
67	Identifies whether entity is in Model Space or Paper Space
68	Identifies whether viewport is on but fully off-screen, is not active, or is off
69	Viewport identification number
70–78	Integer values such as repeat counts, flag bits or modes
210, 220, 230	x,y,z components of extrusion direction (fixed)
999	Comments

Group code	Value type
1000	An ASCII string (up to 255 bytes long) in extended entity data
1001	Registered application name (ASCII string up to 31 bytes long) for XDATA (fixed)
1002	Extended entity data control string ("{" or "}") (fixed)
1003	Extended entity data Layer name
1004	Chunk of bytes (up to 127 bytes long) in extended entity data
1005	Extended entity data database handle
1010, 1020, 1030	Extended entity data x,y,z coordinates
1011, 1021, 1031	Extended entity data x,y,z coordinates of 3D world space position
1012, 1022, 1032	Extended entity data x,y,z components of 3D world space displacement
1013, 1023, 1033	Extended entity data x,y,z components of 3D world space direction
1040	Extended entity data floating-point value
1041	Extended entity data distance value
1042	Extended entity data scale factor
1070	Extended entity data 16-bit signed integer
1071	Extended entity data 32-bit signed long

Comments

The 999 group code indicates that the following line is a comment string. DXFOUT does not currently include such groups in a DXF output file, but DXFIN honors them and ignores the comments. Thus, you can use the 999 group to include comments in a DXF file you've edited. For example,

```
999
This is a comment.
999
This is another comment.
```

File Sections

As you learned earlier in this appendix, the DXF file is subdivided into four editable sections, plus the END OF FILE marker. You use file separator groups to delimit these file sections. The following is an example of a void DXF file with only the section markers and table headers present:

```
 0           (Begin HEADER section)
SECTION
 2
HEADER
            <<<<Header variable items go here>>>>
0
ENDSEC      (End HEADER section)
 0          (Begin TABLES section)
SECTION
 2
TABLES
 0
TABLE
 2
VPORT
 70
(viewport table maximum item count)
            <<<<viewport table items go here>>>>
0
ENDTAB
0
TABLE
2
```

```
 APPID, DIMSTYLE, LTYPE, LAYER, STYLE, UCS, VIEW, or VPORT
70
(Table maximum item count)
             <<<<Table items go here>>>>
0
ENDTAB
0
ENDSEC       (End TABLES section)
0            (Begin BLOCKS section)
SECTION
2
BLOCKS
             <<<<Block definition entities go here>>>>
0
ENDSEC       (End BLOCKS section)
0            (Begin ENTITIES section)
SECTION
2
ENTITIES
             <<<<Drawing entities go here>>>>
0
ENDSEC       (End ENTITIES section)
0
 EOF          (End of file)
```

HEADER Section

The HEADER section of the DXF file contains settings of variables associated with the drawing. These variables are set with various commands and are the type of information displayed by the STATUS command. Each variable is specified in the HEADER section by a 9 group giving the variable's name, followed by groups that supply the variable's value. Table C-3 shows the header variables and their meanings.

NOTE: $AXISMODE and $AXISUNIT are no longer functional in Release 12.

Table C-3. DXF system variables

Variable	Type	Description
$ACADVER	1	The AutoCAD drawing database version number; AC1006 = R10, AC1009 = R11 and R12
$ANGBASE	50	Angle 0 direction
$ANGDIR	70	1 = clockwise angles, 0 = counterclockwise
$ATTDIA	70	Attribute entry dialogs: 1 = on, 0 = off
$ATTMODE	70	Attribute visibility: 0 = none, 1 = normal, 2 = all
$ATTREQ	70	Attribute prompting during INSERT: 1 = on, 0 = off
$AUNITS	70	Units format for angles
$AUPREC	70	Units precision for angles
$AXISMODE	70	Axis on if nonzero (not functional in Release 12)
$AXISUNIT	10, 20	Axis X and Y tick spacing (not functional in Release 12)
$BLIPMODE	70	Blip mode on if nonzero
$CECOLOR	62	Entity color number: 0 = BYBLOCK, 256 = BYLAYER
$CELTYPE	6	Entity linetype name, or BYBLOCK or BYLAYER
$CHAMFERA	40	First chamfer distance
$CHAMFERB	40	Second chamfer distance
$CLAYER	8	Current layer name
$COORDS	70	0 = static coordinate display, 1 = continuous update, 2 = "d<a" format
$DIMALT	70	Alternate unit dimensioning performed if nonzero

Variable	Type	Description
$DIMALTD	70	Alternate unit decimal places
$DIMALTF	40	Alternate unit scale factor
$DIMAPOST	1	Alternate dimensioning suffix
$DIMASO	70	1 = create associative dimensioning, 0 = draw individual entities
$DIMASZ	40	Dimensioning arrow size
$DIMBLK	2	Arrow block name
$DIMBLK1	1	First arrow block name
$DIMBLK2	1	Second arrow block name
$DIMCEN	40	Size of center mark/lines
$DIMCLRD	70	Dimension line color: range is 0 = BYBLOCK, 256 = BYLAYER
$DIMCLRE	70	Dimension extension line color: range is 0 = BYBLOCK, 256 = BYLAYER
$DIMCLRT	70	Dimension text color: range is 0 = BYBLOCK, 256 = BYLAYER
$DIMDLE	40	Dimension line extension
$DIMDLI	40	Dimension line increment
$DIMEXE	40	Extension line extension
$DIMEXO	40	Extension line offset
$DIMGAP	40	Dimension line gap
$DIMLFAC	40	Linear measurements scale factor
$DIMLIM	70	Dimension limits generated if nonzero
$DIMPOST	1	General dimensioning suffix
$DIMRND	40	Rounding value for dimension distances
$DIMSAH	70	Use separate arrow blocks if nonzero
$DIMSCALE	40	Overall dimensioning scale factor
$DIMSE1	70	First extension line suppressed if nonzero

Variable	Type	Description
$DIMSE2	70	Second extension line suppressed if nonzero
$DIMSHO	70	1 = Recompute dimensions while dragging, 0 = drag original image
$DIMSOXD	70	Suppress outside-extensions dimension lines if nonzero
$DIMSTYLE	2	Dimension style name
$DIMTAD	70	Text above dimension line if nonzero
$DIMTFAC	40	Dimension tolerance display scale factor
$DIMTIH	70	Text inside horizontal if nonzero
$DIMTIX	70	Force text inside extensions if nonzero
$DIMTM	40	Minus tolerance
$DIMTOFL	70	If text outside extensions, force line extensions between extensions if nonzero
$DIMTOH	70	Text outside horizontal if nonzero
$DIMTOL	70	Dimension tolerances generated if nonzero
$DIMTP	40	Plus tolerance
$DIMTSZ	40	Dimensioning tick size: 0 = no ticks
$DIMTVP	40	Text vertical position
$DIMTXT	40	Dimensioning text height
$DIMZIN	70	Zero suppression for "feet & inch" dimensions
$DWGCODEPAGE	70	Drawing code page. Set to the system code page when a new drawing is created, but not otherwise maintained by AutoCAD
$DRAGMODE	70	0 = off, 1 = on, 2 = auto
$ELEVATION	40	Current elevation set by ELEV command

Variable	Type	Description
$EXTMAX	10, 20, 30	x,y,z drawing extents upper-right corner (in WCS)
$EXTMIN	10, 20, 30	x,y,z drawing extents lower-left corner (in WCS)
$FILLETRAD	40	Fillet radius
$FILLMODE	70	Fill mode on if nonzero
$HANDLING	70	Handles enabled if nonzero
$HANDSEED	5	Next available handle
$INSBASE	10, 20, 30	Insertion base set by BASE command (in WCS)
$LIMCHECK	70	Nonzero if limits checking is on
$LIMMAX	10, 20	XY drawing limits upper-right corner (in WCS)
$LIMMIN	10, 20	XY drawing limits lower-left corner (in WCS)
$LTSCALE	40	Global linetype scale
$LUNITS	70	Units format for coordinates and distances
$LUPREC	70	Units precision for coordinates and distances
$MAXACTVP	70	Sets maximum number of viewports to be regenerated
$MENU	1	Name of menu file
$MIRRTEXT	70	Mirror text if nonzero
$ORTHOMODE	70	Ortho mode on if nonzero
$OSMODE	70	Running object snap modes
$PDMODE	70	Point display mode
$PDSIZE	40	Point display size
$PELEVATION	40	Current Paper Space elevation

Variable	Type	Description
$PEXTMAX	10, 20, 30	Maximum x,y,z extents for Paper Space
$PEXTMIN	10, 20, 30	Minimum x,y,z extents for Paper Space
$PLIMCHECK	70	Limits checking in Paper Space when nonzero
$PLIMMAX	10, 20	Maximum X and Y limits in Paper Space
$PLIMMIN	10, 20	Minimum X and Y limits in Paper Space
$PLINEGEN	70	Governs the generation of linetype patterns around the vertices of a 2D Polyline: 1 = linetype is generated in a continuous pattern around vertices of the Polyline; 0 = each segment of the Polyline starts and ends with a dash
$PLINEWID	40	Default Polyline width
$PSLTSCALE	70	Controls Paper Space linetype scaling: 1 = no special linetype scaling; 0 = viewport scaling governs linetype scaling
$PUCSNAME	2	Current Paper Space UCS name
$PUCSORG	10, 20, 30	Current Paper Space UCS origin
$PUCSXDIR	10, 20, 30	Current Paper Space UCS X axis
$PUCSYDIR	10, 20, 30	Current Paper Space UCS Y axis
$QTEXTMODE	70	Quick text mode on if nonzero
$REGENMODE	70	REGENAUTO mode on if nonzero
$SHADEDGE	70	0 = faces shaded, edges not highlighted; 1 = faces shaded, edges highlighted in black; 2 = faces not filled, edges in entity color; 3 = faces in entity color, edges in black
$SHADEDIF	70	Percent ambient/diffuse light, range 1–100, default 70
$SKETCHINC	40	Sketch record increment

Variable	Type	Description
$SKPOLY	70	0 = sketch lines, 1 = sketch polylines
$SPLFRAME	70	Spline control polygon display: 1 = on, 0 = off
$SPLINESEGS	70	Number of line segments per spline patch
$SPLINETYPE	70	Spline curve type for PEDIT Spline (see your *AutoCAD Reference Manual*)
$SURFTAB1	70	Number of mesh tabulations in first direction
$SURFTAB2	70	Number of mesh tabulations in second direction
$SURFTYPE	70	Surface type for PEDIT Smooth (see your *AutoCAD Reference Manual*)
$SURFU	70	Surface density (for PEDIT Smooth) in M direction
$SURFV	70	Surface density (for PEDIT Smooth) in N direction
$TDCREATE	40	Date/time of drawing creation
$TDINDWG	40	Cumulative editing time for this drawing
$TDUPDATE	40	Date/time of last drawing update
$TDUSRTIMER	40	User elapsed timer
$TEXTSIZE	40	Default text height
$TEXTSTYLE	7	Current text style name
$THICKNESS	40	Current thickness set by ELEV command
$TILEMODE	70	1 for previous release compatibility mode; 0, otherwise
$TRACEWID	40	Default Trace width
$UCSNAME	2	Name of current UCS
$UCSORG	10, 20, 30	Origin of current UCS (in WCS)

Variable	Type	Description
$UCSXDIR	10, 20, 30	Direction of current UCS's X axis (in World coordinates)
$UCSYDIR	10, 20, 30	Direction of current UCS's Y axis (in World coordinates)
$UNITMODE	70	Low bit set = display fractions, feet-and-inches and surveyor's angles in input format
$USERI1 - 5	70	Five integer variables intended for use by third-party developers
$USERR1 - 5	40	Five real variables intended for use by third-party developers
$USRTIMER	70	0 = timer off, 1 = timer on
$VISRETAIN	70	0 = don't retain Xref-dependent visibility settings, 1 = retain Xref-dependent visibility settings
$WORLDVIEW	70	1 = set UCS to WCS during DVIEW/ VPOINT, 0 = don't change UCS

Writing DXF Interface Programs

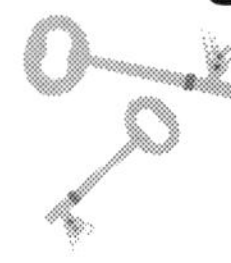

Writing a program that communicates with AutoCAD via the DXF mechanism often appears far more difficult than it really is. The DXF file contains a seemingly overwhelming amount of information, and examining a DXF file manually may lead to the conclusion that the task is hopeless.

As an example, the following is a Microsoft BASIC program that reads a DXF file and extracts all the line entities from the drawing (ignoring lines that appear inside blocks). It prints the end points of these lines on the screen. As an exercise you might try entering this program into your computer, running it on a DXF file from one of your drawings and then enhancing it to print the center point and radius of any circles it encounters. This program is not put forward as an example of clean programming technique nor the way a general DXF processor should be written; it is presented as an example of just how simple a DXF-reading program can be.

```
1000   REM
1010   REM Extract lines from DXF file
1020   REM
1030   G1% = 0
1040   LINE INPUT "DXF file name: "; A$
1050   OPEN "i", 1, A$ + ".dxf"
1060   REM
1070   REM Ignore until section start encountered
1080   REM
1090   GOSUB 2000
1100   IF G% <> 0 THEN 1090
1110   IF S$ <> "SECTION" THEN 1090
1120   GOSUB 2000
1130   REM
1140   REM Skip unless ENTITIES section
1150   REM
1160   IF S$ <> "ENTITIES" THEN 1090
1170   REM
1180   REM Scan until end of section, processing LINEs
1190   REM
1200   GOSUB 2000
1210   IF G% = 0 AND S$ = "ENDSEC" THEN 2200
1220   IF G% = 0 AND S$ = "LINE" THEN GOSUB 1400 : GOTO 1210
1230   GOTO 1200
1400   REM
1410   REM Accumulate LINE entity groups
1420   REM
1430   GOSUB 2000
1440   IF G% = 10 THEN X1 = X : Y1 = Y : Z1 = Z
1450   IF G% = 11 THEN X2 = X : Y2 = Y : Z2 = Z
1460   IF G% = 0 THEN PRINT "Line from (";X1;",";Y1;",";Z1;") to+
(";X2;",";Y2;",";Z2;")":RETURN
1470   GOTO 1430
2000   REM
2010   REM Read group code and following value
2020   REM For X coordinates, read Y and possibly Z also
2030   REM
2040   IF G1% < 0 THEN G% = -G1% : G1% = 0 ELSE INPUT #1, G%
2050   IF G% < 10 OR G% = 999 THEN LINE INPUT #1, S$ : RETURN
```

```
2060   IF G% >= 38 AND G% <= 49 THEN INPUT #1, V : RETURN
2080   IF G% >= 50 AND G% <= 59 THEN INPUT #1, A : RETURN
2090   IF G% >= 60 AND G% <= 69 THEN INPUT #1, P% : RETURN
2100   IF G% >= 70 AND G% <= 79 THEN INPUT #1, F% : RETURN
2110   IF G% >= 210 AND G% <= 219 THEN 2130
2115   IF G% >= 1000 THEN LINE INPUT #1, T$ : RETURN
2120   IF G% >= 20 THEN PRINT "Invalid group code";G% : STOP
2130   INPUT #1, X
2140   INPUT #1, G1%
2150   IF G1% <> (G%+10) THEN PRINT "Invalid Y coord code"; G1% :+
STOP
2160   INPUT #1, Y
2170   INPUT #1, G1%
2180   IF G1% <> (G%+20) THEN G1% = -G1% ELSE INPUT #1, Z
2190   RETURN
2200   CLOSE 1
```

Error Occurrences with DXFIN

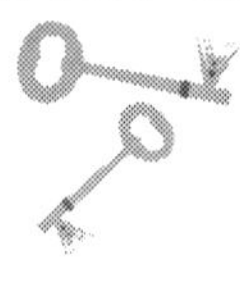

If you encounter an error while loading a DXF file using DXFIN, AutoCAD reports the error with a message indicating the nature of the error and the last line processed in the DXF file before the error was detected. This may not be the line on which the error occurred, especially in the case of errors such as omission of required groups.

Programming References

In this appendix you'll learn about the following:

- ADS library subroutine lists
- Proteus code list
- ACAD.INI file
- SQL command list

ADS LIBRARY

Synopsis of Basic ADS Library Subroutines

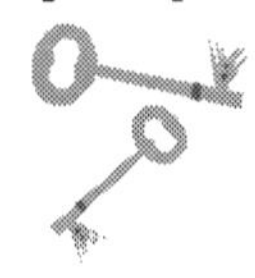

The first part of this appendix summarizes all of the functions provided by the library of the BASIC ADS Interface. Function names are grouped by topic and each is followed by a brief description.

Except where otherwise noted, the functions described here behave like their counterparts in the C-language ADS library; the *AutoCAD Development System Programmer's Reference Manual* has full details.

NOTE: Most functions in the BASIC ADS Interface library are integer functions that return a function result code which indicates their status; a few functions, such as ADSDISTANCE, return a value directly.

For C ADS functions that return a result buffer, the corresponding BASIC ADS function has an additional <llhandle> argument to which the function assigns a linked list.

Establishing the Interface to AutoLISP

ADSINIT (argc, argv)
Initializes the interface to AutoLISP.

ADSLINK (cbc)
Signals AutoLISP that the application is ready for a request and returns AutoLISP request codes.

External Function Handling

ADSDEFUN (sname, funcode)
Defines an external function.

ADSUNDEF (sname, funcode)
Undefines an external function.

ADSGETFUNCODE
Gets code number of requested external function.

ADSGETARGS (llhandle)
Gets arguments to requested external function.

ADSREGFUNC (fhdl, fcode)
Registers a (reentrant) external function.

ADSINVOKE (args, result)
Calls an external function in another ADS application.

Error Handling

ADSFAIL (str)
Prints an error message.

ADSABORT (str)
Prints an error message and then aborts the application.

ADSEXIT (stat)
Exits the ADS application.

Linked List Handling

Control of dynamic data structures is less convenient in BASIC than it is in C, so the BASIC ADS Interface includes this function package to handle the lists employed by the ADS library and AutoCAD.

You'll find a complete discussion on how to use these subroutines included in the *AutoCAD Development System Programmer's Reference Manual,* Section 5.4, "Handling Linked Lists."

REMINDER: The subroutines summarized here *do not* correspond to functions in the C-language ADS library.

RewLL (llhandle)
Rewinds the linked list.

DelLL (llhandle)
Deletes the linked list.

DelLLNode (llhandle, node, flag)
Deletes a node. The <flag> argument must equal either PRENODE or POSTNODE.

GetNodeType (llhandle, node)
Gets the type of the current node.

NextLLNode (llhandle, node)
Gets a value and then advances to the next node.

NextStringNode (llhandle, node)
Gets a string and then advances to the next node.

NextNameNode (llhandle, node)
Gets an entity name and then advances to the next node.

NextShortNode (llhandle, node)
Gets a short integer and then advances to the next node.

NextLongNode (llhandle, node)
Gets a long integer and then advances to the next node.

NextPointNode (llhandle, node)
Gets a point (2D or 3D) and then advances to the next node.

NextRealNode (llhandle, node)
Gets a real (floating-point) value and then advances to the next node.

ApndNameNode (llhandle, value)
Appends a node that contains an entity name.

ApndStringNode (llhandle, value)
Appends a node that contains a string.

ApndShortNode (llhandle, value
Appends a node that contains an integer.

Apnd3DPointNode (llhandle, v**alue)**
Appends a node that contains a 3D point.

Apnd2DPointNode (llhandle, value)
Appends a node that contains a 2D point.

NOTE: Apnd2DPointNode automatically sets the point's Z element to zero.

ApndRealNode (llhandle, value)
Appends a node that contains a real (floating-point) value.

ApndLLNode (llhandle, type, value)
Appends a node of the specified type and value.

AutoCAD Queries & Commands

ADSCMD (rbp)
Executes AutoCAD commands via a linked (result buffer) list.

NOTE: Because BASIC does not support functions with a variable-length argument list, there is no direct counterpart to the ads_command() function. Use the ADSCMD function instead.

ADSGETVAR (sym, llhandle)
Gets the current value of an AutoCAD system variable.

ADSSETVAR (sym, llhandle)
Gets the value of an AutoCAD system variable.

ADSFINDFILE (fname, result)
Searches for a filename.

ADSOSNAP (pt, mode, result)
Finds a point via object snap.

Geometric Utilities

ADSDISTANCE (pt1, pt2)
Finds the distance between two points.

ADSANGLE (pt1, pt2)
Finds the angle between two lines.

ADSPOLAR (pt, angle, dist, result)
Finds a point via polar coordinates.

ADSINTERS (from1, to1, from2, to2, teston, result)
Finds the intersection of two lines.

User Input

ADSGETINT (prompt, result)
Prompts for user input of an integer.

ADSGETREAL (prompt, result)
Prompts for user input of a real (floating-point) number.

ADSGETSTRING (cronly, prompt, result)
Prompts for user input of a string.

ADSGETPOINT (pt, prompt, result)
Prompts for user input of a point.

ADSGETCORNER (pt, prompt, result)
Prompts for user input of the corner of a rectangle.

ADSGETDIST (pt, prompt, result)
Prompts for user input of a distance.

ADSGETANGLE (pt, prompt, result)
Prompts for user input of an angle.

ADSGETORIENT (pt, prompt, result)
Like ADSGETANGLE, but takes into account the current value of the ANGBASE system variable.

ADSGETKWORD (prompt, result)
Prompts for user input of a keyword.

ADSGETINPUT (result)
Retrieves a keyword passed to a user-input function other than ADSGETKWORD.

ADSINITGET (val, kwl)
Determines what is valid user input for the next call to an ADSGET*xxx* function.

ADSUSRBRK
Checks whether the user has pressed Ctrl-C.

External Function Value Returns

ADSRETINT (ival)
Returns an integer.

ADSRETREAL (rval)
Returns a real (floating-point) number.

ADSRETPOINT (pt)
Returns a point.

ADSRETSTR (sval)
Returns a string.

ADSRETNAME (aname, type)
Returns an entity or selection set name.

ADSRETVAL (llhandle)
Returns a value contained in a result buffer.

ADSRETNIL
Returns nil.

ADSRETVOID
Returns void, which is not displayed.

ADSRETLIST (llhandle)
Returns a list.

Conversion

ADSRTOS (val, unit, prec, str)
Formats a real (floating-point) value as a string.

ADSANGTOS (v, unit, prec, str)
Formats an angle as a string.

ADSCVUNIT (value, oldunit, newunit, result)
Converts between real-world units.

Coordinate System Transformation

ADSTRANS (pt, from, to, disp, result)
Translates a point or displacement from one coordinate system to another.

Display Control

ADSPRINTF (string)
Prints a message on the text screen.

NOTE: The BASIC library version of this function takes a single string that possibly includes embedded string values rather than a format string followed by a variable number of value arguments.

ADSPROMPT (string)
Displays a message on the prompt line.

ADSMENUCMD (str)
Displays and activates menus.

ADSREDRAW (llhandle, mode)
Redraws the current graphics screen.

ADSGRAPHSCR
Displays the current graphics screen.

ADSTEXTSCR
Displays the current text screen.

ADSTEXTPAGE
Same as ADSTEXTSCR, but clears the text screen first.

Low-Level Graphics

ADSGRCLEAR
Clears the graphics screen.

ADSGRDRAW (from, to, color, hl)
Draws a vector in the current viewport.

ADSGRREAD (track, type, llhandle)
Reads from an input device.

ADSGRTEXT (box, text, hl)
Displays text in the menu, mode or status area of the graphics screen.

Wild-Card Matching

ADSWCMATCH (string, pattern)
Matches a string to a wild-card pattern.

Selection Sets

ADSSSGET (str, pt1, pt2, entmask, ss)
Gets a selection set.

ADSSSADD (ename, sname, result)
Adds an entity to a selection set (or creates a new set).

ADSSSDEL (ename, ss)
Deletes an entity from a selection set.

ADSSSFREE (sname)
Frees a selection set.

ADSSSLENGTH (sname, len)
Returns the number of entities in a selection set.

ADSSSNAME (ss, i, entres)
Returns the name of an entity in a selection set.

ADSSSMEMB (ename, ss)
Checks whether an entity is a member of a selection set.

Entity Handling

ADSENTGET (ent, llhandle)
Gets the definition data of an entity.

ADSENTMOD (ent)
Modifies the definition data of an entity.

ADSENTMAKE (ent)
Makes a new entity and appends it to the drawing database.

ADSENTDEL (ent)
Deletes (and undeletes) entities in the drawing.

ADSENTNEXT (ent, result)
Finds the next entity in the drawing.

ADSENTLAST (result)
Finds the last entity in the drawing.

ADSHANDENT (handle, entres)
Finds an entity by its handle.

ADSENTSEL (str, entres, ptres)
Prompts user to select an entity by specifying a point.

ADSNENTSEL (str, entres, ptres, xformres, refstkres)
Like ADSENTSEL, but returns additional data for nested entities.

ADSENTUPD (ent)
Updates the screen image of an entity.

Extended Entity Data

ADSREGAPP (appname)
Registers the application's extended entity data.

ADSENTGETX (ent, apps, llhandle)
Gets entity data, including extended entity data that is registered to the application.

ADSXDSIZE (xd)
Returns the amount of memory (in bytes) that a list of extended entity data will occupy.

ADSXDROOM (ent)
Returns the amount of memory (in bytes) that an entity has available for extended data.

Symbol Tables

ADSTBLNEXT (tblname, rewind, llhandle)
Finds the next item in a symbol table.

ADSTBLSEARCH (tblname, sym, setnext, llhandle)
Searches for a symbol in a symbol table.

PROTEUS CODE LIST

Programmable Dialogue Box Functions

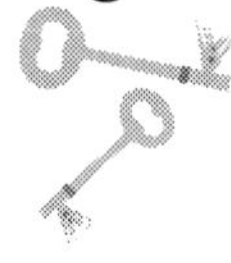

Each PDB (Programmable Dialogue Box) function is listed below with arguments. Only AutoLISP functions are shown. You can find ADS PDB functions in the *AutoCAD Customization Manual.*

(action_tile *key action-expression*)
Associates tile identified by *key* with *action-expression.*

(add_list *item*)
Adds to current list.

(client_data_tile *key clientdata*)
Associates application-managed data with tile specified by *key.*

(done_dialog *[status]*)
Terminates current dialogue box and stops displaying it.

(end_image)
Ends creation of currently active image.

(end_list)
Ends processing of active list.

(fill_image *x1 y1 x2 y2 color*)
Draws filled rectangle in currently active image.

(get_attr *key attribute*)
Gets attribute of tile identified by *key.*

(get_tile *key*)
Gets current value of tile specified by *key.*

(load_dialog *dclfile*)
Loads DCL file.

(new_dialog *dlgname dcl_id [action-expression [screen-pt]]*)
Initializes dialogue box and displays it.

(set_tile *key value*)
Sets value of tile specified by *key.*

(slide_image *x1 y1 x2 y2 sldname*)
Draws AutoCAD slide in active image.

(start_dialog)
Starts accepting user input for current dialogue box.

(start_image *key*)
Starts creation of image in tile specified by *key.*

(start_list *key [operation [index]]*)
Starts processing list in list box.

(term_dialog)
Terminates all dialogue boxes as if user pressed Ctrl-C.

(unload_dialog *dcl_id*)
Unloads DCL file associated with *dcl_id.*

(vector_image *x1 y1 x2 y2 color*)
Draws vector in active image from *x1,y1* to *x2,y2* with *color.*

ACAD.INI LISTING

This file listing courtesy of Autodesk, Inc.

Example File Listing

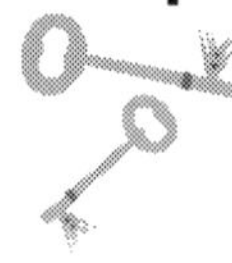

The functions in the ACAD.INI file, as shown below, control the customization of the AutoCAD for Windows toolbar, toolbox, etc.

```
[AutoCAD General]
ToolBarSize=16
ToolBar1=\3\3TOOLBOX ^TOOLBOX1^
ToolBar2=\3\3OPEN ^OPEN^
ToolBar3=\3\3QSAVE ^SAVE^
ToolBar4=\3\3PLOT ^PLOT^
ToolBar5=ZOOM WINDOW ^ZOOM^
ToolBar6=
ToolBar7=
ToolBar8=
ToolBar9=
ToolBar10=
ToolBar11=
ToolBar12=
ToolBar13=
ToolBar14=
MonoVectors=0
ToolBar15=
ToolBar16=
ToolBar17=
ToolBar18=
ToolBar19=
ToolBar20=
ToolBar21=
ToolBar22=
ToolBar23=
ToolBar24=
ToolBar25=
ToolBar26=
UseControlPanelPrinter=1
ACAD=C:\ACADWIN\SUPPORT;C:\ACADWIN\FONTS
Drawing1=C:\ACAD12\DEV\DIA_DEMO
```

```
Drawing2=C:\ACADWIN\SAMPLE\NOZZLE3D
Drawing3=C:\ACADWIN\SUPPORT\SHAFT
Drawing4=C:\ACADWIN\ATTJUNK

[AutoCAD Graphics Screen]
WindowState=5
WindowPosition=Left 0, Top 0, Right 703, Bottom 576
Font=Helv 10 400 0
StatusLine=1
ScreenMenu=1
CommandPrompt=3
ScreenRepair=0
DigitizerArbitration=0
GraphicsBackground=255 251 240
TextBackground=255 255 255
TextForeground=0 0 0

[AutoCAD Text Screen]
WindowPosition=Left 2, Top 30, Right 1022, Bottom 766
Visible=0
TextLines=400
LogFile=acad.log
LogFileOpen=0
Font=Courier 10 400 0
Background=255 255 255
Foreground=0 0 0

[AutoCAD Toolbox]
ToolBox1=UNDO ^UNDO^
ToolBox2=\3copyclip ^COPY_VECTORS^
ToolBox3=\3redraw ^REDRAW^
ToolBox4=\3line ^LINE^
ToolBox5=\3pline ^POLYLINE^
ToolBox6=\3arc ^ARC^
ToolBox7=\3circle ^CIRCLE^
ToolBox8=\3ellipse ^ELLIPSE^
ToolBox9=\3polygon ^POLYGON^
ToolBox10=\3point ^POINT^
ToolBox11=\3dtext ^TANGENT^
ToolBox12=\3ddim ^DIM^
```

```
ToolBox13=MOVE ^MOVE^
ToolBox14=copy ^COPY^
ToolBox15=erase ^ERASE^
ToolBox16=scale ^SCALE^
ToolBox17=rotate ^ROTATE^
ToolBox18=change ^CHANGE^
ToolBox19=mirror ^MIRROR^
ToolBox20=\3break ^BREAK^
ToolBox21=\3extend ^EXTEND^
ToolBox22=stretch ^STRETCH^
ToolBox23=\3trim ^TRIM^
ToolBox24=fillet ^FILLET^
ToolBox25=chamfer ^CHAMFER^
ToolBox26=align ^ALIGN^
ToolBox27=endp ^ENDPOINT^
ToolBox28=int ^INTERSECTION^
ToolBox29=mid ^MIDPOINT^
ToolBox30=center ^CENTER^
ToolBox31=quad ^QUADRANT^
ToolBox32=near ^NEAREST^
ToolBox33=per ^PERPENDICULAR^
ToolBox34=tan ^TANGENT^
ToolBox35=\3\3 ^CANCEL^
ToolBox36=\3pedit ^PEDIT^
TBoxOption=1
TBoxWidth=6
TBoxStart=1
TBoxLocation=437 300
```

SQL COMMAND LIST

This fourth appendix section looks at:

- ADS library subroutine lists
- Proteus code list
- ACAD.INI file
- SQL command list

SQL Syntax

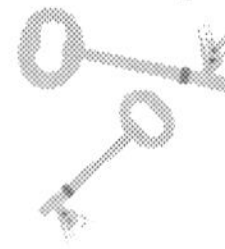

This final part of Appendix D contains a summary of SQL commands and argument syntax. You'll find a more detailed summary of SQL in the *AutoCAD SQL Extension Reference Manual.*

As you read the command listing, notice the SQL command is followed by one or more arguments. When you type an SQL command, some arguments are required, some are not:

- Arguments enclosed in braces **{...}**
  Request information in sequential order.
- Arguments enclosed in brackets **[...]**
  Are not required.
- Arguments shown in parentheses **(...)**
  You may repeat elements more than once.

NOTE: When you type a command with its arguments, you don't type the brackets or braces. They are only shown in the command list. You do type parentheses when you wish to group several arguments so they will be handled at the same time.

Arguments in upper case must be typed exactly as written. Arguments in italics should be replaced by the argument you choose.

The pipe ¦ character separates argument choices. You can type the choice on the left of the ¦ or the choice on the right.

SQL Commands

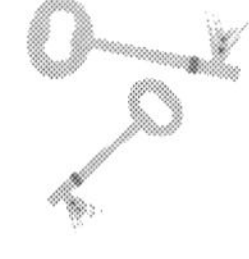

The command statements listed below can all be used by DOS database programs such as dBASE III, dBASE IV and PARADOX. Autodesk supplies drivers for these DBMS programs.

Other drivers are available for running the Sun SPARC workstations with INFORMIX and ORACLE programs. Command statements for these Sun SPARC programs are not listed.

- **CREATE [UNIQUE] INDEX** *index_name* ON *table_name* (*column_name* [*order*],...)

You use this command to create an index for a table.

- **CREATE TABLE** *table_name* (*column_name type* [*modifier*],...)

You use this command to create a table in the database and define its columns and other properties. Database table names **must** be unique.

- **DELETE** FROM *table_name* [WHERE *condition*]

This command deletes rows from the table specified by *table_name*. If you omit the WHERE option, all rows will be deleted from the table.

- **DROP INDEX** *index_name*

Use this command to delete the index specified by *index_name* from the database.

- **DROP TABLE** *table_name*

Use this command to delete the table specified by *table_name* from the database.

- **INSERT** INTO *table_name* [(*column_name, column_name,...*)] {VALUES (*value, value,...*) | *query*}

Use this command to add a new row to the table specified by *table_name*. Values are added to the specified columns.

- **SELECT** *select_list*

This command will:

- Recover a subset of the rows in a table.
- Recover a subset of columns in a table.
- Link rows in multiple tables.
- Retrieve data common to multiple tables.

Example: To use multiple selection sets.

```
SELECT arg1 FROM arg2 [WHERE arg3] [GROUP BY arg4] [HAVING arg5]
[ORDER BY arg6]  <Return>
arg1 = ALL
  or item name
arg2 = Table_name
  or table_name1, table_name2,...
arg3 = Search_condition
arg4 = Column_name
  or column_name1, column_name2,...
arg5 = Search_condition
arg6 = Sort_specification
  or sort_spec1, sort_spec2,...
```

- **UPDATE** *table_name* SET *column_name* = *expression*[, *column_name* = *expression*,...] [WHERE *search_condition*]

Use this command to change the values of fields in the table specified by *table_name*.

Companion Disk Sneak Preview

Outside AutoCAD was designed to be a time-saver; that's why I've created the *Outside AutoCAD Companion Disk*. This disk contains every time-saving program in the book, including programs for finding text, attributes and blocks throughout your drawing, scaling blocks in a single direction, building your own dialogue boxes with AutoCAD's new Proteus system and creating your own real-mode ADS application without buying expensive tools to do the job.

You'll find sample drawing files to help you build the applications described in the book, including building your own ASE (AutoCAD Sequel Extension) application. The files will also be helpful when you begin to customize your AutoCAD for Windows menus, toolbar and toolbox.

And here's a major time-saver: all the *Outside AutoCAD* appendices are also on the disk. You'll be able to refer to them online—a powerful and easy-to-use reference! The appendices include the AutoCAD database codes for use in AutoLISP; the DXF file structure; the Proteus programmable dialogue box command list; information on all included drawing files; the Basic ADS subroutine reference list and more! With the *Outside AutoCAD Companion Disk*, you can immediately use all the programs in the book. You won't waste time creating large drawing or program files, so learning applications will be easy. The companion disk is definitely programmed productivity!

INDEX

A

ACADASE layer 167, 201–2
ACAD.DCL file 282
ACAD.INI file
  example 350–53
  modifying 130–32
ACAD.LSP file 289–90
ACAD1.MNU file
  modifying 133–34
Accelerator keys 134
Add pull-down menu 213
Add Row dialogue box 191, 214, 225
ADS (AutoCAD Development System) 237–44
  advantages 237
  BASIC programs 248–59
    examples 249–50, 255–59
    interface functions 341–49
      See also BASIC ADS Interface
  communicating with AutoCAD 248–49, 254
  compared to AutoLISP 241–44
  concepts 247
  creating sample programs 251–53
  defined 237, 241, 247
  demonstration program 238–41
  knowledge required 248
  linking files 253
  programming languages 241
  protected mode programs 238–41, 247
    loading and running 254
  real mode programs 247, 251–59
    creating sample 251–53
    example 255–59
    loading and running 254, 258–59
  required elements 248–51
  strengths 243–44
  weaknesses 244
ADSINIT function 248
APPLOAD command 10, 289
Arcs
  entity codes 315
ASCII characters
  AutoCAD commands 130
ASCII files 74
  assigning to attributes 97–107, 306–9
  importing into AutoCAD 97–107
  See also DXF
ASE (AutoCAD SQL Extension) 153–59
  adding rows to databases 210–16, 225
  advantages 161
  applications 157–59
  defined 156
  deleting rows in database 217–18
  editing rows in database 215–17, 219–20
  exiting 174
  hands-on exercises 195–232
  initializing 165–67, 202
  preparing DOS 197–98
  See also SQL
ASE (AutoCAD SQL Extension)
  commands 161–93
  accessing 161–62
  administrative 162–75
    defined 162
  categories 161
  link 183–90
    defined 183
  manipulative 190–93
    defined 190
  utility 175–83
    defined 175
  See also Specific names of commands
ASE File pull-down menu 161–62
ASE Make Report dialogue box 177
ASE Make Report History dialogue box 178
ASEADDROW command 190–91
ASECLOSEDB command 162–63
ASEDELLINK command 183–84
ASEDELROW command 191, 217
ASEEDITLINK command 184–87
ASEEDITROW command 191–92
ASEERASEALL command 163
ASEERASEDB command 163–64
ASEERASEDBMS command 164–65
ASEERASETABLE command 165
ASEEXPORT command 176, 232
ASEINIT command 165–67
ASEMAKEDA command 187–89
ASEMAKELINK command 189
ASEMAKEREP command 176–78, 232
ASEPOST command 178
ASEQEDIT command 193
ASEQLINK command 189, 222
ASEQMAKEDA command 189

ASEQVIEW command 193
ASERELOADDA command 189
ASESELECT command 178–79
ASESETDB command 167–68
ASESETTABLE command 173–74
ASESQLED command 179–83
ASETDBMS command 168–69
ASETERM command 174
ASETERMDBMS command 175
ASETROW command 169–73
ASEVIEWLINK command 189–90
ASEVIEWROW command 193
(Assoc function 22–23, 26, 31, 94
Association lists 21–23
  changing values 24–28
  copying 23
  creating 26
  defined 22
  entity codes 313–24
    See also Specific entities
  See also Entity data lists
ATLAST programming language 241
ATTDEF command 51
ATT_DEFF.LSP program 68–69
  listing 300–301
ATTDIA variable 62
ATTDISP command 67
ATTEDIT command 65
ATTEXT command 78–79
ATTREQ variable 62
Attribute Definition dialogue box 51–61
  Attribute dialogue area 55–57
  Insertion Point dialogue area 59–60
  Mode dialogue area 53–55
  Text Options dialogue area 57–59
Attribute Extraction dialogue box 78–79
Attributes 49–70
  changing layer assignments 88–91
  changing layers 303–4
  constant values 54–55
  coordinate selection 59–60
  default values 57
  defined 49–50, 71
  defining 51–61
  dialogue boxes 274–75
  displaying 68
  editing definitions 66–68
  editing values 65
  entering 63–64
  entering values 68–69, 300–301
  entity codes 318–20
  exporting to spreadsheets 148
  extracting 71–80
    creating template files 74–76
    defined 71
    file formats 72–73
    loading into DBMS 80
    planning 76
  finding text strings 91–97, 305–6
  importing ASCII text 97–107, 306–9
  inserting blocks 62–64
  justifying 58
  preparing for exporting
    See Attributes—extracting
  preset values 55
  prompt 57
  rotation 59
  speeding text entry 97, 306–9
  tags 56
  text height 59
  text modes 50, 53–55
  text options 57–59
  text styles 58
    changing 81–88, 301–3
  verifying when inserting 55
  visibility 54
AutoCAD database 1–11
  benefits of understanding 1
  codes 313–24
  defined 1
AutoCAD Development System
  See ADS
AutoCAD for Windows
  advantages 117–22
  customizing 123–40
    cascading menus 139–40
    pull-down menus 132–38
    toolbar 127–30
    toolbox 130–32
  Edit menu 120
  features 117–22
  help 122
  initial screen 123–24
  multiple sessions running 124
  screen capture 119–21
  tools 122

AutoCAD Sequel Extension
  See ASE
AutoCAD SQL Extension
  See ASE
AutoLISP 13–33
  advantages 13
  comments 29
  Companion Diskette programs
    23–24, 285–309
  compared to ADS 241–44
  files
    finding 290–91
    loading 286, 288–89
      multiple 289–93
  functions
    defined 14
    examples 14–18
    listed 311–13
    nested 31
    user-defined 30
    See also Specific names of functions
  interactive input 18–21
  modifying entities 24–28
  multiple expressions treated as one 31
  program listings
    ATT_DEFF.LSP 68–69, 300–301
    BLK_LIST.LSP 28–33, 295–96
    BLK_NAME.LSP 295
    BLK_NAM.LSP 28
    BLK_SCAL.LSP 27, 294
    CA_STYLE.LSP 82–88, 301–3
    CH_LAYER.LSP 88–91, 303–4
    DBTOOLS.LSP 292–93
    FILL_ATT.LSP 97–107, 306–9
    FIND_ATT.LSP 91–96, 305–6
    FIND_BLK.LSP 43, 297
    FIND_TXT.LSP 44–46, 298–300
    LINE_MOD.LSP 27, 293–94
    MOD_BLK.LSP 277–81
  programs
    creating 285
    entering 285, 287
    list 286–87
    loading
      See AutoLISP—files—loading
  prompting user 18–21
  running Dynamic Data Exhange 146–49
  strengths 242
  variables
    coordinates 17–18
    defined 14
    entering 14–18
    integers 14–15
    point values
      See AutoLISP—variables—coordinates
    printing 14–15
    real numbers 15–16
    text strings 16
  weaknesses 243

B

BASE.DCL file 282
BASIC ADS Interface 341–49
  AutoCAD queries and commands 344
  conversion 346
  coordinate system transformation 346
  display control 346–47
  entity handling 348
  error handling 342
  establishing 341
  extended entity data 348–49
  external function handling 342
  external function value returns 345–46
  geometric utilities 344
  graphics 347
  linked list handling 342–44
  selection sets 347–48
  symbol tables 349
  user input 344–45
  wild-card matching 347
BASIC programming language 241, 248–59
  ADS interface functions 341–49
    See also BASIC ADS Interface
  sample program 249–50, 255–59
Bill of materials
  creating with ASE 157
Bitmapped images
  editing 120–21
BLK_LIST.LSP program 10–11
  explained 30–33
  listing 29–30, 295–96
Blkname variable 32
BLK_NAME.LSP program
  listing 28, 295

BLK_SCAL.LSP program
  listing 27, 294
Blocks
  changing single coordinates 27
  coordinates 9
  creating 62
  creating with attributes 76–78
  entity codes 317–18
  entity data lists 7–10
  exploding 66
  finding and listing 10–11, 28–33, 295–96
  finding by name 43, 297
  inserting 62–64
  insertion point 9
  modifying 27, 294
  names 9
    list 10–11, 32
  rotation 9
  substituting in drawing 28, 295
BMP
  See Bitmapped images
Buttons
  programming 128–30

C

C programming language 241, 248
(Caddr function 25
(Car function 24
Cascading menus
  See Menus—cascading
CA_STYLE.LSP program
  explained 84–88
  listing 81–83, 301–3
  loading and running 83–84
Catalogs
  creating with ASE 158
CDF (Comma Delimited File) format 72
(Cdr function 31
Cells 144
CHANGE command 67–68
Check marks
  menu items 135–38
CH_LAYER.LSP program
  explained 89–91
  listing 88–89, 303–4
  loading and running 89
CHPROP command 38
Circles
  center point 7
  entity codes 315
  entity data lists 3–4, 6–7
  radius 7
Client/server concept 126
Clipboard
  copying images to 119–21
CMDECHO variable 93
Columns
  key values 174, 187, 209
  selecting 174
Comma Delimited File
  See CDF
COMMIT command 174
Companion Disk
  ADS program written in BASIC 255–59
  ASE hands-on exercises 195–232
  AutoLISP programs 23–24, 285–309
(Cons function 26
Control databases
  creating 165–67, 201–2
  deleting 163
  deleting tables 165
Coordinates
  attributes 59–60
  changing single values 24–28
  displaying 17–18
  entering 21
  entering in AutoLISP 17
Cost estimates
  creating with ASE 157

D

Database linking
  See ASE; Entities—linking to databases
Database Management System
  See DBMS
Database pull-down menu 205
Database software selecting
  See DBMS drivers
Database system
  See DBMS
Databases
  adding rows through ASE 210–16, 225
  closing 162–64

creating template files 74–76
defined 153
deleting rows through ASE 217–18
designing 71–76, 154, 198–201
See also Attributes—extracting
editing data through ASE 215–17, 219–20
example 154
finding conflicts with drawings 178
linking to AutoCAD
See ASE
passwords 206
selecting 167–68, 204–6
viewing portions in drawings
See Displayable attributes
See also AutoCAD database; Control databases
DBMS (Database Management System)
access 197
defined 153
loading AutoCAD files 80
standards 155
DBMS (Database Management System) drivers
deleting 164–65
selecting 168–69, 203
status 169
terminating 175
DBMS pull-down menu 203
DBTOOLS.LSP program 291–93
listing 292–93
DBTOOLS.LSP program 290
DCL (Dialogue Control Language) 264–66
loading and running applications 266
DCL (Dialogue Control Language) files 263
controlling 273, 277–81
example 273–77
structure 282
DDATTDEF command 51
DDATTE command 65
DDATTEXT command 78–79
DDE
See Dynamic Data Exchange
DDE Initiate Conversation dialogue box 142
DDEDIT command 66–68
(Ddedone function 148
DDE.LSP program 146–49
(Defun function 30, 288
Desktop
defined 116
Dialogue boxes
abbreviations 268
attributes 274–75
components 264 See also Tiles
controlling 277–81
creating 267
guidelines 268–69
sample 264–66
testing programs 282
default values 269
definitions for Release 12 282
designing 271–73
factors to consider 272–73
edit boxes 275–76
editing 267
key values 275
layout 268, 272–73
loading and running 281–82
making portable 269
names 274
nesting 269
programming languages 263–64
sample file 273–77
size 268
text 268
turning on 201
See also Specific names of dialogue boxes
Dialogue Control Language
See DCL
DIESEL 136
Dimensions
entity codes 322–24
Dispatch loop
ADS programming 249
Displayable attributes 227–30
creating 227–29
from database info 187–89
defined 227
editing linked 193
updating 230
from databases 189
Dofun 250
DOS
customizing menus 116
disadvantages 115
preparing for ASE 197–98

Dotted pair
  defined 5
Drawing Interchange File
  See DXF
Drawings
  creating sample 195–97
  finding conflicts with databases 178
  linking to databases
    See ASE; Entities—linking to databases
  linking to spreadsheets
    See Dynamic Data Exchange
  updating
    automatically in outside applications
      See Object Linking and Embedding
    from spreadsheets 143, 145
DXF (Drawing Interchange File) 73, 144
  comments 330
  defined 325
  errors in loading 340
  example of file separators 330–31
  group code ranges 326–27
  group codes 327–30
  HEADER section 331–38
  maximum string length 327
  organization 325–26
  sample program 338–40
  variables 332–38
Dynamic Data Exchange 122, 141–49
  applications 141
  controlling output to spreadsheets
    144–48
  export modes 147–48
  filters 146
  how to do 142–44
  menu 144–46
  shutting down 144, 148
  unloading 146
  using AutoLISP 146–49

E

EDATA variable 95
Edit Attribute Definition dialogue box
  66–67
Edit Attributes dialogue box 65
Edit Link dialogue box 185
Edit Link Key values dialogue box 187
Edit Link Options dialogue box 186
Edit pull-down menu 216
Edit Row dialogue box 192, 217, 220
Edit SQL Selection Set dialogue box 181
Embedding
  compared to linking 126–27
  defined 125
  updating object 126–27
Enter Attributes dialogue box 63–64
(Entget function 31, 85
Entities
  changing single coordinate 24–27
  codes for association lists 313–24
    See also Specific entities
  defined 2
  defining
    See Entity data lists
  displaying definitions
    See Entity data lists
  exporting link information from
    database 176, 232
  group codes in DXF files 327–30
  layers 5
  linking to databases 219–27
    creating 189
    deleting 163–64, 183–84
    editing 184–87
    multiple rows 222–26
    Quick Link 222, 226
    viewing 189–90, 221
    See also ASE
  linking to spreadsheets
    See Dynamic Data Exchange
  listing data
    See Entity data lists
  modifying in AutoLISP 24–28
  names 5, 30
  selecting with dialogue box 35–39
  selection sets
    See Selection sets
  type 5
Entity data lists 2–10
  blocks 7–10
  circles 3–4, 6–7
  codes 313–24
    See also Specific entities
  explanation 7
  identifier key 22

lines 2–3
components 5–6
See also Association lists
Entity Selection Filters dialogue box
See Selection Set Filters dialogue box
(Entmode function 26
(Entnext function 30, 32, 85, 94
(Entsel function 24
ENTTYP variable 94
(Entupd function 87
(Equal function 31
Erase DBMS Driver dialogue box 164–65
Erase Table dialogue box 165
EXPLODE command 66
Extrusion direction 6

F

Field
alphanumeric 154
date 154
defined 154
Files
formats 72–73
See also Specific types of files
FILL_ATT command 103
FILL_ATT.LSP program
explained 102–7
listing 97–99, 306–9
loading and running 100–102
Filter list 37
FIND_ATT.LSP program
explained 93–96
listing 91–93, 305–6
loading and running 93
FIND_BLK.LSP program
listing 43, 297
FIND_TXT.LSP program 298–300
listing 44–46
(Foreach function 32

G

(Getint function 18–19
(Getpoint function 21
(Getreal function 19
(Getstring function 19–21
Graphical User Interface 112, 123
Graying out menu items 138
GUI
See Graphical User Interface

H

Help
AutoCAD for Windows on-screen 122
context-sensitive 114–15, 122
Windows environment 114–15
HIGHLIGHT variable 106
History of SQL Statements dialogue box 182, 232
Hot link 143

I

Identifier key
defined 22
(If function 31
Integers
See Numbers
Inventories
creating with ASE 158

K

Key values
columns 174, 187, 209
dialogue boxes 275
rows 171, 215–16
Keyboard commands 134

L

Layers
changing attribute assignments 88–91, 303–4
entities 5
LINE_MOD.LSP program
listing 27, 293–94
Lines
ending point 6
entity codes 314
entity data lists 2–3
components 5–6

extrusion direction 6
modifying 24–27, 293–94
starting point 6
Linking
compared to embedding 126–27
defined 125
updating object 127
Linking drawings
to databases
See ASE; Entities—linking to databases
to other applications
See Object Linking and Embedding
to spreadsheets
See Dynamic Data Exchange
(List function 32
(Load function 288
Loadfuncs 250–51

M

Make Displayable Attribute dialogue box 188, 228
Make file 253
Make Link pull-down menu 220
Maps
creating with ASE 158
Menus
accelerator keys 134
cascading 139–40
copying standard AutoCAD 132
customizing 116–17
Dynamic Data Exchange 144–46
pull-down
checked items 135–38
control codes 134–38
customizing 132–38
graying out items 138
toggled items 135–38
Microsoft Windows
See Windows (software)
MOD_BLK.LSP program
explained 280–81
listing 277–79
Modify Block dialogue box 272

N

Names
blocks 9, 43
list 10–11, 32
dialogue boxes 274
entities 5, 30
Nested functions 31
New_style variable 85
Numbers
entering in AutoLISP 14–16

O

Object Linking and Embedding 124–27
defined 124
how to do 125
rules 126
See also Embedding; Linking
OLE
See Object Linking and Embedding
Outside AutoCAD Companion Disk
See Companion Disk

P

Parentheses 31, 285
Passwords
databases 206
+Plus sign 285
Point values
See Coordinates
Points
entity codes 314
Polylines
entity codes 320
(Princ function 32–33
Print Screen key 120
(Progn function 31, 95
Program header
defined 241
Programming languages
dialogue boxes 263–64
See also Specific programming languages
Programs
See Specific names or subjects
Protected mode
See ADS—protected mode programs

Proteus 263–83
code list 349–50
defined 263
See also DCL; Dialogue boxes
Pull-down menus
See Menus—pull-down; Specific names of menus
PWEDGE.EXP program 254

Q

Quick Link pull-down menu 222
QuickBasic compiler 248

R

Raster images
copying to Clipboard 120
Real mode
See ADS—real mode programs
Record
defined 154
Relational databases
See Databases
Reports
generating in ASE 176–78, 232
Rows
adding 190–91
adding through ASE 210–16, 225
deleting 191, 217–18
editing data 191–92, 215–17, 219–20
navigating 181
selecting 169–73, 210, 224
key values 171, 215–16
search criteria 172, 212, 217–19
viewing 193
viewing non-current 193
Rubber banding 21

S

Safety management plans
creating with ASE 159
Schedules
creating with ASE 157
Screens
capturing 119–21
SDF (Space Delimited File) format 72–73
Select Key Columns dialogue box 174, 209
Selection Link dialogue box 226
Selection Set Filters dialogue box 35–39
Selection sets 35–46
creating 35–42, 178–79, 230
defined 32
tools for creating 39–42
Sentences
entering interactively 20–21
Sequence end
defined 73
Sequends
entity codes 320
Set Current Database dialogue box 167–68, 205
Set Current Row by Key Values dialogue box 171, 215–16
Set Current Row by Search Criteria dialogue box 172, 212, 219, 223
Set Current Table dialogue box 173, 208
Set Database Please Enter dialogue box 206
Set DBMS Driver dialogue box 168–69
Set Row Options dialogue box 170, 211, 215
Set Row pull-down menu 210
(Setq function 24, 31
Settings pull-down menu 137
Solids
entity codes 315–16
Source code
compiling 252
Space Delimited File
See SDF
Spreadsheets
controlling output from AutoCAD 144–48
importing AutoCAD data 142–44
by attributes 148
by entity handle 148
by name 147–48
See also Dynamic Data Exchange
updating AutoCAD 143, 145
SQL editor 230–32
SQL Editor dialogue box 180, 231
SQL Filename dialogue box 183
SQL (Structured Query Language)
advantages of combining with AutoCAD 155–56
defined 155

SQL (Structured Query Language)
commands 179–83
entering 354
list of previously executed 182
listed 354–56
(Ssget function 32, 39–42
adding X argument 41–42
examples 40–41
(Ssget "X" function 41–42
(Ssname function 85
Strings
See Text strings
Structured Query Language
See SQL
(Subst function 25–26

T

Table pull-down menu 207
Tables
deleting 165
selecting 173–74, 207–9
Template files
creating 74–76
format and rules 74–76
Terminate DBMS Driver dialogue box 175
Text
entering interactively 19–21
entity codes 316–17
finding user-specified 44–46, 298–300
See also Attributes
Text editors 117–19
visible with drawing 118–19
Text files
creating 176
See also ASCII files
Text strings
entering 19–21
entering in AutoLISP 16
finding attribute 91–97
3DFACE
entity codes 322
Tiles
defined 268
pre-defined 273, 275, 282
Toggling menu items 135–38
Toolbar
customizing 127–30
Toolbar Customization dialogue box 128–30
Toolbox
customizing 130–32
Tools 122
defined 116
Tracings
entity codes 321–22

V

Values
comparing 31
See also Key values
Variables
entering in AutoLISP 14–18
Vector images
copying to Clipboard 120
Vertices
entity codes 321
View Link dialogue box 190, 221
View Row dialogue box 193, 224

W

(While function 30
Windows
resizing 124
Windows (software)
advantages 111–12
customizing menus 117
features 116
File menu 112
help 114–15
loading applications 112–13
Paint utility 120–21
See also AutoCAD for Windows
Write text editor 117–19

The AutoCAD Productivity Book

The world's most widely used reference on customizing AutoCAD. You'll find step-by-step chapters on simple methods for creating your own dialogue boxes, revising screen and tablet menus, using DOS to customize AutoCAD and much more!

Companion disk:

- 30 productivity-enhancers AutoCAD forgot about, including metric conversion, copy from Paper Space, Break, Merge and Bold text, exploding all polylines and more!

$27.95 for book only
$77.90 for book with diskette
369 pages, illustrated
ISBN: 1-56604-026-4

AutoLISP in Plain English

At last, an AutoLISP reference that anyone can understand! This basic guide introduces you to the tools you'll need to create simple, useful AutoLISP programs that solve everyday drawing tasks.

Companion disk:

- All lesson programs in the first ten chapters.
- 20 "working" programs featured in Chapter 11.
- Plus 7 programs not found in the book!

$23.95 for book only
$43.90 for book with diskette
272 pages, illustrated
ISBN: 1-56604-009-4

AutoCAD: A Concise Guide to Commands & Features

Completely updated and revised for Release 12, this book offers beginners the most complete, easy-to-read introduction to AutoCAD, including all essential terms and techniques, step-by-step operating instructions on setting up, drawing, editing, saving and more!

Companion disk:

- All drawings and exercises in the book, enabling you to load them without reconstructing them by hand.

$24.95 for book only
$44.90 for book with diskette
447 pages, illustrated
ISBN: 1-56604-008-6

$29.95 for book only
$79.90 for book with diskette
327 pages, illustrated
ISBN: 1-56604-004-3

Solid Modeling With AutoCAD

The first book that helps you understand AutoCAD's Advanced Modeling Extension (AME). Completely updated for AME 2.1, you'll learn how to produce realistic-looking 3D drawings, use these drawings to calculate volume, center of gravity and other mass computations. Your one stop guide to AME!

Companion disk:

- Time-saving batch files.
- Pausing scripts.
- 19 AutoLISP programs from Chapter 11.
- Plus 7 programs not found in the book!

Available through your authorized AutoCAD dealer, bookstores or Ventana Press, P.O. Box 2468, Chapel Hill, NC 27515. 919/942-0220; FAX 919/942-1140. For orders and sales inquiries, call us toll-free at 1-800-743-5369.

TO ORDER additional copies of *Outside AutoCAD*, or other books in the Ventana Press AutoCAD Reference Library™, please fill out this order form and return it to us for quick shipment.

	Quantity		Price		Total
Outside AutoCAD	______	x	$29.95	=	$______
Outside AutoCAD Disk	______	x	$49.95	=	$______
The AutoCAD 3D Companion Book	______	x	$27.95	=	$______
The AutoCAD 3D Companion Disk	______	x	$49.95	=	$______
The AutoCAD Productivity Book	______	x	$27.95	=	$______
The AutoCAD Productivity Book Disk	______	x	$49.95	=	$______
Solid Modeling With AutoCAD	______	x	$29.95	=	$______
Solid Modeling With AutoCAD Disk	______	x	$49.95	=	$______
AutoLISP in Plain English	______	x	$23.95	=	$______
AutoLISP in Plain English Disk	______	x	$19.95	=	$______
1,000 AutoCAD Tips & Tricks	______	x	$27.95	=	$______
1,000 AutoCAD Tips & Tricks Disk	______	x	$49.95	=	$______
AutoCAD: A Concise Guide	______	x	$24.95	=	$______
AutoCAD: A Concise Guide Disk	______	x	$19.95	=	$______
All seven books & seven disks (30% off! Includes shipping—continental U.S. only.)	______	x	$317.00	=	$______

Please specify disk size: ___3 1/2" ___5 1/4"

Also available from Ventana Press: bestselling presentation and desktop publishing design titles:

The Presentation Design Book	______	x	$24.95	=	$______
Harvard Graphics Design Companion	______	x	$23.95	=	$______
Looking Good in Print	______	x	$23.95	=	$______

Shipping: Please add $4.50/first book for standard UPS, $1.35/book thereafter;
$8.25/book UPS "two-day air," $2.25/book thereafter.
For Canada, add $8.10/book.
International orders subject to international air mail rates. = $______

Send C.O.D. (add $4.50 to shipping charges) = $______

North Carolina residents add 6% sales tax = $______

Total = $______

Name ______________________________

Company ______________________________

Address (No P.O. Box) ______________________________

City______________________ State________ Zip ____________

Daytime Phone ______________________________

___ Payment enclosed ___VISA ___MC Acc't # ______________________

Expiration Date__________ Signature ______________________

Please mail or fax to:
Ventana Press, P.O. Box 2468, Chapel Hill, NC 27515
800/743-5369 (orders only); 919/942-0220; FAX: 919/942-1140